What Christians Believe

What Christians Believe

THE STORY OF GOD AND PEOPLE IN MINIMAL ENGLISH

Anna Wierzbicka

OXFORD
UNIVERSITY PRESS

OXFORD
UNIVERSITY PRESS

Oxford University Press is a department of the University of Oxford. It furthers
the University's objective of excellence in research, scholarship, and education
by publishing worldwide. Oxford is a registered trade mark of Oxford University
Press in the UK and certain other countries.

Published in the United States of America by Oxford University Press
198 Madison Avenue, New York, NY 10016, United States of America.

© Oxford University Press 2019

Library of Congress Cataloging-in-Publication Data
Names: Wierzbicka, Anna, author.
Title: What Christians believe : the story of God and people in minimal English /
Anna Wierzbicka.
Description: New York, NY : Oxford University Press, [2019] |
Includes bibliographical references and index.
Identifiers: LCCN 2018034096 (print) | LCCN 2018040600 (ebook) |
ISBN 9780190855291 (updf) | ISBN 9780190855307 (epub) |
ISBN 9780190940591 (online content) | |
ISBN 9780190855284 (cloth :alk. paper)
Subjects: LCSH: Language and languages—Religious aspects—Christianity. |
English language—Religious aspects—Christianity. | Theology, Doctrinal.
Classification: LCC BR115.L25 (ebook) | LCC BR115.L25 W54 2019 (print) |
DDC 230—dc23
LC record available at https://lccn.loc.gov/2018034096

9 8 7 6 5 4 3 2 1

Printed by LSC Communications, United States of America

For the participants of my weekly seminar on "Christianity and translatability" at the Australian National University in 2016–2018, with gratitude and love.

CONTENTS

ACKNOWLEDGMENTS

Although this book bears a single author's name on the cover, its core part—"The Story of God and People"—is, in a very real sense, the outcome of collective work. It is the fruit of sustained, persistent, patient search for the truth by a group of deeply engaged participants of a weekly seminar at the Australian National University, conducted over three years. It is impossible to draw a full list of these participants, but some names must be mentioned.

The original group of "founding members" were Mary Besemeres, Helen Bromhead, Gian Marco Farese, and Bert Peeters. In the last year or so, the core group included, in addition to three of those first four (with Gian Marco Farese back in Italy), Irena Dennis, Debbie Hill, Peter Hill, Denis Fisher, Catherine Hudson, and Paul Jordan. The student population is naturally transient, however, Gian Marco Farese, Carlo dalle Ceste, and Rui Shen were with the group for a very long time. Visiting scholars are also a transient population, but some of the visitors including Christoph Harbsmeier, Hilary Chappell, and Zuzanna Bułat Silva were with us for extended periods and contributed a great deal. Throughout the three-year period, our discussions benefitted enormously from intensive involvement (by email and telephone) of a long-distance participant, Cliff Goddard.

From my perspective, our discussions were a striking illustration, and confirmation, of the words of the great Russian scholar Mikhail Bakhtin: "Truth is not (. . .) to be found inside the head of an individual person, it is born between people collectively searching for truth, in the process of their dialogic interaction." "Process" is an operative word here: getting closer to the truth through dialogic interaction is a long process. But in our experience, if the goal is the same for all the members of the group (searching for the truth patiently, humbly, and with an open mind), consensus steadily grows, errors of interpretation are gradually identified, and the shared sense of getting closer to the truth gets stronger and stronger.

I was truly blessed to have this opportunity for a long-term dialogical interaction, and I am deeply indebted to all the participants. The book is dedicated to them, with gratitude and love.

PREFACE

Many people today—both Christians and non-Christians, believers and non-believers—are unclear or confused about the essentials of the Christian faith. "The Story of God and People," which is at the heart of the present book, sets out these essentials in narrative form, in very simple words, without assuming any previous knowledge. On one level, then, the "Story of God and People" is a simple introduction to the basics of Christian faith in a form accessible to anyone. It is, however, unlike any other such introductions because it systematically uses very simple words and syntax, and does not assume any previous familiarity with either "the Christian story" or Christian vocabulary (e.g., words like "grace," "salvation," "resurrection," or "crucifixion"). Furthermore, the words used in this "Story" are not only simple but also, for the most part, universal: While it is written in English, it is not phrased in "full English," shaped by history, culture, and tradition, but in "Minimal English," in words most of which have exact semantic equivalents in all, or nearly all, languages.

Readers who are interested in the "science" behind the notion of "Minimal English" can find the key answers to their questions in chapter 4 of Part I of the book. The main point is that the discovery of the shared core of all (or most) languages is the result of wide-ranging cross-linguistic investigations conducted over many years by many linguists (see Part I, chapter 4, and the references cited there). Some readers, however, may want to read "The Story of God and People" simply as a story, without asking about the "science" behind the unusually restricted vocabulary and syntax used in it. And some may want to read "The Story" first, focusing on its content (laid bare through the Minimal English), and only later turn to the explanations in Part I.

"The Story of God and People" is not tied to any particular cultural tradition and can be understood by readers of any cultural and ethnic background. But while the language is very simple and transparent, great care has been taken to avoid any simplistic or distorting formulations: The aim of "The Story" is to convey the essentials of Christian faith accurately, making every word count and be justifiable from a theological and historical, as well as a linguistic, point of view. (Because every word counts, each of the forty chapters of "The Story" has gone through many versions, in most cases, at least twenty, each version discussed with colleagues and students.)

For a word to be justifiable from a linguistic point of view means here, above all, being cross-translatable—or having been previously explained through cross-translatable words. The assumption is that no words can be taken for granted as intelligible to anyone, regardless of the person's cultural background, if they do not meet one of these two essential conditions.

Surprisingly, perhaps, experience suggests that for many people even seemingly simple words like "cross" can present obstacles to understanding. The fact that Jesus died on the cross is at the heart of Christianity, and the image of the cross is the central Christian symbol. Yet for many twenty-first-century speakers of English (both children and adults), the word "cross" often brings to mind little more than a "tee shape," or one of the two options in the game of "noughts and crosses." A book for everyone, that is, one with no prior assumptions, needs to explain even the meaning of the word "cross." As chapter 26 of Part II shows, this, too, can be done with very simple and cross-translatable words that all English-speaking readers know and understand, even if their knowledge of English is fairly basic.

I have also used in this "Story" a limited number of words which are not universal and which have no equivalents in many languages of the world. These words are integral to the story told in the Gospels and are deeply rooted in the culture and history of first-century Palestine. They include, for example, "shepherds," "fishermen," "soldiers," "king," "river," "bread," "wine," and "lamb." While "The Story of God and People" can be easily translated into most, if not all, languages of the world, words like those listed above would in some cases need to be included in a glossary and explained through simpler, locally available words.

As for words of Latin origin such as "creator," "incarnate," or "salvation," which are important for Christian liturgies and worship, they do not need to be used in order to convey the essence of Christian belief to people living in the secularized and globalized modern world, where words of Latin and Greek origin cannot be taken for granted as part of essential cultural literacy. As I see it, if Christianity wants to make itself intelligible to anyone in the globalized world who might want to hear it out, it needs to speak, at times, without such words, and to try to rely instead, as far as possible, on universal (readily cross-translatable) words. "The Story of God and People" hopes to serve this need.

Surprisingly, perhaps, the reliance on a limited vocabulary of very simple words allows us not only to present the same faith in different languages but also to articulate that faith with greater precision than it would be possible in one particular language, with all its culture-specific richness. The point is so important that I will illustrate it with an extended example.

The Nicene-Constantinopolitan Creed which was agreed on as an expression of Christian faith by the undivided church in the fourth century opens with the statement: "I believe in one God, the Father almighty, maker of heaven and earth." Or so says the English version, in which the word "almighty" corresponds (more or less) to the word *omnipotens* in the Latin version. But the original version, agreed on in Constantinople in 381, was formulated in Greek, not in Latin, and the Greek word which was used—*pantokrator*—did not mean the same as either *omnipotens* or "almighty." To show with precision what the intended meaning was we need to go beyond complex and language-specific terms like "almighty," *omnipotens*, and *pantokrator* and to reconstruct that meaning in phrases made up of simple and shared human concepts, such as "do," "happen," and "want."

The Latin word *omnipotens* (on which the English "almighty" is based) suggests that God can do anything he wants. But the Greek word *pantokrator* (as it was used in the creed) does not mean that. It has more to do with what will happen (in the end) than with what God can do. *Pas* (genitive *pantos*) means "all," and *krateo* means, roughly, "to hold something firmly and securely." Thus God described as *pantokrator* was seen as someone who is holding everything in his hands and whose will would, ultimately, prevail.

A broadly based collective book entitled *Confessing One Faith: An ecumenical explication of the apostolic faith as it is confessed in the Nicene-Constantinopolitan Creed* (2010) says this about the word *pantokrator*: "It does not mean 'one who can do anything he wants' in an unqualified way, but rather 'one in whose hands all things are.'" The reference to God's hands is of course a metaphor; but it is not a metaphor referring to what God can do ("with his hands") but, rather, to how all things are going to turn out in the end (as God wants). This way of thinking about God is thoroughly biblical. For example, it is consistent with what the prophet Isaiah (55:11) says, on God's behalf: "so is my word that goes out from my mouth: It will not return to me empty, but will accomplish what I desire and achieve the purpose for which I sent it" (New International Version). It is also consistent with what the book of Revelation (1:8) says at the very outset: "I am the Alpha and the Omega, says the Lord God, who is and who was and who is to come, the Pantokrator."

In the English version of the Bible, the last word in this sentence is given as "almighty" (both in the King James Version and the Revised Standard Version). But this is not what the Greek original means. "Pantokrator," as used here, is connected with the symbolism of the Alpha and the Omega, the beginning and the end: In the beginning, God created the world ("I believe in one God, the Father Pantokrator, the maker of heaven and earth"), and in the end, as Isaiah prophesied, God will achieve all his purposes.

Thus, the meaning that the creed sought to express was not (1): "if God wants to do something, God can do it," but (2): "If God wants some things to happen, after some time they will all happen, as God wants." For Christians, the purpose of the creed is not only to express their faith, in unity with past generations of believers, but also to "give glory to God." For many, professing that God is the *Pantokrator* in whose hands, ultimately, all things are and who will accomplish all his purposes, gives more glory to God than calling God "almighty." (Given the scale of human suffering and the problem of evil, a God who is a *Pantokrator* is not alienating in the way that one described as "almighty" can be.)

The difference in meaning between *Pantokrator* and "Almighty" is highlighted by the existence of the common Greek phrase *Christos Pantokrator* and the virtual absence of the corresponding English phrase "Christ Almighty" (or Latin *Omnipotens Christus*). As the Wikipedia article on "Christ Pantokrator" says, "The image of Christ Pantokrator was one of the first images of Christ developed in early Christian Church and remains a central icon of the Eastern Orthodox Church. (. . .) In the West the equivalent image in art is known as Christ in Majesty."

Like the words "Lord" and "King," the word *Pantokrator* is compatible with the Christian image of the risen Jesus (of whom the Creed says that he "will come again in glory to judge the living and the dead and his kingdom will have no end"); but the word "almighty" is not. This is a good illustration of the fact that *pantokrator* in the original Greek version of the creed did not mean what the English word "almighty" suggests. An explanation couched in simple and universal words can help us to identify that intended meaning and to articulate the "Nicene-Constantinopolitan" faith more accurately and more authentically, as well as more cross-translatably, for a global world.

In addition to a very small vocabulary, another unusual feature of "The Story" is the virtual absence of metaphors—except those, which, evidence shows, are universally understood, such as "God is someone above people" and "people can live with God."

The New Testament tells the story of God and people largely through metaphors. This way of telling it has always been, and will always be, indispensable. Yet there is also, I believe, a place for a non-metaphorical re-telling and re-thinking, especially when trying to explain the Christian story and Christian faith to young people, and to non-Christians, in today's globalizing but culturally still very diverse world—a world where numerous metaphors that many speakers of languages like English have for a long time taken for granted are unfamiliar and may not be understood.

To take first a very simple example, in Luke's Gospel (2:19) we read that when the shepherds told Mary what they saw and heard in the fields near Bethlehem on the night when Jesus was born, "she kept all these things, pondering them in her heart" (Revised Standard Version of the Bible, RSV). Later in the same chapter (Luke 2:51) we read about the disappearance of the twelve-year-old Jesus in Jerusalem during the Passover, Mary's and Joseph's anguished search for him, finding him in the temple, and his words of explanation: "How is it that you sought me? Did you not know that I must be in my Father's house?" Here, the sentence about Mary is rendered as: "his mother kept all these things in her heart" (RSV).

What exactly do these sentences mean, someone may ask. "The Story" offers the following non-metaphorical paraphrase (couched in simple and cross-translatable words): "Mary often thought about these words when Jesus was a child, she often thought about these words when Jesus wasn't a child anymore" (v. 19) (a paraphrase which would also apply to Jesus's words in v. 51). Experience suggests that such paraphrases (which help explain how other people, including Luke, could know later what the shepherds said, and what the boy Jesus said) can be helpful to first-time readers of the Gospels, and that they can also be useful to long-term Christians.

To illustrate, a translation of the New Testament published by the Bible Society of India, subtitled "Contemporary English Version" (1995), renders Luke's verses 19 and 51 as follows:

> Mary kept thinking about all this and wondering what it meant. (v. 19)
> His mother kept thinking about all that had happened. (v. 51)

But this is not what the verses in question mean. The point is not that Mary "wondered what it meant" or "kept thinking about all that happened," but, rather, that she preserved the memory of what was *said* (in the Greek original of the Gospel, "rhemata," "sayings"): she thought continuously about these words, "treasured" these words, and protected them from oblivion (in Minimal English: "she often thought about these words when Jesus was a child, she thought about these words when Jesus was not a child anymore").

To take a more complex example, here is a passage from Mark's Gospel:

> (14) Now after John [the Baptist] was arrested, Jesus came into Galilee, preaching the Gospel of God, (15) and saying, "The time is fulfilled, and the Kingdom of God is at hand. (Mark 1:14–15)

For many non-Christians, both Jesus's sayings in verse 15 ("the time is fulfilled" and "the kingdom of God is at hand") would be totally incomprehensible; and in fact, they are likely to be hard to understand for many Christians too.

The paraphrase in Minimal English included in chapter 15 of the "The Story of God and People" relies on the non-metaphorical concepts "God" and "the Prophets," which are introduced, respectively, in chapters 1 and 7. As for the metaphors of "the time being fulfilled" and "the kingdom of God being at hand," they are elucidated through words and phrases which, evidence suggests, are cross-translatable into all languages:

> I want you to know something very good:
> Something is happening in this country now like never before.
> It is happening as the Prophets were saying.
> People can live with God now like never before, God is near now.

Certainly, this paraphrase does not remove the mystery. In particular, it does not explain in what way, exactly, "people can live with God like never before" and in what way "God is near now." (It takes the whole New Testament to explain that.) But the mystery is not compounded by difficult-to-understand English words and phrases, as often happens in more conventional commentaries on the Gospels.

For example, according to Adela Yarbro Collins's (2007) massive scholarly volume *Mark: A Commentary*, the sentence "The time is fulfilled" refers to "the time of eschatological fulfilment," whereas the sentence "the kingdom of God is at hand" "implies that the prophesies of scripture and the hopes of the people are in the process of being fulfilled" (p. 154). As for the phrase "the kingdom of God" itself, Yarbro Collins says that "the historical Jesus was an eschatological prophet who proclaimed the kingdom of God," that "he [Jesus] probably taught (. . .) that a heavenly Messiah would establish the kingdom of God, as God's agent, in the near future" (p. 94), and that "Jesus acts as a herald of God" (p. 79). As I see it, words like "eschatological," "proclaim," "herald," and even "heavenly," and phrases like "God's agent" and "in the process of being fulfilled" create unnecessary barriers for a great many people, both Christians and non-Christians, who would be interested to learn what Jesus meant and how Mark understood Jesus's words.

Thus, "The Story of God and People in Minimal English" hopes to reach out, in a fresh way, and without using traditional religious (or academic) language, to anyone who may want to find out what the Christian faith is all about. It can serve as an aid for religious education, for the teaching of "cultural literacy," and as a spiritual resource for anyone, whether they believe in God or not.

From a linguistic point of view, "The Story of God and People" can be seen as an experiment testing the power of Minimal English—a minimal language based on simple and cross-translatable words and phrases. Such an experiment is likely to be of great interest not only to linguists but also to anthropologists, philosophers, educationalists, those interested in communication studies or translation studies, specialists in language technologies, and so on.

The purpose of using a limited vocabulary of simple and intelligible words is not to "dumb down" religious ideas and truths but, on the contrary, to elucidate them, and to articulate their components with clarity and precision. In fact, "The Story of God and People" presented in Part II of the present book hopes to demonstrate the spuriousness of the widespread view that complex and sophisticated ideas can only be adequately expressed in complex language.

Other readers, however, can ignore the value of the text as a scholarly experiment and as a test for the explanatory power of Minimal Languages and simply move with the flow of the story (Part II). The commentaries in Part III will answer many of the questions which may occur to the readers of the forty short chapters in Part II and whet their appetite for further reflections included in Part IV. Hopefully, both "The Story" itself, and the surrounding material (Parts I, III, and IV) can encourage readers to think more deeply about things that matter greatly to millions of people, to dip into other books, and also to read, and reflect on, the Gospels.

PART I

Introduction and Overview

1

Who are "Christians"?

1.1 The creeds

The question "What do Christians believe?" presupposes a prior question: "Who are Christians?"; and although the second one may seem easier to answer than the first one, even this second one is not unproblematic. As discussed by C. S. Lewis in his classic work *Mere Christianity* ([2001] 1952):

> The world does not consist of 100 per cent Christians and 100 per cent non-Christians. There are people (a great many of them) who are slowly ceasing to be Christians but who still call themselves by that name: some of them are clergymen. There are other people who are slowly becoming Christians though they do not yet call themselves so. There are people who do not accept the full Christian doctrine about Christ but who are so strongly attracted by Him that they are His in a much deeper sense than they themselves understand. (. . .) And always, of course, there are a great many people who are just confused in mind and have a lot of inconsistent beliefs all jumbled up together. (pp. 108–109)

Given the complex situation described above, how can we sensibly approach the question, what do Christians believe? Presumably, a good starting point would be to think of people who *want* to call themselves Christians (for example, for the purpose of a census).

There is no doubt a considerable diversity of belief among Christians (in the sense specified above), but presumably most of them would agree that some two thousand years ago, there lived a man called Jesus, who taught people what God was like and showed it in his own life, who died on the cross, was buried, and on the third day rose from the dead.

Trying to move further, beyond those first and basic points, we could ask: Is there some shared core of beliefs that many Christians (in the sense specified above) would want to identify with, either fully or at least partially, a core that has been stated in a publicly available document?

3

Here, the answer is: yes. The common basis for what Christians in the West and in the East profess to believe in, is stated in two "creeds," one called the Apostles' Creed, and the other, the Nicene Creed. The Apostles' Creed, which is believed to summarize the faith of the Apostles, is an elaboration of Jesus's words to the Apostles (Matthew 28:19), "Go, therefore and make disciples of all nations, baptizing them in the name of the Father and the Son and the Holy Spirit," and of Apostle Peter's speech at Pentecost (Acts 2:14–42):

> *The Apostles' Creed*
> I believe in God, the Father almighty,
> Creator of heaven and earth,
> and in Jesus Christ, his only Son,
> our Lord,
> who was conceived by the Holy Spirit,
> born of the Virgin Mary,
> suffered under Pontius Pilate,
> was crucified, died, and was buried;
> he descended into hell;
> on the third day he rose again from the dead;
> he ascended into heaven,
> and is seated at the right hand of God the Father almighty;
> from there he will come to judge the living and the dead.
> I believe in the Holy Spirit,
> the holy catholic Church,
> the communion of saints,
> the forgiveness of sins,
> the resurrection of the body,
> and life everlasting. Amen.

To clarify, the sentence "he descended into hell" (where the word "hell" is a rendering of the Hebrew word *sheol*) means, essentially, "for some time he didn't live" or "he was with the dead." (Pope Benedict XVI (2009: 90) uses the phrase "dwelt in death" in this context.) "Hell" does not imply here anything like "eternal damnation." The phrase "the resurrection of the body" means that after they die, people can live with God, with other people, as people (recognizable to those who knew them before they died), and not as disembodied spirits. (Their bodies will be transformed but recognizable.)

As British theologian Alister McGrath (2013) notes in his book *FAITH and the CREEDS*, for the first two centuries Christians didn't have, and couldn't have had, any formal "creeds" recognized throughout the Christian world.

> It's not hard to see what the problem was. At its height, in the early second century, the Roman Empire included the entire Mediterranean region. Christianity spread through this area with astonishing speed, but because

it was an illegal religion, its believers were forced to meet in secret to worship. There was no way Christian leaders could gather together to discuss a common set of beliefs: the risk of arrest by the Roman authorities was simply too great. (p. 61)

And yet common understanding, and consensus on most important points, appears to have been steadily growing during the first two centuries. McGrath (2013) writes:

Yet the historical records show a remarkable degree of consensus emerging within the Christian world of the late second century. For reasons that are not fully understood, believers throughout the Roman Empire were beginning to converge on a particular set of writings that they read aloud in public worship and regarded as authoritative in matters of life and thought. There were local variations of course, but by around 190 we can begin to see collections of texts very similar to the modern New Testament taking shape, along with "confessions of faith" that looked a lot like the modern Apostles' Creed. (p. 66)

As for the Nicene Creed, as McGrath tells the story, by the time it was formulated, the status of Christianity had changed radically, from an illegal religion to a legal one, following the conversion of the Roman emperor Constantine. This meant the end of persecutions, no need for Christians to meet in secret places anymore, and a possibility for Christian leaders to travel to meet, and to work together toward explicitly formulating a consensus on matters of faith.

Constantine summoned a council of Christian bishops. They met in 325 at the town of Nicaea in Asia Minor (modern-day Turkey), and the agreement they reached on these matters formed the basis of a new creed. (What we now know as the "Nicene Creed" is actually a later version of the creed of 325, agreed at the Council of Chalcedon in 451.) This 325 creed was imposed on the Church by its bishops and the emperor. Notably, it did not initially command the strong popular consensus that the Apostles' Creed has won over many generations. (p. 70)

Thus, the two creeds developed in very different ways, the first one gradually, over many generations, within widely dispersed Christian communities, and the second one, formulated at official councils, by bishops. As McGrath notes, "there has always been a sense in which the Apostles' Creed is a 'people's creed,' whereas the Nicene Creed is a 'bishops' creed'" (p. 70). (No doubt this explains why a word like "consubstantial" appears in the Nicene Creed, and not in the Apostles' Creed.)

The Nicene Creed owes its continuing prestige to the fact that it resulted from the great councils of the Church when it was still undivided (before the

East–West schism), and is still regarded as a common basis for Christians in the East and the West. I will only adduce here the part about Christ, significantly expanded in relation to the Apostles' Creed:

The Nicene Creed (the part about Jesus Christ)
I believe in one Lord Jesus Christ,
the Only Begotten Son of God,
born of the Father before all ages.
God from God, Light from Light,
true God from true God,
begotten, not made,
consubstantial with the Father;
through him all things were made.
For us people and for our salvation
he came down from heaven,
and by the Holy Spirit was incarnate
of the Virgin Mary,
and became man.
For our sake he was crucified under Pontius Pilate,
he suffered and was buried [*pathonta kai tafenta*],
and rose again on the third day
in accordance with the Scriptures.
He ascended into heaven
and is seated at the right hand of the Father.
He will come again in glory
to judge the living and the dead
and his kingdom will have no end.

Commenting on the continuing importance of the creeds, McGrath (2013) notes that "the creeds do not add anything to the Bible" but rather "summarize its leading themes" (p. 72); they "are primarily communal confessions of faith" (p. 77); they "are a reminder of the importance of intergenerational transmission of faith" (p. 77); and "the creeds were a way in which Christian identity could be affirmed, maintained and safeguarded." McGrath quotes important fourth-century Christian writer Cyril of Jerusalem (Catechesis V, 12):

The synthesis of faith was made . . . to present the one teaching of the faith in its totality, in which what is of the greatest importance is gathered together from all the scriptures. And just as a mustard seed contains a great number of branches in its tiny grain, so also this summary of faith brings together in a few words the entire knowledge of the true religion which is contained in the Old and New Testaments. (p. 72)

And here is a modern quote on the Nicene ("Nicene-Constantinopolitan") Creed as a touchstone of core Christian belief, from a book entitled *Credo* and co-authored by three Polish theologians: the Catholic theologian Wacław Hryniewicz, the Lutheran theologian Karol Karski, and the Orthodox theologian Henryk Paprocki (with different sections written by single authors):

Confession of faith has become in our times a question of fundamental significance—doctrinal, ecumenical, and existential-pastoral. The churches have come to realise that in their striving for a reconciled diversity there exists in the past a solid point of reference. It is the early Christian Nicene-Constantinopolitan Creed. (. . .) I am convinced that Christianity of the future will slowly, not without resistance, become more and more an ecumenical Christianity. Many Catholics, Protestants and Orthodox think today about such a Christianity. (Hryniewicz 2009: 319, 322)

Russian Orthodox theologian Alexander Men' (1996), in his "Credo for Today's Christian," writes in a similar vein. He starts with the central point which unites all Christians: "A Christian centres his or her faith on Jesus Christ by whom all is measured and evaluated (Gal. 2:70; Rev. 1:8)" (p. 69). Then he continues:

A Christian (. . .) experiences the division among Christians as a sin which is common to all and a violation of Christ's will (John 10:16); believes that in the future this sin will be overcome not by a sense of superiority, pride, complacency, or hatred, but rather through a spirit of brotherly love without which the Christian calling cannot be fulfilled. (Matt. 5.23-24). (p. 71)

1.2 What do the creeds mean?

But can these creeds be understood in the same way by Christian communities across time and space? This question, too, runs into many difficulties. One of these difficulties is language. As Nicholas Ostler (2016) argues forcefully with regard to religions in his recent book *Passwords to Paradise* (and as many other linguists have argued before him), languages color what is said in them, and so "the same" faith expressed in different languages is not exactly the same faith. Furthermore, it is now widely accepted that the traditional language of theology—including that of dogmatic formulations such as those included in the creeds—is historically conditioned and for this reason often difficult to understand. To quote biblical scholar Raymond Brown (1975):

The battle of biblical criticism has been to get Christians and the church to recognize that the books of the Bible contain the word of God phrased in the words of men and that therefore to discover God's revelation one must take into account the historical situation, the philosophical worldview, and the theological limitations of the men who wrote them. The same battle has to be won in relation to the dogmas of the church, where once again God's revelation has been phrased by men. (p. 116)

Commenting on the difficulties that many Christians have today with understanding the creeds, Marcus Borg, a well-known writer on, and popularizer of, Christianity, emphasizes that the tenet that Jesus is the only begotten Son of God, who is of one substance with the Father, was formulated in language shaped by its historical context (fourth-century theological debates, the need to rebut a heresy called Arianism, etc.). Borg (1999: 154) refers in this connection to his encounter with black seminarians in South Africa as an occasion when "the cultural relativity of creedal and biblical language hit home": in that particular culture, he discovered, the status of the oldest brother is higher than that of an only son, and so it is seen as a more appropriate way of speaking about Jesus. Borg adds, "To say the obvious, if the creed has been formulated in a different culture, its language would have been very different. This awareness relativizes the creed and the Trinity."

Borg's (1999) observation about the cultural underpinnings of the language of the creed is indisputably true. But his references to the relativity of the creed and to its being a culturally relative product of the ancient church seem somewhat ambiguous: Is there or is there not a stable, constant, culture-independent set of beliefs that all Christians who are reciting the creed can share? Borg says that when he, as a practicing Christian, recites the creed, he understands himself "to be identifying with the community which says these words together . . . [and] not only with the community in the present, but also with the generations of long-dead Christians who said the same ancient words as they stood in the presence of sacred mystery" (p. 154). He also suggests that "we would understand the purpose of the creed better if we sang it or chanted it" (p. 155). No doubt this statement would resonate with many Christians (even if they didn't necessarily agree).

But the crucial question is this: Does one identify with the universal church by reciting the same words or by affirming the same faith? And if it is a matter of shared faith, *what* is this shared faith and how can it be articulated? Despite the ambiguity of Borg's (1999) formulations, it appears that he does mean a shared set of beliefs and not only a shared string of words; and he summarizes ("as he has thus far been able to understand") "what the creed and the [dogma of the] Trinity affirm about Jesus" (p. 154) in three points: (1) "the living risen Christ is a divine reality," (2) "the risen living Christ is . . . not a second God but is one with God," and (3) "what happened in Jesus was 'of God'" (p. 154). This summary, however, could not be said to adequately express the shared faith of Christians across all centuries, languages, and cultures.

First, expressions like "divine reality" could not be translated into most human languages because no counterparts for the English words "divine" and "reality" could be either found or easily forged. Expressions of this kind are no less language- and culture-bound than the Latin phrase *consubstantialem Patri* ("of one substance with the Father") of the Nicene Creed. Second, the expression "one with God" relies on English idiom and could not be readily rendered in many other languages either. Third, the meaning of the sentence "what happened in Jesus was 'of God' " is not fully clear even in English, and in any case could not be readily translated into all languages, as it is heavily dependent on the grammatical structure of languages like English.

As was argued by seventeenth-century thinkers such as Leibniz (1903) and Descartes ([1931] 1701), not everything can be explained and not everything can be defined. Ultimately, the only way to truly explain anything is to explain it in terms of concepts that themselves are intuitively clear and do not require further definitions. Otherwise, all explanations lead to an infinite regression and ultimately explain nothing. This simple and incontrovertible principle— that what is complex and obscure can be explained only in terms that are themselves simple and clear—applies to metaphorical language as much as to anything else.

Consider, for example, the following explanation of the concept of the Trinity in a book entitled *Essential Truths of the Christian Faith: 100 Key Doctrines in Plain Language*:

> The historic formulation of the Trinity is that God is one in essence and three in person. Though the formula is mysterious and even paradoxical, it is in no way contradictory. The unity of the Godhead is affirmed in terms of essence or being, while the diversity of the Godhead is expressed in terms of person. . . . The term *person* does not mean a distinction in essence but a different *subsistence* in the Godhead. (. . .) Subsistence is a difference within the scope of being, not a separate being or essence. All persons in the Godhead have all the attributes of deity. (Sproul 1992: 35)

Explanations like this—ostensibly formulated in plain language—are in fact incomprehensible to most people and they are certainly not cross-translatable into many languages of the world. Not everything can be explained; religious faith can legitimately include mysteries or affirm that while God can know everything about people, people cannot know everything about God. One can agree with Sproul (1992: 35) that "human analogies such as one man who is a father, son, and a husband fail to [fully] capture the mystery of the nature of God" (with a stress on the word "fully," which I have added to the original quote). What one cannot agree with is the assumption that high-register English words like "subsistence" or "essence" can explain it better. Not everything can be explained, but if, as philosopher Ludwig Wittgenstein ([1974] 1922: 3) says, "what can be said at all can be said clearly," whatever can be explained at all can also be explained clearly.

In his book *The Plain Man Looks at the Apostles' Creed*, the theologian and Church of Scotland minister William Barclay ([1990] 1967) has written (with special reference to the Apostles' Creed):

> It is close on eighteen hundred years old. The Church has come a long way in experience and in thought since the latter half of the second century. There are unquestionably difficulties in the Apostles' Creed for the modern mind. It is a fact of history that all great creeds of the Church have what might be called an apologetic basis, and that they were wrought out to face the particular theological dangers of their time. It may well be that a first reaction today is that it is high time that there was a restatement of faith, . . . made in twentieth century terms, and made specifically for twentieth century man. . . . But there are formidable difficulties. . . . It may be natural to long for such a creed stated in modern terms; it will probably prove impossible ever to construct it. (p. 381)

The twentieth century is now gone, and now that we are in the new century, and the new millennium, it is natural to long for more—not just for a statement of faith "for twentieth century [European] man" but also for a statement of faith for all people, that is, one intelligible in a global and universal perspective: in Africa, South America, Asia, or Oceania. It may be impossible to formulate a tenable creed "in modern terms" because "modern" is constantly becoming dated, and in any case what is modern for some will be culturally alien for others. But although we cannot find *terra firma* in modernity, we can find it in universality: Universal human concepts give us a stable and firm reference point that no localized, transient modernity could ever provide. If Christianity aims to be (in the words of the Nicene Creed) one universal church, Christians need to strive for a universal rather than a local and culture-specific statement of their faith.

As the quote from Marcus Borg adduced earlier illustrates, after centuries of Christianity, there is a sense among many Christians that the creeds that congregations recite in churches each week are not fully comprehensible even to those congregations. It would, of course, be a mistake to assume that people who publicly professed their faith in the past always fully understood the creeds of their churches. But perhaps the need to understand in order to believe was felt less acutely then than now. As individual reasoning has increasingly become in many parts of the earth the arbiter of what can and should be accepted as true, understanding has increasingly become essential to faith.

Of course, commentaries abound, but almost as a rule, they are formulated in a way which fails to give a clear and intelligible answer. For example, the *Catechism of the Catholic Church* (1994) explains the first affirmation of the Apostles' Creed ("I believe in God") and of the Nicene Creed ("I believe in one God") as follows:

We firmly believe and confess without reservation that there is only one true God, eternal, infinite (*immensus*) and unchangeable, incomprehensible, almighty, and ineffable, the Father and the Son and the Holy Spirit; three persons indeed, but one essence, substance or nature entirely simple. (p. 55)

Infinite? Ineffable? One essence, substance or nature? Who can understand that? The simplified and youth-oriented version of the Catechism, YOUCAT (2010: 31), doesn't use those particular words, but it explains that "God is a unique, absolute and personal being, ultimate ground of everything"—this is perhaps a bit clearer, but not by much.

To my mind, there is little doubt that the two versions of the Creed—the Apostles' Creed and the Nicene Creed—that many millions of people recite in their churches in the twenty-first century, as they have done for centuries, still provide the best reference point for explaining "what Christians believe." As Alister McGrath (2013) says:

For this reason, reciting the creeds is to be seen as an act of corporate witness, not simply a personal confession of faith. It is not I alone who has put my trust in God; it is the community of faith down the ages that shares this faith with me. In using the creed to frame my faith, I am aligning myself with this community and affirming that I belong to it. (p. 84)

For me, as for McGrath, reciting the creeds means identifying with a community of faith, and not just a community of ritual. The phrase "What Christians believe" as used in the title of this book is intended to refer to that community of faith. At the same time, it seems obvious that the creeds by themselves do not sufficiently explain what those who recite them want to profess, first, because they are extremely compressed summaries of the faith, and second, because they are not self-explanatory. "The Story of God and People," told in Part II of the present book in simple and cross-translatable words, aims at articulating these beliefs in a clearer, fuller, and universally accessible form. At the same time, the use of minimal vocabulary (and minimal syntax) can defamiliarize the Christian story, and enable the readers familiar with it to hear it as if for the first time.

1.3 "Mere Christianity"

Speaking to friends about his wartime broadcasts (1942) which later became part of *Mere Christianity*, C. S. Lewis (1952) said that "he accepted the task because he believed that England, which had come to consider itself part of a "post-Christian" world, had never in fact been told in basic terms what the religion is about" (Norris 2001: xix).

I believe that the task of articulating in basic terms what Christianity is about, is still with us, and no doubt will be for a long time, if only because what is "basic" for one audience may not be basic for another. Lewis was "asked by the BBC to explain to his fellow Britons [in the 1940s] what Christians believe" (Norris 2001: xvii) and he could reasonably assume that, for example, the terms "right" and "wrong," "decency" and "fair play" (which he used quite a lot) were "basic" for his audience. (In fact, *Mere Christianity* opens with a chapter entitled "Right and wrong as a clue to the meaning of the Universe," and in the first chapter introduces not only "the Law of Right and Wrong" but also "the Law of Decent Behaviour," using the words "decent" and "decency" in a moral, "British," sense of the word.) But since these terms don't have semantic equivalents in other languages, not even European ones, they would not be helpful for those outside English-speaking countries. On the other hand, evidence suggests that words like "good" and "bad," "do" and "happen," "want" and "know," or "the same" and "like" (as in the phrase "like this") do have exact equivalents in all languages, and so they can really be used as basic terms for explaining what Christians believe to anyone anywhere.

It has often been pointed out that Lewis's vision of "plain, central Christianity" (Lewis 2000: 435) reflects, in some ways, the culture of a particular place and time ("a southern English middle-class culture during the Second World War," McGrath 2013: 228). His conceptual reliance on terms like "decency" and "fair play," and even "right" and "wrong," is consistent with such comments (although "right" and "wrong" characterize Anglo culture in a much broader sense). Still, the idea that it should be possible, in principle, to articulate the core of Christian faith with clarity and coherence, and in an ecumenical fashion, is one the present book is deeply in sympathy with.

Lewis borrowed the phrase "mere Christianity" from the Puritan English writer Richard Baxter (McGrath 2013). Having lived through "a period of tumultuous religious controversy and violence during the seventeenth century— including the English Civil War and the execution of Charles I," Baxter came to believe in "mere Christianity, Creed and Scripture." He wished to be known as a "mere Christian," equating "mere Christianity" with "catholic Christianity," in the sense of a universal vision of the Christian faith, untainted by controversies and theological partisanship" (McGrath 2013: 219–220, spelling modernized).

Lewis held that to be a Christian one needed a commitment to a specific form of Christianity, and personally he identified with the Church of England, and he famously compared "mere Christianity" to a hall "out of which doors open into several rooms, but which is not itself a place to live in: it is in the rooms, not in the hall, that there are fires and chairs and meals." Nonetheless he thought that a basic, transdenominational form of Christianity *could* be formulated, and that was what he was aiming at. This is also the aim of the present book.

Lewis's aspiration to identify "the scaffolding of a simple and genuinely Christian faith" (McGrath 2013: 221) was clearly linked with his wish to "translate theology into the vernacular," and his realization that to be so "translated," theology had to be re-thought in simple and intelligible words and phrases:

> You must translate every bit of your Theology into the vernacular. This is (. . .) essential. It is also the greatest service to your own thought. I have come to the conviction that if you cannot translate your thoughts into uneducated language, then your thoughts were confused. Power to translate is the test of having really understood one's own meaning. (Lewis 2000: 155)

This is also my experience. Trying to articulate "what Christians believe" for a wide audience, and in widely accessible language, is not a matter of "popularization," but above all, an exercise in clear thinking.

Minimal English, in which "The Story of God and People" (Part II of this book) is written, is, of course, something quite different from Lewis's "vernacular," but the idea that to re-tell the basic tenets of Christian faith in a new, more intelligible language one needs to re-think them through simpler, more intelligible words and phrases, is the same, and so is the discovery that the power to translate one's thoughts into "uneducated language" is the test of having really understood one's own meaning.

Before leaving the theme of "mere Christianity," let me take up Lewis's metaphor of a hall out of which many doors opens onto several rooms, and to point to the room in which I myself live. To quote from my 2001 book, *What Did Jesus Mean*:

> should the reader be interested in where I personally stand, I am a believing and "practising" Roman Catholic. At the same time, my perspective on the Gospels has been strongly influenced by the writings of Jewish, as well as Christian, scholars, and it is broadly ecumenical, which for me includes not only the Catholic and Protestant approaches but also the Eastern Christian tradition. In fact, in my attempts to understand what Jesus meant, I feel I learned most from a saint of the Eastern Church, the seventh-century scholar and mystic Isaac the Syrian (see, e.g. 1981, 1995). Isaac's distinction between "interior" meanings of the Scriptures' "discourse about God"— as opposed to the "outer meanings" and the "bodily exterior of the narratives"— and his insights into the symbolic meaning of apocalyptic images, warnings, and threats are, I find, more illuminating than many hermeneutical theories of the late twentieth century. (p. 23)

In her essay "Theology," American writer and theologian, and by her own description, "arch-Protestant," Marilynne Robinson (2015: 222) closes her discussion with the following sentence: "I have spent all this time clearing the ground so that I can say, and be understood to mean, without reservation, that I believe in a divine Creation, and in the Incarnation, the Crucifixion, the

Resurrection, the Holy Spirit, and the life to come." For me, too, this is core Christianity, which, as Robinson (2015: 216) says, "is expressed succinctly in the Apostles' Creed." As another woman theologian, Dorothy Sayers, put it in the title of her 1947 book, for nearly two millennia the question was—and is—*Creed or Chaos?*

A parting comment. Like many other words describing human groups, the word "Christians" can be used in a number of different ways. If I use this word, broadly speaking, to refer to people who accept (at least) the Apostles' Creed, I fully recognize other people's right to use it in other ways. On this point, too, I would like to quote Marilynne Robinson (2015):

> In the seventh chapter of Matthew [Gospel] there is a text I have never heard anyone preach on. There Jesus says that in the last day "many will say to me, 'Lord, Lord, did we not prophesy in your name, and cast out demons in your name, and do many mighty works in your name?' And then will I declare to them, 'I never knew you; depart from me.'" It is for Christ to decide who the Christians are, who has in fact done the will of his Father. (p. 105)

The parable of the Last Judgment in Matthew's chapter 25 also shows that from God's point of view, how people live is more important than what they say and what they believe.

And yet, as Robinson says in the same essay (referring to her experience as a public speaker), "a mistake is still a mistake. And its consequences can be very grave indeed." She illustrates this point with the following vignette:

> Once, in a discussion of the passage in [St Paul's letter to] Ephesians where Paul speaks of "the sword of the Spirit, which is the word of God", a woman in the audience (. . .) said: "But if you have a sword, you're supposed to smite somebody." Where to begin. (pp. 104–105)

(Robinson's point is that the phrase "the sword of the spirit" as used by St Paul is metaphorical and has nothing to do with killing; and also, that if anybody was ever radically against killing, it was Jesus, who taught love, forgiveness, and "turning the other cheek.")

So while the word "Christians" can be used in different ways, it is important to recognize that it can be legitimately used in the way that, for example, Chesterton, Dorothy Sayers, Benedict XVI, Alister McGrath, Alexander Men', and Marilynne Robinson, used it, and to link it with Jesus's teaching as preserved in the New Testament and "codified" in the Apostles' Creed and the Nicene Creed. It is also important to recognize that both the New Testament and the creeds rely on metaphors, that these metaphors need to be well understood, that they can be understood through cross-translatable words, and, last but not least, that they need to be interpreted in their proper cultural context. It is to this last point that I will now turn.

2

God and cross-cultural communication

2.1 Jesus's "incarnation" in Jewish culture

The story of God and people as told in the many books of the Bible (both the Hebrew Bible and the New Testament) is embedded in one particular speech culture. To understand this story properly, we need to know some things about that speech culture. In order to highlight this crucial point, I will adduce here part of the Abstract of a paper entitled "Jewish cultural scripts and the interpretation of the Bible," which I published more than a decade ago in a linguistic journal called *The Journal of Pragmatics* (Wierzbicka 2004):

> Reading stories can be an exercise in cross-cultural communication—and it can involve miscommunication. When we read texts belonging to other epochs, lands, peoples, and traditions, we need to know something about the "cultural scripts" which shaped the ways of thinking and the ways of speaking reflected in those texts. If these cultural scripts are to be made intelligible to us they must be explained in terms that the culture alien to us shares with our own (. . .). As [Russian literary scholar] Bakhtin (1979: 257) put it, in speaking "we 'pour' our speech into ready-made forms of speech genres (. . .) These forms are given to us in the same way in which our native language is given". Accordingly, to understand ways of speaking which belong to a culture alien to us we must learn to "hear" them in their proper cultural context and with some knowledge of this culture's ready-made speech forms; in other words, we must try to understand the underlying cultural scripts. Mainstream Anglo culture, with its cherished traditions of rationality and empiricism, and with its emphasis on science and scientific discourse, values consistency, accuracy, logical formulations, absence of contradictions (on any level), absence of exaggeration, dispassionate reasoning, and so on. As I have discussed in my book *What Did Jesus Mean?* (2001), these are not the values of the culture of Hosea, or the

culture of Jesus, just as they are not the values of the culture reflected in the stories of Sholom Aleichem or Isaac Bashevis Singer. (p. 575)

The key point that we need to grasp here is Jesus's cultural, and linguistic, Jewishness—a point which has only recently begun to be fully appreciated in the literature on the essentials of Christian faith. Commenting on the influence of Jewish ways of speaking on Jesus's mode of expression, Russian biblical scholar and Bible translator, Sergei Averintsev (2007) writes:

> Such facts of verbal coincidences (. . .) localise, in a concrete way, Him, who, according to the dogmatic statement of the Chalcedon Council, is in his incarnation true man (*alethos anthropos*), who lived his earthly life, like all other people, inside the space at a particular culture and who said entirely novel things in the established language of that culture. "And let the heretics not say that he was incarnated 'in a dream'" [in the words of a liturgical Orthodox chant]. (p. 495)

The words "was incarnated" ("*voplotilsja*") are very helpful here. Incarnation means not only being born in a particular body but also being born in a particular family, country, epoch, culture and language. For Jesus, this included Jewish culture and the linguistic traditions of the Jewish prophets. To quote Averintsev again:

> It is absolutely necessary to understand that facts which testify to a deep anchoring of Jesus' speech style in the biblical tradition (including the already mentioned verbal coincidences)—that if such facts are rightly understood (. . .), not only do they provide serious proof of a concrete historicity of the Gospel narratives, but also give—in full agreement with the (. . .) authoritative commentaries of ancient exegetes (beginning with the Fathers of the Church)—an example of Christ's fidelity to the living tradition [of his people]. (p. 495)

At this point, Averintsev quotes the remark of eighteenth-century Orthodox saint, Theophilact of Bulgaria, in relation to Jesus's words on the Cross: "Eloi, Eloi, lama sabachthani!" (Mark 15:34): "The Lord utters these words in Hebrew, showing that to his last breath, he reveres what is Jewish."

The metaphor of "incarnation" in relation to language and culture is also aptly invoked in Marilynne Robinson's (2015) essay "Son of Adam, Son of Man":

> He spoke the language of his time and people, in awareness of the associations particular words and phrases acquired, through scriptural contexts and their elaborations, and in the streets as well. In the ordinary course of things, embedded as they were in centuries of use, their senses would interact. It is surely among the mysteries of Incarnation that Jesus

could take on human language as well as human flesh, and that he could find it suited to his uses. (p. 253)

To dot the "i" here, too, what Jesus took on was not only "human language" in general, but also a particular "linguaculture," with its own words, phrases, discourse patterns, and cultural scripts. To illustrate, first, with a very simple example, in Luke's Gospel (14:26), Jesus says to the crowd accompanying him:

> If any one comes to me and does not hate his own father and mother and wife and children and brothers and sisters, yes, and even his own life, he cannot be my disciple.

This echoes the book of Genesis (29:31), where we hear that Jacob, who had two wives, Leah and Rachel, "hated Leah." This follows directly a line (29:30) which says that he "loved Rachel more than Leah." "Hating Leah" means "loving Rachel more." "Speaking the language of his people," Jesus means something similar here: He is not telling his disciples to "hate" their own fathers and mothers, but to "love him more" (see also Matthew 10:37).

2.2 Jewish cultural scripts and the interpretation of the Bible

In her introduction to an English edition of a volume of Yiddish short stories by the Jewish writer Sholom Aleichem the translator, Frances Butwin (1958), writes:

> There are as many types of curses as there are people cursing, but the hardest to explain is the mother cursing her child. The child may be crying because he is hungry. The mother bursts out, "Eat, eat, eat. All you want to do is eat. May the worms eat you. May the earth open up and swallow you alive." This mother loves her child, she is only pouring out the bitterness that's in her heart in the only way she knows. But in translation she sounds like a monster. (p. 9)

As the translator's comment shows, reading stories can be an exercise in cross-cultural communication—and it can involve serious miscommunication. If on the basis of cultural practices that a given piece of literature reflects we can formulate some rules of interpretation, we can help to minimize such miscommunication and build cross-cultural bridges between readers and writers.

As I argued in the paper "Jewish cultural scripts," cross-cultural misunderstandings arising from misinterpretation of culturally alien texts can have particularly far-reaching consequences in the area of religion. If a reader of Sholom Aleichem's stories takes the poor Jewish mother for a "monster," it is a pity, but it is not necessarily a matter of vital importance for anyone. If, however, a reader of the Hebrew Bible takes God as portrayed by the Hebrew prophets for a monster, it is a different story. And yet, if the reading glasses of the reader of the Hebrew Bible have Anglo lenses, the Yahweh presented there may well seem at times to be astonishingly vindictive and cruel. For example, in the Book of Hosea God speaks like this about Israel (13:7–8):

> So I will be to them like a lion;
> Like a leopard by the road I will observe them;
> I will meet them like a bear deprived of her cubs;
> I will tear open their rib cage,
> And there I will devour them like a lion.
> The wild beast shall tear them.

Yahweh's anger is great and its consequences are presented in apocalyptic terms ("the sword shall slash in his [Israel's] cities, devour his districts, and consume them"). Immediately after these dire images, however, comes a renewed outpouring of love (11:8–9), which cancels the threats:

> How can I give you up, Ephraim?
> How can I hand you over, Israel? (. . .)
> My heart churns within me;
> My sympathy is stirred.
> I will not execute the fierceness of my anger;
> I will not again destroy Ephraim.
> For I am God, and not man,
> The Holy One in your midst;
> And I will not come with terror.

Who is this God, then? From a modern Anglo perspective he seems to be if not a monster of vindictiveness then, at the very least, a monster of inconsistency and contradictions. The inconsistency and contradictions are, however, in the eye of the beholder: In fact, Yahweh is not contradicting himself at all, because he is not making any factual statements. His "illocutionary purpose" (cf. Austin 1962; Searle 1969) throughout his discourse is not that of threat, but above all, that of appeal ("O Israel, return to the Lord your God").

In his book *The Language and Imagery of the Bible*, G. B. Caird (1980) called the phenomenon in question "prophetic hyperbole," and he commented: "Prophecy deals more often than not in absolutes. The prophets do not make carefully qualified predictions that the Israelites will be destroyed unless they repent. They make unqualified warnings of doom, accompanied by unqualified calls to repentance. . . . What appears to be an unconditional verdict turns out to contain an unexpressed conditional clause" (p. 112). Jewish theologian Abraham Heschel (1962) spoke of this phenomenon in terms of the "mysterious paradox of Hebrew faith": "The All-wise and All-mighty may change a word that He proclaims. . . . The anger of the Lord is instrumental, hypothetical, conditional, and subject to his will. . . . The message of anger includes a call to return and to be saved. The call of anger is a call to cancel anger. . . . Its purpose and consummation is its own disappearance" (p. 286).

As I have argued at length in *What Did Jesus Mean?* (2001), an appreciation of the cultural scripts of Jewish prophetic speech is also necessary for the understanding of Jesus' speech preserved in the Gospels. As emphasized, in particular, by the Jewish scholar Pinchas Lapide (1985), Jesus spoke very much in the manner of the Hebrew prophets with whose discourses he had lived from early childhood. (Lapide (1985: 97) says that he spoke "exactly like the prophets before him.") It is true that we do not find in the Gospels "threatening" speeches like that of Yahweh in Hosea chapter 13 ("So I will be to them like a lion"), but the underlying principle of painting images of the future in order to appeal for some actions in the present is clearly in evidence.

Accordingly, when Jesus says in Matthew's Gospel (5:23) that whoever says to his brother "You fool!" shall be in danger of hell-fire, it is a cross-cultural misunderstanding to interpret his words as predictions of what is actually going to happen, or as threats made on God's behalf. In light of the discourse strategies of Hebrew prophets, Jesus's words ought to be read as expressing the following message:

> If you do this [say to your brother e.g., "You fool!"] it is very bad for you.
> God wants you not to do it.

The core idea here is not "if you do this, something very bad will happen to you because of this," but "if you do this, it is very bad for you."

On the surface, Jesus's talk about God (especially in Matthew's Gospel) is as inconsistent and full of contradictions as Hosea's portrayal of Yahweh speaking to Israel. In fact, however, all these contradictions are in the eye of the beholder, unfamiliar with the cultural scripts of Jewish prophetic discourse. Jesus' teaching about limitless forgiveness is made perfectly clear in parables like that of the Unforgiving Servant (Matthew 18:21–35). Not that that parable, in contrast to various other parables and sayings, is free of contradictions in its words and images. Here too, the "king's" forgiveness does not extend to the "unforgiving servant": Everything can be forgiven, except a failure to forgive. But does this mean that, according to Jesus, NOT everything can be forgiven? Obviously not: Saying that everything can be forgiven except a failure to forgive is a paradoxical, vivid, dramatic way of saying that everything *should* be forgiven (a point which nothing could highlight better than Jesus's words on the cross: "Father, forgive them, for they do not know what they are doing," Luke 23:24). Thus, to speculate what kinds of sins are, according to Jesus's teaching, unpardonable, is like arguing whether God can forgive seventy-eight offenses ("didn't Jesus draw a line at seventy-seven?" and "didn't he draw a line at a 'sin against the Holy Spirit?'") To interpret exhortations and appeals as judgments or predictions is to misunderstand the illocutionary force of the utterances in question.

This is, of course, not to say that Jesus's teaching about God is identical in content with the teachings in the Hebrew Bible. My point is that to understand what Jesus meant we have to take into account the cultural scripts which had shaped the speech of the Hebrew prophets. Remarkably, despite all the intervening centuries, indeed millennia, and despite all the differences in genre and register, we can still catch some echoes of those scripts in the everyday speech of the people in the Yiddish stories of East European Jewish writers such as Sholom Aleichem or Isaac Bashevis Singer.

In the case of a Jewish mother, a "bad feeling" ("when I think about you now, I feel something very bad") can be expressed as a "bad wish" ("I want something very bad to happen to you"). In the case of the Hebrew prophets, a "bad feeling" ("when I think about what you do I feel something very bad") can be expressed as a vengeful intention ("I [God] want to do something very bad to you because of this"). In the case of the Gospels, a "bad feeling" is associated with an announcement of a forthcoming doom sanctioned by God ("something very bad will happen to you because of this," perhaps even "God will want it to happen"). The details of the relevant speech acts are in each case different, but clearly, there are also some important common threads. Above all, in each case the illocutionary force is different from what the surface form of the utterances suggests.

The idea of the limitlessness of God's forgiveness was conveyed by Jesus in a positive way through the image of the Father in the parable of the Prodigal Son, and in a negative way, through the image of the king in the parable of the Unforgiving Servant. It was also conveyed, in a non-parabolic way, in his teaching on prayer: "For if you forgive men their trespasses, your heavenly Father will also forgive you. But if you do not forgive men their trespasses, neither will your Father forgive your trespasses" (Matthew 6:14-15); and in Luke (6:37): "Forgive, and you will be forgiven." All these references to the future—what God will forgive and what he will not forgive—are likely to be misunderstood if they are not interpreted in their proper cultural context, that is, in the context of Jewish prophetic speech.

Like Hosea, Jesus spoke, hyperbolically and dramatically, of the limits of God's forgiveness. In both cases, the images of a future doom must be interpreted as exhortations for the present. "O Israel, return to the Lord your God," pleads Hosea (14:1), having just assured Israel, on Yahweh's behalf, that it was too late for any return. Jesus teaches unlimited forgiveness in a non-parabolic way through his model prayer ("and forgive us our trespasses as we forgive those who trespass against us," cf. Matthew 6:12, Luke 11:4), as well as through his own life, that is, through his final prayer on the cross: "Father, forgive them, for they do not know what they are doing" (Luke 23:34).

The Christian tradition has recognized the forgiveness of sins as an essential part of Christianity in the Apostles' Creed: "I believe in the forgiveness of sins," "credo in remissionem peccatorum." Nonetheless, the surface contradictions in the Scriptures have often baffled Christian commentators and led them to contradictory statements in their own commentaries, for example, that, on the one hand, God's mercy is limitless, but on the other, it is limited in this or that way. A better understanding of Jewish cultural scripts, and in particular, of the scripts behind Jewish prophetic discourse, can lead to the resolution of exegetical problems which in the past have tended to obscure some of the most central aspects of Jesus's teaching.

While Jesus often spoke according to the scripts of Jewish prophetic discourse, he also—as has often been pointed out—used some rhetorical devices which were characteristically his own. These devices, variously described as "striking," "pithy," "paradoxical," "riddle-like," "hyperbolic," "absurd," and "humorous" (cf., e.g., Caird 1980; Chesterton 1925; Funk, Hoover et al. 1993), can be identified more clearly in terms of universal human concepts, as can the interplay between Jesus's own style and the rhetorical strategies of his culture.

In essence, then, Jesus urged people to act like God, and he sometimes said so in plain words (cf., e.g., Matthew 5:48). At other times, however, he formulated the same message in a paradoxical manner, by saying, as it were, that if people don't imitate God in his goodness, then God will imitate people in their badness, a warning with some of the grotesque humor of the admonition "let the dead bury their dead." For example, if people don't imitate God in being *always* ready to forgive everyone, then God will imitate people and will not be willing to forgive *some* people, or *some* sins.

Clearly, people couldn't imitate God in being *always* willing to forgive if God were not himself *always* willing to forgive. This clash is not a sign of contradiction in the substance of Jesus's teaching; rather, it is an instance of Jesus's paradoxical style of teaching—in some ways, very much his own, but in others, drawing on the same cultural scripts which had shaped the speech of Hosea and the other great Jewish prophets. When a Jewish prophet says that God "will do something very bad to people" if they live in a certain way, this means that this prophet is calling on people, urging people, pleading with people, on God's behalf, not to live in this way. "God will do something very bad to you if you live like this" means, in essence, that "God wants you to live not like this," that "it is very bad for you to live like this," that "it is very good for you to live with God," that "you can live with God," that "God wants it."

Just as when a Jewish mother screams at her child something that, on the face of it, means "I want something very bad to happen to you," it would be ethnocentric to take it literally, so too when a Jewish prophet says something like "God will do something very bad to you" it would be ethnocentric to interpret it literally.

There are undoubtedly important differences between the New Testament and the Hebrew Bible, both in content and in style. But there are also continuities. An important aspect of these continuities was illuminated by the seventh-century Syrian biblical scholar and mystic St Isaac of Niniveh, who wrote the following about the Scriptures as a whole:

> That we should imagine that anger, wrath, jealousy or the such like have anything to do with the divine Nature is something utterly abhorrent to us. . . . Nor again can we possibly say that He acts thus out of retribution, even though the Scriptures may on the outer surface posit this. Even to think this of God and to suppose that retribution for evil acts is to be found in Him is abominable. (Isaac of Niniveh 1995: 162)

Isaac of Niniveh took particular care to distinguish the external form of the Bible ("the bodily exterior" of its discourse about God) from the meanings concealed inside it:

> Many figurative terms are employed in the Scriptures of God, terms which are far removed from his (true) nature. And just as (our) rational nature has (already) become gradually more illumined and wise in a holy understanding of the mysteries which are hidden in (Scripture's) discourse about God—that we should not understand everything (literally) as it is written, but rather that we should see (concealed) inside the bodily exterior of the narratives, the hidden providence and eternal knowledge which guides all—so too we shall in the future come to know and be aware of many things for which our present understanding will be seen as contrary to what it will be then. (Isaac of Niniveh, 1995: 171)

In a book entitled *The Old Testament in the New*, biblical scholar Steve Moyise (2001) writes: "Christianity did not spring out of a vacuum but is in direct continuity with the religion enshrined in what Christians call the Old Testament" (p. 1). This continuity—reflected in quotations, allusions, and echoes—applies as much to the style as to content. As Moyise puts it, "the biblical authors were so immersed in scripture that they naturally used many of its idioms and expressions as their own" (p. 6). And so of course did Jesus.

In his book *Simply Good News*, British theologian and biblical scholar Tom Wright (2015) speaks of various Bible passages as written in "dramatic first-century, picture language that is difficult to decode today" (pp. 89–90). Referring in particular to the belief of early Christians that "Jesus would come back again," Wright comments that "many western Christians in our own day have quietly abandoned the belief altogether, preferring to see such language as a bit of ancient mythology we can do without today."

But although that "first-century picture language" may indeed be "difficult to decode today," we do need to try to "decode" it. It was not only early Christians who used "first-century picture language." Jesus did too.

As for "Jesus's returning," this is included in the Apostles' Creed: "He will come again, in glory, to judge the living and the dead." To understand what Jesus and the Apostles meant by such sentences we do need to try to translate the "pictures" they used into words, as far as possible, cross-translatable words, and this is what "The Story of God and People" (Part II of this book) aims to do. (To see how this can be done for "Jesus' returning," see Part II, chapter 40.)

It also needs to be said that such dramatic picture language was characteristic not only of first-century Palestine but also of the Jewish prophets for many centuries before (for example, Hosea). To understand such language we need to interpret it in its cultural context, in accordance with the traditions of biblical prophetic speech and, generally, with Jewish cultural scripts.

2.3 Cross-cultural communication and the concept of "hell"

All this of course has profound implications for the interpretation of the traditional doctrine of "hell" and "eternal damnation." In the creeds, Christians profess their faith in "the forgiveness of sins and life everlasting," and there is no mention of any "everlasting hell," but the hyperbolic and figurative language of the Gospels does include references to "hellfire" (e.g., Matthew 5:22), and even "unquenchable fire" (e.g., Mark 9:44) and "eternal fire" (Matthew 25:41). Taken out of their cultural context, such references have often been interpreted as affirming the prospect of "eternal damnation" for some people, incompatible with Jesus's teaching of unlimited forgiveness. Commenting in particular on the reference to an "unpardonable sin" (a sin against the Holy Spirit) in Mark's Gospel (3:79), Catholic theologian and biblical scholar Wacław Hryniewicz (2012) writes:

> Here we come close to one of Jesus' eschatological sayings whose understanding requires cross-cultural awareness. Those to whom the cultural linguistic traditions of such sayings were alien would find this text profoundly disturbing. If such readers are familiar with obvious metaphors and paradoxes they are prepared to understand images, but reading about "no forgiveness" and about an "eternal sin" they tend to take these words literally. (p. 79)

Emphasizing the Gospels' key theme of limitless forgiveness, Hryniewicz (2012) comments:

> What Jesus says about God may seem, as in the case of Hosea, inconsistent and full of contradictions. Are there exceptions to the divine readiness to forgive? Does it mean that God ceases to love people who have committed the sin against the Holy Spirit, and does not try to reconcile them with himself? Is he on the one hand infinitely merciful, while on the other his mercy has some fixed limits?
>
> Again, these contradictions appear only to those who are not familiar with the prophetic discourse and Jesus' paradoxical style of

teaching. It is true that in the parable of the unforgiving debtor which follows Peter's question and Jesus' answer (Mt 18:23-35), the "king's" forgiveness is categorically refused to the "unforgiving servant". Does this mean that not everything can be forgiven or that it is unforgivable not to forgive? (p. 80)

Rejecting such an interpretation as due to a lack of cross-cultural understanding, Hryniewicz appeals, again, to the conventions of Jewish prophetic speech, which are totally at variance with the norms of modern Anglo speech culture:

Jesus' often repeated call for trust in merciful God should not be misinterpreted as a threat or prediction of an irrevocable and unhappy future, which can only cause fear and despair. Such misinterpretations would contradict the conventions of the Jewish prophetic speech. (p. 81)

In this context, Hryniewicz adduces a quote from *What Did Jesus Mean?*:

Even now, when most readers have come to realize that images like "the furnace of fire", "outer darkness", and "weeping and gnashing of teeth" should not be taken literally, the hyperbole of words like "everlasting" often continues to be unrecognized. And yet even in colloquial English, phrases like "for ages" or "forever" can be used as a hyperbole for "a long time" (especially when referring to waiting). If this is possible in modern Anglo culture, which values understatement and on the whole is inimical to hyperbole, how much more should it be seen as possible in the context of the Jewish prophetic "Drohrede" (. . .), that is, the language of rhetorical threats and warnings. In fact, this is precisely how it was seen by early Fathers of the church such as Clement of Alexandria, Origen, and St. Gregory of Nyssa, who held that all suffering ("punishment") after death has a spiritual, healing, and purifying character and must therefore come to an end." (Wierzbicka 2001: 457)

"The Story of God and People" (Part II of this book) does not engage in abstract arguments such as those quoted above but simply re-tells the biblical story in a way which is informed by them. (See, in particular, chapter 40, Part II.)

As far as I can see, the resulting text, formulated in simple, intelligible and cross-translatable words and phrases, is free from any apparent inconsistencies and incoherencies. At the same time it can stand on its own: it does not require a critical and historical commentary to convey the relevant tenets of the Christian Creed: "I believe . . . in the forgiveness of sins, . . . and life everlasting." (The interested reader can find such a commentary in *What Did Jesus Mean* and the references cited there, but "The Story" presented here, in Part II of *What Christians Believe*, can be read on its own.)

In his book *The Everlasting Man,* G. K. Chesterton (1925) commented that the story told in the Gospels "is anything but (. . .) 'a simple Gospel'" (p. 120). "It is by no means (. . .) a story that is easy to get to the bottom of. (. . .) The Gospel as it stands is almost a book of riddles" (pp. 119–120). Some of Jesus's most important teachings about what the creed calls "the forgiveness of sins" and "life everlasting" is formulated in the form of parables, like the parable of the Lost Sheep and the parable of the Prodigal Son. Such parables are very clearly intended as "riddles" whose solution could be worked out by the listener. Jesus did not formulate their solution explicitly, leaving it to his listeners to figure it out for themselves and, presumably, expecting them to look for coherence—not a coherence at the surface level, in what St Isaac of Nineveh called "the bodily exterior of the narratives," but at a deeper level, where the intended meaning could be found.

St Isaac (1995), who was closer in culture and tradition to Jesus than Western theologians such as St Augustine, rejected a literalist reading of an "everlasting damnation" as a deplorable misunderstanding and an insult to God:

> It is not (the way of) the compassionate Maker to create rational beings in order to deliver them over mercilessly to unending affliction (in punishment) for things of which He knew even before they were fashioned, (aware) how they would turn out when He created them—and whom (nonetheless) He created. (p. 165)

In view of this, Gehenna can only be, according to St Isaac, temporary and part of God's overall love and mercy; to deny that both the kingdom and Gehenna were foreseen by God for the purpose of our good would be blasphemy:

> That we should further say or think that the matter is not full of love and mingled with compassion would be an opinion full of blasphemy and insult to our Lord God. (By saying) that He will even hand us over to burning for the sake of suffering, torment and all sorts of ills, we are attributing to divine Nature an enmity towards the very rational beings which He created through grace. . . . Among all His actions there is none which is not entirely a matter of mercy, love and compassion: this constitutes the beginning and the end of His dealings with us. (p. 172)

A recent echo of these words can be heard in Marilynne Robinson's essay "Theology": "Granting all complexities, is it conceivable that the God of the Bible would shackle himself to the worst consequences of our worst behaviour? Reverence forbids" (2015: 216).

In his chapter in *Universalism and the Doctrine of Hell* (1992), Protestant theologian Paul Helm quotes Charles Darwin:

> I can hardly see how anyone ought to wish Christianity to be true, for if so, the plain language of the text seems to show that the men who do

not believe, and this would include my Father, Brother, and almost all my best friends, will be everlastingly punished. And this is a damnable doctrine. (p. 257)

What this poignant quote illustrates is how much damage can be done by mistaking exhortations for predictions, and how misleading the "plain language" of a distant culture can be if one is not familiar with its "cultural scripts."

Before concluding, let me quote, once more, Hryniewicz (2012):

The culture of Jesus' times was profoundly influenced by the tradition of the biblical prophets. He spoke a language of the prophets shaped by Jewish scripts and cultural rules which contained certain shared linguistic patterns. (. . .)

The failure to understand the Jewish prophetic discourse may obscure some of the central aspects of Jesus' teaching. To many Western Christians, especially those who insist on the infallibility of the letter of the Bible, the paradoxical sayings of Jesus present insurmountable difficulties and become great stumbling-blocks. How can one be a true disciple of Christ, if one does not faithfully obey what he commands us to do in order to be saved? Can the Bible err? Because of its linguistic paradoxes the Bible has suffered much violence from all kinds of literalists who, forgetting the Jewish prophets, took the eschatological threats found in the Gospels at their face value. The lack of familiarity with the Jewish rhetorical tradition has often led to misunderstanding of Jesus' universal message about God whose greatest concern is the salvation of all. (pp. 72–73)

Crucially, the point about "eschatological threats" meant as appeals applies also to "eschatological parables" such as the parable of the Last Judgment in St Matthew's Gospel (25:31-46), with its apparent division of people into "the sheep" and "the goats." As discussed by Hryniewicz in an earlier book (*A Hope of Salvation for All: From an Eschatology of Fear to an Eschatology of Hope*, 1990), the intended message of this parable is not that there are, and always will be, two categories of people, "the sheep" and "the goats." Rather, it is a personal message to everyone: You are both like a sheep and like a goat, God wants you to be like a sheep, not like a goat; from now on, try to live like a sheep, not like a goat.

The parable of the Lost Sheep offers a different image, but its message is closely related to that of the Last Judgment. The point is not that that there are, and always will be, two categories of sheep, those with the flock and those that are lost, but that everyone is, or can be, like a lost sheep, and that God wants all the "sheep" to be together, with the shepherd, and will not let any "sheep" remain lost forever. This is why the final lines of the last chapter of "The Story of God and People" (Part II of this book) read:

God feels something very good towards all people,
God wants to do very good things for all people.
All people can live with God if they want to.
After people die, they can live with God, with other people, forever.
God wants it

These lines are consistent with the concluding lines of the Apostles' Creed: "I believe in the communion of saints, the forgiveness of sins, the resurrection of the body, and life everlasting. Amen."

I will add that the images of the shepherd and the lost sheep highlight perhaps better than anything else Jesus's cultural Jewishness and his ongoing conversation with the Old Testament. "The Lord is my shepherd, I shall not want," says the Psalmist (Psalm 23). Jesus takes up this image: "I am the good shepherd (. . .) I lay down my life for the sheep" (John 10:14–15), thus identifying himself with the Psalmist's God, and at the same time expressing his own mission. "I am a lost sheep, seek thy servant," says the Psalmist (Psalm 19:176), and Jesus responds (as it were) with the words "For the Son of Man is come to save that which was lost" (Matthew 18:11), and with the parable of the Lost Sheep, in which the shepherd leaves ninety-nine sheep to go and seek the one which has gone astray (Matthew 18:12–14; Luke 15:4–7). Unmissably, the parable echoes the words of the prophet Isaiah: "All we like sheep have gone astray (. . .); and the Lord hath laid on him the iniquity of us all" (53:6)—a sentence in which Christians see the image of Jesus dying on the cross for all people.

To modern readers of the New Testament, the metaphor of sheep may be misleading, and it could hardly be congenial: if they think that the New Testament encourages them to be "like sheep" this can only be off-putting, even though, on reflection, they should be able to recognize that in the parable one lost sheep—an individual—has a greater value than ninety-nine.

3

God and language

3.1 Can we say something true about God with ordinary human words?

In his little book *What Do We Mean by "God"?* (2015), Anglican theologian Keith Ward asks: "Who or what is 'God'?" (title of the first chapter); and he answers: "God is something which is completely indescribable."

As a former Regius Professor of Divinity at Oxford, Ward knows, of course, that in the Christian understanding God is not "something" but "someone," yet he is apparently so anxious to repudiate the idea of God as an old man with a beard and to stress that God cannot be adequately described in human language that if he has to choose, he seemingly prefers to call God "something" rather than "someone."

In this chapter, I will try to illustrate how the approach taken in "The Story of God and People" (Part II of this book) differs from others by comparing some ways of speaking about God and Jesus (for Christians, the Son of God) with those presented in two recent Christian books published in a series called "A little book of guidance": Ward's *What Do We Mean by "God"?* is the first one, and the second is *What Is Christianity?* written by the former Archbishop of Canterbury Rowan Williams (2015). My purpose is not to criticize these two "little books of guidance," but to use them as points of reference, to be able to show more clearly what is different, and unusual, about the approach taken here (and also, in my 2001 book *What Did Jesus Mean?*, to which the present book is a successor).

I will, however, engage with Ward's statements such as "God is something which is completely indescribable" and use them as a point of departure for presenting a different view of the power of language and in particular, of the ability of languages to express what Christians believe, and to do so clearly, intelligibly, and truthfully.

So what, according to Ward (2015), can be said about this indescribable "something" called God? Ward writes: "You could say—though it might be a little misleading—that God is the infinite source or origin of the universe. God is the infinite being which is expressed through the finite beings in the universe" (p. 6).

From my point of view, one big problem with such statements is that they cannot be expressed in languages other than English, since the keywords on which they depend—such as "infinite" and "finite"—have no equivalents in most languages of the world. Accordingly, whatever the merits of the passage above, its meaning is locked in English (and other European languages).

It is not that Ward doesn't try to explain what he means by "infinite" and "finite," but unfortunately his explanation is also locked in English and cannot be rendered in most other languages of the world:

> When we say that God is infinite, we mean that God is not limited by anything else. There is nothing which sets limits to God and so makes God finite. God is not just one thing among other things of the same sort. But that means that we cannot think of God as a being, even as a very large being, who exists in addition to the universe—because if God were outside the universe, God would be limited by it and excluded from it. (p. 3)

Even in a language like English, to explain "infinite" as "not limited by anything else" is not very helpful if we don't know what "limited by something else" might mean. Similarly, to explain "finite" by saying that "there is nothing which sets limits to God" is not very helpful if we don't know what "setting limits to God" might mean. Furthermore, words and expressions like "limited," "limitless," and "set limits to" have no counterparts in most languages of the world (just as "infinite" and "finite" don't). So even if such explanations could help some highly educated Europeans, they certainly would not help speakers of most non-European languages. Are there, then, no "human" (rather than high-register European) terms with the help of which God could be characterized across languages and cultures?

Empirical cross-linguistic investigations suggest that there *are* such terms. Indeed, there are whole phrases which, evidence suggests, have their counterparts in all languages and which could be used to say some things (the same things) about God in any language. For example, cross-linguistic investigations show that apart from the word "God" itself, in any language one can say the exact equivalents of the English sentences "God is now, God always was, God always will be"; "God is everywhere"; and "there is no one else like God." (See, e.g., Goddard and Wierzbicka 2014a, and the Natural Semantic Metalanguage (NSM) Homepage, bit.ly/1XUoRRV; Wierzbicka 2018a.)

We may indeed be unable to explain "the reality of God" (Ward 2015: 7) in human words (the only kind we have), but does this mean that we humans can't say anything true about God at all, or that we can't say anything true about God in prose, as Ward would have it? ("The language about God is something like the language of poetry" (p. 7).) Trying to explain this point, Ward relies on the culture-specific English words "revelation," "reality," and "experience":

> "Revelation" is the important word here. It literally means an unveiling, a drawing-apart of the veils of appearance to disclose the reality which underlies them. You can say that you have an experience of God when that revelation occurs, when the veils of the finite world are, as it were, drawn aside and you see the infinite reality which underlies them. But you cannot describe that reality in prose. (p. 10)

This may sound like a resonant and poetic passage, but conceptually, and linguistically, it is entirely locked in English. "Revelation" may be an important word in English—as "reality" and "experience" certainly are (see Wierzbicka 2010)—but none of these words could be translated into most languages of the world.

I will return to "revelation" in the next section. Here, let me comment on Ward's objections to the phrase of the Nicene Creed describing God as "the maker of heaven and earth." The picture implied by this phrase, he says, "almost irresistibly makes us think of the bearded muscle-man with his compasses, moulding the sky and the ground out of some sort of clay or primeval energy. But we know by now that we must discard such pictures once we have left the nursery school" (pp. 8–9). In his own account of creation, Ward replaces the phrase "the maker of heaven and earth" with some sentences in philosophical English likely to be incomprehensible to most English speakers and certainly untranslatable into most languages of the world. Here is his proposal:

> What we have to say is that there is an infinite, literally indescribable reality which is the source and origin of all finite things, which expresses its character in and through them, and which is the true and enduring basis of whatever reality they have. To say that there is a 'maker of heaven and earth' is to say that the world of finite things is seen most truly when it is seen as the expression of a source and origin which is its essential truth and reality. (p. 9)

I agree that by themselves, phrases like "maker of heaven and earth" are not sufficient and that they require a commentary, and I offer such a commentary in chapter 2 of "The Story" (Part II of the book). In contrast to Ward's commentary quoted above, however, that chapter seeks to articulate the Christian understanding of creation in words and phrases which have their counterparts in all languages, and which in fact can be understood even by young children (not only in English-speaking countries but in all parts of the world). If we want to explain creation in a way intelligible through any language, then I would suggest, as a first approximation, the following: "The Earth exists because God wants it to exist; everything exists because God wants it to exist."

Like many other theologians, Ward (2015) does express concern for humanity as a whole, and he acknowledges the need to speak about God clearly and non-parochially: "The Christian religion, like most religions, is basically a search for God; and the search for God is the search for those finite expressions of the infinite reality which will be clearest and most fulfilling for us and for humanity as a whole" (p. 12).

Unfortunately, this very passage is itself both unclear and conceptually "parochial" (because concepts like "infinite" and "reality," well established in English, are unknown to speakers of most other languages around the globe). I am not sure what "finite expressions" that would be "clearest (. . .) for humanity as a whole" Ward has in mind here. As I see it, however, the expressions which are clearest to humanity as a whole are those which occur, with exactly the same meaning, in all human languages and which can therefore be seen as humanity's shared conceptual language, or "Common Human."

As the present book seeks to demonstrate, saying true things about God (in simple and intelligible prose) is possible. Moreover, it is possible to say such things in words, phrases, and sentences which, as evidence suggests, are cross-translatable into all languages, and which can therefore tell a story accessible to humanity as a whole.

Many of these phrases may sound naïve and unsophisticated, but arguably this reflects their strength rather than weakness. For example, the first lines of chapter 1 of "The Story" ("God") read: "There is someone not like people. This someone is someone above people. This someone is now, always was, always will be. This someone is everywhere. There is no one else like this someone. God is this someone." This may sound less sophisticated, and therefore less satisfactory, than "God is the infinite being which is expressed through the finite beings in the universe" (Ward 2015: 6), but it is fully understandable, fully cross-translatable, requires no further explanations, and doesn't need to be taken as poetry rather than plain, intelligible prose.

Ward makes claims about language which from a linguistic point of view seem arbitrary and unfounded. For example, he says:

> All our words are about finite things. When we use a word for something like a table or a chair, we use that word to pick out something which is different from other things, which marks out the limits of the thing, which refers to a finite reality. All our words have to do that; for they pick out slices of reality by marking off their limits from other things. So none of our words can apply properly to God. If God is infinite, and if all our words must apply to finite things, then none of our words are going to describe God properly. (p. 5)

What, however, is the basis for the claim that "all our words are about finite things"? Evidence strongly suggests that all languages have a word for "all." How is "all" a word about "finite things"? And when God says to Moses in

Exodus, "I am who I am," presumably he is using the Hebrew words for "I" and for "be" without implying that he is a "finite thing." What, then, is the basis for the claim that "none of our words can apply properly to God"? Ward (2015) says that "the idea that God is infinite is a very hard one to grasp" (p. 4), but the question arises whether this is a helpful thing to say about God in the first place. Why not try to say, instead, things that *can* be understood, for example, that God is now, always was, and always will be? (Cf. "Revelation," 2:8).

I agree that a sentence like "God is now, always was, and always will be" may not exhaust all the implications of "I am who I am," and in *What Did Jesus Mean?* (Wierzbicka 2010) I suggested a further, "timeless," component: "God exists because God exists, not because of anything else." I still think that this is something that can be meaningfully said about God (preferably using "is" instead of "exists"). But the word "always" is a good start, and can also be used meaningfully about God.

In a book of essays by Alexander Men' (1996), *Christianity for the Twenty-First Century*, we find a defense of words which is both inspired and down-to-earth:

> It may be that at the higher level of the human spirit or at moments of special inner elevation, words are superfluous. But as a rule, we cannot manage without words, without concepts or without thinking.
>
> We may readily understand why the theologian William Hamilton or the mystic Jiddu Krishnamurti rejected all definitions of God and even the very word "God" itself on the ground that words tend to become fetishized. But on the other hand, their attempt to rise above words was destined to failure. People are not only creatures who contemplate and experience, but beings who think and speak. To reject concepts and words is to go against human nature, against the human need to give meaning to life and experience. (p. 43)

Arguing against theologians who reject the word "God" Men' cites, as an example, the eminent Protestant theologian Paul Tillich:

> In rejecting the idea of God "up in heaven", another contemporary theologian, Paul Tillich, has suggested that we speak about God as "inexhaustible depth". In doing so he failed to see that "depth" is the same kind of conventional spatial metaphor as "heaven". (p. 44)

Defending the absolute necessity of words for making sense of our experience as well as sharing it with other people, Men' rejects the claims of so-called apophatic (i.e., negative) theology, according to which people can only say what God is not, but cannot affirm anything about God in words.

> . . . people cannot be restricted to this "negative" theology. God manifests himself in life so actively, so powerfully, so vitally, and so

concretely that simple negation is not enough. Religious life and thought need words of affirmation as well. They may need to be constantly accompanied by riders and qualifications, but they are a necessity to us as human beings. (p. 46)

Saying amen to all that, I would add that the words in which we try to articulate our experience, and our faith, need to be well chosen. As I have tried to show in earlier publications (e.g. Wierzbicka 2001, 2018a), words which can be particularly helpful in this endeavor are those which are simple, intuitively clear, and universally cross-translatable.

3.2 Can we say something true about God with words like "want" and "feel"?

The word "revelation" is, as Ward notes, an important Christian word (I would add: for speakers of English). It is not, however, one which has counterparts in all languages of the world. If one wanted to explain to speakers of most non-European languages what the part of the New Testament called "The Revelation to John" is about, one would have to come down from the high register of English divinity studies to the level of simple human words such as "want," "do," "say," and "know."

The first line of that part of the New Testament says: "The revelation of Jesus Christ, which God gave him to show to his servants what must soon take place; and he made it known by sending his angels to his servant John" (Revelation 1:1). It seems clear that a core part of the meaning expressed here is that "God wanted people to know what would happen after some time." If it sounds too naïve, or too anthropomorphic, to say that God wanted people to know some things, and if a word like "revelation" is of the essence here, then Jesus's "Good News" would be accessible only to English speakers, and only to those among them who are versed in academic, and philosophical, registers of English.

Plainly, this is not the case. The very idea of "Good News" is that God wants all people to know some things. The word "want" is indeed of the essence here. As the Prologue to John's Gospel puts it in relation to Jesus's birth, "the true light that enlightens every man [human being] was coming into the world" (John 1:9). In other words, Jesus was born on earth because God wanted all people to know what is true. High-register English words like "revelation" or "incarnation" are not necessary to say that, but the words "want," "know," and "true," which can be found in any human language and are known to children as well as adults, *are* necessary. As I will illustrate shortly, the word "feel" is also necessary to explain how the New Testament wants people to think about God.

Unfortunately, saying that God wants something or feels something is precisely the kind of statement that Ward condemns, apparently thinking that such statements somehow cheapen God and make him sound too much like humans.

> If, as I have said, none of our words can give an exact, correct description of God, so that we cannot say that God is thinking or feeling or desiring or willing, in the way that we think, feel or will; (. . .) does that mean that we cannot really say anything true about God at all? In one way it does. And that is a very important fact about God. Anything we say about God is only partially or inadequately true, in the sense we must mean it. All our words are inadequate to express the reality of God. (p. 7)

The idea that it is somehow naïve or unjustified to say that God *wants* something is clearly at variance with how Jesus spoke about God. How could we possibly understand Jesus's prayer in the Garden of Olives: "My Father, if it is possible, let this cup pass from me; yet not what I want but what you want" (Matthew 26:39 NRSV, New Revised Standard Version), if the word "want" was inapplicable to God?

The same applies to God's feelings. Leaving aside, for the moment, the whole gamut of emotions attributed to God, anthropomorphically, in the Hebrew Bible ("the Old Testament"), in the New Testament, too, a great deal is said about God's feelings—especially love, and in some of the key lines of the Gospels, Jesus speaks of God's feelings. Thus, in one of the best known lines of the Gospels, Jesus says: "God so loved the world that he gave his only son so that whoever believes in him should not perish but have eternal life" (John 3:16).

The Greek verb *agapao* used in this sentence and glossed in the English translations as "love" does not have an exact equivalent in all human languages, but two main components of its meaning can be articulated in any language as follows: "to want to do good things for someone" and "to feel something very good towards someone" (Wierzbicka in press). Accordingly, the sentence "God loved the world" (where "the world" stands for "all people") can be explained in any language as a combination of these two components: "God wanted to do good things for all people" and "God felt something very good towards all people." Such statements will not necessarily be equally colloquial or idiomatic in all languages, but they will be understandable.

According to Mark's Gospel, God himself speaks of his feelings during Jesus's baptism, when he says to Jesus: "You are my Son, the Beloved, with you I am well pleased" (Mark 1:11). Not every language has a word matching the English "beloved" or the Greek word *agapetos* (as in Mark 1:11), but obviously people who believe this scene to be part of God's revelation need to try to understand what God is saying here. Further, in trying to explain these words to speakers of languages which don't have a word matching *agapetos* Christian commentators need to find some other words capable of carrying the central message "I feel something very good towards you." For example, the Pitjantjatjara (Central Australia) version, *Tjukurpa Palya*, uses here the word *mukuringanyi*, which Goddard's (1996) dictionary glosses as "love" (sense 3 of the verb, the other two senses are glossed as "want/like" and "be fond of, fancy, desire, like"). (For further discussion, see Wierzbicka, in press.)

The exact meaning of the word translating the Greek word *agapetos* may differ from language to language, but the essence of what God says to Jesus in this sentence—"I feel something very good towards you"—can be expressed in any language. Surely, it is this essence expressible in any language which the text—and the speaker behind the text—wants readers to take as God's message. What applies to the scene of Jesus's baptism in Mark's Gospel applies also to Jesus's "Transfiguration" in Matthew's Gospel (17:5), where the three Apostles, Peter, John, and James, hear God say about Jesus: "This is my beloved Son, with whom I am well pleased." (Again, the Greek word used in this scene is *agapetos*.)

According to the part of the New Testament known as John First Letter, God is love:

> Beloved, let us love one another, because love is from God; everyone who loves is born of God and knows God. Whoever does not love does not know God, for God is love [*agape*]. God's love was revealed among us in this way: God sent his only Son into the world so that we might live through him. (. . .) God is love and those who abide in love, abide in God, and God in them. (1 John 4:7–9, 16)

To convey this message of the New Testament in languages which don't have a word corresponding to the Greek words *agape* ("love," noun) or *agapao* (verb), we need to break its meaning into components based on the concepts "want" and "feel." Since, evidence suggests, these concepts are present as words in all languages, the central and most distinctive message of the New Testament that "God is love" can be conveyed through all languages—provided that the words "want" and "feel" do apply to God.

One final comment on the applicability of "mental verbs" like "want" and "feel" to God. According to the Bible, and to mainstream Christianity, God created people "in our [God's] image," "after our [God's] likeness" (Genesis 1:26). What can creation "in God's image" possibly mean if it doesn't have anything to do with wanting and feeling? Essentially, as chapter 1 of "The Story" puts it, "God is someone not like people" (more precisely, "There is someone not like people, God is this someone.") And yet, God created people "in his own image." According to the interpretation articulated in cross-translatable words in chapter 2 of "The Story," in people God wanted to have creatures who could want to "talk back" to him, and who would "love" as they were "loved." That is, people could want to say something to God, as God wants to say something to people, and they could feel something very good toward

God, as God feels something very good toward people, and they could feel something very good toward people, as God feels something very good toward people. They could also want to do good things for people, as God wants to do good things for people. Some aspects of this interpretation are open to discussion, but it seems clear that the "similarity" of people to God stressed in the phrase "in his own image" must refer to the human capacity for "wanting" and "feeling" rather than to anything physical. If so, however, then God, too, wants and feels. (Of course, animals can also "want" and "feel," but this is beside the point: Presumably it is the content of what people can "want" and "feel" which makes people "created in the image of God.")

Certainly, not all human words apply properly to God; and, when, for example, words like "wrath" or "hate" are used by people about God (e.g., in Psalm 1:5: "thou hatest all workers of iniquity," KJV, King James Version), we must not take them literally. As seventh-century scholar and mystic St Isaac of Nineveh (1995: 171) has written, "Just because [the terms] wrath, anger, hatred, and the rest are used of the Creator, we should not imagine that He [actually] does anything in anger or hatred or zeal. Many figurative terms are employed in the Scriptures of God which are far removed from His true nature."

But if *all* words—including "someone," "you," "I," "want," and "feel"— were inapplicable to God, so that no possibility of dialogue between people and God (no "I" and "you") were left, then even Jesus's statements about God, and Jesus's model prayer ("Our Father . . . your kingdom come") would have to be rejected. Surely, this would be a case of *reductio ad absurdum*.

In an essay entitled "Theology," included in the volume *The Givenness of Things*, American novelist, essayist, and Protestant theologian, Marilynne Robinson (2015: 220) writes: "To oversimplify greatly, the argument in Western civilization has been about whether the sense of an Other, an order of Being that exists in meaningful relationship with humankind, or that at least can be described in human terms, is or is not a meaningful intuition." As this quote illustrates, for Robinson, God is self-evidently "someone other than people," who nonetheless can be described in human terms. There can be some debate as to how exactly the meaningful relationship between people and this someone "Other than people" should be described, but the fact that it *can* be described in human terms is for her a given. On this point, as on many others, I am at one with Robinson.

I would add that just as people can talk *about* God in human terms, God can speak *to* people in human terms. Robinson mentions in this context "the problem, if that is the word, of putting divine utterance into plain language" (p. 253). In fact, however, putting divine utterance into "plain" language is not as great a problem as it might seem (if by "plain" we understand a language that relies on cross-translatable words and can therefore be understood by all people). For example, when God says "I am who I am," we can put this into "plain" language intelligible anywhere in the world as "I am now, I always was, I always will be." It is a far greater problem to put some *human* utterances into "plain" language intelligible anywhere in the world, because "human utterances" are often steeped in particularities of history and culture, and because they often carry with them, in a highly condensed form, "local" cultural experiences. (I will return to this point in chapter 4, in section 4.4).

Commenting on his portrayal of Jesus in his book *Jesus of Nazareth* (Benedict XVI 2007a: xix) and acknowledging the importance of the "historical-critical interpretation of every biblical text," Pope Benedict XVI also expresses his confidence in the Gospels as a whole: "I trust the Gospels" (p. xxi). In a similar spirit, I would like to say: I trust the shared core of human languages. In particular, I have confidence in shared human concepts such as "someone," "good," "true," "want," and "feel," with the help of which the Gospels, and the Christian faith based on them, can be interpreted, and interpreted in the same way, in all human languages.

3.3 How did Jesus speak about God?

According to Ward, "God is beyond human concepts," but this was clearly not Jesus's view. Jesus spent most of his public life speaking to people about God—relying, in doing so, on human concepts. Usually, however, he did not rely, in speaking about God, on adjectives—and he certainly did not say that God was "infinite," "unfathomable," "ineffable," "absolute," or "transcendent." In fact, nearly the only adjectives he did use to talk about God were very simple ones: "good" (*agathos*), "living" (*zon*) and "true," or "truthful" (*alethinos*)—the first two, universally cross-translatable, and the third, very widespread across languages of the world.

> "No one is good [*agathos*] but God alone." (Luke 18:19)
> "The living [*zon*] Father sent me." (John 6:57)
> "He who sent me is true [*alethinos*]." (John 7:28)

One other adjective that Jesus (as remembered in the Gospels) used about God is "perfect" (*teleios*): "You therefore must be perfect as your heavenly father is perfect" (Matthew 5:48). The meaning of the word "perfect," as Jesus uses it here about God, is made clear by the context: God wants to do good things for all people, God wants to do good things for bad people as he wants to do good things for good people.

> But I say to you, Love your enemies, and pray for those who persecute you, so that you may be sons of your Father who is in heaven; for he makes his sun rise on the evil and on the good, and sends rain on the just and the un-just. (Matthew 5:44–45)

Jesus's favorite way of speaking about God, however, relied on the universal phrase "like this," which he liked to use to introduce his explanations about what he called "the kingdom of God," and also, his shorter or longer explanatory stories about God. For example:

a. the kingdom of God is like a merchant who, when he had found one pearl of great price, went and sold all that he had and bought it. (Matthew 13:45)
b. And again he said, "to what shall I liken the kingdom of God? It is like yeast, that a woman took and mixed in with three measures of flour until all of it was leavened." (Luke 13:21)
c. The kingdom of heaven is like a mustard seed that someone took and sowed in his field; it is the smallest of all the seeds but when it has grown it is the greatest of shrubs and becomes a tree, so that the birds of the air come and make nests in its branches. (Matthew 13:32)

Jesus's stories about God, explaining what God is like, are also extended similes, based on the universal concepts "like" and "like this" (sometimes rendered in English as "just so"). To illustrate with the twin parables of the Lost Sheep (Luke 5:3–7) and the Lost Coin (Luke 15:8–10):

The parable of the Lost Sheep
So he told them this parable: "What man of you, having a hundred sheep, if he has lost one of them, does not leave the ninety-nine in the wilderness, and go after the one which is lost, until he finds it? And when he has found it, he lays it on his shoulders, rejoicing. And when he comes home, he calls together his friends and neighbors, saying to them, 'Rejoice with me, for I have found my sheep which was lost.' Just so, I tell you, there will be more joy in heaven over one sinner who repents than over ninety-nine righteous persons who need no repentance.

The parable of the Lost Coin
Or what woman, having ten silver coins, if she loses one coin, does not light a lamp and sweep the house and seek diligently until she finds it? And when she has found it, she calls together her friends and neighbors, saying, 'Rejoice with me, for I have found the coin which I had lost.' Just so, I tell you, there is joy before the angels of God over one sinner who repents.

It might be argued that in talking about God (and about the kingdom of God) in similes, Jesus acknowledges that one can't really say anything true about God with words. This cannot be the case, however; the very fact that Jesus often used twin similes (two different images making the same point) highlights the importance he attached to the message hidden behind the images—a message which he wanted his listeners to figure out for themselves. Arguably, this is what the so-called parable of the Lamp (Luke 8:16–18) is all about:

Parable of the Lamp

No one lights a lamp to cover it with a bowl or to put it under a bed. No, he puts it on a lamp-stand so that people may see the light when they come in. For nothing is hidden but it will be made clear, nothing secret but it will be known and brought to light. So take care how you hear.

Meanings are "hidden" in parables and similes, but they are not intended to remain hidden forever. They are to be brought to light, and this requires careful listening on the part of the listeners, so that the message can be "heard" (understood) well.

It is not my purpose here to articulate the full meaning of the twin parables of the Lost Sheep and Lost Coin (I tried to do this in Wierzbicka 2001: 298–299), but the message that God wants something, does something, and feels something is clear enough:

God knows all people.
All people can live with God, God wants it.
At the same time, it is like this:
    If someone doesn't want to live with God,
    this someone *can* not live with God.
If someone doesn't want to live with God, this is very bad for
    this person.
God feels something because of this.
God doesn't want it to be like this forever, God does many things
    because of this.
If after some time this person wants to live with God, God feels
    something very good because of this.
God is like this.

Thus, the powerful conceptual tool of "like," for which there is a word in every language, is not meant to be a substitute for a supposedly ineffable meaning that cannot be expressed in words; rather, it is a pointer to a clear meaning which can be conceived in "Common Human" and expressed in every known language.

I will illustrate the importance of the conceptual set of tools including the word "like," the phrase "like this," and the mini-sentence "it is like this" with one other example: the key Christian expression "the Son of God." Theologians have often tried to explain this expression in ways that lock its significance into English. To illustrate, here is a quote from Rowan Williams (2015):

We call him the Son of God. But we do not mean by this that God is physically his father, or that he is made to be another God alongside the one God. (. . .) God is first the source of everything, the life from which everything flows out. But then we say that this one God is also living and real *in* that "flowing-out". The life that comes from him is not something different from him. It reflects all that he is. (. . .) his glory and beauty and communicates them. Christians say that God has a perfect and eternal "image" of his glory, sometimes called his "wisdom", sometimes called his "Word", sometimes called his "Son", though this is never to be understood in a physical or literal way. (p. 3)

Whatever merits one can find in this passage, the fact is that the explanation offered here is not translatable into most languages of the world, because they do not have words like "physical," "real" and "literal," or phrases like "life from which everything flows out" or "living and real in that flowing out." Linguistic evidence, however, suggests that in any language one could tell the following story:

> It can be like this:
> A man wants some things to happen somewhere far from the place where he is.
> Because of this, he says to his son:
> "I want you to go to that place, I want you to do some things there as I say."
> After this, this man's son does these things, as his father wanted.

If we take this little story as our point of reference, we don't have to engage in elaborate and untranslatable explanations denying God's "physical paternity" and the like. Rather, we can say that Jesus was "like a son sent by a man to a faraway place, to do some things as his father wanted." It is important to note in this context that Jesus often spoke about himself as being "sent" by the Father to do some things and say some things (to people), and that in fact the metaphors of "son" and of "being sent" went hand in hand for him. For example:

a. God sent the Son into the world, not to condemn the world,
   but that the world might be saved through him. (John 3:17 RSV,
   Revised Standard Version)
b. He who sent me is with me. (John 8:29)
c. I came not of my own accord, but he sent me. (John 8:47)
d. this charge I have received from the Father. (John 10:18)
e. I have not spoken on my own authority; the Father who sent me has himself given me the commandment what to say and what to speak. (John 12:49)
f. the works which the Father has granted me to accomplish, these very works which I am doing, bear me witness that the Father has sent me. (John 5:36)

In an extended form, the same simile of a man who sends his son to a distant place to get some things done as he (the father) wants is presented in Matthew's Gospel (21:33–39) in the parable of the Vineyard and the Tenants. Briefly, the story goes as follows: A man planted a vineyard, let it out to tenants, and went to another country, and "when the season of fruit drew near," he first sent his servants and then his son to the tenants "to get his fruit." But the tenants first killed the servants and then the son. (See chapter 28 of "The Story"). When Jesus speaks of himself as being "sent by the Father," he clearly wants to say: "God is like that man [in the story], I am like that son"—and this, too, can be said, with exactly the same (or only minimally different) meaning, in any language.

I am not saying that this is all there is to the concept "the Son of God." Rather, I am suggesting that whatever else there is, we should try to explain it in equally simple, intelligible, and cross-translatable words and phrases. Phrases like "life from which everything flows out" are not sufficient because they are hard to understand even in English and impossible to translate into other languages.

Ward's statement that "God is something completely indescribable" seems to reflect a philosopher's frustrated desire to describe God. But why should anyone (other than a philosopher) want to "describe" God? Jesus didn't ask: "Is God describable?" Rather, he asked: "What is God like?" This is one of the main things that Jesus wanted to talk to people about—not in philosophical discourse with words like "absolute," "infinite," or "transcendent," but with the simple words "God is like this . . . ," accompanied by a simple story, often about a father, a housewife, a king, a landowner, or a shepherd.

It is essential to recognize, however, that these simple similes and parables are used to help the listeners to understand the intended message, and to remember it, not because the intended message cannot be put into "literal prose." When Jesus tells a story in order to show what God is like, he leaves it to the audience to figure out in what way God is like the characters in the story, and wants them to translate the message of the story into non-figurative language in their own minds.

The need for translating images into words is particularly clear in the case of "mixed characters" to whom Jesus liked to compare God, such as the "unjust judge" in Luke's Gospel (18:1–8). Briefly, the judge is known to be unjust, but the widow who pesters him for a just solution gets her way because she wears him down with her persistence. Jesus's strategy employed here is sometimes described with the words "how much more": God is being compared to the unjust judge not because God, too, could be unjust but, rather, because if even the unjust judge does as asked if someone is persistent, how much more will God, who is just, be willing to do good things for someone who perseveres in prayer!

It is not enough, then, to say that "God is like that unjust judge"; it is also necessary to say in what ways God is like that judge. This, too, can be articulated in words and phrases available in all human languages, along the following lines:

God wants to do good things for all people,
    God *can* do good things for all people.

At the same time, God wants people to often speak to him,
    to tell him what they want.
God is like this.

As this example illustrates, translating stories which liken God to various human characters into clear, non-figurative messages is possible only because we are able to say that God *wants* something or *feels* something. It is important, therefore, to recognize that Jesus had no qualms about using human words like "want" and "feel" (or "love") in relation to God. To illustrate:

If a man loves me, he will keep my word, and my Father will love him. And we will come to him and make our home with him. (John 14:23)

As the Father has loved me, so I have loved you. (John 15:9)

For the Father himself loves you, because you have loved me and have believed that I came from the Father. (John 16:27)

Abba, Father, for you all things are possible; remove this cup from me; yet, not what I want, but what you want. (Mark 14:36)

3.4 "Speaking in tongues" and human understanding

To reiterate the main point of this chapter ("God and language"), there are no good reasons to think that human words are not good enough to speak about God, and not good enough to enable people to say anything true about God. This was clearly not Jesus's view. In particular, Jesus did not share the view of those theologians who see words like "want" and "feel" as inapplicable to God.

At the same time, there are good reasons to think that many words used about God in theological and philosophical commentaries are obscure and un-helpful, and create barriers to human understanding—both within particular linguistic and cultural spheres and across languages and cultures. This applies not only to technical philosophical vocabulary of English and other European languages but also to culture-specific English words like "reality," "experience," and "limitless," and to "European" words like "infinite" and "almighty."

In a beautiful little book entitled *Qui est le Dieu des chrétiens* (*Who Is the God of Christians?*), two French philosophers, Brague and Batut (2011), try, as they say, to answer the title question in a clear and non-technical way, in-telligible to outsiders, and useful for interreligious dialogue. The key answer put forward by one of the two authors is that the God that Christians believe in is, as the creed put it, "le Père tout-puissant" ("Father Almighty"). This is followed by a further explanation:

So what does it mean, "Almighty Father"? Well, it doesn't mean a God who would do difficult things in order to show that he is able of doing them and to impress us. Rather, it is a God who does everything, even what at first sight seems impossible to us, to make us his sons ["les fils", presumably, meaning "his children"]. He uses his omnipotence to make whatever can enter into a relationship of filiation with him into his children [lit. "sons"].

[C'est pour faire de ce qui peut entrer avec lui dans un rapport de filiation, justement des fils, qu'il s'épolie de cette toute-puissance]. (p. 19)

This explanation may seem clear to a European philosopher, but it is doubtful that it would be helpful in interreligious dialogue or in explaining Christian faith to young people—even if they are native speakers of French or English.

In "The Story of God and People" words like "filiation" are avoided like the plague, phrases like "enter into a relationship" (which no child would be likely to understand) are also avoided, metaphors like "Father" are not used without an explanation, and even seemingly intelligible words like "almighty" are replaced with clearer and more explanatory paraphrases built out of simple words available in all languages, such as "can," "want," "if," and "happen."

To illustrate with the creed's word "almighty" ("I believe in almighty God"), the use of such simple words not only allows us to explain complex concepts like "almighty God" (*omnipotens deus*) to speakers of languages which do not have any words corresponding to "almighty," it forces us to be more precise in our own thinking by deciding whether we mean (a), or (b), or (c): (a) Everything that happens because God wants it to happen; (b) If God wants something to happen, it happens; or (c) If God wants something to happen, it can happen because of this. Thus, not even familiar Christian words like "almighty" can be taken for granted. They are not self-explanatory; only trying to explain them to ourselves through words that *are* self-explanatory can ensure that we do understand what we mean.

The importance of clear understanding in all Christian talk about God was strongly emphasized by St Paul, in the context of the early Christian practice known as "speaking in tongues." According to Paul, this practice could be valuable and inspired, but it is not understandable:

If even lifeless instruments, such as the flute or the harp, do not give distinct notes, how will anyone know what is played? And if the bugle gives an indistinct sound, who will get ready for battle? So with yourselves; if you in a tongue utter speech that is not intelligible, how will anyone know what is said? For you will be speaking into the air. There are doubtless many different languages in the world, and none is without meaning; but if I do not know the meaning of the language, I shall be a foreigner to the speaker and the speaker a foreigner to me. (1 Corinthians 14:7–11)

God may be "incomprehensible" to people, as the *Catechism of the Catholic Church* puts it, but this doesn't mean that human writings about God need to be incomprehensible, and especially, that Christians' explanations of what they believe in, need to be incomprehensible.

St Paul's familiarity with a number of different languages and his eager-ness to bring the Gospel of Jesus Christ to many nations is likely to have played a role in this insistence on intelligibility and clear understanding: "I thank God that I speak in tongues more than all of you; nevertheless, in church I would rather speak five words with my mind, in order to instruct others also, than ten thousand words in a tongue" (First Letter to the Corinthians 14:19). Naturally, those who, like the present author, believe in "Minimal Languages" as a path to human understanding, can find these words congenial and inspiring.

I would like to close this chapter, "God and language," with another quote from Marilynne Robinson (2015: 182), who in her essay entitled "Value" says: "I speak with all due respect for my academic brothers and sisters when I say I often doubt that they look deeply enough into the meaning of the words they use." I would add that if one wants to look deeply into the meaning of words, it helps to have a good semantic microscope, and a trusty set of procedures. The approach to language and thought, on which "The Story of God and People" is based, provides, I believe, both such a set of procedures and such a microscope.

4

Minimal English

4.1 What is Minimal English?

Minimal English is a highly reduced version of English which can ensure maximum translatability without compromising intelligibility. This means that any sentence formulated in this version of English should be fully intelligible to all speakers of English and at the same time (with some, but not many, exceptions) be readily translatable into any other language. (For discussion of these exceptions, see section 4.4.)

The core of Minimal English consists of words and grammatical constructions which, evidence suggests, have their equivalents in most, if not all, other languages. This means that the core of Minimal English matches the core of most, if not all, other languages: We have good reasons to believe that all, or nearly all, human languages share a common core, that is, a matching set of words and a matching set of grammatical constructions.

A search for such a common core of all languages has been, for decades, at the center of a program of cross-linguistic investigations guided by the so-called NSM approach to language and culture.[1] In the course of this search,

---

[1] The acronym "NSM" stands for "Natural Semantic Metalanguage," and also for the approach to the study of language, thought, and culture which has the Natural Semantic Metalanguage at its center. To quote from Goddard (2010: 817):

> The Natural Semantic Metalanguage (NSM) is a (. . .) system of meaning representation based on empirically established universal semantic primes, i.e., simple indefinable meanings which appear to be present as word-meanings in all languages (Wierzbicka 1996; Goddard 1998; Goddard and Wierzbicka eds. 2002; Peeters ed. 2006; Goddard ed. 2008). Originated with Wierzbicka (1972), the system has been developed and refined over some 35 years. There is a large body of descriptive-analytical work in the framework, not only about English, but Russian, Polish, French, Spanish, Malay, Japanese, Chinese, Korean, Ewe, East Cree and other languages. (. . .) The NSM metalanguage can be thought of as a highly disciplined and standardised subset of natural language. (. . .) The NSM metalanguage itself represents a very substantial set of claimed findings about language universals. (. . .) In tandem with this claim about linguistic universals there is a

very specific hypotheses about this common core were formulated, repeatedly put to the test, and either revised or upheld depending on the findings. As a result, there are good reasons to believe that we now know what the shared conceptual, lexical, and grammatical core of all, or nearly all, languages looks like. (See sections 4.2 and 4.3.)

Furthermore, researchers now believe that, if slightly augmented, different language-specific versions of this common core can function as minimal languages and be used for practical purposes. In particular, being radically reduced and thus pruned of any "cultural baggage," such minimal languages can be useful for articulating knowledge and ideas without special cultural biases, and for furthering cross-cultural and cross-temporal understanding.

Thus, Minimal English is a highly reduced version of English which to a very large extent matches similarly reduced versions of other languages, for example, Minimal Polish, which is now also fairly well developed. (For samples of Minimal Russian, Minimal Chinese, Minimal Ewe, and Minimal Tok Pisin, see section 4.2.)

To illustrate, there are no words like "right" and "wrong" in Minimal English, because most languages of the world do not have exact semantic equivalents of these words. On the other hand, the words "good" and "bad," which, evidence suggests, have exact semantic equivalents in all languages, do belong to Minimal English. Similarly, the words "far" and "near," which evidence suggests have exact semantic equivalents in all languages, belong to Minimal English, whereas the word "distance" (with no counterparts in most languages of the world) does not.

As the subtitle of this book indicates, "The Story of God and People" is written in Minimal English. (A parallel "Story of God and People" written in Minimal Polish was published in Poland (Wierzbicka 2017a).) This means that this "Story" shows Minimal English in action, and can give the reader a good idea of what it is, how it works, and what can be done with it. To prepare the reader for the unconventional style of "The Story," I will mention, by way of example, two facts.

The first fact is the complete absence (most unusual in an extended piece of English prose) of the words "and," "but," and "or." The reason is that, indispensable as these words may seem to most speakers of English, they are in fact not always cross-translatable. By contrast, the words "if" and "because," which are fully cross-translatable, are present in "The Story" on virtually every page.

---

corresponding claim about universals of cognition, because the mini-language of semantic primes embodies the fundamentals of linguistic cognition, i.e. cognition as it can be carried out with and expressed through language. A bibliography of NSM publications, along with a number of downloadable papers, is available at the NSM Homepage <https://intranet.secure.griffith.edu.au/schools-departments/natural-semantic-metalanguage> [short URL bit.ly/1XUoRRV].

The second fact that I want to mention at this point has to do with the grammar of Minimal English, which is also highly reduced. Notably, the only form of "reported speech" that is available in Minimal English is so-called direct discourse, or direct quotation. For example, in reporting the dialogue between John the Baptist and Jesus in chapter 13, "The Story" says: "John said to Jesus: 'I can't baptize you,'" and "Jesus said: 'I want you to do it.'" "Indirect discourse," as in "John told Jesus that he couldn't baptize him" and "Jesus said that he wanted him to do it," would not be allowed in Minimal English, because it is not universal, and there are no instances of it in "The Story of God and People." (Incidentally, the language of "The Story" matches here the language of the Gospels, where Jesus's words are virtually always given in the form of direct quotations, and not as "indirect discourse.")

The notion of Minimal English is contrastive. It presupposes a distinction between different forms of English, and especially, between "maximum English," such as "Anglo English," and a radically pruned version of it. The first has been shaped by the history and culture of one particular part of the world, and still bears the imprints of its origins. The second is derived from the first, but being radically reduced it can come very close to the shared core of all languages. It has been built not only by systematic reduction of English but also by decades of empirical cross-linguistic investigations, aimed at identifying that common core.[2] Accordingly, Minimal English is not another simplified version

---

[2] The range of languages studied in the NSM framework is illustrated in the table (from Goddard and Wierzbicka 2014b, references to the sources can be found there).

Language family/type	Language(s)	Sources
Austronesian	Malay, Mbula, Longgu, Samoan	Goddard (2001a, 2001b, 2002), Bugenhagen (2001, 2002), Hill (1994), Mosel (1994)
Indo-European	Spanish, Danish, French, Polish, Russian	Travis (2002, 2004, 2006), Levisen (2012), Peeters (2006, 2010), Wierzbicka (2002), Gladkova (2007, 2010)
Semitic	Amharic, Arabic, Hebrew	Amberber (2008), Habib (2011a, 2011b)
Finno-Ugric	Finnish	Vanhatalo et al. (in press)
Sinitic	Chinese (Mandarin), Cantonese	Chappell (2002), Ye (2006, 2007, 2010), Tong et al. (1997), Tien (2009), Leung (2012), Wakefield (2011)
Algonquian	East Cree[†]	Junker (2003, 2006, 2008), Junker and Blacksmith (2006)
Niger-Congo	Ewe	Ameka (1994, 2006, 2009)
Japonic	Japanese[†]	Hasada (1998, 2001, 2008), Asano-Cavanagh (2009, 2010)

of English analogous to Ogden's 1930 "Basic English" or Jean-Paul Nerrière's "Globish" (2004), both pruned for practical purposes but not reduced to the bare essentials. Building a mini-language that would, for the most part, match the lowest common denominator of all languages is an entirely different undertaking. Neither Ogden nor Nerrière aimed at identifying a minimal set of words with counterparts in many (let alone all) languages, and in fact they were not looking at English from a cross-linguistic perspective at all.

Given such a skeletal lexicon, Minimal English cannot of course be an all-purpose practical global means of communication. It can be, however, a global minimal lingua franca for the elucidation of ideas and explanation of meanings—and not only in scholarship but also in international relations, politics, business, law, healthcare, education, ethics, and indeed in any context where it is important to explain precisely what one means (see Goddard ed. 2018). As I wrote in *Imprisoned in English* (Wierzbicka 2014):

> Theoretically, a mini-version of any language (Russian, Chinese, Arabic, etc.) could fulfil such an auxiliary function; but given the realities of today's globalizing world, at this point it is obviously a mini-English that is the most practical way out (or down) from the conceptual tower of

Korean	Korean	Yoon (2006, 2008)
Tai-Kadai	Lao	Enfield (2002)
Papuan	Koromu, Kalam, Makasai	Priestley (2002, 2008, 2102a, 2012b), Pawley (1994), Brotherson (2008)
Pama-Nyungan (Australia)	Pitjantjatjara/ Yankunytjatjara, Arrernte	Goddard (1991, 1994), Bromhead (2011a), Harkins and Wilkins (1994), Harkins (2001)
Non-Pama-Nyungan (Australia)	Bunuba	Knight (2008)
Creoles	Hawaii Creole English, Roper Kriol	Stanwood (1997, 1999), Nicholls (2009)

The broad range of NSM-based cross-linguistic investigations on which the common core of all languages is based has often been acknowledged by outsiders. For example, philosopher David Chalmers (2012: 9) comments, referring to NSM, that it has been "used to analyse an extraordinary range of expressions in many different languages." Well-known typologist Nicholas Evans (2010), who is not an NSM practitioner and who has sometimes expressed doubts about a few NSM primes as proposed lexical universals, acknowledges the status of NSM as a most highly developed system for cross-linguistic identification of meaning:

> NSM practitioners have produced a vast body of semantic analyses across dozens of languages, and at present can lay claim to having developed the approach that has gone deepest into the possibilities of setting up a cross-linguistically valid set of basic semantic categories in which all meanings can be stated. (pp. 516–517)

Babel that the cultural evolution of humankind has erected, for better or for worse. (. . .)

There are good reasons for a mini-English to be, in today's world, the paramount auxiliary language of interpretation, explanation, and intercultural communication. There are no good reasons, however, for historically shaped Anglo English to be treated as the voice of Truth and Human Understanding. (p. 196)

This applies to religion and theology as much as to any other domain. To elucidate what Christians believe, it is good to try to think, at times, in a minimal language. To be able to convey this understanding to anyone who is interested, across geographical, linguistic, and cultural boundaries, it is particularly useful to be able to explain it through Minimal English—the closest there can be at the moment to a global auxiliary lingua franca.

In his introduction to a volume entitled *Universals of Human Thought*, philosopher Ernest Gellner (1981) wrote: "Unconvertible currencies are not suitable for trade" (p. 9). A key characteristic of Minimal English is that (unlike "Basic English," "plain English," so-called "Simple English," or any other reduced form of English) it is almost fully "convertible." (For an explanation of the qualification "almost," see section 4.4.)

4.2 Universal semantic primes

The innermost core of Minimal English and of all other Minimal Languages (in the sense in which the phrase "Minimal Language" is used here) is a set of sixty-five words which match in meaning an identical set of sixty-five words in every other language, and which are so simple in meaning that they cannot be further explained through other words, without circularity. These words are known as "semantic primes."

To illustrate, SEE, which is a semantic prime, cannot be defined, and all attempts to do so lead to vicious circles. For example, the *Longman Dictionary of the English Language* (1987) defines *see* via "eye" ("to see: to perceive by the eye"), then defines *perceive* via *see* ("to perceive: to become aware of through the senses, especially to see"), and *eye* via *sight* ("eye: any of various usually paired organs of sight"), and then defines *sight* as "something seen."

The set of elementary meanings which cannot be further explained includes, in addition to verbs like SEE, HEAR, WANT, KNOW, FEEL, and SAY, the adjectives BIG, SMALL, GOOD, BAD, and TRUE (but not "false"), and more than fifty others, as shown in Table 1, where all these elements are divided into twelve thematic categories. (By convention, these elements, which are called "semantic primes," are often represented in writing by small capitals.)

TABLE 1.

Universal words which are also semantic primes

1.	I, YOU, SOMEONE, SOMETHING~THING, PEOPLE, BODY, KIND, PART
2.	THIS, THE SAME, OTHER
3.	ONE, TWO, MUCH~MANY, LITTLE~FEW, SOME, ALL
4.	GOOD, BAD, BIG, SMALL
5.	THINK, KNOW, WANT, DON'T WANT, FEEL, SEE, HEAR
6.	SAY, WORDS, TRUE
7.	DO, HAPPEN, MOVE
8.	BE (SOMEWHERE), THERE IS, BE (SOMEONE/SOMETHING), (IS) MINE
9.	LIVE, DIE
10.	WHEN~TIME, NOW, BEFORE, AFTER, A LONG TIME, A SHORT TIME, FOR SOME TIME, MOMENT
11.	WHERE~PLACE, HERE, ABOVE, BELOW, FAR, NEAR, SIDE, INSIDE, TOUCH
12.	NOT, MAYBE, CAN, BECAUSE, IF, VERY, MORE, LIKE

To call such words "universal words" is of course an abbreviated way of speaking. For example, in Polish the words matching the English words "big" and "small" in meaning are *duży* and *mały*: the sound is different, but the meaning is exactly the same.

As we will see in chapter 1 of "The Story," the Christian concept of "God" can be portrayed, essentially, with thirty such elements, including words meaning "someone," "not," "like," "people," "above," "now, "before," "after," "place," "else (other)," "can," "see," "the same," "time," "know," "some," "something," "this," "because," "want," "good," "if," "do," "happen," "say," "true," "all," "feel," "very," and "live." The exact correspondence between the thirty English words listed above and the words occurring in the explanation of "God" in chapter 1 may not be immediately visible, because that explanation includes, for example, the words "everything" and "everywhere," which are not listed here. This lack of perfect correspondence, however, is more apparent than real: for example, "everywhere" is really a shorthand for "all places," and "everything" for "all things," and the words "all," "place," and "something" ("thing") do occur among the thirty listed above, and among the sixty-five in Table 1.

It is also very important to say that there are certain combinations of the 65 elementary concepts which recur in all languages. For example, in every language one can say that "someone wants to do something good for someone else," or that "someone wants to do good things for all people."

Many questions about the individual elements and their combinations may occur to the reader at this point. This is not, however, the place to discuss them, and if someone is sufficiently interested, they will be able to find the answers to most of their questions in the linguistic literature mentioned in the

References. Here, I will show how one can speak about God in Minimal English by presenting six components from chapter 1 of "The Story," formulated exclusively in semantic primes:

An extract from chapter 1 of "The Story" ("God")

There is someone not like people.

This someone is someone above people.

This someone is now, this someone always was, this someone always will be.

This someone is everywhere.

There is no one else like this someone.

God is this someone.

I will now illustrate the universal cross-translatability of such semantic components by presenting their exact semantic equivalents from four different languages: [A] Russian, [B] Ewe (West Africa), [C] Tok Pisin (Oceania), and [D] Chinese. In each case, the text was provided by an expert: Anna Gladkova (Monash University, Russian), Felix Ameka (Leiden University, Ewe), Carol Priestly (Wollongong University, Tok Pisin), and Emily Fong and Zhengdao Ye (Australian National University, Chinese).

[A] Russian

Есть кто-то не такой как люди.

Этот кто-то – кто-то над людьми.

Этот кто-то есть сейчас, этот кто-то всегда был, этот кто-то
    всегда будет.

Этот кто-то везде.

Нет никого другого такого как этот кто-то.

Бог это этот кто-то.

[B] Ewe

Ame áɖé li, méli abé ame-gbetɔ́wó ené o.

Ame sia fo amewó kátã́ ta

Ame sia li fífíá, ame sia nɔ(a) anyí ɖáá, ame sia anɔ anyí ɖáá

Ame sia le afí siáa afí

Ame áɖéké méli abé ame sia ené o.

Máwúé nyé ame sia.

[C] Tok Pisin

I gat wanpela i no olsem manmeri.

Em wanpela i stap antap long manmeri.

Em wanpela i stap nau, em wanpela i stap olgeta taim bipo,
    em wanpela em bai i stap oltaim oltaim.

Em wanpela i stap long olgeta ples.

I no gat narapela i olsem dispela.

God em i dispela.

[D] Chinese

有谁，他与人不同
他于人之上
他昔在，今在，永在
他无处不在
他独一无二
上帝就是他

Having introduced in this way the non-universal concept of "God," we can say a great deal *about* God using no words other than universal semantic primes, as shown by these further sentences from chapter 1 of "The Story."

> God is good.
> If God wants something, it is something good.
> If God does something, it is something good.
> If God wants something to happen, it can happen because of this.
> If God says about something: "I want it to happen," it happens
>   because of this.
> If God says about something: "It is like this," it is true.
> God knows everything.

4.3 Universal semantic molecules

The sixty-five semantic primes are not the only meanings which are expressed as words in all languages. Evidence suggests that next to these "atoms of meaning," there is also a comparable number of meanings which could be called "universal semantic molecules": they are complex (i.e., they can be broken down into "atoms") but they, too, appear to occur as words in all languages (see Table 2).

TABLE 2.
Universal semantic molecules (partial list)

hands, mouth, eyes, head, ears, nose, face, legs, teeth, bones, blood

be born, children, men, women, mother, father, wife, husband

long, round, flat, hard, sharp, heavy

fire, water, wood, stone, light

be on something, at the top, at the bottom, in front, around

sky, earth, ground, sun, stars, moon, during the day, at night

creature, grow (in ground)

be called

hold; laugh, sing, play; kill

Several words from this second set occur in chapter 2 of "The Story of God and People," devoted to God as "creator of the world" as the three extracts below (a, b, and c) illustrate. Neither the English word "create" nor the English word "world" have their equivalents in all languages of the world. On the other hand, evidence suggests that "earth," "sun," "moon," and "stars" do have their equivalents in all languages. Similarly, the English words "animals" and "plants" do not have their equivalents in all other languages. On the other hand, the words "grow" and "creature" do have such equivalents, and so do the phrases "something growing" and "living creatures of many kinds." Most importantly (from a human point of view), not only do all languages have an indefinable word matching "people" (in sentences like "God wants to do good things for all people'), but also, they all have words matching "men," "women," and "children." All this is illustrated below by an extended extract from chapter 2 of "The Story."

a. It is like this now:
    There are many people living on earth, there are many things on earth,
        many things are happening on earth.
    There is the sky above the earth, there is light, there is the sun, there
        is the moon, there are stars.
   It is like this because God wants it to be like this.
   It wasn't always like this. A very very long time ago, it was like this:
    There was no earth, there was no sky, there was no light,
        there were no places as there are now, there were no people,
    there was nothing anywhere, nothing was happening anywhere.
    There was God.
b. For a very long time many things were happening to the earth,
        they were happening because God wanted it.
   For a long time, it was like this:
    no things were growing on earth,
    no living creatures were living on earth.
   After this, it was not like this anymore, it was like this:
    things of many kinds were growing on earth,
    living creatures of many kinds were living on earth.
   All this was as God wanted. God said: "This is very good."
   When it was like this, for a long time there were no people on earth.
   After this, there were people living on earth.
   It was like this because God wanted it. God said: "This is very good."
c. When there were people on earth, it was not like before,
        because people were not like other creatures.
    It was like this:
    People wanted to know many things about many things,
        not like other living creatures.

People could think about many things, not like other living creatures.
They could think like this: "After some time, I will die,"
    other living creatures could not think like this.
They could think: "I can do good things, I can do bad things,"
    other creatures could not think like this.

In chapter 26, on the crucifixion of Jesus, we encounter the body part words "head," "face," and "hands"; the "material" word "wood"; the physical property word "heavy"; the verb "kill"; and the "topological" words "top" and "bottom" (adapted from the adverbials "at the top" and "at the bottom"). To show how universal semantic molecules can be broken down into semantic primes, I will adduce one example: "creature."

creature
something living
something like this can move
something like this can feel something

For the purposes of Minimal English, however, we can simply use the cross-translatable word (molecule) "creature."

4.4 Non-universal words in Minimal English

As we saw in sections 4.2 and 4.3, many things can be said about "God and people" in universal words. Some of these things can be said in semantic primes alone (as the first three blocks in chapter 1), and others require also universal semantic molecules (as in chapter 2). Naturally, all words and phrases that are universal (that is, match in meaning across languages) are also cross-translatable. For this reason, evidence suggests, chapters 1 and 2 are fully cross-translatable.

Many other chapters of "The Story" are not as completely cross-translatable as those two. For example, chapter 3 includes the words "sheep" and "shepherd," which are quite prominent in the language of the Bible. Not all human groups, however, are familiar with sheep, and those which are not, do not have words like "sheep" and "shepherd." For example, in the Pitjantjatjara language of Central Australia until recently there were no such words. It is not surprising, therefore, that biblical sentences like "God is my shepherd" (Psalm 23) are rendered in the Pitjantjatjara Bible, *Tjukurrpa Palya*, with words borrowed from English, "sheep" and "shepherd." For example, when Jesus says in John's Gospel "I am the good shepherd," this is rendered in *Tjukurrpa Palya* as "Ngayuluma [I am] shepherd palyanya [good]." Speakers of many other languages of the world still have no words corresponding to "sheep" and "shepherd," and no experiential basis for interpreting biblical metaphors based on these concepts.

The importance of words like "sheep" and "shepherd" in biblical language and thought is easy to understand: After all, Abraham, Isaac, and Jacob were all pastoralists, and so were many of their descendants, for many generations. "The Story of God and People" cannot do without these two words (or without the word "lamb").

As shown in NSM-based literature (see, e.g., Goddard 2011; Wierzbicka 1985, 1996), words of this kind can be defined (explicated) through universal semantic primes and molecules, but it would not make sense to try to define them within the text of "The Story of God and People." Instead, they can be listed in a separate "cultural lexicon," and given there either full or partial definitions couched in cross-translatable words, as appropriate. Here, I will only sketch a general picture of the kinds of non-universal vocabulary used in "The Story of God and People."

Thus, to continue with "biology," there are two other kinds of living creatures that are mentioned in "The Story": "dove" (which symbolizes the Holy Spirit) is mentioned in chapter 13, where John the Baptist baptizes Jesus, and "rooster" is mentioned in chapter 24, where Apostle Peter is denying Jesus in the courtyard of the chief priest's house. The word "oxen" occurs in chapter 10 ("Jesus is born"), where one reads that "Jesus was born in a cave . . . where there were oxen at night (because there was no place in a house where they [Mary and Joseph] could be for some time)." In chapter 6, God speaks to Moses from inside a bush, so in the Minimal English version of "The Story" the word "bush" is mentioned. However, not all languages have a words for "bush" different from the word for "tree." (For example, Pitjantjatjara doesn't.)

Geographical and environmental words which appear in "The Story" include "mountain," "river," "lake," "desert," "cloud," and "rock." For example, God speaks to Moses and gives him the Ten Commandments on a mountain called Mount Sinai; and Jesus often spends time, either alone or with his disciples, on a mountain called the Mount of Olives. John the Baptist lives in the desert, and baptizes people in a river called Jordan. A lake called Gennesaret plays a key role in Jesus's life in Galilee.

Several non-universal words in "The Story" belong to the material culture. They include "bread," "wine," "table," "cup," and "linen." Several other non-universal words used in "The Story" have to do with people. They include "carpenter," "fishermen," "soldiers," "king," and "slaves." (Mary's husband Joseph is a carpenter, several Apostles are fishermen; Roman soldiers whip, mock, and crucify Jesus; David is the king of Israel; Israelites are slaves in Egypt.)

Two non-universal kinship terms used in "The Story" deserve a special mention: "son" and "brother." Thus, in chapter 9, the angel tells Mary that she will give birth to a son, and that people will call him the "Son of God," and in English, the same word "son" is used in both cases. In some languages, however, (for example, in the Australian language Yolngu) the word for a woman's son is different from the word for a man's son, so one word would be used for "son" in relation to Mary and another in relation to God.

As for the word "brother," it is, strictly speaking, not translatable into languages like Pitjantjatjara. Many Australian languages make a lexical distinction between older brothers and younger brothers, treating these two relationships as different, and don't have a general term for "brother" (independent of seniority). For example, in Pitjantjatjara, an older male sibling is called *kuṯa* (glossed in Goddard's 1996 dictionary as "senior brother or close male cousin"), whereas a younger sibling, whether male or female, is called *maḻanypa* (described in the same dictionary as "junior brother, sister or cousin"). So when the risen Jesus tells Mary Magdalene in John's Gospel: "go to my brothers [i.e. the Apostles] and say to them, I am ascending to my Father and your Father, to my God and your God" (John 20:17 RSV), the *Tjukurpa Palya* version of Jesus's message says "go to my *maḻanypa*," that is, as it were, "go to my junior siblings." This presents the risen Jesus as taking an attitude of superiority toward the Apostles, whereas the English translation of John's Gospel, and the Minimal English account of the encounter in chapter 31, do not.

One deliberate omission which may escape the reader's attention concerns words like "descendants," "ancestors," "genealogy," and "generation." Themes related to these words play an important role in the Bible (see, e.g., the Gospel of Matthew chapter 1). The words as such, however, are not cross-translatable, and they are absent from "The Story," written, as it is, in Minimal English. The themes linked with these words are very much present in "The Story," but they have been dealt with the help of other, cross-translatable, words and phrases.

Turning now to non-universal verbs, I will note that the two most important ones occurring in "The Story" are "read" and "write." Throughout "The Story" (beginning with the last segment of chapter 1), there are repeated references to the Bible, and to what people can know if they read this or that part of the Bible. In chapter 6, Moses brings from Mount Sinai two big flat stones on which he had written the Ten Commandments. In chapter 26 ("Jesus is nailed to the cross"), people can see the words "Jesus of Nazareth King of the Jews" written on something that is nailed to the cross above his head; and in chapter 39 ("An Apostle called Paul"), we hear that Paul said many things about Jesus "in writing." Other non-universal verbs used in "The Story" include "nail" (as in "they nailed his hands to the cross, they nailed his feet to the cross") in chapter 26, "wrap" in chapter 29 ("What happened with Jesus's body after he died"): "they wrapped Jesus's body in some linen," and "carry" in chapter 26, where we read that "Jesus had to carry a cross."

To illustrate how seemingly basic words like "carry" may be less than fully cross-translatable—and yet be nearly cross-translatable—I will adduce here some information about the Austronesian language Longgu. As shown by Deborah Hill (2016), this language has no general verb like "carry." Instead,

it has a number of more specific verbs, one of which is *ango'ihia* "carry something on the shoulder." As Hill explains, this verb is only used when the carrier
is a man, because women don't carry things in this way. It is clear that this verb
fits the sentence about Jesus carrying a cross perfectly well and that while not
identical in meaning to the English verb "carry," in context, the differences do
not affect the cross-translatability of the sentence as a whole.

Two other verbs which play an important role in the Minimal English version of "The Story of God and People" are "eat" and "drink." These verbs, too,
are not universally cross-translatable, because in some languages (for example,
the Papuan language Kalam) one verb corresponds to both "eat" and "drink."
Thus, in chapter 22 of the Minimal English version of the Last Supper, Jesus
says to his disciples "Take, eat, this is my body" about the bread, and "Drink
from it, all of you, this is my blood" about the wine, whereas in a Kalam version, the same verb would be used in both cases. Strictly speaking, therefore,
"eat" and "drink" are not fully cross-translatable, but practically speaking, in a
context like this, they are.

I will not try to present here the full list of non-universal words occurring
in "The Story of God and People" (although this list does not extend very
much beyond what has been mentioned in this section). Most of these words
embody concepts which are deeply anchored in local history, geography, and
culture, so it is hardly surprising that they do not have their counterparts in all
languages. As already mentioned, such words can be listed in a "cultural lexicon," with full or partial explanations, as appropriate.

On the other hand, I would like to say something here about some words
which embody concepts belonging to "spiritual culture" and which refer to
invisible and intangible beings and entities. These words, too, are not cross-
translatable. In "The Story of God and People" this group of words includes
"God," "angel," "soul," "Satan," and "spirit." The most important of these,
of course, is the word *God*, which recurs throughout "The Story." This concept is introduced, through semantic primes, in chapter 1 of "The Story," and
expanded upon in chapters 2, 3, and elsewhere. It is also a concept partially
rendered in section 4.2 of the present chapter, in four additional languages
from four different continents.

The concept of "angel" is introduced, without much explanation, in
chapter 9 ("A woman called Mary says "yes" to God"). Enough is said, however (in universal words), to enable anyone unfamiliar with this concept to understand as much as is needed in order to be able to follow the story: We hear
in this chapter that Mary saw someone not like people, and that she knew that
it was someone good and that God wanted to say something to her. We are
also given the Hebrew/Aramaic word with which, presumably, she would have
thought about this someone.

In chapter 13, where John the Baptist baptizes Jesus, we hear that after the
baptism, in the desert, Jesus saw someone not like people, and that he knew that

it was someone bad. We also hear with what word the relevant part of the Bible describes this someone: "Satan."

The word "soul" is mentioned in chapter 15 ("Jesus teaches people what is good for them"), where it appears as part of something that Jesus says. The word is not fully explained, but everything that matters is explained in the adjacent lines: "it is good for you if you often think like this: 'I have a body, at the same time, I have something else, a soul; because I have a soul, I can live with God, after I die I can live with God forever.'" The Hebrew/Aramaic word which Jesus would have, presumably, used here is also provided (*nepesh*).

It is important to stress that the six lines with the word "soul" in chapter 15 are not meant to define the full meaning of the English word "soul," or even of the Hebrew, and Aramaic, word *nepesh*, as used in the Hebrew Bible, but rather, of the word that Jesus used (in the new sense in which he was using it) when he contrasted a person's body with that invisible, and indestructible, "something else." (More fleetingly, the word "soul" appears also in chapters 23 and 33.)

Thus, while the English word "soul" as such is not fully cross-translatable (because its closest counterparts in other languages do not match its meaning exactly), the word "soul" as used in chapter 15 and elsewhere in "The Story" can be rendered in other Minimal Languages by the closest counterparts of "soul" in the corresponding "full" languages (*psyche* in Greek, *dusha* in Russian, *Seele* in German, etc.), because the meaning intended by Jesus is, in a sense, special (his own), and this special meaning is clear from the context, and thus, essentially, cross-translatable.

Another important word in the area of "spiritual culture" which proved indispensable in "The Story" is "spirit." The concept of "the Holy Spirit" is partially explained in the text of chapter 36, but the word "spirit" recurs throughout "The Story," and not always in the phrase "the Holy Spirit." For example, in chapter 27, the last words that the dying Jesus utters on the cross (Luke 22:46) are—as the King James Bible translated them—"Father, into your hands I commit my Spirit." "The Story" renders this as "Father, I want my Spirit to be in your hands." But are both these concepts, "soul" and "spirit," distinguished in the languages of the world?

At this stage, the answer to this question must be that we don't really know. What we do know is that in some languages, the Greek words "psyche" and "pneuma," usually rendered in English translations of the Gospels with "soul" and "spirit," are rendered with the same word. For example, in the translation of the Bible into the Pitjantjatjara languages of Central Australia, both "psykhe" and "pneuma" are rendered with the word *kurunpa* (also used for the Holy Spirit).

This doesn't mean, however, that in this language the two concepts in question cannot be distinguished, because on closer inspection *kurunpa* may turn out to be polysemous, and have two (or more) distinct meanings, used in different grammatical frames. The matter requires further investigation.

4.5 Expanding the lexicon of Minimal English through the "called-mechanism"

In any thematic domain, the lexicon of Minimal English can be significantly expanded beyond that of "Common Human" (that is, beyond the set of universal semantic primes and molecules) by what I will call the "called-mechanism." The simplest, and almost trivial, example is that of "proper nouns." Thus, since the first line of chapter 9 says: "Jesus's mother was called Mary," the word "Mary" can later be used in "The Story" without any explanation and the reader will know that it refers to the woman who was Jesus's mother. Many such words are used throughout "The Story" to refer to major figures, including Abraham, Isaac, Jacob, Moses, Joseph (Mary's husband), Caiaphas, Pilate, Mary Magdalene, and the Apostles Peter, John, Thomas, and Paul, as well as Judas.

The same mechanism allows "The Story" to introduce many geographical concepts, for example, "a country called Egypt," "a mountain called the Mount of Olives," "a river called Jordan," "a lake called Gennesaret," "a city called Jerusalem," and "a town called Nazareth." There is also a historical-cum-geographical concept "the Roman empire" and "historical-cum-religious" concept "the day of the year called Passover." Other concepts which could be described as "historical-cum-religious" include "the book called the Bible," "the part of the Bible called Genesis," "the things (which God spoke to Moses and which Moses wrote down on two big flat stones) called the Ten Commandments," and "something called the Temple." Below, I will show in more detail how, for example, the concept of "the Temple" is introduced in "The Story" (in chapter 8):

> There was something called the Temple in Jerusalem.
> The people of Israel thought about it like this:
>> "This place is like no other place,
>> God speaks to the people of Israel in this place."
> Israelites felt something very good toward the Temple.

Not all words introduced in "The Story" through the "called-mechanism" would be treated by dictionaries as "proper names." For example, of the three important groups of people introduced in "The Story" through this mechanism (the prophets, the Apostles, the Sanhedrin) the first two would normally not be so treated. In chapter 7 of "The Story" the concept of "a prophet" is introduced as follows:

> After Moses died, it was like this:
>> When God wanted to say something to the people of Israel,
>> God said it to someone not like many other people,
>> after this, this someone said it to the people of Israel;
> Someone like this was called a prophet.

> Many prophets spoke to the people of Israel at many times
>   (some were women).
> They spoke not like other people. When they said something,
>   they wanted people to think: "God says this to us."

As this example illustrates, although the words "prophet" and "prophets" are not cross-translatable, enough information is provided in cross-translatable words for the reader to be able to follow the narrative. The same applies to the word "Apostles" (in chapter 17), which is also introduced with a great deal of information, including the following lines:

> When Jesus didn't live in one place anymore
>   some people were always with him, wherever he went.
> These people were called the Apostles. (…)
> The Apostles were all men, there were twelve of them,
>   as there were twelve sons of Jacob.
> It was like this because Jesus wanted it to be like this. (…)
> Jesus wanted these men to always be with him,
>   he wanted them to know him.
> He wanted them to know well what he did, what he said,
>   what happened to him.
> He wanted them to say to many people later:
>   "We were there, we saw it, we heard it."
> At the same time, he wanted them to know who he was,
>   to know that he said to God: "Father," "Abba."

"The prophets" were not a group who lived together as "the Apostles" did, and the two concepts are introduced in "The Story" in different ways, but the word "called" plays an important role in both cases. The concept of "the Sanhedrin" is introduced (in chapter 20) in yet another way, but also relying on the "called-mechanism":

> There were many people like Caiaphas in Jerusalem,
> because the Temple was in Jerusalem.
> There were many priests, many scribes, many Pharisees.
> Some of these people were above the other people in that country.
> They were called the Sanhedrin.
> When these people wanted something to happen, they could say:
> "We want this to happen," as one person can say about something:
> "I want this to happen."
> Many things were happening in that country at that time
>   as these people wanted.
> The Romans thought about the Sanhedrin like this:
>   "These people are above the other people in this country. . . .
>   If we want some things to happen in this country, we can speak to them."

As the short text above shows, the word "Sanhedrin," like the word "Apostles," stands for a group of people who lived at the same time and were often together. It is not, however, a word which can also refer to the individual members of the group, as in the case of "Apostles" (one Apostle, two Apostles, three Apostles), and it stands for what in English legal language is called "a corporate person": The Sanhedrin can make decisions, like one person.

Looking back at all the words discussed in this section so far, we can now ask: what do the words introduced into Minimal English through the "called-mechanism" have in common? And why aren't words from the "cultural lexicon" (mentioned in section 4.4) introduced through the "called-mechanism" whereas those in section 4.5 are? For example, why aren't the non-universal words like "shepherd," "bread," "city," or "soldiers" introduced into "The Story" as "someone called shepherd," "something called bread," and "people called soldiers"?

Roughly speaking, the answer is that the words introduced through the "called"-mechanism are thought of by the speakers as referring to people, places, and things that are either unique or special. This is very clear in the case of the names of people and places: phrases like "a woman called Mary" or "a man called Joseph" are understood as referring to unique individuals identified through a particular word ("Mary," "Joseph"). Similarly, phrases like "a country called Egypt," "a city called Jerusalem," and "a lake called Gennesaret" are understood as referring to unique places identifiable through the words "Egypt," "Jerusalem," and "Gennesaret." Words like "shepherd," "city," or "soldiers," on the other hand, are not intended to identify anything, and this is why one can speak of "two shepherds," "two cities," and "two soldiers," though (normally) not of "two Marys," "two Jerusalems," or "two Gennesarets."

Using Minimal English, we can explain this "identifying" function of words like "Mary," "Jerusalem," and "Gennesaret" as follows:

A woman called Mary
People can think about this woman like this:
> "when I want other people to know that I'm thinking about this woman, not another woman, I can say the word Mary"

The same explanation does not apply, however, to words like "Prophets," "Apostles," "Temple," or "Church" (in English, often with the definite article "the") or to phrases like "the Ten Commandments." Here, what matters is not that the referent is thought of as unique, but rather, that it is thought of as "special." For example, in chapter 7, the concept of "prophets" is followed by the phrase "someone not like many other people," "the Temple" is introduced in chapter 8 with the sentence: "people of Israel thought about it like this: 'this place is like no other place'."

Thus, it is the fact of being thought of as something or someone "special" that often leads to the introduction of a "special" word, a word which is not exactly a "name" (an "identifier") but which works somewhat like a "name." The matter cannot be pursued here any further, but what has been said should be enough to indicate that the use of the "called"-strategy in Minimal English is not arbitrary but corresponds to a mechanism widely used also in ordinary language.

4.6 Metaphors and Minimal English

To understand the Gospels one needs to understand, inter alia, the metaphors in the Gospels. Many of these metaphors are so familiar in European art and literature that they seem to be self-explanatory. This ease of understanding, however, is often an illusion, and to the extent to which theological commentaries have tried to explain them, they came up with different interpretations.

Chesterton's remark (quoted earlier) that "the Gospel as it stands is almost a book of riddles" (1909: 120) applies, above all, to the metaphors in the Gospels. A good example is provided by the metaphor of the keys given by Jesus to Peter in Matthew's Gospel (16:18–19 RSV):

> And Jesus answered him, (. . .) And I tell you, you are Peter, and on this rock I will build my church, and the powers of death shall not prevail against it. I will give you the keys of the kingdom of heaven, and whatever you bind on earth shall be bound in heaven, and whatever you loose on earth shall be loosed in heaven. [In Greek, the first of these lines links the word *Petros* (Peter) with the word *petra* (rock) as follows: "You are *Petros*, and on this *petra* I will build my church." In Aramaic, it would have been "You are *Kefas*, and on this *kefas* I will build my church."]

Chesterton recognizes the significance of this metaphor when he writes: "Christ founded the Church with two great figures of speech in the final words to the Apostles who received authority to found it. The first was the phrase about founding it on Peter as on a rock; the second was the symbol of the keys" (p. 137).

The metaphor of the rock is, according to Chesterton, rather self-explanatory, but the metaphor of the keys (and its extension "binding" and "loosening") is not self-explanatory at all, as shown by the different interpretation assigned to it by different commentators.

Pope Benedict XVI (2007a) comments on this passage as follows:

> The three metaphors which Jesus uses here are very clear: Peter will be the "rock" on which the edifice of the church will be built; he will possess the "keys" to the kingdom of heaven, to open or close it for everyone as he sees fit for a given person; finally he will be able to 'bind' or 'unbind', in the sense that he can enjoin or forbid what he regards as necessary for the life of the Church, which is and remains the church of Christ. The church

is always the church of Christ and not of Peter's. Thus it is described here in very vivid images, what in later theological reflection was described with the concept of "primacy of jurisdiction." (p. 63)

The images are indeed very vivid but they are not self-explanatory, and neither are the explanations. Catholic commentator (and well-known critic of papacy) Garry Wills (2003) offers a different explanation (which may or may not be compatible with Benedict XVI's):

> The ability to set rules is indicated, and the connection with the "keys" indicates that these are the rules for inclusion in or exclusion from the community (. . .) This is precisely the activity of the church in deciding norms of inclusion—whether that of non-Temple observers in Jerusalem (Acts 7:48), non-kosher Christians in Antioch (Gal. 2:12) or Gnostics in the time when Matthew's and John's Gospels were written. (p. 67)

Wills elaborates:

> The power of inclusion or exclusion is given to Peter, as first of the apostles—but not exclusively to him (. . .) All the disciples are included in Jesus's words in Mt 18: 18: "Solemnly I tell you (*hymon*, plural) that whatever you tie on earth will have been tied in heaven and whatever you untie on earth will be untied in heaven." (p. 67)

The words "exclusion" and "inclusion" sound right here, and the etymological link between the Latin noun *clavis* "key" and the verbs *excludere* and *includere* supports this, but who or what is meant to be excluded, and from what exactly?

Wills speaks of the "exclusion from the community," but I don't think this is persuasive. As I see it, the clearest and most cogent interpretation of the metaphor of the keys can be found in Chesterton's *The Everlasting Man*, where he develops the idea of a creed as a key. According to Chesterton, in order to preserve Jesus's Good News, Christianity needed to define itself against a swarm of other beliefs circulating in the ancient world.

> When the Faith first emerged into the world, the very first thing that happened to it was the was caught in a sort of swarm of mystical and metaphysical sects, mostly out of the East; like one lonely golden bee caught in a swarm of wasps. (Chesterton 1908: 143)

Thus, to distinguish the bee from all the wasps someone needed to be able to say authoritatively: this **is** part of Christianity and that is **not**.

Provocatively using the words "dogmatic" and "anathemas" in a positive sense, Chesterton speaks here boldly of "dogmatic definitions and exclusions," which in his view were essential for the preservation of Jesus's message and for a clear outline of Christian faith. Thus, for Chesterton (1908) it was the creed that was like a key, and a key that every Christian could have, so to speak, a copy of: because every Christian could, so to speak, carry the creed in his or her pocket, like a key: "The Early Christian was very precisely a person carrying about a key, or what he said was a key" (p. 137).

Furthermore, according to Chesterton, the whole Christian movement consisted in claiming to possess a key.

> It was not merely a vague forward movement, which might be better represented by a battering-ram. It was not something that swept along with it similar or dissimilar things, as does a modern social movement. As we shall see in a moment it rather definitely refused to do so. It definitely asserted that there was a key and that it possessed that key and that no other key was like it; in that sense it was as narrow as you please. (p. 137)

In a chapter entitled "The witness of the heretics," Chesterton pays a special tribute to the "heretics," because it was the need to distance itself from their doctrines that led the early church to articulate its own teaching clearly and unambiguously, in a pure form. As Chesterton further emphasizes, many of these doctrines were deeply pessimistic and regarded the creation of the world as the work of an evil spirit.

> Now that purity was preserved by dogmatic definitions and exclusions. It could not possibly have been preserved by anything else. If the Church had not renounced the Manicheans it might have become merely Manichean. If it had not renounced the Gnostics it might have become Gnostic. (. . .)
>
> The condemnation of the early heretics is itself condemned as something crabbed and narrow; but it was in truth the very proof that the Church meant to be brotherly and broad. It proved that the primitive Catholics were especially eager to explain that they did not think man utterly vile; that they did not think life incurably miserable; that they did not think marriage a sin or procreation a tragedy. (. . .)
>
> In the very thunder of their anathemas they affirmed forever that their asceticism was not to be anti-human or anti-natural; that they did wish to purge the world and not destroy it. And nothing else except those anathemas could possibly have made it clear, amid a confusion which still confuses them with their mortal enemies. (p. 144)

In my view, these are great ideas and great observations, which offer us a better basis for a semantic interpretation of the metaphor of the keys than the alternative explanations advanced in the literature. Still, they only offer a basis for a precise semantic interpretation, not the interpretation itself. To arrive at an interpretation which is precise, clear, and cross-translatable, I would suggest linking the image of the keys with the notion of the "Holy Spirit," explained by Jesus (in John's Gospel) on the night before he died as "the Spirit of truth." Here are the most relevant lines:

I will pray the Father, and he will give you another Counsellor [Paraclete] to be with you forever, even the Spirit of truth. (. . .) (John 14:16–17)

the Counsellor [Paraclete], the Holy Spirit, whom the Father will send in my name, he will teach you all things, and will bring to you remembrance of all that I have said to you. (John 15:25–26)

. . . when the Spirit of truth comes, he will guide you into all the truth. (John 16:13)

. . . if I do not go away, the Counsellor [Paraclete] will not come to you; but if I go, I will send him to you. And when he comes, he will convince the world concerning sin and righteousness and judgment (. . .) When the Spirit of truth comes, he will guide you into all the truth (John 16:6–13)

In chapter 36 of "The Story of God and People," the corresponding section looks as follows:

> On the night before he died Jesus had said many things to the Apostles
>   like never before.
> He knew that in a very short time they would feel something very very bad.
>   He said to them then:
> "I want you to know that when I am not with you on earth like before,
>   there *will* be someone with you."
> Jesus spoke about this someone with the words: "the Paraclete,"
>   "the Spirit," "the Holy Spirit."
> The Apostles didn't know well at that time
>   what he wanted to say with these words.
> (When the prophets said: "the Spirit," "the Holy Spirit,"
>   "the Spirit of the Lord," they didn't say "someone.")
>
> Jesus had said things like this to them at that time:
> "I want the Holy Spirit to be with you, I will say it to my Father.
>   I can't always be with you like before.
> When the Holy Spirit is with you, *I* will be with you,
>   I will be with you in another way."
> At the same time Jesus said something like this:
> "When the Holy Spirit is with you, you will know well
>   what I wanted to say to you before.
> If someone says some things about God then, you will know
>   what is true, what is not true.
> If someone says some things about me, you will know
>   what is true, what is not true.
> If someone says about something: 'it is very bad if people do this,'
>   you will know what is true, what is not true."

The "dogmatic definitions" and "exclusions" that Chesterton is talking about refer, it seems to me, to the early Church's authority to say "this is true" and "this is not true" about statements defining Christianity, that is, directly or indirectly, statements about God, statements about Christ (in Jesus's words, "about me") and, broadly speaking, statements about people's behavior ("he will convince the world concerning sin, and righteousness, and judgment," John 16:8).

When Jesus is saying to Simon Peter (in Matthew 16:18): "You are Peter, and on this rock I will build my church," he is speaking about Simon Peter individually. When, however, he speaks about the keys, and about the "binding" and "loosening" (Matthew 16:19), he is clearly speaking about the church. This church is defined (in John 15:13) in terms of the Holy Spirit: "When the Spirit of truth comes, he will guide you into all truth" (John 16:13). This promise of the coming of the Holy Spirit, or the spirit of truth, is fulfilled on the day of Pentecost, when . . .

> suddenly a sound came from heaven like the rush of a mighty wind, and it filled all the house where they [the Apostles] were sitting. And then appeared to them tongues as of fire distributed and resting on each of them. And they were all filled with the Holy Spirit . . . (Acts 2:2–4)

Henceforth, the "Holy Spirit" or "the Spirit of truth" will be with the Apostles and will lead them into "all truth": about God, about Jesus, about people. The "keys" will be given to the Apostles (and their successors), so they can articulate the creed and know what to include and what to exclude. After that, every Christian could be, in Chesterton's words, "a person carrying about a key, or what he said was a key."

In her 1949 book *Creed or Chaos*, which I have already mentioned, Dorothy Sayers calls the Christian faith "the most exciting drama that ever staggered the imagination of man," and (like Chesterton) provocatively uses the word "dogma" in a positive sense when she affirms that "the dogma [summarized in the Creeds] *is* the drama": "The drama is summarized quite clearly in the creeds of the Church, and if we think it dull it is because we either have never really read those amazing documents, or have recited them so often and so mechanically as to have lost all sense of their meaning" (p. 1).

Thus, trying to articulate what Christians believe, one has to be guided, to a large extent, by the creeds (the Apostles Creed and the Nicene Creed). At the same time, to understand the meaning of these creeds, one needs to be guided, to some extent, by what can be said (and therefore thought) in all languages. To make another use of the metaphor of the keys while at the same time drawing on the phrase used by the Yanomami shaman Davi Kopenawa (Kopenawa & Albert 2013), universal human words can provide keys with the help of which many hidden, or semi-hidden, meanings and ideas can be "opened out" for everyone to understand.

PART II

The Story of God and People

CONTENTS

1. God

There is someone not like people.
This someone is someone above people; this someone is above everything.
This someone is now, always was, always will be. This someone is everywhere.
There is no one else like this someone.
God is this someone.
People can't see God; at the same time, people can know some things about God.
They can know these things because God wants it.
People can know that it is like this:
God is good.
If God wants something, it is something good, if God does something,
it is something good.
If God wants something to happen, it can happen because of this.
If God says about something: "I want it to happen," it happens.
If God says about something: "It is like this," it is true.
God knows everything.

At the same time, people can know that it is like this:
God knows all people.
God feels something very good toward all people.
God wants to do good things for all people.
God wants to speak to all people.
All people can know God, God wants it.
All people can live with God, God wants it.

People can know many things about God if they read a book called the Bible.
It is a book not like any other books. God speaks to people in this book.
This book has two parts, one is called "The Old Testament,"
the other is called "The New Testament."
The Old Testament has many parts; it is like one book,
at the same time many books are parts of it.
Many people wrote these books over a very long time,
they wrote about things of many kinds.
The New Testament is not like this.
Not many people wrote it, these people didn't write it over a very long time.
They didn't write about things of many kinds.
They all wrote about someone called Jesus.
When people read the New Testament,
after some time they can know this someone (Jesus).
At the same time, they can know that when they know this someone (Jesus),
they know God.

2. The world exists because God wants it to exist

It is like this now:
>   There are many people living on earth, there are many things on earth,
>   many things are happening on earth.
>   There is the sky above the earth, there is light, there is the sun,
>   there is the moon, there are stars.

It is like this because God wants it to be like this.
It wasn't always like this. A very very long time ago, it was like this:
>   There was no earth, there was no sky, there was no light;
>   there were no places as there are now,
>   There were no people, there was nothing anywhere,
>   nothing was happening anywhere.
>   There was God.

Before there was anything anywhere, God said something.
God said:
>   "I want there to be places of some kinds;
>   I want some things to be happening in these places."

When God said this, something happened, it happened as God wanted.
God said: "I want there to be light." When God said this, there was light.
God said: "This is very good."
After this, many other things were happening for a very long time,
   as God wanted.
After some time, it was like this:
>   There were places of many kinds,
>   many things were happening in these places.
>   There was the earth, there was the sky, there was the sun,
>   there was the moon, there were stars.
>   It was like this because God wanted it to be like this.

God said: "This is very good."

For a very long time many things were happening to the earth,
   because God wanted it. For a long time, it was like this:
>   No things were growing on earth.
>   No living creatures were living on earth.

After this, it was not like this anymore, it was like this:
>   Things of many kinds were growing on earth.
>   Living creatures of many kinds were living on earth.

All this was as God wanted. God said: "This is very good."
When it was like this, for a long time there were no people on earth.
After this, there were people living on earth.

It was like this because God wanted it. God said: "This is very good."
When there were people on earth, it was not like before,
   because people were not like other living creatures.
It was like this:
      People wanted to know many things about many things,
         not like other living creatures.
      People could think about many things, not like other living creatures.
      They could think like this: "After some time, I will die,"
         other living creatures could not think like this.
      They could think: "I can do good things, I can do bad things,"
         other creatures could not think like this.
At the same time, it was like this:
      People could want to speak to God, as God wants to speak to people.
      People could feel something very good toward other people,
         as God feels something very good toward people.
      People could want to do good things for other people,
         as God wants to do good things for people.
God wanted it to be like this. God wants the same now.

People can think like this:
      "The earth is something very good, many good things happen on earth."
At the same time people know that many very bad things happen on earth.
They know that it is like this:
      People die, often people feel something very very bad,
      often living creatures feel something very very bad.
They can think about it like this:
      "God knows why it is like this,
      we can't know it now, we can know it after we die."
At the same time, they can think:
      "One day, it will not be like this anymore, it will be like this:
      People will not die anymore, they will not feel anything bad,
      living creatures will not feel anything bad."
They can think: "One day, all will be well, God wants this."

3. People can live with God

God knows all people, feels something very good toward all people,
    wants to do good things for all people.
Because of this, it is like this: all people can live with God, God wants it.
If someone lives with God, it is very good for this person,
    nothing else is like this.
People can always live with God if they live like this:
        They feel something very good toward other people,
        as God feels something very good toward all people,
        They want to do good things for other people,
        as God wants to do good things for all people.
God wants people to live like this.
When people live like this, they can live with God because God is like this.

People often don't live with God. It is like this now, it has always been like this.
Often, they do something when they know that it is something very bad.
Often, they don't want to think about God.
At the same time, they often live like this:
        They want to do bad things to other people,
        They don't want to do good things for other people.
        They feel something very bad toward other people.
        They don't feel something very good toward any other people.
When people live like this, they can't live with God,
    because God is not like this.

Some parts of the Bible say things like this about it:
        There is someone not like people, this someone is bad.
        This someone wants people not to live with God,
            because of this, this someone does many things.
        This someone says many things to people, these things are not true.
        If people live as this someone wants them to live,
            they can't live with God.
Some parts of the Bible call this someone: "Satan," some say: "the devil."

It is like this: people *can* not live with God if they don't want to.
At the same time, it is like this: if someone doesn't live with God,
    it is very bad for this someone.
If someone doesn't live with God, God feels something because of this.
God wants it not to be like this, God does many things because of this.

People can think about God like this:

God is like a shepherd.

A shepherd thinks about many sheep. He knows all these sheep.

These sheep can know him.

When they hear his voice, they can know that it is his voice.

The shepherd wants these sheep to be with him.

He wants them to be always in places where there is good grass to eat.

He thinks like this: "I don't want bad things to happen to any one of them."

He does many things because of this.

God is like such a shepherd.

In one country people thought like this about God for a very long time.

Many people in that country had many sheep, many were shepherds.

Many people in that country thought a lot about God.

At many times, God spoke to the people in that country.

People in all countries can know a lot about it if they read the Bible.

4. God wants to live for some time with people on earth

All people can live with God, nothing else is like this, God wants this.
At the same time, God doesn't want it to be like this:
    People live with God because they have to (can't not) live with God.
God wants it to be like this:
    People know God, because of this they want to live with God.
God has always wanted it to be like this.
All people can know God, people are born like this;
    they are born like this because God wants this.
At the same time, often people don't know God well.
God wanted it to be like this:
    All people know God well, all people want to live with God.
Because of this, a long time ago some things happened in one country
    not like anywhere else.
It was like this:

God wanted to live for some time on earth, with people, like people live.
God wanted to live on earth at one time, in one country,
    not at many times in many countries.
God wanted to live like people lived in that country,
    to speak like people spoke in that country.
God wanted to speak to these people.
God wanted it to be like this:
    First, these people can know God well,
    some time after this, people in other countries can know God well.
Because of this, a very long time ago God did many things,
    many things happened because of this.
People can know many things about it if they read the Bible.

One part of the Bible is called Genesis, it is before all the other parts.
If people read this part, they can know that a very long time ago,
    God spoke to a man called Abraham.
They can know that Abraham was born in a city called Ur
    in a country called Chaldeia, in a part of the earth called Mesopotamia.
They can know that God wanted Abraham to go to another country,
    far from the country where he was born.
They can know that God wanted Abraham to live in that other country.

People can think about it like this:
> In Chaldea, people thought like this:
> "The Moon is like someone, this someone is above people,
> this someone is above us.
> We have to do many things as this someone wants.
> If we don't do it, something very bad can happen to us."
> In other parts of Mesopotamia, people thought like this about the Sun.
> God wanted people not to think like this about the Moon,
>> not to think like this about the Sun.
>
> God wanted people to think like this:
>> "God is above people, God is above us;
>> we want to live as God wants us to live."
>
> At the same time, God wanted people to know *how* to live.
> Because of this, when God wanted to speak to Abraham,
>> God wanted Abraham to go to another country.
>
> God wanted him to live far from Chaldea, far from Mesopotamia.

At the same time, people can think like this:
> God wanted Abraham to think like this:
> "God will do very good things for me.
> Very good things will happen because of this to many other people.
> After some time, very good things will happen because of this
>> to people everywhere on earth, God wants it."

If people read Genesis, they can know that it was like this:
> God felt something very good toward Abraham.
> God wanted to live on earth with people in the same country
>> where, some time before, Abraham lived.

5. God speaks to Abraham

When God spoke to Abraham, God said something like this to him:
"I want you not to live anymore in the country where you live now,
   I want you to live in another country.
If you live in that other country, after some time it will be like this:
   many many people will be born in that country because of this.
Look at the sky at night; there are many many stars there,
   you can't say how many; these people will be like this.
All these people can be born because sometime before, you were born.
Because of this, all these people will think about you like this:
   'Abraham is our father.'
I will do very good things for you,
   very good things will happen to all these people because of this.
After some time, very good things will happen because of this
   to people in all parts of the earth."

Abraham did as God wanted.
Because of this, some time after this, Abraham lived in that other country.
Because of this, some time after this, many people were born in that country,
   they all thought like this: "Abraham is our father."
When Abraham lived in that country, it was called Canaan,
   later it was called Palestine.
Now a big part of that country is a country called Israel.
For a long time people said the word "Israel" about some people,
   not about a country.
It was like this (so says the part of the Bible called Genesis):

Abraham was the father of Isaac, Isaac's mother was called Sarah.
Isaac was the father of Jacob, Jacob's mother was called Rebecca.
Isaac lived in Canaan, like Abraham.
Jacob had to live for many years in another country.
After this, when he could live in Canaan, something happened to him.
Genesis says this about it:
   God spoke to Jacob in a place called Jabbok. God said:
   "You will not be called Jacob anymore, you will now be called Israel;
   I want you to be the father of many people;
   these people will live in the country where I wanted Abraham to live."
After this, the Bible often says about Jacob: "Israel."
Jacob had two wives, one was called Leah, the other was called Rachel.
He had many sons (twelve), these sons had wives,
   they were the fathers of many children.

After some time many people lived in that country because of this.
Often the Bible speaks about them as people can speak about one person,
     it calls them "Israel."
Other people called them Hebrews, Israelites, Jews.
They spoke Hebrew.

The people of Israel (the Israelites) thought like this: "We are people of one kind."
They thought:
     "If someone's father is someone of this kind,
     this person is someone of the same kind.
     Jacob was someone of this kind, Isaac was someone of this kind,
     Abraham was someone of this kind.
     These are our fathers."
At the same time they thought like this:
     "God feels something very very good toward the people of Israel.
     God spoke to Abraham many times.
     God felt something very very good toward Abraham.
     Abraham could know God before other people could know God,
     God wanted it to be like this."

Abraham knew God.
He knew well what God had said to him, he thought about it like this:
     "God (El, Elohim) said these things to me,
     because of this I know that it is all true."
He wanted to think like this.
At the same time, he thought like this:
     "God (El, Elohim) is like no one else, God is above everything;
     I want to listen to God."

6. God speaks to Moses

After Jacob died, for a long time Israelites didn't live in Canaan,
    they lived in a country called Egypt.
For a long time, they could live there as they wanted to live
    (they were shepherds).
After this, they couldn't live there anymore as they wanted, they were slaves;
    very bad things happened to them.
The king of Egypt wanted many Israelites (many men) to die,
    he wanted many children to die.
One Israelite felt something very very bad because of this,
    not like all the others. It was a man called Moses.
God wanted Moses to do some things.
Because of this, one day God spoke to Moses. It happened like this:

> Moses was living in a desert at that time (near Egypt, not in Egypt),
>   near a big mountain called Mount Sinai.
> One day, Moses saw fire inside a bush. It was like this:
>   the fire was touching the bush for some time;
>   at the same time nothing was happening to the bush.
> Then Moses heard God's voice from inside the bush: "Moses, Moses!"
> Then God said to Moses:
>   "I want to speak to you, as I spoke to Abraham, to Isaac, to Jacob.
>   Very bad things are happening to the people of Israel in Egypt,
>   I feel something because of this.
>   I don't want the people of Israel to live in Egypt anymore,
>   I want the people of Israel to live in Canaan.
>   I want you to do some things because of this.
>   Go back to Egypt. Speak to the people. I will be with you.
>   I want the people of Israel to know that I said these things to you.
>   Then speak to the king of Egypt."
> Moses said to God:
>   "How can I do this?
>   When I say to the people of Israel: "God said this to me,"
>   they will say: "Who is this God? What is his name?"
>   What can I say to them then?"
> God said:
>   "My name is: 'I AM.' Say to them: 'I AM wants me to say this to you.'"

After this, Moses did everything as God wanted.
Many things happened in Egypt because of this.
Then, God did something very good for the people of Israel.
(A part of the Bible called Exodus says a lot about it.)

After this, Israelites didn't live in Egypt anymore.

For a long time, they lived in a desert, not in one place all the time.

Moses wanted them to go to Mount Sinai, where God spoke to him before.

He wanted God to speak to them.

When they were there, God spoke to Moses on the mountain.

God said to Moses:

"Say to the people: God says:

'If you live as I want, I will always be with you,

not like with other people, I'll be very near to you; I want this.'"

Moses said this to the people. They said to him then:

"We will do everything as God says, say this to God."

Then Moses built something called an altar ("God's place").

The people killed some animals, as Moses wanted.

Then Moses sprinkled the blood of these animals on the altar,

after this, he sprinkled some blood on the people.

He wanted to say in this way: "God says: I want it, we say: we want it;

when people see this blood, they can know that it is true."

God said some other things, Moses wrote them on two big flat stones.

They all said: "I (God) say: Live like this."

After this, Israelites could know how God wanted people to live.

These things were called the Ten Commandments.

The first said: "Think like this about me: 'God is above us, God is above me;'

don't think like this about anyone else."

Another, like it, said: "Don't think like this about anything anywhere;

don't think like this about any thing."

Some others said: "Don't kill people," "Don't steal,"

"Don't say anything bad about someone else if it is not true."

One said to men: "A husband can do something with his wife,

as men often want to do, because he is her husband.

Don't do this with another man's wife; don't think: I want to do this with her."

Many people think about the Ten Commandments like this:

there was never anything like this before anywhere on earth.

Before he died, Moses said to the people of Israel:

"After some time, someone else like me will live with you, God said so.

When this someone speaks, people can know well

what God wants to say to people, what God wants people to do."

For a long time, Israelites spoke about this someone.

They thought: "When will this happen? When will he be born?"

When Jesus lived on earth, many Israelites thought:

"Moses said this about Jesus, Jesus is like another Moses."

(In the Gospel of John, Jesus says: "Moses was speaking about me.")

7. God speaks through the prophets

For a very long time, God often spoke to the people of Israel.
Before Moses died, it was like this:
>When God wanted to say something to the people of Israel.
>God said it to Moses, after this, Moses said it to the people of Israel.
After Moses died, it was like this:
>When God wanted to say something to the people of Israel,
>God said it to someone not like many other people,
>after this, this someone said it to the people of Israel.
Someone like this was called a prophet.
Many prophets spoke to the people of Israel at many times
(some were women).
They spoke not like other people. When they said something,
>they wanted people to think: "God says this to us."
The prophets wanted the people of Israel to want to live with God at all times,
>to think about God at all times.
People can know what many prophets said
>if they read the part of the Bible called the Prophets.
Often the prophets said things like this about something:
>"after some time, something like this will happen in this country,
>God wants it."
Two prophets called Isaiah said things like this to the people of Israel:

"God says:
>'I feel something very good toward you, Israel.
>I want to do very good things for you.
>I want you to think about me. I want you to want to live with me.
>I want you to know me well. If you know me well,
>after some time people in other countries can know me well, I want this.'
God says:
>'Very bad things are happening to many people on earth.
>I feel something very good toward all people on earth.
>After some time, I will do something very good for all people on earth,
>as I did something very good for you when you were in Egypt.
God says:
>'After some time, someone not like other people will be born in this country.
>A woman will be this someone's mother, this someone will be her son,
>>no man will be his father.
>His name will be "Emmanuel" (in Hebrew, "God with us").
God says:
>He will be like the light, people everywhere on earth will see this light.
>He will want to do good things for all people on earth.

God says:

>   He will be like a lamb, he will not want to do anything bad to anyone.
>   Other people will do very bad things to him.
>   He will feel something very bad because of this, he will die because of this.
>   When these people are doing this to him, he will not say: I don't want this.'"

Some other prophets spoke about someone not like other people.
Someone else spoke about someone not like other people,
>   this someone else was called David.

David was a king of the people of Israel, before he was a king he was a shepherd.
He felt something very good toward God,
>   he often wanted to say some things to God.

He often said some things to God when he was a shepherd,
>   he often said some things to God when he was a king.

Often when he wanted to say some things to God,
>   he said these things with something of one kind called a psalm.

When he wanted to speak to God in this way, he sang, he played music.
People can know how David spoke to God
>   if they read a part of the Bible called Psalms.

Afterwards, when the Israelites spoke to God, they often said Psalms.
(Many other people do the same now.)
God felt something very good toward David.
A prophet called Nathan said to David: "God says this to you:

>   'I want to do very good things for you.
>   You will be like the father of many people.
>   Some of these people will be kings of the people of Israel;
>   one of these people will be king forever.'"

(When Jesus lived on earth, many Israelites thought like this:
"God was saying this about Jesus." Many people think like this now.)

8. It all happened as the prophets said

For a very long time, the prophets said things like this to the people:
"After some time, someone not like other people
    will be born in this country.
Very bad things are happening to the people of Israel,
    this someone will do very good things for the people of Israel.
Very bad things are happening to all people,
    this someone will do something very good for all people."
Sometimes the prophets said:
"This someone will be the king of the people of Israel."
For a very long time the people of Israel often spoke about it.
They called this someone "the Messiah."
(Before, this word meant something else, every king was called a "messiah."
Later, it was not like this anymore.)
They didn't know when "the Messiah" would be born. They wanted it to be soon.

It happened as the prophets said.
(People can know a lot about it if they read some parts of the Bible;
these parts are called the Gospels, in Greek, "Evangelion",
This word means "good news.")
A long time after David lived, a long time after both prophets called Isaiah lived,
    someone not like other people was born in that country.
This someone's name was Jesus, in Hebrew Yeshua.
The name Yeshua means something like this:
"When something very bad happens to people,
    God does very good things for them."
The Gospel of Matthew calls this someone (Jesus) "the Son of Abraham,"
"the Son of David."

Jesus was born at a time when the country where the people of Israel lived
    was one small part of something very very big.
This something was called the Roman empire.
It was something not like anything else at that time,
    many countries in many parts of the earth were part of it.
There was a big city called Rome in this empire.
The people in Rome were called Romans, they spoke Latin.
Often people called the Roman empire: "Rome," like the city.
When Jesus was born, someone called Caesar Augustus lived in Rome.
He was someone above all the people in the Roman empire,
    like the king of a country is someone above all the people in that country.
Later, someone like this was always called Caesar.
When Jesus died, someone called Tiberius was "Caesar."

Jesus was born in a small town called Bethlehem in Judea.

Judea was one part of Palestine, another part was Galilee.

Someone called Herod was at that time king of Judea, as the Romans wanted (not as the people of Israel wanted).

The people of Israel knew that King David was born in Bethlehem.

At the same time they could know that the Messiah would be born there (One of the Prophets said so.)

The small town called Bethlehem was near a big city called Jerusalem.

King David lived in Jerusalem, often when Israelites thought about Jerusalem, they thought about King David.

Later, there was something called the Temple in Jerusalem.

The people of Israel thought about it like this:

"This place is like no other place, God speaks to the people here."

Israelites felt something very good toward Jerusalem.

They thought about it like this:

"Jerusalem is a city not like any other city,

God feels something very good toward Jerusalem."

The prophets often spoke about Jerusalem.

The prophet called Ezekiel said: "Its name will be 'God is there.'"

When Jesus was a boy (not a child), he often went to Jerusalem with his parents, perhaps every year.

Later, he often spoke to people in Jerusalem;

like other prophets, sometimes he spoke about Jerusalem.

He felt something very good toward Jerusalem.

He knew that very bad things would happen to it,

he knew that the Romans would do very bad things to it.

When he thought about it, he wept.

Many things happened to Jesus in Jerusalem. He died in Jerusalem.

(This "Story" will say more about it later.)

9. A woman called Mary says "yes" to God

Jesus's mother was called Mary (in Aramaic, Mariam).
She lived in a town called Nazareth in Galilee.
(People spoke Aramaic in Galilee at that time.)
Mary didn't have a husband; at the same time she knew
   that a man called Joseph would be her husband in a short time.
Sometime before Jesus was born, something happened to Mary.
Before it happened, she didn't know that something like this could happen to her.
It happened like this:

One day Mary saw someone not like people, she thought:
   "this is an angel" (in Aramaic, "mal'ak").
Then the angel spoke to her.
Mary knew then that God wanted to say something to her.
The angel said:
   "I want to say something very good to you, Mariam.
   God is with you, God feels something very good toward you."
Mary didn't know why this was happening to her,
   she didn't know what she could think about it.
Then the angel said:
   "Don't think like this, Mariam: 'something bad can happen to me now.'
   Think like this: 'something very good is happening now.'
   In a very short time, something will happen to you;
      it will happen because God wants it to happen.
   Because of this, after some time you will give birth to a child (a son).
   You will call him Jesus.
   He will not be like other people, people will call him the Son of God.
   He will be a king, like David.
   Sometimes people will call him 'Son of David.' He will be king forever."
Mary said: "How can this happen to me? I don't have a husband."
The angel said:
   "God wants it to happen. Because God wants it to happen, it can happen."
Then the angel said:
   "You know Elizabeth, the wife of Zechariah.
      you think about her like this: 'She is like my mother's sister.'
   You know that for a very long time, people said about her:
      'She can't give birth to a child.'
   Now she knows that she will soon give birth to a child.
   If God wants something to happen, it can happen."

Mary knew that she could say at that moment: "I don't want it to happen to me."
She didn't say this. She said:
"I want it to happen to me as you say.
I want it to happen because God wants it."
After this, the angel was not with her anymore.

A very short time after this, Mary went to the place in Judea
    where Elizabeth lived with her husband Zechariah.
Mary felt something very good toward Elizabeth,
    she wanted to be with her for some time at that time.
She knew that Elizabeth would give birth to a child soon,
    because the angel said so.
("The Story" will say more about this child later, it was a son,
    his name was John, he was a prophet.)
When Elizabeth saw Mary, she felt something like never before.
She said this to her then (she spoke like a prophet):
"You are a woman not like other women. God is with you.
You are the mother of the Son of God."

Then *Mary* spoke like a prophet, she spoke like this (not with these words):
"It is like this in my soul now: I think very very good things about God,
I feel something very very good toward God.
I want to say very very good things about God.
God has done very very good things for me.
Everywhere on earth people will always say this about me.
God did this not because I am someone above other people.
God did this because God is good.
If people think about God when bad things are happening to them,
    God does good things for them.
Some people think like this:
'We are not like other people, we are above other people;
God wants to do good things for us, not for others.'
God doesn't want people to think like this.
God wants people to think *like this*:
'I can live because God does good things for me;
God wants to do good things for all people.'
God will do very good things for the people of Israel,
    as he said to our father Abraham."
Mary was with Elizabeth for three months. Then she went back to Nazareth.

10. Jesus is born

When Mary said to the angel: "I want it to happen to me as you say,"
    something happened in her body.
Because of this, some time after this, she gave birth to a child (a son);
    she called him Jesus, as the angel said.
Joseph was then Mary's husband.
Joseph knew that no man was this child's father.
God wanted him to know it.
Joseph wanted to do good things for Jesus like a child's father can do.
Jesus was not born in Nazareth, he was born in Bethlehem, like King David.
It happened like this:

At that time all men in Palestine had to go to the place where they were born
    because Caesar Augustus said so.
Caesar Augustus wanted the Romans to know some things about them.
He wanted this because he wanted the Romans to know well
    how much money someone could pay them each year.
He wanted some Romans to write this about every man,
    he wanted them to it in the place where this man was born.
Joseph was born in Bethlehem, because of this, he had to go to Bethlehem,
    Mary went with him.
They knew that she would give birth to a child very soon,
    at the same time they knew that they had to go.

When they were in Bethlehem, Jesus was born.
He was born in a cave where there were oxen at night, not in a house.
(There was no place in a house where they could be for some time,
no place in a house where Mary could give birth.)
When Jesus was born, Joseph was with Mary.
There were no other people with them at that time. It was night.
There were some shepherds near that place at that time,
    they were looking after their sheep at night.
At one moment, the shepherds saw an angel, the angel said to them:
    "I want you to know that something very good happened tonight,
    the Messiah was born in Bethlehem."
The next moment the shepherds could see many angels.
The angels were singing, they were singing to God.
The shepherds went then to Bethlehem:
    there they saw Mary, they saw Joseph, they saw child Jesus.
Some time after this (we don't know when)
    three other people went to Bethlehem to see child Jesus.
(So says the Gospel of Matthew.)
They were not Israelites, they lived far from Judea, they knew a lot about stars.

When they saw a star not like any other stars, they thought like this:
> "Something happened in Judea.
> A child not like other children has been born, this child will be a king.
> He will be a king not like other kings."

They wanted to see this child, to kneel before him, as before a king,
> as before God. So they went.

In Judea, they went first to Jerusalem, then to Bethlehem.
In Bethlehem they saw Mary, Joseph, child Jesus.

Forty days after Jesus was born, two very old people knew
> that a child not like other children had been born.

(So says the Gospel of Luke.)
One was a man called Simeon, the other, a woman called Anna, a prophet.
They saw the child Jesus in the Temple in Jerusalem
(they were often in the Temple, Anna was there every day).
They saw him there because forty days after she gave birth,
> Mary went to the Temple with the child in her arms.

All women had to do in that country at that time (the Law said so).
Joseph went with her.
When they saw child Jesus, they thought: "This is the Messiah"
(God wanted them to know who this child was).

Simeon held the child in his arms, then he spoke to God.
He said (he said it with the words of Isaiah, he was speaking like a prophet):
> "God, you are good. I can die now because I saw this child, as you said."

(He knew that before he dies, he would see the Messiah.
God wanted him to know it.)
Then he said this to God:
> "Because this child was born, all people can know you well.
> First, the people of Israel can know you well,
> after this, people in all parts of the earth can know you well because of this.
> This child will be like the light."

After this, Simeon said to the child's mother, Mary:
> "Because this child was born, many things will happen in this country.
> Some people will feel something very bad because of this,
> > others will feel something very good.
> Some people will do very bad things to him.
> You will feel something very very bad because of this.
> You will feel something like someone can feel
> > when something very very bad is happening to their body.

Mary often thought about these words when Jesus was a child,
> she often thought about them when he was not a child anymore.

11. Jesus lives in Nazareth

When Jesus was a child, he lived in Nazareth in Galilee;
    later, people called him Jesus of Nazareth.
(A long time before Jesus was born, prophet Isaiah said:
"People in Galilee will see a light not like any other light.")
Jesus's mother Mary lived in Nazareth with her husband Joseph,
    Jesus lived with them.
During that time, something happened once like never before.
It happened like this:

Every year, they went to Jerusalem before the day called Passover,
    with many other people.
(This "Story" will say more about this day of the year later).
One year, when Jesus was not a small child anymore, they did the same,
    Jesus went with them.
When they were going back, Jesus wasn't with them.
(He was in Jerusalem, as before, they didn't know it.)
They thought like this:
    "he is with other people, with other children, we will see him later."
After one day, they knew that it was not like this, no one knew where Jesus was.
They went back to Jerusalem, they went to many places there,
    they didn't see him in any of these places.
They felt something very bad at that time.
After three days they saw him in the Temple.
He was there with some other people, these people knew the Bible very well.
Jesus was talking to them about the Bible.
They all thought like this: "How can this child know so much?"
Mary said then to Jesus:
    "Son, why did you do this to us?
    We didn't know where you were, we felt something very bad."
Jesus said to them:
    "You didn't know where I was?
    Didn't you know that I have to be in my Father's house?"
They didn't know at that time why he spoke like this.

Mary thought about these words for a very long time.
She thought about them when Jesus was a child,
    she thought about them when he was not a child anymore.
When they went back to Nazareth, Jesus went with them.
After this, he lived with them as before.

When they wanted him to do something, he did it,
  when they wanted him not to do something, he didn't do it.
God was with him, people in Nazareth felt something very good toward him.

When Jesus was not a child anymore, for a long time he lived in Nazareth,
  like before.
During that time, he lived like many other people in that town lived.
He did many things every day like Joseph did. He was a carpenter, like Joseph.
At the same time, he often read the Bible.
He wanted to know well what God said to Abraham, what God said to Moses,
  what God said to David.
He wanted to know well what the prophets said to the people of Israel.
He wanted to know well what God wanted to say to him,
  he wanted to know well what God wanted him to do.

After some time, Jesus didn't want to live in Nazareth anymore.
He wanted to speak to people in many places.
He wanted to say something like this to them:
    "For a very long time the prophets said:
    'At some time some things will happen in this country like never before.
    At that time God will do very good things for the people of Israel.
    At the same time, God will do very good things for all people.'
    I want you to know that these things are happening now.
    It is like this: people can live with God now not like before,
      people can know now that God is near."
Jesus wanted many people in many places to hear this.

12. The prophet called John the Baptist

Jesus wanted something to happen to him
    before he spoke about God to many people in many places.
He wanted many people to see it.
It happened as he wanted. It happened like this:

A prophet called John was saying some things to many people
    at that time near the river Jordan, in Judea.
John didn't live like other people lived at that time in that country,
    he lived in the desert.
When John was saying these things in that place near the river Jordan,
    many people wanted to hear it.
These people lived in many places in Judea,
    they all wanted to go to that place near the river Jordan.
They knew that a prophet was saying some things to people there,
    they wanted to hear it.

John was saying things like this to people near the river Jordan:
    "As you know, for a long time the prophets said:
    'At some time, someone not like other people will live in this country,
    this someone will do very good things for the people of Israel,
    at the same time he will do very good things for all people.'
    As you know, some of the prophets said:
    'Before this someone is here, someone else here will say:
    He will be here in a very short time.'
    I say to you now: I am this someone else.
    I live because God wants me to say some things to people.
    God wants me to say to you now:
    'This someone will be here in a very short time.
    Do some things because of this now.'
    He is someone above me, I am someone below him.
    I touch you with water, he will touch you with fire."
(When John said "fire," he was speaking about the "Holy Spirit."
This "Story" will say more about it later.)

At the same time, John was saying things like this to people:
    "God wants something to happen in you before this someone is here.
    It can happen if you want it to happen.
    If it happens, after this you will think not like before.
    If you think not like before, you can live not like before.

God wants you to think like this now:
'Before, I didn't live as God wants people to live,
I was doing very bad things.
I don't want to live like this anymore.
I want to live now as God wants people to live.'"

When John was speaking like this to people, he wanted people to do some things.
He wanted everyone to be in the river for a short time.
When the water was touching someone's body,
 he wanted this someone to say about some things:
  "I did this. When I was doing it, I was doing something very bad.
  I don't want to do it anymore."
Many people were doing as John said.
People thought: "John does something as no other prophet did before."
They said about John: "John 'baptizes' people."
Because of this they called him John the Baptist.
(In Greek, "baptizo," "I baptize," meant something like this:
"I want [you] to be under water for a short time.")

Jesus wanted John to baptize him as he was baptizing other people.
John did it, because Jesus wanted it. He didn't know why Jesus wanted it.
He knew that Jesus didn't do anything bad.
People can think about it like this:
Jesus wanted it because he wanted to say something like this to people:
  "I want this to happen to me as it happens to other people.
  I want to be with other people.
  I feel something very good toward all people.
  I think like this about people: all people are one."
When John baptized Jesus, some things happened like never before.
(More about it in the next chapter.)

13. John the Baptist baptizes Jesus

One day when John was baptizing people in the river Jordan,
    he saw Jesus in that place.
Jesus said then to John:
    "I want you to baptize me, as you are baptizing other people."
John thought then: "He is not someone like other people,
    he is someone above me, I am someone below him."
Because John thought like this, he said to Jesus:
    "I can't baptize you, you can baptize *me*."
Jesus said to John:
    "I *want* you to do it. It will be good if it happens.
    It will be as God wants."
Because Jesus said this, John baptized him, as Jesus wanted.

A very short time after, something happened in that place like never before.
It was like this:
There was something like a dove above Jesus, it was very close to him.
It was there for some time; Jesus saw it.
Jesus knew that it was God's Spirit, "the Holy Spirit."
(This "Story" will say more about "the Holy Spirit" later).
At the same time he heard a voice above this place,
    he knew that it was God's voice.
The voice said:
    "You are my Son, I feel something very very good toward you.
    You know that I want you to do some things.
    You want to do it as I want, this is very very good."
John saw the dove, he knew that it was God's Spirit, he heard the voice,
He knew it was God's voice.
He wanted people to know what he saw, what he heard.
He wanted people to know who Jesus was.

The next day John saw Jesus in the same place; he said about him then:
    "This is the Lamb of God."
At the same time, he said something like this about Jesus:
    "He wants all people to live with God."
(A long time before, prophet Isaiah said about someone:
"He is like a lamb; he will die because people do very bad things."
John was saying this about Jesus.)
Before he baptized Jesus, some people said to John:
    "Who are you? Are you the Messiah?" He said: "I am not."
(These people were people of one kind called "priests."
This "Story" will say more about people of this kind later.)

John said to these people at that time:

"I am like a voice, the voice says: 'someone will be here soon.'"

When John saw Jesus the day after he had baptized him, he said:

"When I baptized him, I saw a dove above him.

It was there for some time. I knew that it was the Holy Spirit.

I had known before that I would see these things.

I had known it because God said it to me.

I knew then who he was. God wanted me to know it.

Because of this I can say now: This is the Son of God, it is true, I know it."

After this, for some time Jesus was not with other people.

He was in the desert, the Holy Spirit was with him.

Some things happened to him then not like at any other time.

The Bible says something like this about it:

Someone spoke to Jesus in the desert, it was someone not like people.

It was someone bad.

(Some parts of the Bible say "the devil" about this someone,

one part says: "Satan.")

This someone wanted Jesus to think like this:

"I am the Son of God. If I say: I want something to happen, it will happen."

Because of this, this someone said to Jesus:

"If you say: 'I want these stones to be bread,' they will be bread."

(This someone knew that Jesus hadn't eaten anything for a long time,

that in the desert he didn't eat anything.)

Jesus said to this someone then: "I don't want to say things like this."

Then this someone said to Jesus:

"If you say: 'I don't want bad things to happen to me,'

they will not happen."

Jesus said: "I don't want to say things like this."

Then this someone said something like this to Jesus:

"Very good things will happen to you if you say to me:

'You are someone above people.'"

Jesus said then: "I don't want to say this to you, Satan.

God is someone above people, not anyone else."

After this, this someone wasn't with Jesus anymore.

After this, Jesus wanted to be with people.

He knew what God wanted him to do. He wanted to do it.

He could think like this then: "I know now: God wants me to do it *now*."

14. What Jesus did when he didn't live in Nazareth anymore

After this, Jesus didn't live in one place anymore,
    because he wanted to speak to people in many places.
He wanted to speak about God because he wanted people to know
    what God is like.
He wanted to speak about people because he wanted people to know
    how it is good for them to live.
At the same time he wanted to say something like this to people in many places:
    "Something very good is happening here now, I want you to know it.
    People can live with God now like never before, God is near."
When Jesus said these things, often people thought like this:
    "Who is he? No one ever spoke like this before."

In all the places where he went, Jesus did very good things for people,
    nobody else could do things like that.
Often, it was like this:
    Someone felt something very bad
        because something very bad was happening in their body.
    Jesus saw this person, he knew what this person felt,
        he felt something because of this.
    He wanted this person not to feel like this anymore,
        he did something because of this.
    After this, this person didn't feel like this anymore.

Often it was like this:
    When Jesus was in a place with other people, someone said to him:
    "I can't do many things like other people
        because something very bad happened to my body.
    I know that you can do something very good for me;
    I know that if you do it, it will not be like this anymore."
    (Some said: "I can't see," some: "I can't hear," some: "I can't move.")
    Jesus said to this person then: "I want it not to be like this anymore,"
        he touched this person's body.
    After this, it wasn't like before: this person *could* see (hear, move).
Often the same happened when someone touched Jesus's robe.
Often if someone couldn't move others carried them to the place where Jesus was
    because they wanted Jesus to touch this person.

Sometimes when Jesus was somewhere with other people, it was like this:
    Someone in this place was doing many things not like other people,
    very bad things were happening to this person because of this.

(At that time people thought about it like this:
"there is someone bad inside this person.")
When Jesus saw someone like this, he said:
  "I want it not to be like this anymore."
After this, it was not like this anymore.

Sometimes when Jesus was in a place, he knew that it was like this:
  a short time before someone had died there;
  some other people there felt something very bad at that time
  because they felt something very good toward that person.
Jesus said to this person then: "I want you to live".
After this, this person lived.

Jesus did many other things like that.
He did these things because he wanted to do something good for people
  when something very bad was happening to them.
When he did something very good for someone,
  he didn't want other people to know that he had done it.
It was never like this:
  He did it because he wanted people to know that he could do it.
It was never like this:
  He did it because he wanted something very good to happen to him.
It was never like this:
  He did it because he wanted something very bad not to happen to him.

15. Jesus teaches people what is good for them

Many many people in the country where the people of Israel lived
    wanted to know what Jesus said to people.
Because of this, many many people went to places
    where Jesus was saying things to people, they wanted to hear it.
Many of them lived in Galilee, many others lived in Judea,
    far from the places where Jesus spoke to people.
When Jesus saw these people, he felt something very good toward them.
He thought about them like this:
        "They are like sheep when there is no shepherd with them."
He wanted them to know what is good for them,
    because of this, he often said things like this to them:

        It is good for you if you often think about God;
            it is good for you if you often think: "I want to live with God."
        It is good for you if you often think like this:
            "Every day I live because God does good things for me."
        When something very bad is happening to you,
            it is good for you if you think like this:
            "God knows that this is happening to me now,
            God knows what I feel now."
        It is good for you if you often think like this:
            "I want to know what God wants me to do now."
        It is good for you if you often speak to God.
        It is good for you if you speak to God every day.

        It is good for you if you often think about other people,
            if you feel something good toward other people.
        It is good for you if you want to do good things for other people.
        If someone says to you: "I want you to do something good for me,"
            it is good for you if you want to do it.
        When you are doing it, don't think like this:
            "I'm doing something good for someone, I want people to know it."

        It is good for you if you often think like this:
        "I have a body, at the same time, I have something else, a 'soul'
        (the Hebrew word was 'nepesh').
        Because I have a soul, I can live with God,
            after I die I can live with God forever."
        Other people can do very bad things to my body,
            they can't do anything bad to my soul.

It is not like this:
　if something bad happens to my body, this is bad for my soul.
It is like this:
　if I think something bad, if I want to do something bad,
　if I feel something bad toward someone, this is bad for my soul."

At the same time, Jesus said things like this to many people in many places:

　It is bad for you if you feel something bad toward someone else.
　It is bad for you if you want to do something bad to someone else.
　It is bad for you if you think like this about someone:
　　"This person did something bad to me,
　　because of this, I want to do something bad to this person."

　It is bad for you if you often think like this:
　　"I want to have a lot of money."
　It is bad for you if you think like this about many things:
　　"I want these things to be mine."

　It is bad for a man if he thinks about women's bodies
　　as people can think about things.
　People often think like this about things: "I want this thing to be mine,"
　　it is bad for a man if he thinks like this about women's bodies.
　If a man thinks like this about a woman's body,
　　he is doing something bad to this woman.
　It is bad for a man if he says to his wife:
　　"I don't want to live with you anymore."
　If a man says this to his wife, he is doing something very bad to her.
　(At that time in that country men could say this to women.
　Women couldn't say this to men.
　Men thought about it like this: "We can do this because Moses said so.")

16. How Jesus lived, what he was like

Jesus wanted to do good things for all people.
He didn't want to do anything bad to anyone.
When people were doing very very bad things to him,
he didn't want to think about them like this:
    "they are doing very bad things to me,"
he wanted to think about them in another way.
He said to God: "I don't feel anything bad toward them,
    I don't want anything bad to happen to them."
He said: "They don't know what they are doing."
(This "Story" will say more about it later.)

Jesus knew that many people in the country where he lived
thought like this about people of some kinds:
      "People like this do very bad things, they are bad people,
      I don't want to be with such people."
He didn't think like this about anyone, he wanted other people to know it.
Because of this, he often wanted to be with people of these kinds,
    he ate with them, he drank with them.

Jesus knew that many Israelites felt something very bad
    toward people of another kind called Samaritans.
He didn't feel anything bad toward people of any kind,
    he didn't feel anything bad toward Samaritans.
When he wanted people to know how to live, he said something like this:
"It was once like this:
    Something very bad happened to an Israelite.
    Other Israelites didn't want to do anything good for him.
    Then a Samaritan did many good things for him.
It will be good if you live like this Samaritan."
He spoke to a Samaritan woman about God
    like he had spoken to no one else before.

Many men in that country thought like this about some women:
    "I don't want a woman like this to touch me."
Jesus didn't think like this about any women.
He didn't think about women as many men thought about women at that time.
He felt something good toward women.
He wanted men not to do bad things to women.
He often wanted to be with women.
He often wanted to speak to women about God.

He said some things to women about God
  before he said these things to any men.
He felt something very good toward children.
He thought about children not as many other people
  thought about children at that time.
He thought like this: "Someone like this can be very close to God."

Jesus felt something very very good toward some people.
One of them was a man called John (another John),
  another one was a woman called Mary Magdalene.
Before they knew Jesus, they both lived in Galilee,
  later, they both wanted to go with Jesus wherever he went.
He felt something very very good toward three people
  in a place called Bethany near Jerusalem.
One of them was a man called Lazarus, two were women, his sisters,
  one was called Mary, the other, Martha.
When he was in Judea, he was often in their house for some time.
(This "Story" will say more about them later.)
He felt something very very good toward his mother, Mary.
When she said to him: "I want you to do something good for me,"
  she knew that he would do it.
(It was like this in a place called Cana, in Galilee.
People can know what happened if they read the Gospel of John.)
When he was dying he thought about her, he knew what she felt,
  he wanted to do something very good for her.
He felt something very very good toward the people of Israel.

Jesus felt something very very good toward God.
Often he spoke to God all night (often, on a mountain).
When he wanted to speak to God, he said "Abba" to him,
  as children in that country said to their father.
He was saying in this way: "I feel something very good toward you,
  I know that you feel something very good toward me."
Jesus always wanted to know what God wanted him to do.
He always wanted to do it.

Jesus lived like this; he was like this.

17. The people who were with Jesus

When Jesus didn't live in one place anymore
    some people were always with him, wherever he went.
These people were called the Apostles. It was like this:
When Jesus was a small child, his mother Mary was always with him,
    she knew what happened to him, she could later say it to someone else.
When Jesus lived in Nazareth, he lived with Mary, with Joseph.
Mary knew well what Jesus did, what he said, what happened to him,
    she could say it later to someone else.
When Jesus didn't live in Nazareth, the Apostles were always with him.
They knew well what he did, what he said, what happened to him,
    they could say it later to many people.

The Apostles were all men, there were twelve of them,
    as there were twelve sons of Jacob.
It was like this because Jesus wanted it to be like this.
In the Bible they are often called the Twelve. Their names were:
    Simon Peter, Andrew, John, James, Philip, Bartholomew, Matthew,
    Thomas, another James, Thaddeus, another Simon, Judas.
Jesus wanted these men to always be with him, he wanted them to know him.
He wanted them to know well what he did, what he said, what happened to him.
He wanted them to say to many people later:
    "We were there, we saw it, we heard it."
At the same time, he wanted them to know who he was,
    to know that he said to God: "Father," "Abba."

Before these men were with Jesus, they lived in Galilee,
    some of them were fishermen.
They were all with Jesus because one day he said to them:
    "I want you to be with me wherever I go."
(Before he said it, he was all night on a mountain, he was speaking to God.)
Before these men were with Jesus, some of them were with John the Baptist,
One of them was Andrew, another was John.
These two men were with John the Baptist when he said about Jesus:
    "This is the Lamb of God."
When they heard this, they followed Jesus (as he walked);
    they were with him for some time that day.
Later the same day Andrew spoke about Jesus to Simon.
He wanted him to be with Jesus for some time.
When Jesus saw Simon, he said to him: "You will be called Peter."
(This "Story" will say more about it later.)

Jesus spoke to the Apostles not like he spoke to other people.
Sometimes he said things like this to them:
    "People will do very bad things to me.
    I will feel something very bad because of this, I will die because of this."
(When he was saying this, he didn't say "I," he said: "The Son of Man.")
For a long time the Apostles didn't know why Jesus said this.
For a long time they didn't know well who he was.
They thought about him like this:
    "He wants to do something very good for the people of Israel,"
They didn't think like this: "He wants to do something very good for all people."

The Apostles spoke to Jesus not like they spoke to other people.
At first, they said to him "Rabbi" (Teacher); later they said "Lord."
For some time, when they said: "Lord," they wanted to say this with this word:
    "You are someone above us, you are someone above other people."
Later, they wanted to say more, they wanted to say:
    "You are someone above us, you are someone above *all* people."

In places where Jesus spoke to people, many women were often with him.
Mary Magdalene was one of them.
There were two other women called Mary, some others were called Joanna,
    Salome, Susanna; there were others.
These women felt something very good toward Jesus.
They wanted to be with him.
When he spoke about God, they wanted to hear it.
At the same time they wanted to do many good things for him.
They did this for a long time. They were with him when he was dying.

18. What happened on Mount Tabor

One day, in Galilee, Jesus said to the Apostles:
"Who am I? What do people say? What do you say?
Peter said: "You are the Messiah, the Son of the living God."
After this, Jesus said things like this to the Apostles:
"After some time I will go to Jerusalem.
People there will do very bad things to me. They will kill me.
Before I die, I will feel something very very bad.
I want you to know that three days later I will live."
At that time, the Apostles didn't know why Jesus was saying this.
They didn't know well at that time who he was.
They thought about him like this at that time:
"He will do something very good for the people of Israel."
Jesus wanted them to know who he was.
Because of this, a short time after Peter said: "You are the Messiah."
    something happened like never before.
It was like this:

Jesus went to the top of a mountain called Mount Tabor with three Apostles.
They were Peter, John, James (John's brother).
(Sometimes Jesus wanted these three to be with him, not all of them.)
When they were there, something happened to Jesus like never before.
It happened like this:

Jesus was speaking to God. The Apostles fell asleep.
When they woke up, they saw something like never before.
Jesus looked like he had never looked before.
When they were looking at him, they saw light.
When they looked at his face, they saw light.
When they looked at his robe, they saw light.
This light was like no other light.
It was not in the place where Jesus was, it was *in* Jesus.
The Apostles didn't know how it could be like this,
    they didn't know what to think.
They knew one thing: when they saw this light, they felt something,
    something very very good, they couldn't not feel it.
Then at one moment they saw two men next to Jesus;
    they were speaking to him, speaking about him.
The Apostles thought: "One of these two is Moses, the other is Elijah."
(Elijah was one of the prophets.) They thought:
"These two don't live on earth anymore; at the same time, they know Jesus.
They are speaking to him, speaking *about* him. How can this be?"

When they thought like this, they felt something very bad;
    at the same time, they couldn't not feel something very very good.
Peter said then to Jesus:
    "Lord, it is very good here now.
    You are here now, Moses is here now, Elijah is here now.
    It will be good if it can be like this for a long time."
He didn't know what he was saying, what he wanted to say.
At one moment, when he was saying this, there was a cloud there.
They saw light inside that cloud; they heard a voice from inside the cloud.
They knew that they were hearing God's voice,
    they didn't know what would happen to them because of this.
The voice said:
    "This is my Son, I feel something very good toward him; listen to him."
At that moment, they fell to the ground, their faces touched the ground.
They felt something like never before.

Then Jesus touched them, he said to them:
    "I don't want you to feel anything bad now."
When they looked at him, they didn't see light anymore.
They didn't see anyone else in that place anymore.
Jesus said to them:
    "Don't say anything about this to anyone now, you can say it later."
Then he said like before:
    "In a short time people will do very bad things to me. They will kill me.
    I want you to know that after I die, I will live.
    You can speak to people about this then."
When Jesus said this to them, he didn't say "I," he said:
    "The Son of Man."

The three Apostles often thought about that day, about that light,
    when Jesus didn't live on earth anymore.
In the first part of John's Gospel, John says about Jesus:
    "We knew him, we saw that light when we were with him that day."
In a part of the Bible called "The Second Letter of Peter," Peter says:
    "We saw that light when we looked at Jesus on Mount Tabor.
    One day, when you don't live on earth anymore, you will all see Jesus.
    You will all see that light."

19. What people said about Jesus, what people thought about Jesus

When Jesus didn't live in one place anymore,
    people in many places were speaking about him.
Many people said:
    "Never before did anyone speak like this, do things like this.
    He is the Messiah!"
At the same time some other people said very bad things about Jesus.
Some of these other people were people of one kind called "scribes".
Many of these people thought like this:
    "We are not like other people; we know well what the Law says,
    what the Bible says."
Some were people of one kind called "the Pharisees".
These people thought like this:
    "We are not like other people, we do everything as the Law says."
Some were people of one kind called "priests".
These people thought like this:
    "We are not like other people, we can do some things in the Temple
    as God wants."

These people (scribes, Pharisees, priests) said things like this about Jesus:
    "The Law says: 'people can't do some things on the Sabbath,'
    Jesus does things like this on the Sabbath.
    He thinks: 'I can do some things like God, I am someone like God.'
    He calls God: 'my Father.'"
These people felt something very bad toward Jesus.
One of them was a priest in Jerusalem called Caiaphas.
He was someone above all the other priests,
    at the same time he was someone above the people of Israel.

When Jesus was in Jerusalem, he often spoke in the Temple.
People like Caiaphas could know what he said there.
One day, when Jesus was in the Temple, some people said to him:
    "How can you know so well what the Bible says?"
Jesus said: "When I say some things to people, these things are true.
    My Father has said these things to me before."
They said to him: "Who are you? Where is your Father?"
Jesus said:
    "*God* is my Father. You don't know God, I know him.
    I was with him before, before there was anything anywhere.
    I am here now because he wants it.
    In a short time, I will be with him like before."

At the same time he said:

"I do everything as my Father wants; he is always with me."

When Jesus said these things, some people there said:

"Maybe he is the Messiah." Others said: "No, he can't be.

He was born in Galilee, the Messiah will be born in Bethlehem."

(Jesus was born in Bethlehem, they didn't know it.)

Another time Jesus said things like this to people in the Temple:

"People don't know how to live, like people don't know where to go

in a place where there is no light.

I am the light. If people want to live as I say, they can know how to live.

They can then live with God.

If people don't live with God, they live like slaves,

they are like slaves of the devil.

If people want to live as I say, they can live not like slaves.

They can live with God. They can then live forever."

They said: "How can you say this? Abraham died, the prophets died,

how can anyone live forever?"

Jesus said: "Abraham knew that after some time I would be here,

he felt something very good because of this."

They said to him: "You saw Abraham? How can that be?

You live now, Abraham lived a very very long time ago."

Jesus said to them: "Before Abraham was, I AM."

When they heard this, they felt something very very bad.

They all knew that God had said to Moses: "My name is I AM."

They picked up some stones, they wanted to throw them at Jesus,

they wanted to kill him.

They couldn't do it then because at that moment he went out of the Temple,

they didn't know how it happened.

When people like Caiaphas knew what Jesus was saying in the Temple,

they thought like this: "This man has to die."

Jesus knew that they thought like this.

He knew that they wanted some people to kill him.

Because he knew this, one day he said to people like Caiaphas in the Temple:

"You can do something very bad to this temple;

if you do it, this temple will not be here as before.

I will do something then;

because of this, three days later there will be another temple here."

No one knew at that time that he was speaking about his body.

(This "Story" will say more about it later.)

20. The Romans

At that time, the country where the people of Israel lived (Palestine)
  was part of the Roman empire.
There were many Roman soldiers in Palestine,
  a Roman called Pilate was someone above all these soldiers.
Many things were happening in Palestine as the Romans wanted.
Israelites felt something very bad because of this.
The Romans spoke Latin. Many of them could speak Greek
(as many other people in all parts of the Roman empire).
Many Israelites could speak Greek, therefore they could speak to the Romans,
  the Romans could speak to them.

There were many Roman soldiers in Jerusalem, Pilate was often in Jerusalem.
People like Caiaphas thought like this:
    "Many people in this country are saying about Jesus:
    'He is the Messiah, the king of the people of Israel.'
    If many people in Jerusalem say things like this, the Romans can know it.
    If they know it, very bad things can happen to the people of Israel,
        very bad things can happen to us."
Many people in Jerusalem said things like this about Jesus
after something happened in Bethany, where Lazarus lived with his two sisters.
Not many people had spoken about Jesus in Jerusalem before this happened.
It happened like this:

    Lazarus died. Jesus was not in Bethany at that time.
    (He was in a place on the other side of the Jordan).
    When Jesus was in Bethany a few days later,
        both sisters wanted to speak to him, they were crying.
    They were saying to Jesus:
        "Lord, you were not here, he died because you were not here."
    Jesus wept then, many people saw it.
    They said: "He felt something very, very good toward him."
    Jesus went to the place where Lazarus's body was (it was in a cave).
    When he was there, he spoke to God.
    Then he said: "Lazarus, get up!," many people heard this.
    At that moment, Lazarus got up. Many people could see him.
    His body was bound with linen, his face was wrapped with a cloth.
    After this, many people in Bethany were saying about Jesus:
        "*He* did this. He is the Messiah."
    Some people spoke about it to people like Caiaphas.

There were many people like Caiaphas in Jerusalem,
   because the Temple was in Jerusalem.
There were many priests, many scribes, many Pharisees.
Some of these people were above the other people in that country.
They were called the Sanhedrin.
When these people wanted something to happen, they could say:
   "We want this to happen," as one person can say: "I want this to happen."
Many things were happening in that country at that time
   as these people wanted.
The Romans thought about the Sanhedrin like this:
   "These people are above the other people in this country.
   If we want some things to happen in this country, we can speak to them."
When the Sanhedrin knew what people said about Jesus, they thought like this:
   "If the Romans know this, something very bad can happen."
They thought: "Something very bad can happen to the people of Israel,
   something very bad can happen to us."
Because of this, they thought like this:
   "We have to do something to this man; what can we do?"
(One of them didn't want to think like this. He was called Nicodemus.
This "Story" will say more about him later.)

Shortly after some people spoke to Caiaphas about Lazarus,
   the whole Sanhedrin was in Caiaphas's house.
(Maybe not Nicodemus, we don't know.)
These people thought like this: "What can we do to this man Jesus?"
They wanted to talk about it. Caiaphas said:
   "It will be good for the people of Israel if this man dies."
After Caiaphas said this, the others said: "He has to die."
They thought like this:
   "It will be good if the Romans kill him, it will be good if this happens soon.
   It will be good if Pilate says to the Roman soldiers: Kill this man."

21. Passover

It happened as the Sanhedrin (people like Caiaphas) wanted.
It happened in Jerusalem, a short time before the day of the year called Passover.
There were many people in Jerusalem at that time
    because Passover was not like any other day of the year.
God once did something very good for the people of Israel on that day.
Before that day, the Israelites had lived in Egypt, they were slaves there.
After that day, they did not live in Egypt anymore,
    they were not slaves anymore.
After this, Israelites wanted to think about this on the same day of the year.

On that day in Egypt, the Israelites killed many lambs, then they ate the meat
(there was one roasted lamb in every house).
They thought: "God wants us to do it like this."
(People can know why it was like this if they read Exodus.)
After this, Israelites wanted to do the same every year on the same day.
When there was a Temple in Jerusalem, they killed the lambs in the Temple.
They did it because they thought: "God wants this."
Because of this, every year there were many people in Jerusalem
    a short time before the Passover day.

When the people in Caiaphas's house said: "This man has to die,"
    Jesus was in Jerusalem with the Apostles.
Jesus knew that in a short time people would kill many lambs in Jerusalem,
    as happened a long time before in Egypt.
At the same time he knew that people would kill *him* then,
    as they would kill the lambs.
People can think about like this:
    "Maybe Jesus thought like this:
    'A long time ago in Egypt, at the time of Passover,
    God did something very good for the people of Israel.
    After this, the people of Israel could live not like before,
        they were not slaves anymore.
    This year in Jerusalem, at the time of Passover,
    God will do something very good for all people,
    After this, all people can live not like before,
        they can live not like slaves anymore.
    At that time, in Egypt, many lambs died at the time of Passover.
    This year, in Jerusalem, the Son of Man will die.'"

Long before Jesus was born, prophet Isaiah spoke like this about someone:
> "God wants this someone to be the light,
> God wants people everywhere on earth to see this light."

(Isaiah was speaking like prophets speak, people couldn't always know what he wanted to say.)
Then Isaiah said things like this about this someone:
> "People did very very bad things to him,
> he felt something very very bad because of this.
> When they were doing these things to him he didn't say anything.
> He was like a lamb when people want to kill it.
> He didn't want to do anything bad to anyone.
> He wanted to do something good for all people,
>   he wanted all people to live with God.
> He died because of this.
> He died because people often didn't want to live with God,
>   because *we* often didn't want to live with God.
> He is now with God.
> He doesn't want anything bad to happen to anyone, he says it to God."

For a long time no one knew who Isaiah was speaking about.
Maybe Isaiah didn't know it: he spoke like a prophet.
John the Baptist thought like this: "Isaiah was speaking about Jesus".
Later, the Apostles thought the same.

As this Story said before, when John the Baptist saw Jesus near Jordan,
    he said: "This is the Lamb of God."
When Jesus didn't live on earth anymore,
    the Apostles often spoke about him in the same way.
In a part of the Bible called "The First Letter of Peter," Peter speaks like this.
In another, "The Revelation," John speaks like this.
In the part of the Bible called "The First letter to the Corinthians,"
    Paul calls Jesus "Christ our Passover."
(The Apostles often called Jesus "Christ" then, sometimes "Jesus Christ,"
"Christos" is the Greek word for Messiah.)

22. What Jesus said to the Apostles on the night before he died

On the Passover day, Israelites did some things not like at other times.
They wanted to do these things like Israelites had done for a very long time.
Everyone thought like this about some people at that time of the year:
    "I want to be with them in the evening on the Passover day,
    I want to eat bread of one kind with them,
    I want to eat the meat of one roasted lamb with them,
    as people do on that day."
Jesus wanted to be with the Apostles in this way one day before Passover,
    not on the Passover day.
(He knew that he would die on the Passover day:
he wanted to say some things to the Apostles before he died.)
Because of this, on that day, in the evening,
    Jesus was with the Apostles in a house near the Mount of Olives.
They were in a room above the other rooms.
There was a table there, there was bread on the table, there was wine.

Jesus wanted the Apostles to know that it would be like this:
    very soon some people would do very bad things to his body,
    he would die because of this,
    before he died, he would feel something very very bad.
He wanted them to know why he would die like this,
    to know that he wanted to do something very good for all people.
At the same time Jesus wanted the Apostles to know that it would be like this:
    After he died, for a short time he would not live;
    after this, he would live, he would never die.

At the table, Jesus took the bread in his hands, then he said to God:
    "Father, you are good, you want to do good things for all people."
After this, he broke the bread into pieces, as he often did,
    he wanted all the Apostles to eat pieces of one bread.
Then he said something to the Apostles like no one had ever said before.
He said: "Take, eat, this is my body."
After this, he took the cup with wine into his hands.
When he was holding it, he said to God, like before:
    "Father, you are good, you want to do good things for all people."
Then he said to the Apostles: "Drink from it, all of you, this is my blood.'
He wanted them to drink from one cup.
After he had done these things, he said:
    "Do the same when I am not with you like before anymore."

When Jesus was doing these things, he said (not with these words):
 "In a very short time people will kill me;
 I want you to know why it will be like this.
 Often people don't live with God, often they don't *want* to live with God.
 This is very very bad for people.
 I want all people to live with God.
 I want all people to *want* to live with God.

When Jesus spoke about his blood, he said something else at the same time.
He said (not with these words):
 "A long time ago at Mount Sinai God spoke to the people of Israel.
 You know that God said:
  'If you live as I want, I will always be with you,
   not like with all other people, I'll be very near to you, I want this.'
 You know that the people of Israel said then:
  'We want to do everything as God wants.'
 You know that Moses sprinkled the blood of some animals on the altar,
  then sprinkled some blood on the people.
 You know that he wanted to say: God says: I want it, we say: we want it.
  When people see this blood, they can know that it is true.'
 I say to you: '*all* people can live with God, God wants it.
  When people see *my* blood, they can know that it is true.'
 At the same time I say to God:
  'Father, I want to do everything as you want.'"

Later, the Apostles could know that when Jesus said this,
 he wanted to say something else at the same time.
The could know that he wanted to say something like this:
 "For a long time, the people of Israel thought like this:
 'On some days, we kill animals in the Temple because God wants it;
  if we do this, we can live with God.'
 God wants the people of Israel not to think like this anymore.
 God wants all people to know that it is like this:
 All people can live with God if they want to; God wants it.
 Everywhere on earth people can say to God: 'I want to live with you';
  God wants people to say it."
The Apostles could know then that on that night Jesus wanted to say:
 "I die because I want people to know this."

23. Gethsemane

Later that night, Jesus was with the Apostles in a garden.
This garden was on the Mount of Olives; they had often been there before.
It was one day before the Passover day.
Because of this, there were many people everywhere in Jerusalem.
Jesus was often on the Mount of Olives at night without the Apostles
    when he wanted to speak to God.
He was often there with the Apostles during the day
    when he wanted to be with them without other people.
The garden was called Gethsemane, there were olive trees there.
(This garden is there now as before, people can see it, they can see olive trees).
Jesus wanted to be there with the Apostles that night.
There was no one else there at that time.
When they were going to that garden Jesus said:
    "The Bible says: 'If something very bad happens to the shepherd,
    the sheep run away.' It will be like this here tonight.
    A short time after this, I will die.
    I want you to know that not long after I die, I will live.
    You will see me in Galilee."

One of the Apostles was not with them in that garden at that time.
This Apostle was called Judas.
Judas was at that time with people like Caiaphas. It was like this:
    The Sanhedrin wanted the Romans to kill Jesus before Passover.
    Because of this, they wanted some soldiers to take Jesus
        to Caiaphas's house that night.
    (They wanted the soldiers to do it at night
    because they didn't want other people to see it.)
    Because they wanted this to happen that night,
        they wanted to know where Jesus would be that night.
    Judas knew this, he said it to them. They paid him for it.
    People don't know well why Judas did it.
    (The part of the Bible called the Gospel of John says:
    "Satan was in him at that time.")
    When Judas thought about it later, he felt something very very bad,
        he wanted not to live anymore.

When they were in the garden, it was late at night;
    the Apostles wanted to sleep.
Jesus went away a little from the place where they were.
He wanted three of them (Peter, John, James) not to sleep.
He wanted these three Apostles to be near him, to know what he felt.

He said to them:

> "It is like this in my soul now: I feel something very very bad,
>> like someone can feel when they are dying.
>
> Be with me now, don't fall asleep."

Then he went away a little from the place where these three were.
He wanted to speak to God.
He knew what would happen to him that night,
  he knew what would happen to him the next day.
He thought about it like this:

> "It is like a cup of wine, God wants me to drink this cup."

He fell to the ground, his face was touching the ground.
He spoke to God like this then:

> "Abba, if this doesn't *have* to happen to me, I want it not to happen.
>
> At the same time I want everything to happen as *you* want, not as *I* want."

He felt something very very bad. The Gospel of Luke says:

> "His sweat fell to the ground like big drops of blood."

After some time he got up; he thought about the three Apostles then,
  he went to them. They were asleep.
He said to Peter then: "You are asleep? Can't you be with me at this time?
  Can't you be awake for a short time?"

A very short time after this, there were many other people in the garden,
  Judas was with them.
Some were Roman soldiers; others were Israelites (temple guards).
One was Caiaphas's slave (called Malchus).
When Judas saw Jesus, he kissed him; all knew then that this was Jesus
(Judas had said: "I'll kiss him.")
Peter didn't want them to do anything bad to Jesus.
He had a sword in his hand; he hit Malchus, he cut off his ear.
Jesus said to Peter: "Don't do anything with a sword.

> My Father wants me to drink this cup.
>
> I *can* not drink it. I can say to my Father: 'I don't want to drink it.'
>
> I don't want to say it. I want to do everything as my Father wants."

Then he touched the man's ear; after this, it was like it was before.
They tied Jesus's hands because they wanted to take him to Caiaphas's house.
Jesus said to all these people then: "You can take me, don't take anyone else."
After this, they took him to Caiaphas's house. The Apostles were not with Jesus.
They ran away.

24. Jesus before Caiaphas

Soon the whole Sanhedrin was in Caiaphas's house.
They wanted to say about Jesus:
>"We know what he did. The Law says: it is like this:
>if someone does things like this, this someone has to die."

Because of this, they wanted some other people to be there,
to say some very bad things about Jesus.
They wanted these people to say about something:
>"He said this, with these words, I heard it."

They wanted to say after this:
>"He said this, these people here heard it, because of this, he has to die."

Some people there said some things about Jesus as the Sanhedrin wanted,
these things were not true.
Two men said something like this:
>"He said: 'I will do something very bad to the Temple,
>after this there will be no Temple here. I will do something else then;
>because of this, after three days there will be another Temple here.'"

These two men couldn't say it with the same words.
One said: "He said: I *will* do," the other said: "He said: I *can* do."
Jesus had said something else with the word "Temple," he said:
>"You can do something very bad to this temple.
>If you do it, I will do something then;
>because of this, after three days there will be another temple here."

(He was saying in this way: "My body is like a temple. You can kill my body.
If you do it, after three days I will live.")

When these people were saying these things about him, Jesus didn't say anything.
Caiaphas then said to Jesus:
>"You don't say anything when these people say such things about you?"

When Caiaphas said this, Jesus didn't say anything, like before.
Caiaphas then said:
>"I want you to say one thing, you can't not say it, we want to hear it:
>Are you the Son of God?"

Jesus said:
>"Yes, I am. You will see the Son of Man on the right hand of God
>—he will come in a cloud full of light."

Then Caiaphas tore his robe, he wanted to say in this way:
>"When I hear this, I feel something very very bad."

They all knew that long before, the prophet Daniel had said:
>"I see someone like a Son of Man—he comes on earth in a cloud full of light
>—he is someone above all people—he will be king forever."

They could know that when Jesus said: "You will see the Son of Man,"
he was saying in this way: "you will see me.")
Then Caiaphas said to the Sanhedrin:

"We have all heard it. We don't have to hear anything more.
If someone says something very bad about God, it is very very bad,
the Law says so.
This man said something like this here now. What will we do now?
What do you say?"

When Caiaphas said this, the whole Sanhedrin said: "This man has to die."
Then some people there spat on Jesus, some hit him in the face.
When they were doing it, they were laughing.

Two Apostles were near Caiaphas's house at that time, one of them was Peter,
the other was John.
There was fire in that place, the men sat on all sides of the fire,
Peter sat with them.
A woman in that place said to Peter: "Were you not with that man Jesus?"
Peter said: "No, I don't know him."
After this, two other people said the same to Peter.
One said: "You were with him, I saw you in the garden."
Peter said, like before: "I don't know that man."
When Peter was saying it for the third time, the cock crowed.
At that moment, Peter saw Jesus, Jesus looked at Peter.
Some people were taking him out of Caiaphas's house.
The day before Jesus had said to Peter:

"Before the cock crows, you will say three times: 'I don't know that man.'"
When Jesus looked at Peter, Peter thought about this
(he wasn't thinking about it before).
He knew at that moment that when he said: "I don't know that man,"
he did something very bad to Jesus.
He felt something very very bad then. He went away, he cried.

A short time after this, the Sanhedrin took Jesus to the place where Pilate was.
(It was called the "Praetorium").
They wanted Pilate to say: "This man has to die".
They wanted him to say to the Roman soldiers: "Kill this man."
(Some people think: "Caiaphas spoke to Pilate about it the night before.
Pilate spoke about it to his wife, she wanted to know what Caiaphas had said;
Pilate knew what would happen the next morning.")

25. Jesus before Pilate

When Caiaphas with the other men brought Jesus to the "Praetorium,"
    they didn't want to go inside, they wanted Pilate to speak to them outside.
Many people were with them there.
When Pilate was outside, he said to them:
    "What do you want to say about this man? What did he do?"
They said to him:
    "We know well what he did. Because of this, we want you to say:
    'This man has to die.'"
Pilate said to them:
    "You want *me* to say this? *You* can do to him as you want, as your law says."
They said to him:
    "Our law says: this man has to die. At the same time we can't kill anyone."
    You can say to the soldiers: "Kill this man." *We* can't say this to anyone."
(It was a Roman law; the Romans wanted it to be like this in the Roman empire:
the Romans could say to soldiers about someone: "kill this man,"
nobody else could say it about anyone.)
Then they said: "This man says to the people: 'I am the king here.'
    He says: 'Don't pay money to the Romans.'"
They knew that Jesus didn't say these things.
They said this because they wanted Pilate to think like this about Jesus:
    "This man wanted to do something bad to the Roman empire,
    he has to die because of this."

Then Pilate went inside the Praetorium, where Jesus was. He said to Jesus:
    "You are the king of the Jews?"
Jesus said:
    "I am a king not like other kings. I am not the king of a country on earth.
    No soldiers have to do as I say."
Pilate said then to Jesus: "Then you *are* a king?"
Jesus said: "You say this." Then he said (not with these words):
    "I say some things to people about God, about people.
    These things are true. I want people to know how to live,
    what is good for them, how they can live with God;
    I want them to know what God wants. I was born because of this;
    I live because of this; I can die because of this.
    If someone wants to know what is true they hear my voice."
Pilate said: "How can people know what is true?"
At the same time, he thought: "This man didn't do anything bad."

A short time after this, Pilate's wife said to him:

    "Don't do anything bad to this good man.

    I saw him in a dream, I felt something very bad then.

    Don't do anything bad to him."

After this, Pilate went outside, like before,

  to the place where Caiaphas with the other men were.

He said to them:

    "I can't say: 'I know that this man did something very bad';

    because of this, I can't say: 'This man has to die.'"

They said then to Pilate:

    "He said: 'I am the Son of God.'

    If someone says this, they have to die."

When Pilate heard this, he felt something very bad.

He thought like this:

    "Who *is* this man? Where is he from?"

    Maybe if I say: 'This man has to die,'

        something very bad will happen to me."

He went inside then. He said to Jesus: "Where are you from?"

When he said this, Jesus didn't say anything.

Pilate thought like this then: "I don't want to say: 'This man has to die.'"

Then Pilate went outside another time.

Caiaphas with the other men were there as before. He said to them:

    "I can't say: 'This man has to die.' He didn't do anything very bad."

When they heard this, they said to Pilate:

    "This man wanted to be the king in this country.

    If you don't say: 'He has to die,' people can know

        that you don't want Caesar to be the king in this country.

    They can say it to Caesar."

When Pilate heard this, he felt something very bad. He thought like this:

    "If I don't say: 'He has to die,' something very bad can happen to me."

After this, Pilate said: "This man has to die."

Then he said to the soldiers: "Kill him."

Before Pilate said this to the soldiers, he washed his hands.

He did it in a place where many people could see it.

At that time, in some countries, people did this when they wanted to say:

"I know that something very bad is happening here. It is happening

  because someone wanted it, I didn't want it."

When Pilate washed his hands in that place at that time,

  he wanted to say something like this in this way.

26. Jesus is nailed to the cross

Jesus died on the same day, he died in Jerusalem.
Before he died, people did many very bad things to him.
After Pilate said to the soldiers: "I want you to kill this man,"
    the soldiers did many very bad things to Jesus's body.
After this, when people looked at him, they saw blood on his body.
The soldiers took off his robes, they wanted something like a king's robe
    to be on him, they wanted something like a crown to be on his head.
(It had many sharp parts, they were thorns.)
When they were doing it, they were laughing.
They were saying things like this to Jesus:
    "We feel something very good toward you.
        You are someone above other people, you are the king of the Jews."
When they were saying this, they were hitting him on the head,
    they were spitting on him.
They wanted to feel something good because of this,
    at the same time they wanted him to feel something very bad.

After this, the soldiers took Jesus to a place called Golgotha, it was on a hill.
When they were taking him there, Jesus had to carry something called a cross.
A cross was made of wood, it was very big, it was very heavy.
It had two long parts, one of them was very long.
When Jesus was carrying the cross,
    he felt something very bad in his whole body because of this.
At the same time he knew that he would die on that cross,
    he knew how he would die.

When a man died on a cross, it was like this:
    There was a cross somewhere in a place where many people could see it;
        it couldn't move.
    The top part of the very long part was high above the ground,
        the bottom part was inside the ground.
    The man's head was near the top of this very long part,
        his feet were near the bottom.
    The other long part had two parts on two sides of the very long part.
    The man's arms were touching the other part,
        one arm on one side, the other on the other side.
    The man's body was hanging on the cross,
        sometimes it was nailed to the cross, sometimes it was tied to it.
    The man's feet were touching one of the two long parts in one place,
        they could not move.

His hands were touching the other long part in two places, on both sides,
　far from body, they could not move.
The man couldn't move as he wanted.
He felt something very bad in his whole body because of this.
Many people could see this man during that time,
　many people could see his face.
Because of this, many people could know what this man felt.
The Romans often wanted a man to die like this
　if they wanted to say something like this to many people:
　"This man wanted to do something bad to Rome,
　the same will happen to anyone if they want to do this."
Many, many people died like this in the Roman empire.
Many slaves died like this. Many Israelites died like this.

When Jesus was on Golgotha, the Roman soldiers nailed his body to the cross.
They nailed his feet to one long part of the cross, his hands to the other.
Then they nailed something at the top of the cross; it said:
　"Jesus of Nazareth king of the Jews," as Pilate wanted.
(Someone had written it on this thing in Latin, Greek, Hebrew,
as Pilate wanted.)
When the soldiers were nailing his body to the cross,
　Jesus felt something very very bad in his body because of this.
He knew that God felt something very very bad at the same time
(he had said before: "Father and I are one").
He said to God then:
　"Father, I don't want anything bad to happen to these people.
　I don't feel anything bad toward them.
　They don't know what they are doing."
When people saw Jesus on the cross, his arms high above the earth,
　his hands far from his body, they could think like this:
　"Jesus loves all people on earth, he wants to draw all people to God."
They could know that a short time before, Jesus said:
　"When I am above the earth, I will draw all people to myself."
One Roman soldier there (he was above all the others) thought:
　"Something is happening here like never before."

27. Jesus dies on the cross

When Jesus was on the cross, he felt something very very bad,
   he felt like this for a long time.
Many people there saw him, they saw his blood, they saw his face;
   they could know well what he felt in his body.
Some people there were saying things like this to him:
      "You are someone above other people, you are a king.
      Why can't you do anything now?"
They wanted to feel something good because of this;
   at the same time, they wanted him to feel something very bad.
At one moment Jesus said in a loud voice:
      "My God, my God, why are you not with me anymore?"
When people heard his voice,
   they knew that at that moment he felt something very very bad.
Some people think about it like this:
      "Jesus thought at that moment: 'God is not with me anymore.'"
Others think: "Jesus didn't think like this, at the same time he *felt*
   like someone can feel when they think like this."
Some think: "Jesus felt at that moment like someone can feel
   if they think: 'I can never be with God.'"

The words: "My God, my God, why aren't you with me anymore?"
   are the first part of a psalm, many people near the cross could know this.
These people could know what David said in the last part of this psalm.
They could know that he said something like this:
"Lord, I know that when I say something to you
   because I feel something very bad, you hear it.
I know that at some time people everywhere on earth will know
   that you want to do good things for all people.
I know that people everywhere on earth will say to you:
   'You are above us, you are above all people on earth.
   You are good, you want to do good things for all people,
   you *can* do good things for all people.'
   We feel something very good toward you
      we want to live with you always.'"
Many people think like this: "When Jesus said the first part of this psalm,
   he was thinking about the whole psalm."

Shortly after this, Jesus saw his mother Mary, she was standing near the cross.
Some other women were with her.
They lived in Galilee; they went with Jesus to Judea, like Mary.

One of them was Mary Magdalene.
One was another Mary, the mother of one of the Apostles.
Another was Salome, the mother of two Apostles.
When Jesus saw his mother, he saw one of the Apostles there, it was John
(the other Apostles were not there).
Jesus knew that when *he* (Jesus) felt something very very bad,
    Mary felt something very very bad because of this.
He said then to Mary about John: "This will now be your son."
Then he said to John: "This will now be your mother."
(If people read the part of the Bible called the Gospel of John,
they can know that it happened as Jesus wanted.
They can know that after Jesus died, Mary lived with John, in John's house.)

Some time after this, Jesus said: "Water!"
People there could know then that he felt something very bad in his mouth.
They could know that he felt like someone can feel
    if they haven't had any water in their mouth for a very long time.
They could know that he was dying.
Before he died, Jesus said to God:
    "Father, I want my spirit to be in your hands."
(The words "I want my spirit to be in your hands" are part of another psalm.
Jesus said more: he said 'Father'. Before, no one said "Father" to God.)
Then Jesus said (not with these words): "I did everything as you wanted."
After this, Jesus died.

The soldiers pierced Jesus's body with something called a spear.
It was something very long, they could touch Jesus's body with it
    when it was high above the ground.
One end of this spear was sharp; they wanted it to be inside Jesus's body,
    on one side of his body, near the heart.
They did this to Jesus's body because Pilate wanted to know well
    that Jesus didn't live anymore.
When they did it, people saw a lot of blood on this side of Jesus's body,
    at the same time, they saw a lot of water.

It all happened as the prophets said.
The Apostle John saw it all. He could say later to other people:
"It happened like this, I saw it, this is true."

28. Why Jesus died on the cross

Jesus died on the cross because he wanted to do something very good
    for all people: he wanted them to live with God.
God didn't want people to kill Jesus.
Jesus said so when he spoke like this about God to people in the Temple:
    "A man wanted his son to do something in a faraway place.
    He felt something very very good toward his son.
    He wanted nothing bad to happen to his son.
    The people in that place killed his son. God is like this man."
God wanted it to be like this: all people would know God;
    when they knew God, they would want to live with God.
Because of this, God wanted it to be like this:
    Jesus would go to many places, would speak to people,
    would do good things for people; people would know him.
    At the same time people would know who Jesus was, who his Father was,
    Jesus would say this to people.
God knew that if Jesus did this, people would kill him,
    he would die on the cross. Jesus knew the same thing.
Jesus could have said to God: "I don't want to do it."
He didn't say it. He wanted to do everything as God wanted.
At the same time, he wanted to do something very good for all people.

Shortly before he died on the cross Jesus said:
    "When I am lifted up from the earth, I will draw all people to myself."
He said: "When someone sees me, they see my Father."
He said: "I am in the Father, the Father is in me."
Jesus knew that when he was on the cross people would see him,
    would see his blood, would know what he felt.
He knew that at some time, *all* people would see him,
    all people would know what he felt on the cross.
They would know that he was on the cross
    because he wanted to do something very good for all people.
They would know that when *he* felt something very very bad,
    God felt something very very bad.
(They would know that he had said about God: "We are one.")
They could feel something very good toward Jesus then,
    they could feel something very good toward God.
It could be like this then: they would think:
    "I want to live with Jesus, I want to live with God."

When Jesus was dying on the cross on Golgotha,
    there were two other crosses there at the same time,
One was on one side, one on the other.

Two other men were dying there at the same time.
One of these men said to Jesus: "Aren't you the Messiah?
Can't you do something good for all of us now?"
The other man said to him:
> "This is happening to us because we did very bad things,
> Jesus didn't do anything bad."
As this other man was looking at Jesus on the cross, he thought:
> "I know what he feels in his body now."
At that moment something happened in him.
He thought then: "I know now who he is, who his Father is."
When he thought like this, he thought at the same time:
> "I want to be with Jesus, I want to be with God."
He said to Jesus at that moment: "Jesus, think about me
when you are with God in the place where you are king."
Jesus said to him then: "It will be as you want.
Today you will be with me, with God."

People can think about it like this:
> "Something can happen in everyone as happened in that man
>> when he was looking at Jesus dying on the cross.
> Everyone can think then: 'I know how Jesus died on the cross;
>> I know now who he is, who his Father is.'
> When they think like this, they can think at the same time:
>> 'I want to live with Jesus, I want to live with God.'"
Some people say:
> "Something like this cannot happen in someone after this someone dies."
Others say: "It *can* happen after someone dies".
Often these people say things like this at the same time:
> "Many many people died before Jesus lived on earth.
> Many of them did very bad things, didn't live with God.
> Before Jesus died, he said:
>> 'In a short time all these people will hear my voice.'
> (The Gospel of John says so.)
> When his body was in the tomb, he was with these people.
> (The First Letter of Peter says so.)
> He wanted them to know that it is like this:
>> all people can live with God if they want to, God wants it.
> Because of this, we can know now that it is like this:
>> Some people don't live with God before they die.
>> After they die, they see Jesus; they know then who he is.
>> At the same time, they know how he died on the cross,
>> they know *why* he died on the cross.
>> Something happens in them then.
>> After this, they *want* to live with Jesus, they *want* to live with God."

29. What happened with Jesus's body after he died

Sometime after the soldiers pierced Jesus's body, a short time before the evening,
    a rich man called Joseph of Arimathea spoke to Pilate:
He said: "Can I now take away Jesus's body?"
Pilate said: "You can."
Joseph of Arimathea was one of the people called the Sanhedrin.
He was not often with Jesus before Jesus died,
    he didn't want people to see him when he was with Jesus.
At the same time, he felt something very good toward Jesus.
Before Jesus died, he thought: "This is the Messiah."
Joseph wanted the body of Jesus to be in a place
    where nothing bad could happen to it, inside something called a tomb.
It was a place inside a rock, like a small cave.
There were many such tombs in a garden near the place where the cross was,
    one of them belonged to Joseph.
Before, Joseph thought about it like this: "After I die, my body will be here."
(No one else's body was there before.)

When Pilate said "You can," Joseph took Jesus's body,
    he carried it to the place where that tomb was.
Another man was with him, that man was called Nicodemus.
Like Joseph, Nicodemus was not often with Jesus before Jesus died.
Like him, he was one of the people called the Sanhedrin,
    he didn't want people to see him when he was with Jesus.
At the same time, like Joseph, he felt something very good toward Jesus,
    he thought: "This is the Messiah."
Once when Jesus was in Galilee, Nicodemus went at night to the place
    where Jesus was, he wanted to speak to him.
Jesus said some things to him then like to no one else.
After this, Nicodemus could know who Jesus was.
He could know how people can know God, how they can live with God.
(People can know what Jesus said to Nicodemus
if they read the part of the Bible called the Gospel of John.)

The men wrapped Jesus's body in linen (one cloth around the body,
    one around the head), then laid it in the tomb.
They put something called myrrh with something called aloes inside the linen,
    as people did then in that country.
They put very very much of it, as people did when a king died.

They did everything very quickly because it was a short time before
the evening before the day called the Sabbath.
(The Sabbath was the last day of the week,
Israelites couldn't do many things on that day because the law said so.
At the same time, Israelites thought like this:
"the evening before the Sabbath is part of the Sabbath.")
Then the two men pushed a very big stone;
after this, this very big stone was in front of the tomb, as they wanted.
Because of this, after this, no one could go inside the tomb,
no one could touch Jesus's body.

Some women saw all this, these women were near the cross
with Mary Jesus's mother when Jesus was on the cross.
They were: Mary Magdalene, Mary the mother of James,
Joanna the wife of Chuza, Salome the wife of Zebedee.
These women felt something very good toward Jesus,
they were often with him before he died.
They wanted to put some oil on Jesus's body, as people did in that country,
they wanted to do it well.
They knew that they couldn't do it on the same day
because it was the evening before the Sabbath.
Because of this, they wanted to do it in the morning
on the first day after the Sabbath.
The next day, on the Sabbath, the women were not near the tomb anymore,
the two men were not there anymore.

On the evening after the Sabbath some people like Caiaphas said to Pilate:
"We want there to be some Roman soldiers in front of the tomb.
This man said: 'Three days after I die, I will live.'
If there are no soldiers in front of the tomb it can be like this:
some people will take his body from the tomb, then they will say:
'It is as he said, after he died, he lives.'"
Pilate said: "Why do you want Roman soldiers to be there?
There can be guards (temple guards) there if you want."
(These guards had to do everything as people like Caiaphas said.)
After this, there were some guards in front of the tomb,
as people like Caiaphas wanted.

30. Jesus lives

After the Sabbath day, before the sun rose,
    something happened in the place where Jesus's body was.
Something happened to Jesus's body.
It happened not because some people did something to it.
It happened because God wanted it to happen.
After it happened, Jesus's body was not in the tomb anymore.
People don't know how it happened.
The part of the Bible called the Gospel of Matthew says this:

On the first day after the Sabbath, before the sun rose,
        the earth shook in that place.
The guards didn't know what was happening.
They felt something very very bad. They thought like this:
        "Something is happening here like never before.
        Something is happening inside the tomb, what can it be?"
They couldn't look inside the tomb
        because there was a big stone in front of it.
Then, they *could* look inside the tomb
        because the stone wasn't there anymore.
(Did they push the stone away? We don't know.
The Gospel of Matthew says: "An angel pushed it away.")
At that moment they knew that Jesus's body was not there anymore.
They felt something very bad then.
They thought like this: "When people like Caiaphas know this,
        something very bad can happen to us."
Because they thought like this, they went to Caiaphas's house,
        they wanted Caiaphas to know what happened.
After a very short time, many people were in Caiaphas's house,
        the whole Sanhedrin (as Caiaphas wanted).
When all these people knew what happened, they talked about it,
        they wanted to know what they could do.
Then they said to the guards:
        "We don't want people to know what happened.
        Don't say it to anyone.
        Say: 'At night, when we slept, some people took Jesus's body.'"
They paid money to the guards because they wanted them to say this.

On the same day, the Apostles knew that Jesus's body was not in the tomb.
Before *they* knew it, the women knew it: Mary Magdalene, Mary wife of Cleopas,
    another Mary, Salome wife of Zebedee, Joanna.

It happened like this:

> When the sun rose, these women were near the place where the tomb was.
> They were there at that time
>> because they wanted to do some good things to Jesus's body.
> (They knew what the two men did before, they wanted to do more.)
> They thought like this: "There is that big stone in front of the tomb,
>> who can push it away? We can't do it."
> When they were in the place where the tomb was,
>> they knew that the big stone wasn't there anymore.
> When they looked inside the tomb,
>> they knew that Jesus's body wasn't inside the tomb anymore.
> (The part of the Bible called The Gospel of Mark says:
> "They felt something very bad because of this,
> they didn't know what happened;
> they didn't know what they could think about it.")

Mary Magdalene ran then to the place where Peter was.
John was there with Peter.
She said to them: "The Lord is not in the tomb anymore, someone took him,
  we don't know where he is."
When the two Apostles heard this, they ran to the place where the tomb was.
A very short time after this, they were in that place.
The part of the Bible called the Gospel of John says this:

> John was in the place where the tomb was before Peter.
> He looked inside, he saw the linen on the ground.
> He didn't want to go inside the tomb before Peter could go inside it.
> Soon after, Peter was there.
> When he went inside the tomb, he knew that Jesus's body wasn't there.
> When he looked at the linen, he knew that it was like this:
>> One of the two linen cloths was folded up.
>> (Before, it was wrapped around Jesus's head).
>> It was away from the other.
>> (Before, that other cloth was wrapped around Jesus's body).
> When John was inside the tomb, he knew the same.
> He thought like this at that moment:
> "It is not like this: someone took Jesus's body;
> it is like this: Jesus lives."

31. Mary Magdalene sees Jesus

A short time after this the two Apostles were no longer in that place
    where the tomb was.
Mary Magdalene was near the tomb as before.
She was looking inside the tomb.
She thought like this then: "Jesus is not inside the tomb anymore
    because someone took him."
She didn't think: "Jesus is not inside the tomb because he lives."
She felt something very very bad at that time. She was weeping.
Then she turned around.

At that moment she saw Jesus; she saw him because he wanted her to see him.
She didn't know that it was Jesus.
Jesus said to her:
        "Woman, why are you weeping? Who do you want to see?"
Like before, when she heard these words she didn't know that it was Jesus.
She said to him:
        "My Lord is not here anymore, did you do something to him?
        I want to know where he is."
Jesus said to her then: "Mary!"(He said it in Aramaic: "Mariam!")

At that moment, Mary Magdalene knew that it was Jesus.
She knew that it was Jesus's voice, she knew that he was there.
She thought then: "He lives."
She thought: "This is true."
She felt something like never before.
She said to Jesus: "Rabboni!" (It was an Aramaic word.)
She was saying something like this with this word: "Teacher!"
At the same time, she was saying something like this with this word:
        "You are someone not like other people.
        You can do very good things for people.
        I feel something very good toward you."
(Israelites didn't often say this word to men, they said: "Rabbi" to men;
some said the word "Rabboni" to God.)
Mary Magdalene felt something very very good at that moment.
She felt something very very good toward Jesus.
She wanted to touch him, she wanted to hold his feet.
She wanted to hold him for some time.

Jesus said to her then:

> "I don't want you to hold me for a long time.
> I want you to do something else now.
> Go to the place where my brothers are.
> I want them to know that I say to them:
>> 'You will see me in a short time.
>> After this, I will go to my Father, my Father is your Father.'"

Mary Magdalene knew that when Jesus said "my brothers,"
> he said it about the Apostles.

She knew that Jesus wanted the Apostles to know that she saw him.
She knew that he wanted them to know that he lives.
She knew that he wanted them to know what he said to her.
Because of this, she ran to the place where the Apostles were.
She said to them: "I saw the Lord, he lives."
When they heard it, they thought like this: "This can't be true."

32. Some other people see Jesus

On the same morning, a little later, the other women saw Jesus,
    they saw him because he wanted them to see him.
Later that day two other people saw him (he wanted them to see him).
They saw him when they were going to a place called Emmaus,
    not far from Jerusalem.
One was a man called Cleopas, we don't know who the other one was.
(Some say: "Maybe it was Mary, Cleopas's wife; she was at the cross,
with Jesus's mother, when Jesus was dying."
Some say: "Maybe it was Luke, the Gospel of Luke says a lot about all this,
Luke knew well what the two felt").
These two felt something very good toward Jesus.
Before he died, they thought like this: "He is the Messiah."
After he died, they thought: "He died, maybe he was not the Messiah";
    they felt something very bad because of this.

They were talking about these things when they were going to Emmaus,
    they felt something very bad at that time.
When they were talking like this they saw Jesus;
    they didn't know at that time that it was Jesus.
He went with them for some time.
When they were going like this, Jesus said to them:
    "What were you talking about? Has something bad happened to you?"
Cleopas said:
    "Don't you know what happened in Jerusalem a very short time ago?
    Something very very bad happened.
    The Romans killed a prophet, Jesus of Nazareth.
    They did it because people like Caiaphas wanted them to do it.
    Before he died, we thought: 'This is the Messiah'.
    Now we don't know what we can think.
    There were some women with us.
    They went to the tomb early today, then they said:
        'We saw the tomb, we looked inside, his body is not there anymore.'
    When the women said this, we thought: 'This can't be true.'
    Then some men went to the tomb (they had always been with us before).
    They said: 'It is as the women said.'
    We don't know what to think anymore."

When Cleopas said this, Jesus said to them both:
    "Oh, why do you think like this!
    Don't you know what the prophets said? It all happened as they said.
    The Prophets knew that the Messiah would die like this,
        that people would kill him in this way.

At the same time they knew that after he died, he would live,
　　that after this, he would not die.
They knew that he would be with God, as he was before he was born;
　　that people would know who he is."
Jesus said many other things to them when he was going with them like this.
He spoke about the Bible, about Moses, about the Prophets.
All this time they didn't know that it was Jesus.
When they were in Emmaus, Jesus wanted to go further that day.
The two said to him: "Don't go further today, it will be night soon, eat with us."
Jesus did as they wanted.
A short time after this, they were inside a house, there was a table there;
　　there was bread on the table.
Jesus took the bread into his hands, then he said to God:
　　"Father, you are good, you want to do good things for all people."
Then he broke the bread into pieces, he wanted the two to eat this bread,
　　he said to them: "Eat it."
At that moment, they knew that it was Jesus.
They felt something then like never before.
A moment after this, Jesus was not with them anymore;
　　they didn't know how it happened.
They were both saying something like this:
　　"Why didn't we know before that it was Jesus?
　　Didn't we feel something like fire, something very good,
　　when he was speaking to us about the prophets?"
The two wanted the Apostles to know that they had seen Jesus,
　　they wanted them to know what had happened.
Because of this, on the same day, they went back to Jerusalem.

33. The Apostles see Jesus

On the same day, in the evening, the Apostles saw Jesus.
They were in the same room in Jerusalem where they had been with Jesus
   on the night before he died.
The door was closed, as they wanted. They were thinking like this at that time:
     "Maybe some people want to do something very bad to us now".
They felt something very bad because of it.
When they were thinking like this, they saw Jesus.
They saw him because he wanted them to see him.
It was like this: At one moment Jesus was not with them in that room,
   the next moment he was there.
The Apostles didn't know how it happened, they didn't know
   how it could have happened.
They thought: "Maybe this is not someone living,
   maybe this someone doesn't have a body like someone living."
When they thought like this, they felt something very bad because of it.

Then Jesus spoke to them.
First he said something like people in Palestine often said to other people
   when they saw them for the first time after some time.
Maybe he said it with the Hebrew word "Shalom,"
   maybe he said it with the Aramaic word "Shlam."
People wanted to say something like this to other people with these words:
     "I want it to be like this: you feel something good in your soul now,
     you don't feel something bad."
When *Jesus* said this, he was saying more, he was saying:
     "If I am with you, it *can* be like this."
(On the night before he died he had said to them:
"I want you not to feel something bad in your soul."
At the same time he said:
"It *can* be like this because I say I want it to be like this.")

After this, Jesus said to them:
     "Why do you feel something bad? I live.
     You could have known that I live because the women saw me.
     When the women said to you: 'We saw the Lord,'
        why did you think: 'this can't be true'?
     It is me. You can see my hands, you can see my feet.
     You can touch my side. You can know that it's me."
The Apostles felt something very very good then.

They thought: "It is Jesus. He lives."
They knew that it was like this:
     his body was not like before, at the same time, it *was* his body.
They didn't know how it could be like this.
They thought: "Something has happened like never before."

Then Jesus said some things to the Apostles
  like he had said to the two before on the way to Emmaus. He said:
     "Everything has happened as the prophets said, as the psalms said.
     The prophets *knew* that it would be like this:
     People would do very bad things to the Messiah;
     he would feel something very very bad because of this;
     people would kill him; on the third day he would live;
     after this, he would never die."
After this, Jesus said to the Apostles:
     "I want people in all parts of the earth to know
       what happened during the time when you were with me.
     I want you to speak about me to people in many countries.
     The Holy Spirit will be with you.
     Because you were with me for all this time, you can say:
       'It all happened like this.'
     When you say it, you can say at the same time:
       'This is true, we know it, we saw it.'"

Before the Apostles saw Jesus on that day, Peter saw him
(he saw him after Mary Magdalene had seen him).
We don't know where Peter was at that time,
  we don't know what Jesus said to Peter.
A part of the Bible called The First Letter of Peter says something like this:
     "On the day when Jesus's body was in the tomb,
     Jesus was with the dead.
     Many, many people had died before Jesus died,
     on that day Jesus was with all those people.
     He wanted them to know that after people die they can live.
     He wanted them to know that all people can live with God forever,
       if they want to."
We don't know how Peter knew this. We can think:
  Maybe Jesus said this to Peter when Peter saw him on that day.

34. The Apostle called Thomas sees Jesus

When the Apostles saw Jesus that evening, on the first day of the week,
    one of the Apostles was not with them.
Because of this, he didn't see Jesus when the other Apostles saw him.
This Apostle was called Thomas.

Thomas felt something very very good toward Jesus.
Some time before, when Jesus wanted to go to Judea,
    where many people wanted to kill him, Thomas wanted to go with him.
He said to the other Apostles at that time:
        "I want to go with him, I want to die with him.
        It will be good if we all go with him, if we all die with him."
(Before that, in Galilee, many many people thought about Jesus like this:
"He is a prophet, God is with him."
It was not like this in Judea.
There, people like Caiaphas said very bad things about him;
they wanted to kill him.
Jesus knew this. At the same time, he *wanted* to go to Judea, to Jerusalem.
He said: "I can't not go to Jerusalem.")

On the night before he died, Jesus said some things to Thomas
    like he had not said to anyone else.
First, he said to all the Apostles:
        "I am going now; you can be with me later, I want this;
        you know the way."
(He wanted to say with these words: "I am going to my Father now,
you can be with me, with my Father, later.")
Thomas said then:
        "Lord, we don't know where you are going, how can we know the way?"
Jesus said then to Thomas: "*I* am the way."

A short time after the other Apostles saw Jesus on that first day,
    they said to Thomas: "We saw Jesus, he lives."
Thomas then said to them:
        "I can't think like this now: 'This is true, Jesus lives.'
        Before I can think like this, I want to see his hands;
        I want to see the places where the nails were.
        If I can't see these places, I can't think: 'this is true,'
            I can't think: 'after he died, he lives.'
        I want to touch his hands in the places where the nails were.
        I want to touch the side of his body where the spear pierced it."

Some time after this, in the same place, the Apostles saw Jesus another time.
This time Thomas was with them. He saw Jesus.
Jesus said to Thomas:
> "You can see my hands now;
> you can touch them in the places where the nails were.
> You can touch my side in the place where the spear pierced it.
> Don't think like this anymore: 'This can't be true.'
> Think like this: 'It is true, Jesus lives.'"

When Jesus said this to him, Thomas knew that when the other Apostles said:
> "We saw Jesus, he lives," it was true.
He said something to Jesus then like never before
(none of the Apostles had said this to Jesus before).
The part of the Bible called The Gospel of John says:
> "Thomas then said to Jesus: 'My Lord and my God.'"
People can think about it like this:
> "Thomas said this to Jesus because he saw Jesus."
They can think: "maybe Thomas wanted to say:
> 'I know now: when I see you, I see God'."
At the same time people can think like this:
> "Maybe Thomas didn't know well what he wanted to say
> when he said 'My Lord and my God.'
> Maybe he wanted to say: 'I know now: when I see Jesus, I see God.'"

Jesus said to Thomas:
> "You think now: 'It is true, Jesus lives' because you have seen me.
> People can think like this *not* because they have seen me.
> It is very good for people if they think like this
> *not* because they have seen me.
> It is very good for people if they *want* to think like this."

35. People can't see Jesus on earth anymore

After this, the Apostles saw Jesus on earth at some other times.
They saw him in Jerusalem, they saw him in Galilee.
During that time, he said things like this to them:
    "You know many things about me, not like other people,
        because you were always with me.
    You know what I did during that time, you know what I said,
        you know what happened to me.
    Say it to other people; say it to people in this country,
        say it to people in other countries, say it to people everywhere on earth.
    When you are speaking to people about these things, you can say:
        'It is true, I know it, I was with Jesus at that time.'
    I want you to say it."
After some time, the Apostles knew
    that people wouldn't see Jesus on earth anymore like before.
They could know it because one day something happened like never before.

On that day they were with Jesus on the Mount of Olives, as he wanted.
He said to them then as before:
    "Because you were always with me, you know what I did, what I said,
        what happened to me.
    I want people in all parts of the earth to know it.
    Go to many places, say it to people in these places.
    At the same time, baptize people in these places.
    When you do it, say:
        'I baptize you in the name of the Father, the Son, the Holy Spirit.'"
The Apostles didn't know well then what Jesus wanted to say with the words:
    "the Father, the Son, the Holy Spirit."
They didn't know then that Jesus was speaking in this way about God.
They thought like this: "God is one."
At the same time they knew that when Jesus was speaking about God,
    he sometimes said: "we."
They knew that he could think about God like this: "We are one;"
    they knew it because he said: "I and the Father, we are one."
They didn't know then that when he said: "the Father, the Son, the Holy Spirit,"
    he could think: "We are all one."

Then Jesus said: "I will be with you always when people live on earth."
(He said: "to the end of days").
The Apostles could know then that when he said "with you"
    he was thinking about many many people.

They could know that many of these people would live
    a long time after Jesus had lived on earth.
They could know that many of them would live
    very far from the country where Jesus lived.
They could know that when he said to God, on the night before he died:
    "I want them to be one, as we are one," he was thinking about all these people.

After that, something happened in that place, it happened in a very short time.
At one moment the Apostles could see Jesus there,
    a moment after they could not see him.
They couldn't see him because there was a cloud
    in the place where he was a moment before.
After a very short time, the cloud wasn't there anymore.
They couldn't see Jesus anymore then.
They knew that he was not there anymore.
They stood there for some time, they looked toward the sky.
They knew then that Jesus wouldn't be with them on earth like before anymore.

The Apostles didn't feel something very bad because of this,
    as they felt at the time when Jesus died; they felt something very good.
They thought like this: "Jesus is with God now."
They knew that they could think about him like they thought about God.
They knew that they could think like this:
        "If he wants something to happen on earth, it can happen because of this.
        If he wants something to happen in other places,
            it can happen because of this."
They knew they could think like this:
        "After some time, we will see Jesus, he said so.
        Before we see him, he will be with us on earth in another way."

36. The Holy Spirit

On the night before he died Jesus said some things to the Apostles
    like never before.
He knew that in a very short time they would feel something very very bad.
He said to them then:
    "I want you to know that when I am not with you on earth like before,
    there *will* be someone with you."
Jesus spoke about this someone with the words: "the Paraclete," "the Spirit,"
    "the Holy Spirit."
The Apostles didn't know well then what he wanted to say with these words.
(When the prophets said: "the Spirit," "the Holy Spirit,"
"the Spirit of the Lord," they didn't say "someone.")

Jesus had said things like this to them at that time:
    "I want the Holy Spirit to be with you, I will say it to my Father.
    I can't always be with you like before.
    When the Holy Spirit is with you,
    I will be with you, I will be with you in another way."
At the same time Jesus said something like this:
    "When the Holy Spirit is with you, you will know well
    what I wanted to say to you before.
    If someone says some things about God then, you will know what is true,
    what is not true.
    If someone says some things about me, you will know what is true,
    what is not true.
    If someone says about something: 'it is very bad if people do this,'
    you will know what is true, what is not true."
After this, Jesus spoke about the Holy Spirit on the day
    when they saw him on earth for the last time.
He wanted them to know then that the Holy Spirit would be with them soon.

A short time after this, it happened as he said.
It happened on a day called (in Hebrew) Shavuot.
Every year, there were many people in Jerusalem on that day.
All Israelites wanted to be in the Temple on that day.
Later, Christians called this day Pentecost (a Greek word);
    many Christians call this day Pentecost now.
When it happened, all the Apostles were in one place, in a house in Jerusalem,
    Jesus's mother Mary was with them.
At one moment they heard something like a big wind in this place.
At the same time everyone saw something above everyone else's heads,
    it was like a small fire.
The Apostles knew that something had happened to them like never before.

They felt something like never before.
They knew then that the Holy Spirit was with them, was *in* them.

After this happened, the Apostles didn't think like before.
Before it happened, they often thought like this:
> "Some people can do something very bad to me
> because I was with Jesus, I don't want this to happen."

When they thought like this, they felt something very bad.
Because they felt like this,
> they didn't want to do many things,
> they didn't want to be in places where there were many people,
> they didn't want to speak about Jesus to anyone anywhere.

After it happened, they didn't think like this anymore, they thought like this:
> "I can say many things about Jesus to many people
> because I was with Jesus, I want to do it."

When they thought like this, they felt something very good.
Because they felt like this,
> they wanted to do many things,
> they wanted to be in places where there were many people,
> they wanted to speak about Jesus to many people in many places.

The Apostles did all these things; they *could* do it
> because the Holy Spirit was with them.

When they were doing it, they knew that the Holy Spirit was with them,
> was in them; they couldn't not know it.

People can know more about it if they read one part of the Bible.
It is called "The Acts of the Apostles."

37. The Church: people who want to live with Jesus, with other people

On the day when the Apostles knew that the Holy Spirit was with them,
    they felt something very very good.
They were saying: "God is very good! God is doing very good things for people!,"
Many people heard this.
There were many people in Jerusalem on that day because it was Pentecost,
    many of them didn't know Aramaic.
(Many Israelites lived in other countries at that time;
many didn't speak Aramaic, many didn't speak Hebrew.)
At the same time, it was like this: When the Apostles spoke in Aramaic,
    everyone knew what they were saying. Everyone thought:
    "These men are speaking like people speak in the country where *I* was born.
    How can this be?"

Then Peter spoke to them all.
He said: "Israelites! I want to speak to you about Jesus of Nazareth."
Then he spoke like this:
    "Listen! Jesus was the Messiah.
    When the prophets spoke about the Messiah, they were speaking about *him*.
    You know what Jesus did, because of this you know that God was with him.
    You know how he died.
    It all happened as the prophets said, as David said.
    When David spoke about the Messiah, he said things like this:
        'He will be someone like my son, he will be king forever.
        After he dies, nothing bad will happen to his body.
        He will live, he will never die. God wants it to be like this.'
    It all happened as David said, we know it, we saw it.
    Jesus lives. He is now with God, very near to God.
    You can all know what we are saying here today
        because the Holy Spirit is with us now, Jesus wants it.
    The Holy Spirit can be with you all if we baptize you.
    Do you want us to baptize you?"
After this, many people said: "I do." Then the Apostles baptized them.
When they were doing it, they said:
    "I baptize you in the name of the Father, the Son, the Holy Spirit."
They were saying with these words:
    "It can be like this now: you will live with Jesus, with other people.
    It can be like this because God wants it: the Father, the Son, the Holy Spirit."

After this, the Apostles spoke about Jesus to many people in many other places.
At the same time, they spoke about Abraham, Isaac, Jacob.
They spoke about Moses, about the prophets.

They said things like this: "Our fathers wanted to live with God;
  if you live with Jesus, you will live with God."
After this, many people in many places said to the Apostles:
  "I want to live with Jesus, I want you to baptize me."
They all often called Jesus "Christ."
Because of this people called them "Christians." Christians thought like this:
  "We are many, at the same time we are one,
  like many parts of someone's body are one body."
When they thought like this, they often said the word "church."
They thought: "We are the church." They thought:
  "Christ lives; this church is something like his body.
  Christ wants the Holy Spirit to be always with this church."
They thought: "The Holy Spirit is God's Spirit,
  at the same time, it is Christ's Spirit; it is one Spirit."
They knew that before he died, Jesus said to God:
  "I want them to be one, as we are one."
After some time, not a very long time, there were many Christians
  in many parts of the Roman empire.

Christians often went to places where someone could speak about Jesus,
  they wanted to hear it.
They wanted to do something with other Christians there,
  as the Apostles did on the night before Jesus died.
They knew that Jesus said about one bread then: "This is my body,"
  they knew that he said: "Eat it."
They wanted to eat parts of one bread with other Christians,
  as Jesus wanted the Apostles to do.
They thought like this: "If we eat one bread, we are like one body,
  we are something like Christ's body."
For a very long time they couldn't do this in many places
  because they couldn't do it anywhere where people could see them.
It was like this because for a very long time
  the Romans didn't want any people in the Roman empire to be Christians.
During that time they killed many many Christians.
Before they killed them, they did very bad things to them.
This didn't happen if someone said: "I don't want to be a Christian."
Many Christians didn't want to say this. They thought like this:
  "After we die, we will live.
  We will live with God, with Jesus, with other people.
  We can live with God, with Jesus, with other people, forever."
Many many people, in many parts of the earth, think like this now.

38. The Apostle Peter

Peter was an Apostle not like the others.
Jesus said some things to Peter like to no other Apostle.
Peter said some things to Jesus like no other Apostle.
Often when all the Apostles wanted to say something to Jesus, Peter said it.
Before, Peter was called Simon.
The first day when Jesus saw Peter, he said to him:
>   "You are Simon son of Jonah? You will be called Kefas"

(In Aramaic, Kefas was rock; the Greek word was Petros).

A short time before Jesus was with three Apostles on Mount Tabor,
>   he said to all the Apostles: "Who am I? What do people say?"

They said: "Some say: John the Baptist, some say: one of the Prophets."
Jesus said to them then: "What do *you* say?"
Peter said: "You are the Messiah, the Son of the living God."
(None of the Apostles had said this to Jesus before.)
Jesus said to Peter then:
>   "God wanted you to know this, Simon son of Jonah.
>   I say to you now: You are Peter (rock).
>   If someone builds something on rock (not on sand),
>   it can be there for a very very long time.
>   You will be such a rock. I will build something on this rock.
>   It will be *my church* [in Greek, "ekklesia mou"].
>   Satan will want it not to be on earth,
>   he will do many very bad things to it because of this.
>   I say to you: It will not be as Satan wants,
>   *my church* will always be on earth as long as people live on earth."

(The Apostles didn't know then what Jesus wanted to say
with the words "my church," they knew it later.)
Then Jesus said something like this to Peter:
>   "If later people want to know how they can live,
>   if they want to live with God, you can say it to them.
>   Your words will be like keys to a place where people can live with God."

Then he said the same to all the Apostles
(not with the word "keys," with some other words).

After this, Jesus said some other things to all the Apostles.
He wanted them to know what would happen to him.
He wanted them to know that people would kill him,
>   as before they killed many prophets.

Peter said to Jesus then:

"Don't say things like this, Lord! Such things will never happen to you!"
When Peter said this, Jesus said to Peter:

"When you say this to me, you are doing something very bad to me.
You speak to me like Satan!"
The Apostles knew that Jesus felt something very bad at that moment,
because he said to Peter: "Satan."

Jesus knew Peter well. He knew that Peter thought like this at that time:

"Very bad things cannot happen to Jesus;
he is the Messiah, he will be the king of the people of Israel."
Jesus knew that when later people would want to kill him, Peter would say:

"I don't know that man."
At the same time, he knew that Peter felt something very very good toward him.
When he wanted the Apostles to know that he was alive,
he wanted Peter to see him before all the others.
He wanted Peter to know that he didn't feel anything bad toward him
(after Peter said: "I don't know that man").

A short time before the Apostles knew that Jesus wouldn't be on earth anymore,
Jesus said something to Peter like never before.
He said: "Simon, son of Jonah, do you feel something very good toward me?
Not like all the others, more?"
Peter said then to Jesus:

"Lord, you know everything,
you know that I feel something very good toward you."
Jesus then said to Peter:

"I want you to be like a shepherd.
Soon, many people will say: 'I want to live with Jesus, with other people.'
I want you to think about them like a shepherd thinks about his sheep."
Later Christians knew what Jesus said to Peter. They talked about it.
They knew what he said with the words "shepherd," "keys," "rock."
They wanted to know well what he wanted to say with these words.
They didn't all think about it in one way.
Christians talk about it now, as before, they don't all think about it in one way.

39. An Apostle called Paul

One of the Apostles spoke about Jesus to people in many countries,
    these people were not Israelites.
This Apostle wanted people everywhere to know Jesus,
    he wanted them to want to live with Jesus.
He wanted them to know that if they wanted to live with Jesus,
    they didn't have to live like Israelites.
He wanted them to know that if they lived with Jesus, they lived with God.
This Apostle was called Paul. Paul was not an Apostle when Jesus lived on earth.
At that time, he was called Saul.
Saul thought like this: "This man Jesus wants us Jews not to live as Moses said;
    he wants us to think not like before. This is very very bad."
Because he thought like this, he felt something very bad toward Jesus,
    he felt something very bad toward Christians.
When Jesus didn't live on earth anymore,
    he did very bad things to many Christians in Jerusalem because of this.

One of these Christians was called Stephen.
He spoke about Jesus like no one else, the Holy Spirit was with him.
After people listened to Stephen, many wanted to be Christians.
Because of this, people like Caiaphas felt something very bad toward Stephen,
    they wanted to kill him, after some time, they did it.
They did it like this: they threw many stones at him.
When they were doing this, Stephen didn't feel anything bad toward them.
He spoke to God about it, like Jesus spoke to God
    when the soldiers were nailing him to the cross.
When these people were throwing stones at Stephen, Saul was with them.
He thought like this: "They are doing something very good."
Then one day something happened to Saul: as he said later, he saw Jesus.

It happened like this:
        Saul was not in Jerusalem , he was going to a city called Damascus.
        He wanted to do very bad things to many Christians there,
            as he did in Jerusalem, he wanted them to be in prison.
        At one moment, he saw light above the place where he was,
            then this light was *in* the place where he was.
        He couldn't see anything in that place because of it.
        He fell to the ground.
        He heard a voice then, the voice said to him:
            "Saul, Saul, why do you want to do very bad things to me?"

Saul said: "Lord, who are you?"
The voice said: "I am Jesus, you are doing very bad things to me."
At that moment something happened in Saul.
He didn't want to do bad things to Christians anymore.

After this Saul wanted to know what the Apostles said about Jesus;
    he wanted to know what Jesus did, what he said.
After a short time, he didn't think about Jesus like before; he thought like this:
    "Jesus was the Messiah. The prophets spoke about him.
    He lives; all people can live with him if they want to.
    We Israelites know that Moses wanted us to live with God.
    I know now that if people live with Jesus, they live with God."
He wanted to be baptized.
He didn't want to be called Saul, like before, he wanted to be called Paul.

Paul wanted people everywhere to know that all people can live with Jesus:
    Greeks, Jews; women, men; slaves, not slaves; all people.
He wanted all people to know that if they live with Jesus, they live with God.
He went to many countries to say this to people.
Often very bad things happened to him because of it.
He didn't think then: "I don't want these things to happen to me,"
    he thought: "I want people to know Jesus."
(People can know more about it if they read "The Acts of the Apostles.")
Paul said a lot about Jesus like no one else, he wrote down much of it.
Many people want to read it, now as before.
He wanted people to know well who Jesus was, why he lived on earth,
    why he died on the cross.
He wanted them to know well what the church is.
He wanted them to know what God wants.

Paul died in Rome, like Peter, the Romans killed them in Rome,
    as they killed many other Christians, when Nero was Caesar.
They killed Paul with a sword, Peter died on a cross, like Jesus.
Many Christians think like this now:
    The other Apostles wanted many people to know Jesus,
    they did many things because of this.
    These two Apostles did more;
    there are many many Christians on earth now because of this."

40. What will happen to all people—what God wants

When Jesus didn't live on earth anymore,
　　the Apostles knew that he was with God, as he was before he was born.
They knew that after some time all people will see him, that when they see him,
　　they will know who he is.
They knew that people will then see a light like no other light,
　　as three Apostles saw once on Mount Tabor.

The Apostles could think about it like this:
　　　　People will know then that when they see Jesus, he sees *them*,
　　　　　　that he knows what they are like inside.
　　　　They will know that he knows how they lived,
　　　　　　at the same time *they* will all know how they lived.
　　　　They will know when they did good things for other people.
　　　　They will know that they were doing good things for God then.
　　　　They will know when they didn't want to do good things for other people.
　　　　They will know that they didn't want to do something good for God then.
　　　　They will think about some things like this:
　　　　　　"When I did this, I did something very bad."
　　　　They will think about some other things like this:
　　　　　　"When I did this, I did something good."
　　　　Jesus will say to some people then:
　　　　　　"You can live with God now, as you are now."
　　　　If he says this to someone, they will feel something very very good.
　　　　He will say to some other people:
　　　　　　"You can't live with God now, as you are now."
　　　　If he says this to someone, this someone can feel something very very bad.

The Apostles could know that when people see Jesus,
　　he will not say to anyone: "You can *never* live with God."
They could know it because they knew how Jesus spoke about God.
They could know what he wanted to say when he said this:
　　　　A man had two sons.
　　　　One of them didn't want to live with his father, he wanted to go away.
　　　　The father didn't say to him: "You can't do it."
　　　　He said: "you can do as you want."
　　　　The son went away.
　　　　He lived for a long time in places far away from his father's house.
　　　　He did very bad things in these places,
　　　　　　very bad things happened to him because of it.
　　　　After some time, he went back to his father, he said to him:

"Father, I want to live with you. I can't live with you now like a son
because I did very bad things.
Many people live in your house, you are someone above them;
maybe I can live with you like these people."
The father said to him then:
"Son, you can always live with me like a son lives with his father."
The father felt something very very good, because he *wanted* this:
He *wanted* his son to live with him, he wanted it very much.
God is like this father.
The Apostles knew that another time Jesus spoke like this about God:
A shepherd had a lot of sheep.
One didn't want to be with him, with the other sheep. It went away.
It was far from the shepherd for a long time,
very bad things happened to it because of this.
The shepherd went to many places
because he wanted to bring that sheep back to the other sheep.
Because he did this, after some time, that sheep was with him,
with the other sheep.
The shepherd felt something very very good because of this,
because he wanted this, he wanted it very much.
God is like this shepherd.

The Apostles wanted other people to know what Jesus said about God,
to know with what words he said it.
People can know these things if they read the Gospels.
The Apostles could know well what Jesus wanted to say,
because the Holy Spirit was with them.
They said it in many places. Later some people wrote it down.
They wrote it in something called the Creed, the Holy Spirit was with them.
Because of this, people everywhere can now know that Christians say this:
Jesus lives. People can live with Jesus, with other people.
When they live with Jesus, they live with God.
God feels something very good toward all people,
God wants to do very good things for all people.
All people can live with God if they want to.
After people die, they can live with God, with other people, forever.
They can feel something very very good forever. God wants it.

PART III

Brief Commentaries on the Chapters of Part II

Commentary on chapter 1: "God"

In his book *The Faith of a Physicist*, scientist and theologian John Polkinghorne (1994: 52) tells the story of an English theologian who was giving a lecture to a group of clergy. "At the end, one of them said, 'Professor X, do you believe in God?' He received a carefully nuanced academic reply. 'No, no,' said his interrogator, 'I just want to know if you believe in God.' Professor X then said, 'I believe, indeed I know, that at the heart of reality is One who reigns and loves and forgives.'" Polkinghorne comments: "It was a splendid reply," and so it was. It was not, however, a reply that could be translated into most languages of the world.

Another definition of God quoted by Polkinghorne comes from theologian D. A. Pailin's (1989: 24) book *God and the Process of Reality*: "A theistically satisfactory concept of the divine must conceive of the divine as being intrinsically holy, ultimate, personal, and agential." Sadly, this second definition is even less cross-translatable than the first, and a good example of a "nuanced academic" explanation which is largely incomprehensible outside academia.

Trying to propose a similarly brief alternative phrased in universal (cross-translatable) human words, I would, to begin with, propose this: God is someone not like people, God is someone above people, God is now, always was, always will be, God is good, there is no one else like God. I think these five very short sentences provide enough meaning to make sense of a Christian's statement "I believe in God" (and also, of the atheist's statement: "I don't believe in God"). Nonetheless, from a Christian point of view this is not enough.

In a book of interviews with Polish theologian Wacław Hryniewicz (2001: 73), the interviewers cite "six truths of the faith" which are the basis of the Catholic teaching of children in Poland. These six truths include the following two: (1) There is one God and (2) God is a just judge, who rewards [people for] good things and punishes [people for] bad things. Hryniewicz agrees that the first is "a fundamental truth of faith," but (referring to the part of the New Testament called The First Letter of John) he objects to the second one: "This one grates on me. I would be inclined to say instead: 'God is love' (1J 4, 8, and 16)."

John's "definition" (or characterization) of God—"God is love"—goes undoubtedly to the heart of Jesus's message, and therefore to the heart of Christianity. It is, however, highly condensed. If we unpack it, what exactly does it mean? John goes on to explain: "God is love, and he who abides in love abides in God, and God in him" (3:165). This has important implications for people: "Beloved, let us love one another, for love is God, and everyone who loves, is born of God and knows God. He who does not love, does not know God, for God is love." (1 John 4:7–8). I have discussed this link between people's love and God's love in chapter 3 of "The Story" and will focus here on the statement "God is love" as such. Is it translatable into all languages?

When I open my copy of *Tjukurpa Palya* (1987), the New Testament (Good News) in the Australian language Pitjantjatjara, I find there the sentence "Godanya mukulya nyinyapai" (1 John 4:8), where "Godanya" is built on the loanword "God," *nyinapai* means, essentially, "is," and *mukulya* is an adjective glossed by Goddard's 1996 dictionary of this language as "fond of, liking, loving." As this rendering of John's sentence in *Tjurkurrpa Palya* indicates, one can't really say in Pitjantjatjara (the equivalent of) "God is love," one can only say something like "God is loving."

The main point here is that "love" (as in "God is love") is an abstract noun and that many languages do not have abstract nouns. In the Greek original of John's letter, the word translated into English as "love" is *agape*. The concept is complex, and I believe that in order to be fully explained in languages which do not have a word corresponding to it, it has to be broken down into its two essential components, based on the universal concepts FEEL and WANT. In chapter 1 of "The Story" this is done by means of the two components: "God feels something very good toward all people" and "God wants to do good things for all people." Such a rendering is consistent with the Judeo-Christian idea that God is not "impassive," incapable of feelings (like the supreme being of ancient Greek philosophers), but on the contrary, is capable of love, compassion, joy, and also suffering.

As Polkinghorne (1994: 62) notes, the idea of a God incapable of feelings "certainly accords ill with the God of the Bible: 'How can I give you up, O Ephraim! How can I hand you over, O Israel? (Hosea 11.8).'" One could add to this the preceding lines from Hosea:

> When Israel was a child, I loved him, and out of Egypt I called my son. The more I called them, the more they went from me; they kept sacrificing to the Baals, and burning incense to idols. Yet it was I who taught Ephraim to walk, I took them up in my arms; but they did not know that I healed them. I led them with cords of compassion, with the bands of love, and I became to them as one who eases the yoke on their jaws, and I bent down to them and fed them. (Hosea 11:1–4)

As these quotes from Hosea indicate, God's very good feelings toward people make him vulnerable: these words breathe love, but also sorrow and suffering. Similarly, Jesus's parable of the Prodigal Son, in which Jesus wants to show what God is like, makes clear that the father (who stands for God) not only "feels something very very good toward his son" but also suffers ("feels something very very bad") when the son goes away. Polkinghorne (1994: 62) comments: "Once God is acknowledged to be vulnerable through his love for his creation, it becomes possible to speak of the mystery of a suffering God."

The idea of a "feeling," vulnerable God raises the question of the meaning of the word "almighty" as used in relation to God (a word which is not included in "The Story"). The Apostles' Creed, which is an essential reference point for Christians, says: "I believe in God, the Father Almighty." What exactly is meant by the phrase "Father Almighty" will be explored throughout the forty chapters of the "The Story." Here, we need to note that as discussed by great fourteenth-century logician and theologian William Ockham, it cannot mean that "God can do anything and everything" (McGrath 1992: 21):

> In his famous discussion of the opening line of the Apostle's Creed—"I believe in God the Father almighty"—Ockham moves in immediately to ask precisely what is meant by that deceptively simple word "almighty". It cannot, he argues, mean that God is *presently* able to do everything, although it does mean that God was *once* free to act in this way. God has established an order of things which reflects his loving and righteous will— and that order, once established, will remain until the end of time. (. . .)
>
> For Ockham, God cannot now do everything. He has deliberately limited his possibilities. In his omnipotence, God chose to limit his own options. Is that a contradiction? No. If God is really capable of doing anything, he must be able to commit himself to a course of action—and stay committed to it. (. . .) Ockham's approach, though long neglected, needs to be recovered and valued; for it represents a responsible, helpful and thoroughly Christian approach to the question of God's omnipotence. (McGrath 1992: 19–20)

Many modern theologians have been thinking along similar lines. I will mention three. Simone Weil (1963: 33) in her *Gravity and Grace* speaks of "a radically transcendent God who has tied his hands in the presence of evil." I would note here that the paradoxical idea of a God who has "tied his hands" seems to accord well with the words of Jesus's model prayer "Our Father" (Matthew 6:9–13): "thy will be done on earth as it in heaven," in the Vulgate's Latin translation "fiat voluntas tua in terra sicut in caelo," that is, "let all things happen on earth according to your will, as they do in heaven." The implication is that currently things don't always happen on earth as God wants (although they do "in heaven"), but that God is able to bring it about that they will (it is a prayer of petition, of request, like "forgive us our trespasses").

Vernon White (1985: 14), meditating in his book *The Fall of a Sparrow* on "the ancient conundrum": "why does a good almighty God allow so much evil?," wistfully uses the phrase "this God of power and love." In the end, he opts for a long-term view and quotes these verses of the prophet Isaiah (as rendered by the English Standard Version of the Bible): "I am God, and there is none like me (. . .) I will accomplish all my purposes (. . .) I have spoken, and I will bring it to pass; I have purposed, and I will do it" (Isaiah 46:9–11).

Theologian and physicist John Polkinghorne (1994) does say that God "can do whatever he wills," which, on the surface, appears to contradict Ockham and McGrath, but he too, links God's "omnipotence" with God's ability to achieve his purposes ("I have spoken, and I will bring it about"):

> God intersects with the world, but is not in total control of its process. The act of creation involves divine acceptance of the risk of the existence of the other, and there is a consequent kenosis [emptying] of God's omnipotence. This curtailment of divine power (. . .) arises from the logic of love, which requires the freedom of the beloved. (. . .) God remains omnipotent in the sense that he can do whatever he wills, but it is not in accordance with his will and nature to insist on total control. (p. 81)

And one last quote, from the Polish theologian Hryniewicz (2001: 318): "We believe that it is God who has the last word, who is creating something astoundingly new."

Chapter 1 of "The Story of God and People" is consistent with such thinking: it does not say that "God can do anything," but instead includes the following lines: "If God wants something to happen, it can happen because of this," and "if God says about something: 'I want it to happen, it happens because of this.'" This does not deny the mysteries of the world we live in, and especially the mystery of suffering and evil, but it is enough to explain why the world exists, why there are people on earth, and what the nature of Christian hope is. As Polkinghorne (2002: 149) puts it, "The only ground for such hope lies in the steadfast love and faithfulness of God that is testified to by the resurrection of Jesus Christ."

Thus, from a Christian point of view, to speak about God one needs to speak about Christ at the same time:

At the heart of Christian faith lies the mysterious and exciting idea that the infinite and invisible God (. . .) has acted to make the divine nature known (. . .) through the life of a first-century Jew in whom humanity and divinity were both truly present. (. . .) It is essential to grasp this belief if we are to understand the proper role that Scripture plays in Christian thinking. The Word of God uttered to humanity is not a written text but a life lived, a painful and shameful death accepted, and the divine faithfulness vindicated through the great act of Christ's resurrection. (Polkinghorne 2010: 2–3)

A final point: images of God in the Bible. The final section of chapter 1 acknowledges that the Bible is a sacred book for Christians—a book in which they believe God speaks to people. At the same time, this section recognizes that from a Christian point of view some parts of the Bible—for example those which celebrate military conquests, and command, as if on God's behalf, acts of cruelty toward the conquered cannot be seen as inspired by God. Further, it recognizes that the Bible requires interpretation, that God's voice has often been misheard, and God's words, misinterpreted. This applies, above all, to Old Testament statements and images of God incompatible with the core Christian belief that God is love, but also, to some images in the New Testament book called the Revelation. To quote the seventh-century Syrian mystic and theologian St Isaac of Niniveh (1995):

That we should imagine that anger, wrath, jealousy or the like have anything to do with the divine Nature is something utterly abhorrent for us: no one in their right mind, no one who has any understanding (at all) can possibly come to such madness as to think anything of the sort about God. Nor again can we possibly say that He acts thus out of retribution, even though the Scriptures may on the outer surface posit this. Even to think this of God and to suppose that retribution for evil acts is to be found with Him is abominable. (pp. 162–163)

Just because (the terms) wrath, anger, hatred, and the rest are used of the Creator, we should not imagine that He (actually) does anything in anger or hatred or zeal. Many figurative terms are employed in the Scriptures of God which are far removed from His true nature. (p. 171)

The seventh-century saint and mystic's insistence that the Bible requires interpretation is echoed by two contemporary theologians, Polkinghorne and Hans Urs von Balthasar:

Just as God does not write universal messages in the sky but works more hiddenly, inspiring and guiding individuals and communities, so in a similar way Scripture is inspired by God but written by human beings, in order to be interpreted and understood by them in their succeeding generations. (. . .) A central task for the Christian interpreter of Scripture is to discern what in the Bible has lasting truthful authority, rightly commanding the continuing respect of successive generations, and what is simply time-bound cultural expression, demanding no necessary continuing allegiance from us today. Absolutely no one is free from having to make judgements of this kind. (Polkinghorne 2010: 13)

Balthasar (1982: 405), for his part, sums up his perspective on the Christian interpretation of the Scripture by invoking "the theological basic principle: Only love is credible."

Commentary on chapter 2: "The world exists because God wants it to exist"

Unlike many other chapters, chapter 2 was not only tested for cross-translatability with linguists in universities but also tested and discussed with a group of native speakers of the Austronesian language Longgu "on the ground." In November 2016, linguist Deborah Hill took a copy of chapter 2, along with one of chapter 9, to a village in the Solomon Islands, where she discussed every line and every word with a group of Longgu consultants. As she reported, the Longgu speakers were extremely interested in the project and keen to render "The Story," as literally as possible, in Longgu. After some lengthy discussions, all those involved reached a consensus and were satisfied with the outcome.

The only phrases of the Minimal English original that the Longgu consultants were not happy with involved a repetition of the word "many" in some lines: "many places of many kinds," "many things of many kinds," and "many creatures of many kinds." In response to these reactions, the Minimal English text has now been adjusted, and, for example, the phrase "many places of many kinds" has been reduced to "places of many kinds" (an outcome beneficial for the Minimal English version, too).

The phrase "living creatures" was rendered by Longgu speakers as "living things." It emerged, however, that this Longgu phrase can be only applied to "living creatures" (in the English sense), and not, for example, to plants, so the meaning of the Longgu phrase is the same as that of the English one.

From a religious point of view, the most challenging aspects of chapter 2 have to do with human uniqueness and with the likeness of people to God. According to "The Story," the unique features of people (in comparison with other living creatures) include human capacity for, and interest in, knowing and thinking, and in particular, the ability to think about the future, to make plans, to foresee one's own death, and to think about one's own actions as either "good" or "bad." On this last point, "The Story" follows Darwin: "Of all the differences between man and the lower animals, the moral sense or conscience is by far the most important" (*The Descent of Man*, 1871: 97, quoted in Suddendorf 2013: 185).

Elaborating (in the same work), Darwin wrote:

> A moral being is one who is capable of reflecting on his past actions and their motives—of approving of some and disapproving of others; and the fact that man is the one being who certainly deserves this designation, is the greatest of all distinctions between him and the lower animals. (Darwin 1871: 610)

Turning now to people's likeness to God, the relevant verses of the Bible, and its creation story, are well known: "Then God said: Let us make man in our image, according to our likeness (. . .). So God created man in his own image, in the image of God he created him, male and female he created them" (Genesis 1:27). Where exactly does this "likeness" of people to God lie, according to the Christian understanding of Genesis? In formulating its answers to this question, "The Story" follows, in particular, Benedict XVI's emphasis on people's ability and desire to speak to God, and an eminent scientist, Francis Collins's emphasis on people's capacity for love.

> The first "thou" that—however stammeringly—was said by human lips to God marks the moment in which spirit arose in the world. Here the Rubicon of anthropogenesis was crossed. For it is not the use of weapons or fire, not new methods of cruelty or of useful activity that constitute man, but rather his ability to be immediately in relation to God. (. . .) The theory of evolution does not invalidate faith, nor does it corroborate it. But it does challenge faith to understand itself more profoundly and thus to help man to understand himself and to become increasingly what he is: the being who is supposed to say "thou" to God in eternity. (Benedict XVI 2009: 46–47)

Francis Collins (2006: 27), the head of the Human Genome Project, writes: "surely most of us have at one time felt the inner calling to help a stranger in need, even with no likelihood of personal benefit. And if we have actually acted on that impulse, the consequence was often a warm sense of 'having done the right thing.'" Collins refers at this point to the key Christian concept of "agape":

> Agape, or selfless altruism, presents a major challenge for the evolutionist. It is quite frankly a scandal to reductionist reasoning. It cannot be accounted for by the drive of individual selfish genes to perpetuate themselves. Quite the contrary: it may lead humans to make sacrifices that lead to great personal suffering, injury, or death, without any evidence of benefit. And yet, if we carefully examine that inner voice we sometimes call conscience, the motivation to practice this kind of love exists within all of

us, despite our frequent efforts to ignore it. Sociobiologists such as E. O. Wilson have attempted to explain this behaviour in terms of some indirect reproductive benefits to the practitioner of altruism, but the argument quickly runs into trouble. (p. 27)

Recalling his experience as a doctor in Africa, Collins reflects (with reference to C. S. Lewis's (1977 [1960]) book *The Four Loves*):

Nothing I had learned from science could explain that experience. Nothing about the evolutionary explanation for human behaviour could account for why it seemed so right for this privileged white man [himself] to be standing at the bedside of this young African farmer, each of them receiving something exceptional. This was what C. S. Lewis calls agape. It is the love that seeks no recompense. It is an affront to materialism and naturalism. And it is the sweetest joy that one can experience. (p. 217)

Two other aspects of "creation" as depicted in "The Story" need to be noted here: first, that "creation" is represented here not only in terms of an initial impulse (corresponding to science's "big bang"), but also in terms of a continuing process; and second, that "creation" is seen, from a Christian (and Judeo-Christian) point of view, as "something good." I will not discuss the first of these points in any detail, apart from drawing attention to the line "God wants the same now," which suggests that God is continually sustaining the world. I will, however, elaborate the second point.

In his book *The Everlasting Man*, G. K. Chesterton (1925) points out that most of the heresies with which the early church struggled through its dogmas and anathemas saw the world as inherently bad, and the creation of the world as the work of an evil spirit, and that, by contrast, Christians (following the tradition of the Hebrew Bible) saw the creation of the world—the work of a good Creator—as inherently good. As physicist and theologian John Polkinghorne discusses in a number of books, this debate—is the world bad and pointless or good and meaningful?—has reignited in recent decades, when scientists have come to agree that (after some billions of years) the world will inevitably end. Does the end of the world mean the end of everything? (In the Orthodox catechism *The Living God* (1989) a character referred to as "Seeker" addresses this question to another character, referred to as "Sage." Sage replies: "Certainly not," quoting the words from Paul's First Letter to Corinthians: "For the form of this world is passing away" (1 Corinthians 7:31) and "The last enemy to be destroyed is death" (1 Corinthians 15:26).)

Polkinghorne (2002: 9) is convinced that the goodness of creation "is supported by science's discernment of the rational beauty and fruitful history of the universe." At the same time, he emphasizes that the Christian understanding of the beginning of the world and the Christian belief in the goodness of creation make sense only in the context of an accompanying expectation of a "new creation" which is to come when the present physical world comes to its inevitable end and in which God will be with people. As the visionary author of Revelation says:

> Then I saw a new heaven and a new earth, for the first heaven and the first earth had passed away (. . .) and I heard a loud voice from the throne saying, "Behold, the dwelling of God is with men. He will dwell with them, and they shall be his people, and God himself will be with them; he will wipe away every tear from their eyes, and death shall be no more, neither shall there be mourning nor crying nor pain any more, for the former things have passed away." (Revelation 21:1–4)

(It should be noted that in the best tradition of Hebrew prophets, Revelation also includes some terrible threats and warnings directed at evil-doers, expressed, according to the cultural conventions of Hebrew prophetic speech, as images of future punishments; properly understood, however, these apocalyptically phrased warnings do not detract from the overall message that "death will be no more," and "pain will be no more.")

Arguably, what matters here is both human suffering and the suffering of animals. According to Polkinghorne (1994: 86), "theological discourse has become unduly human-centred. (. . .) In fact, humanity and the physical world belong together. (. . .)." St Paul's words that "the whole creation has been groaning in travail until now" (Romans 8:22) and that "the creation itself will be set free from bondage to decay" (Romans 8:21) certainly indicate a concern going far beyond humanity. In chapter 2, this concern and care is reflected in the line referring to living creatures: "One day, it will not be like this anymore, it will be like this: (. . .) living creatures will not feel anything bad."

"And what about streptococcus, and other bacteria?" it might be asked. (Polkinghorne (1998: 86) quotes the couplet: "He loveth all, who loveth best/ the streptococcus is the test"). Minimal English allows us to deal with this question too: human concern for living creatures extends only to those "living things" which are regarded in ordinary language as living creatures, that is, living things that can feel. From a human point of view, bad things happen to sparrows (for which Jesus expressed concern in Matthew's Gospel 10:29) but not to (living) things like viruses and bacteria.

The words "All will be well" are a well-known quote from the revelations of the fourteenth-century mystic Julian of Norwich (nearly all of which came to her in the context of what would now be called a near-death experience, Sweetman 2011: 69).

I will close the commentary on the chapter about creation with one more (extended) quote from Polkinghorne (2002: 149), which explains in sophisticated non-minimal language the same points that the last segment of chapter 2 of "The Story" tries to make in poorer but cross-translatable words of Minimal English:

1. If the universe is a creation, it must make sense everlastingly, and so ultimately it must be redeemed from transience and decay.
2. If human beings are creatures loved by their Creator, they must have a destiny beyond their death.
3. There must be sufficient continuity to ensure that individuals truly share in the life to come as their resurrected selves and not as new beings given the old names. There must be sufficient discontinuity to ensure that the life to come is free from the suffering and mortality of the old creation.
4. The only ground for such a hope lies in the steadfast love and faithfulness of God that is testified to by the resurrection of Jesus Christ.

Commentary on chapter 3: "People can live with God"

If chapter 1 of "The Story" is primarily about God, and chapter 2, about the world, chapter 3 is primarily about people. A crucial thing about people that is in focus here is that they can all live with God, and that it is very good for people to live with God: Nothing else is like this.

But how are people to live, if they are to live with God? In this chapter, the necessary conditions for living with God are presented not as some arbitrary rules but, rather, as something that follows naturally from what God is like. God loves people; it follows that to be able to live with God, people too need to love people. In cross-translatable words, this means that the main focus is not on what people do but on what they feel and want: God feels something very good toward people and wants to do very good things for people; to be able to live with God, people, too, need to feel something very good toward people and to want to do very good things for people. (Of course if people *want* to do good things for other people, they *will* do some such things, but the focus is not so much on the actions as on "the heart": the feeling and the wanting.)

Further, it follows from what God is like that people cannot live with God when they live in ways contrary to what living with God is all about ("love"), that is, when they live feeling something very bad toward other people, wanting to do bad things to other people, not feeling anything very good toward other people, and not wanting to do good things for other people. In essence, this is what in traditional Christian language is called "sin." In modern times, Christian theologians often prefer to speak not of "sin" but of "alienation from God." In cross-translatable language, we can speak about "not living with God." According to the New Testament, "not living with God," that is, in effect, living without love, is very, very bad for people—worse than anything that can happen to people's bodies.

But is "sin"—or "not living with God"—really primarily about the absence of love? According to many Christian commentators, both in the past and today, the answer is yes. For example, Benedict XVI (2006) starts his book *Credo for Today* with a chapter entitled "What it means to be a Christian—Over Everything: Love," the first sentence of which (a heading) is "Love is enough." (He then goes on to discuss the relationship between love, faith, and hope.) Thus, the stress that chapter 3 of "The Story" places on "love" (rendered in cross-translatable words of Minimal English), is, I think, justified. Nonetheless, there are two other sentences in this chapter which present "alienation from God" (or "not living with God") from two other points of view as well: "often, they [people] don't want to think about God" and "often, they [people] do something when they know that they are doing something very bad."

God, who created people, knows what is best for people, and according to the New Testament, what is best for people is "eternal life," that is, living with God, with other people, forever. This is what God, who loves people, wants for all people—and this is what God wants people to want too.

The New Testament, which follows the tradition of the Hebrew Bible in this respect, often speaks about people's life with—or without—God using the image of sheep and a shepherd. The shepherd knows and loves his sheep, and wants what is best for them, but the sheep often go astray. When this happens, the shepherd patiently and tirelessly searches for the lost sheep. The image of God as a shepherd is a leitmotif of the Bible and, arguably, the best clue to its interpretation.

Finally, it may be asked: and what about "the Fall"? What about Adam and Eve? In chapter 3, the "Fall" is represented mainly in the line "People often don't live with God. It is like this now, it has always been like this." There is no reference there to a first couple, or a first sin. Many Christians do think, of course, that there was such a first couple, and such a first sin. Others take such references to be a figurative way of speaking about all people, at all times. Importantly, the Christian creeds make no pronouncement on this matter, so there is no "normative" Christian view here, and often Christians keep their minds open on this point. I will illustrate this with two interesting quotations, one from physicist and theologian Polkinghorne, and one from the Orthodox catechism *The Living God* (1989). Polkinghorne (1991) speaks from the position of a scientist who is also a deeply believing Christian:

> If I were asked what is the major Christian doctrine that I find most difficult to reconcile with scientific thought, I would answer: the Fall. I do not mean the status of humankind as sinful. It seems only too clear that something is awry in the lives of men and women; that there is an innate bias frustrating good intentions and tarnishing hopes (. . .) Even less do I mean

the Christian diagnosis that this state of affairs arises from an alienation from God, the attempt to live autonomous lives by those who are by nature spiritually dependent upon the grace of their Creator. These insights seem to me to be plausible and illuminating.

The difficulty arises from picturing this situation as having arisen subsequent to an unfallen state, with the associated notion that a radical change occurred as the consequence of some disastrous ancestral act. (. . .) How does this square with our knowledge that *homo sapiens* evolved from more primitive hominids? (p. 99)

Polkinghorne's "alienation from God" corresponds to "The Story's" line "people often don't live with God," and his phrase "the attempt to live autonomous lives by those who are by nature spiritually dependent upon the grace of their creator," to the line "often, they don't *want* to think about God." The Orthodox catechism starts from a different perspective, but it does not disagree:

Seeker: What proof do we have that everything happened in the way that the Bible describes?
Sage: We have no proof. The truth of this narrative is no more historical in nature than is the existence of the garden in space or the couple Adam and Eve in time.
Seeker: But don't we say that Adam and Eve are the first people, our common ancestors?
Sage: Were Adam and Eve actually the first couple or do they represent humanity as a whole? Neither revelation nor science permits us to answer this question with certainty. What is certain is that all men [people] can recognize themselves in Adam, as St Paul tells us (see Rom 5:12-14). There are elements in all of us which made the temptation and fall of Adam and Eve possible. (*The Living God*, 1989: 12, vol. 1)

From a Catholic perspective, Wacław Hryniewicz (2001: 21) reaches similar conclusions: "It is significant that the [Second Vatican] Council constitution Gaudium et Spes (no. 13) describes general human sinfulness without using the concept of the original sin."

Commentary on chapter 4: "God wants to live for some time with people on earth"

Chapter 4 focuses on what in traditional Christian language is often referred to as "God's plan of salvation," where "salvation" translates the Greek word "sotēria" used in the New Testament. Religious writer Garry Wills (2007: 189) in his book on Saint Paul renders this word in English as "rescue": "The revelation is that all the nations (. . .) are to be saved (*sōzesthai*). (. . .) Rescue [i.e. 'salvation', *sotēria*] was for him [Paul] a divine initiative, God's raid on enemy territory, bringing the people out from captivity. It was a massive liberation act, like the breaking open of every prison, and only God's energy can accomplish this."

Why did people need to be "rescued," or "liberated"? In Minimal English, the answer is that people often don't live with God, and can't live with God, because of the way they live (such as wanting to do bad things to other people and hating other people). God's "plan" (or "initiative") was to do something that could "liberate" people from that kind of life, and induce them to want to live with God. The key to people's wanting to "live with God" was people knowing God, and knowing the truth about God.

So this is what Christians call "incarnation": In order to make himself known to people God decided to live with people on earth, for some time, like people live, that is, to be born on earth like people are born (without being conceived like other people are conceived), to live like people live, and to die like people die (without, however, remaining dead for a long time).

Living with God is "life," living without God is "death." To understand this, people need "light"—the "light of truth," and the words "life," "light," and "truth" come closely together in the New Testament, in relation to Jesus (particularly in John's Gospel). For example:

"In him was life; and the life was the light of men." (John 1:4)

"The people who sat in darkness have seen a great light, and for those who sat in the region and shadow of death light has dawned." (Matthew 4:16)

"I am the way, and the truth, and the life." (John 14:6)

Further, these three key concepts—"life," "light," and "truth"—are also closely associated in the New Testament with the concept of "being free"—as Paul says in his Letter to the Romans, "free from the law of sin and death" (Romans 8:2). As Jesus tells his opponents in the Gospel of John, when people understand who he is, and why he lives on earth, they will know the truth about God, and the truth about people, "and the truth will make you free" (John 8:32). Jesus's opponents reply then: "we (. . .) have never been in bondage to anyone. How is it that you say, 'You will be made free?'" (John 8:33). And Jesus answers: "Truly, truly I say to you, everyone who commits sin is a slave to sin (. . .). If the Son makes you free, you will be free indeed" (John 8:34).

But abstract nouns like "life," "truth," and "freedom" are not cross-translatable: many languages don't have such words; and many don't have an equivalent of "free" either. Chapter 4 of "The Story" explains God's goal with the help of the cross-translatable concepts "know," "want," and "live with": "God wanted it to be like this: people know God, because of this, they want to live with God." To explain God's "plan" for achieving this goal we need the same three concepts: "God wanted to live for some time on earth, with people, like people live" and "God wanted it to be like this: first, people in one country know God well, some time after this, people in other countries can know God well because of this."

The idea of God choosing one particular country and one particular time in which "to live on earth with people, like people live" strikes some modern Western writers as unacceptable, but this is precisely what Christians have always believed. As the Nicene Creed puts it, "I believe in one Lord Jesus Christ, the Only Begotten Son of God. (. . .) For us men [people] and for our salvation he came down from heaven, and by the Holy Spirit was incarnate of the Virgin Mary, and became man."

Jesus's mother was a Jewish girl who lived in Palestine at the time when Caesar Augustus was the Caesar of Rome and Herod the Great was the king of Judea. So according to the Christian understanding, God came to live on earth, with people, as a Palestinian Jew. He lived on earth immersed in one particular culture (Jewish culture), he spoke the local language (Aramaic), and he read one people's sacred book (the Hebrew Scriptures) in that people's sacred language (Hebrew).

The phrase "Only Begotten Son of God" insists that God's "incarnation" and life on earth as a human being happened only once, a claim which for some contemporary Western writers is impossible to believe and contrary to "modern historical consciousness" (Kaufman 2005 [1987]). In a book entitled *The Gospel in a Pluralist Society*, British theologian and missionary Leslie Newbigin (1989) writes:

> It is not easy to resist the contemporary tide of thinking and feeling which seems to sweep us irresistibly in the direction of an acceptance of religious pluralism, and away from any confident affirmation of the absolute sovereignty of Jesus Christ. (. . .) The overwhelming dominance of relativism in contemporary culture makes any firm confession of belief suspect. To the affirmation which Christians make about Jesus, the reply is, "Yes, but others make similar affirmations about the symbols of *their* faith; why Jesus and not someone or something else?" (p. 169)

As Newbigin comments, there is an aspiration to humility in such critiques of the Christian belief in Jesus's uniqueness, but there is also a relativist rejection of the notion of truth, which for Christians is non-negotiable. Often, the implication appears to be that if I believe that something is true, and some other people believe that something else is true, then what I believe is true cannot be true, in fact, nothing can be true, there is no truth, there are only different opinions, different points of view: one thing can be "true for me," and a different one "true for you." Opposing such a relativist attitude to the truth in his encyclical *Veritatis Splendor*, Pope John Paul II (1993: 10) speaks of the "yearning for absolute truth" that always remains in the human heart, and of "a thirst to attain full knowledge of it." Similarly, John Polkinghorne (1998: 47) insists that "in both science and theology, the central question is, and remains, the question of truth."

Why do Christians believe in Jesus's uniqueness as God's "incarnation" on earth? Primarily, because in the light of the Gospels, it is clear that this is what Jesus himself believed and taught. When Christians read the Gospels, they "hear" (as they think) Jesus's voice, and this voice rings true to them. This is not an objective, scientific "proof" of Jesus's uniqueness, but faith. (As Jesus says to Pilate in John's Gospel, "everyone who is of the truth hears my voice," John 19:37, see chapter 25 of "The Story.")

"The Story of God and People" seeks to articulate what Christians *believe*, not what Christians claim they know or what Christians claim they can prove. Christians think that what their creeds say is indeed true, and they *want* to think like this: in essence, this is what the concept of "faith" means for Christians, as Minimal English allows us to state in clear and cross-translatable words: "I think like this: this is true, I know it, I want to think like this." (But I have *reasons* to want to think like this, and a key reason is, so to speak, Jesus's voice.)

Christians' belief in Jesus's uniqueness as God's "incarnation" on earth is of course closely related to their belief in God's unique relationship with the Jewish people and with God's choice of one man as his "special friend," namely, Abraham. If this looks to some modern Western readers of the Bible as favor-itism on God's part, or as a groundless and self-serving claim on the part of Abraham's (and Isaac's, and Jacob's) descendants—well, so be it. Evidently, this is what Jesus and those who were close to him believed. A special love for Abraham and his descendants, and, also, for a particular place on earth, is an undeniable aspect of the story of God and people as outlined in the Bible—both the Hebrew Bible and the New Testament.

Does this mean that God loved Abraham more than other people? The short answer is no, it is not a *greater* love but a *special* love. The question applies not only to Abraham but also to the people of Israel: There can be no doubt that according to the Bible, and to Christian belief, "Israel" was, and is, God's "chosen" people; Abraham was "chosen" as the people of Israel was "chosen" by God. I will return to the question of God's "special love" for Abraham, and for the people of Israel, in Appendix B.

As American author George Weigel (2009 [1999]: 157) writes in his massive biography of Pope John Paul II, when a group of bishops from different parts of the world visited what Christians call the Holy Land during the Second Vatican Council in 1964, "The mystic starkness of the Judean wilderness left a lasting impression on Wojtyła, as on so many others. Here he was powerfully struck by the fact that God, in order to redeem the world, had entered history at one time and one place. As he put it in a poem, 'You seek out people every-where/You had to stop in some place. This one is chosen by You.'" This is the perspective reflected in chapter 4 of "The Story."

Commentary on chapter 5: "God speaks to Abraham"

From a linguistic point of view, the greatest challenges in the chapter on Abraham have to do with key concepts such as "descendants," "promise," "faith," and "blessings": How can one tell Abraham's story without relying on such complex and anything but cross-translatable words without missing anything that is essential to it?

The Orthodox catechism *The Living God* (1989, vol. 1) writes:

> The first eleven chapters of the Book of Genesis, the first book of the Bible, are not, properly speaking, historical. It is only with the twelfth chapter, which speaks of God's promise to Abraham, that we are dealing with history, that is, with the description of events which can be placed in time and space. God promises to intervene in the life of mankind, and with this promise begins the history of the people of God, Israel, which will lead us up to Christ, the King of Israel. (pp. 43–44)

God of course entered into a dialogue with humanity (or so Christians believe) from the moment the first people appeared on earth, but as *The Living God* (1989) says, we have no historical records of those earlier people and conversations. In the case of Abraham, however, we are dealing with history: We know where and when Abraham was born (in the middle of the nineteenth century BC, in the city of Ur in southern Mesopotamia), who his father was, who his brothers were, and who his wife was. It is of this historical figure, then, that we hear what God said to him and how he responded. If in the quote above the key word is "promise," in the quote below the key word is "faith": "Beginning with this first narrative we become aware of the faith of Abraham, an exemplary faith which is both the gift of God and the human acceptance of this gift. It is both free and freeing, leading to a willing cooperation in God's work, and unhesitating 'yes." (p. 43).

In the next quote, a key concept is that of "descendants" (Abraham's descendants): "Thus Abraham sets out for the land of Canaan (. . .) and tirelessly pursues his goal, encountering many adventures on the way. Once again the Lord speaks to Abraham, promising him many descendants" (p. 44). The first key figures among these descendants are Abraham's son Isaac and Isaac's son Jacob, the latter mysteriously renamed by God as Israel, according to Genesis 32:26, 28.

> Jacob, the son of Isaac, returns to Canaan, the land of his birth, after an absence of twenty years. It is an imposing caravan: twelve sons, four wives, with servants and animals. He leads his family through the ford of the Jabbok and stays alone for the night. Here an awe-inspiring spectacle takes place from which Jacob emerges transformed, and from which the chosen people will receive through Jacob (. . .) their new name of Israel. (*The Living God*, 1989: 46, vol. 1)

But the "promise" given by God to Abraham extends through him and his "descendants" to all humankind: "In thee shall all the families of the earth be blessed" (Genesis 12:3, KJV). The catechism goes on to comment:

> By choosing Abraham, Isaac, and Jacob, God chose a people for Himself, the people of Israel. Yet He allies Himself to these people so as to address Himself to all humanity through them and to call all peoples to salvation. Christ will be born of this race. That is why Christians are truly sons of Abraham, Isaac, and Jacob, as St Paul wrote: "And if you are Christ's, then you are Abraham's offspring, heir according to promise" (Galatians 3:29). Abraham, then, is the father of all believers. (p. 47)

Chapter 5 of "The Story" introduces all these motifs, without any of the complex and non-cross-translatable words. Thus, in "The Story" God says to Abraham: "I will do very good things for you," "very good things will happen to all these people [Israelites] because of this," and "after some time, very good things will happen because of this to people in all the parts of the earth."

Perhaps the most challenging words in the story of Abraham are those like "descendants" and "offspring," and also, in biblical language, "thy seed" (KJV). Unlike "mother," "father," and "be born," words such as "offspring," "ancestors," and "descendants" do not have equivalents in most languages of the world and embody highly culture-specific ways of thinking. In this chapter of "The Story," what is really important to convey is expressed with the help of the word "be born," and also the word "father" used figuratively: "all these people will be born because sometime before, you [Abraham] were born" and "all these people will think about you like this: 'Abraham is our father.'"

As for Abraham's "faith," it fits in with the explication of "faith" in the commentary to chapter 4: Abraham thought like this: "I think like this: this is true, I know it, I want to think like this." Abraham's "monotheism" (faith in one God) is rendered in the line: "Abraham thought like this: 'God (El, Elohim) is like no one else, God is above everything' (people in other countries did not think like this at that time)." (This is how God reveals himself to the people of Israel in other books of the Hebrew Bible, for example, "Hear, o Israel, the Lord our God is one Lord" (Deuteronomy 6:11) and "there is no other" (Isaiah 45:5).)

The concept reflected in the Minimal English phrase "this God is above everything" also reverberates throughout the Hebrew Bible, starting with the words of the mysterious figure called Melchizedek (Genesis 14:18), described as "the priest of the most high God," who recognizes and blesses Abraham in the name of "the most high God, creator of heaven and earth" (Genesis 14:19).

But although in Genesis God—"the most high"—promises Abraham that he will become the father of "a great and mighty nation" (Genesis 18:18), God also promises him that "all the nations of the earth shall be blessed in him" (Genesis 18:18) and [speaking directly to Abraham] "in thy seed shall all the nations of the earth be blessed" (Genesis 22:18).

The New Testament writers, and in particular Paul, often reflect on the theme of a great promise made by God to Abraham, and through him, to all nations, as the following quotes from Paul's Letter to the Galatians illustrate:

> Now the promises were made to Abraham and to his offspring. It does not say, "And to [your] offsprings," referring to many; but, referring to one, "And to your offspring," which is Christ. (Galatians 3:16)

> There is neither Jew nor Greek, there is neither slave nor free, there is neither male nor female; for you are all one in Christ Jesus. And if you are Christ's, then you are Abraham's offspring, heirs according to promise. (Galatians 3:28–29)

Thus, as Christians believe, four thousand years ago God—"the God of Abraham, Isaac and Jacob"—entered into a dialogue, and a special loving relationship, with one man, Abraham, and one family (the family of Abraham, Isaac and Jacob). From that family came, two thousand years later, Jesus of Nazareth, so that through him, as Paul put it, "the blessing of Abraham might come on the Gentiles" (Galatians 3:14), "and in thee shall all the families of the earth be blessed" (Genesis 12:3, KJV).

Commentary on chapter 6: "God speaks to Moses"

The Story of Moses, as summed up in chapter 6, includes—apart from the Exodus from Egypt—three major themes: the burning bush, the "Covenant," and the Ten Commandments. Chapter 6 largely omits the details of the Exodus from Egypt (referring the reader to the part of the Bible called "Exodus") and focuses, above all, on what God said to Moses, and through Moses, to the people of Israel, that is, on the "burning bush," the covenant, and the Decalogue.

I will start, then, with a few comments on the "burning bush" exchange, where the most arresting, and challenging element is God's revelation as "I AM." In his *History of Religion* (on which I will draw throughout this chapter), Alexander Men' (1991) writes:

> It will remain a secret for us forever what the Egyptian fugitive experienced in the silence of the Sinai mountains, but we know that from then on he would be a faithful servant of the God Invisible, the Lord and Master of human fates, the God who had entrusted him, Moses, and his people with a mysterious, historic mission. It was that God to whom people had prayed since time immemorial. Faith in Him had been the sacred legacy of the forefathers of Israel. He was the God who had revealed himself to Abraham, the God of the forefathers. He has his being beyond the everyday and beyond life itself. He is the One Who *Is* ["Suščij"], whose name is Yahweh. This new name of God indicates a new level of revelation.

Abraham did not know this name. Nonetheless Yahweh is that one who summoned the ancient patriarch to his presence and gave him the Promise. (p. 210)

The use of the word "Yahweh" in the Hebrew Bible is the subject of extensive literature, as is also the relation between "Yahweh" and "El"/"Elohim" (see, e.g., the entry on "Names of God in the Hebrew Bible" in *The Oxford Companion to the Bible*) and neither of these topics can be discussed here. What matters most from the point of view of "What Christians believe" is that God presents himself to Moses as "I AM," in the Greek of the Septuagint, "ego eimi," and that this is, as Men' puts it, a new level of Revelation. In Exodus (6:3, RSV), God says to Moses: "I am the Lord: And I appeared unto Abraham, unto Isaac, and unto Jacob, by the name of God Almighty, but by my name JE-HO-VAH was I not known to them."

From a Christian point of view, the most important aspect of the name "I AM" ("ego eimi") is that in the Gospels, especially in the Gospel of John, "ego eimi" (I AM) is often used by Jesus, with, as many Christian commentators put it, "a claim to divinity" (see, e.g., Packer 2001: 106; cf. Brown 1994: 137). The topic of the meaning and significance of this phrase as "the divine name" will be discussed in the commentaries on chapters 23 and 34.

Here, I will only note two points: first, that Men's frequent rendering of "Yahweh" with an ordinary-sounding word "Suščij" is very felicitous in Russian and works as a kind of name for "Yahweh," but it doesn't work in English (clearly neither "the One Who IS" nor "the EXISTING ONE" sounds like names.) The second point is that biblical phrases such as "the God *of* Abraham" cannot be reproduced as such in Minimal English, and that in chapter 6, God's statement "I am the God of Abraham" has been interpreted as referring, primarily, to a relationship based on speaking: "I want to speak to you, as before I spoke to Abraham." Clearly, this self-identification could be expanded and elaborated, but in the present context, it seems sufficient.

Turning now to the concept of "covenant," I will start again with a quote from Men' (1991).

A few days after they made camp at Sinai, the leader ordered everyone to prepare for a great moment: people were concluding a solemn covenant with God. It was something unheard of, because in the thinking of the peoples in the [Near] East, humans were as nothing in comparison with God and making a "pact" or covenant between them would be an act of incredible impudence.

But here the Lord of Life himself, through the mouth of his prophet, announces the conditions for this startling agreement: "If you will listen to my voice and keep my precepts, you will be my chosen people above all other nations, my kingdom of priests and my holy nation. (p. 222)

Men' goes on to cite the nineteenth-century Russian theologian, Vladimir Solov'ev (1901):

> Having separated themselves from paganism, and risen, by their faith, above Chaldean magic and Egyptian wisdom, the fathers and chiefs and leaders of the Jews became worthy of God's choice. God chose them, revealed himself to them, and concluded a covenant with them. The covenant between God and the people of Israel is the centrepoint of Jewish religion. (quoted in Men' 1991: 222)

But what exactly does the covenant consist in? Exodus (19:4–6) puts it like this: "Now therefore, if ye will obey my voice, and keep my covenant, then ye shall be a peculiar treasure unto me above all people: for all the earth is mine. And ye shall be unto me a kingdom of priests, and an holy nation." This message, addressed by God, through Moses, to the people of Israel, is rather mysterious; and while it is often discussed by commentators, it tends to be explained in words that are complex and far from self-explanatory. In chapter 6, I have interpreted the phrase "holy nation" in terms of an if-clause: "if you live as I want" and the sentence: "ye shall be unto me a kingdom of priests," in terms of an offer and a promise: "I will always be with you, not like with other people, I will be very near to you, I want this."

The commentary provided by the editors of the Polish "Millennium Bible" (1971: 84) states: "Among all nations, Israel is the closest to Yahweh, (. . .). This closeness imposes on Israelites an obligation of aiming at 'holiness', that is, of trying to be faithful in fulfilling God's commands." I have not followed the part of the commentary indicated by the ellipsis: "Israel is the closest to Yahweh because it gives the right sacrifices." As emphasized by Men', in the Ten Commandments, sacrifices or rituals are not even mentioned: "Moses didn't reject external forms of cult. (. . .) But in the Decalogue, there is no mention of them. It seems hard to believe, but it is simply a fact: in the main Law given to the whole of Israel, the text of which people learnt by heart, there is complete silence about any external forms of worship."

Two fairly specific words used in chapter 6 are likely to catch the reader's attention: "altar" and "sprinkle." Surely, these two don't have equivalents in all languages? Indeed, they do not. Yet they are both important for the story of the "covenant" between God and the people of Israel, ratified with the blood of some animals, sprinkled first on the altar and then on the people: "And Moses took the blood, and sprinkled it on the people, and said, 'Behold the blood of the covenant which the Lord hath made with you . . .'" (KJV) In chapter 6, the altar represents God (as one of the two parties to the agreement), and the word "altar" has been defined simply as "God's place." The word "sprinkle" refers here to a symbolic action, whose main purpose is to create a visible sign of the agreement: "God wants it, we want it; when people see this blood they can know that it is true." (I note that in the translation of the Bible into the Pitjantjatjara language of Central Australia, the verb *kurpini* "to wet" is used instead of "sprinkle": not exactly the same, but close enough.) Significantly, the expression "the blood of the covenant," used in Exodus in relation to Moses's action, is quoted by Jesus at the Last Supper (Mark 14:24; Matthew 26:28; Luke 22:20; Paul 1 Corinthians 11:25). Here, the "blood of the covenant" refers to Jesus's own blood, symbolically ratifying the *new* covenant, the covenant between God and the whole humankind.

Turning now to the third major theme of chapter 6, the Decalogue—its content and its significance—I will also start with a quote from Men' (1991). Having summarized the "ten commandments," Men' comments:

> What simple words are these at first glance! But if they seem somehow self-evident to us, for the ancients, they carried the force of an unimaginable revelation. It is sufficient to recall the relationship that prevailed between people and the divine in Egypt, Babylon or Greece to understand how extraordinary the sacred laws inscribed on the tablets must have seemed to the people of those times. These two plain roughly hewn stones had greater significance for the spiritual history of humanity than all the thousands of elaborately decorated Assyrian and Egyptian monuments. There is something deeply symbolic in the fact that the most ancient fragment of the Old Testament that has survived to our times is the Nash papyrus containing the Ten Commandments of Moses. (p. 227)

From a semantic, as well as cross-linguistic, point of view, it is remarkable how easily most of the "ten commandments" translate into universal human concepts, some straight into semantic primes (e.g., "don't say something bad about someone else if it is not true"), and some, into universal, or nearly universal, semantic molecules (e.g., "don't kill," "don't steal"). The first commandment, however, is a challenge: "I am the Lord thy God (. . .). Thou shalt have no other gods before me."

It is by no means self-evident what exactly Moses meant by this sentence. Presumably, the word "God" as used here meant something very close to what the first half of chapter 1 of "The Story," "God," says (in simple and cross-translatable English). The phrase "*your* God," however, takes us beyond cross-translatable English: undoubtedly, "God" was for Moses "someone not like people," but "*your* God" cannot stand for "*your* someone" (the word ""someone" does not combine with the word "your").

In chapter 6, this "your" has been interpreted in terms of "thinking"—*your* thinking: I want you to "think like this about me [says God to the people of Israel]: 'God is above us, God is above me.'" Thus, the phrase "your God" is based on a certain understanding of the word "God" (which includes, among others, the components "this someone is not like people" and "this someone is above everything"), and the phrase "your God" commands the Israelites to think about this "someone" as Someone who is "someone above people" and "someone above us."

God's "new name" revealed to Moses takes one of the components of that concept and gives it a special emphasis. In chapter 1, this component was phrased like this: "this someone is now, always was, always will be." Presumably, it was also part of Abraham's concept of "God" ("El"), but it didn't have the same prominence in it as in Moses's concept, where it becomes God's "new name."

So this is how Israelites are to think about God (that Someone who is now, always was, and always will be): "this Someone is above people, this Someone is above us, this Someone is above me"—and they are *not* to think like this about anyone else. This is, I suggest, the core meaning of the first commandment, stated in a form which is both intuitively clear and cross-translatable into all languages.

The second commandment is really an extension of, and an elaboration on, the first one. In the simplest, and probably earliest, form (as given by Men', who draws on biblical scholars like Gerhard Kittel quoted in Men' 1999: 226) it says: "You shall not make for yourself a graven image, or likeness, of God." Considered in that short form, without later accretions, it appears to extend the first commandment from "don't think like this about anyone else" to "don't think like this about anything (any things)."

The later, expanded form of the second commandment ("you shall not make for yourself a graven image or any likeness of anything that is in heaven above, or that is in the earth beneath, or that is in the water under the earth," Exodus 20:4) is clearly aimed at different forms of idolatry common in the ancient Near East. As *The Oxford Companion to the Bible* (1993: 260) notes, "Hebrew [word] *pesel* is variously translated as 'graven image', 'idol', or 'statue'. Three-dimensional images of metal, stone, wood, or clay were ubiquitously venerated in antiquity."

So this is what Moses's second commandment was evidently aimed at: people "venerating" objects (as *The Oxford Companion to the Bible* puts it without distinguishing "worshipping" from "venerating")—either things made by people or things "in the heaven above," like the moon or the sun. It forbade thinking about anything, whether man-made or part of the visible world, like this: "this thing is something above us," "we have to do some things because of this [such as performing certain rituals, bringing offerings etc.]." As any reader of Exodus will know, this is in fact how the Israelites came, at one point, to think about the "Golden Calf," which they asked Aaron, Moses's brother, to make for them (Exodus 32:1–8):

> And when the people saw that Moses delayed to come down out of the
> mount, the people gathered themselves together unto Aaron, and said unto
> him, Up, make us gods, which shall go before us; for as for this Moses, the
> man that brought us up out of the land of Egypt, we wot [know] not what is

become of him. And Aaron said unto them, Break off the golden earrings, which are in the ears of your wives, of your sons, and of your daughters, and bring them unto me. And all the people brake off the golden earrings which were in their ears, and brought them unto Aaron. And he received them at their hand, and fashioned it with a graving tool, after he had made it a molten calf: and they said, These be thy gods, O Israel, which brought thee up out of the land of Egypt. And when Aaron saw it, he built an altar before it; and Aaron made proclamation, and said, Tomorrow is a feast of the Lord. And they rose up early on the morrow, and offered burnt offerings, and brought peace offerings; and the people sat down to eat and to drink, and rose up to play. And the Lord said unto Moses, Go, get thee down; for thy people, which thou broughtest out of the land of Egypt, have corrupted themselves. They have turned aside quickly out of the way which I commanded them: they have made them a molten calf, and have worshipped it, and have sacrificed thereunto, and said, These are the gods, O Israel, which have brought thee up out of the land of Egypt.

As could be expected, after this betrayal by Aaron and the people, Moses gets exceedingly angry, to the point of breaking the two sacred tablets with the Ten Commandments ("and Moses' anger waxed hot, and he cast the tables out of his hands, and brake them beneath the mount," Exodus 3:19); whereupon the Israelites turn back to Yahweh, the true God who had really brought them out of Egypt, and God replaces the tablets with the Ten Commandments. As this story illustrates, the main point of the first two commandments was essentially the same: that people are not to think about anyone or anything in the way they are to think about God; and consequently, they are not to worship anyone or anything other than God. Speaking of Moses's rejection of all forms of idolatry, Men' comments:

> The whole ancient world couldn't give up the idea of God as a being looking like humans or like animals, or at least having some visible form. Moses decidedly rejects any such notions. God is invisible. (. . .) It seems incredible that in such a distant epoch such an elevated, spiritual notion of deity could have emerged. (. . .) Yet there is good evidence that, on the whole, Jews remained faithful to Moses' testament. (p. 229)

Listing all kinds of things that archaeologists found in the soil of Palestine (including representations of cherubs, lions, birds, and Canaanite deities), Men' concludes: "But no representations of Yahweh were found" (p. 229).

And yet, as Christians believe, the invisible God, whose voice Abraham and Moses had heard but whose face they could not see, did want people on earth to see him, in a way. He wanted more: to *live* with people on earth, for some time, like people live, and to become, for some time and for ever more, "God with us." This is the theme of the next four chapters of "The Story."

Commentary on chapter 7: "God speaks through the prophets"

As the little *Compendium of the Catechism of the Catholic Church* (2005: 21) puts it, "The people descended from Abraham would be the trustees of the divine promise made to the patriarchs [i.e. Abraham, Isaac, and Jacob]." Out of this promise arose an expectation. The Orthodox catechism *The Living God* (1989) speaks of this expectation thus:

> The history of Israel is that of a slow and painful ascent toward Christ, with moments of hesitation, rebellion, and human weakness, but also with demonstrations of God's love. (. . .) The secret meaning of this history, which we shall slowly discover, is the mystery of the promise of Jesus Christ, a promise which is announced to the Israelites and for which they have been prepared. (vol. 1, p. 47)

The Hebrew word was not "Christ" (which is a Greek word) but "Messiah" (literally, "the Anointed one"). The anticipation of the Messiah is evident in the Books of the Prophets in the Hebrew Bible, hundreds of years before Jesus was born. When in the Gospel of Luke the last prophet of the Old Testament, John the Baptist, sends his messengers to Jesus with the question: "Are you he who is to come, or shall we look for another?" (Luke 7:20), he is referring to that anticipation voiced by most of the earlier prophets. Jesus replies to the question with a quote from the prophet Isaiah, citing Isaiah's description of what is to be expected when the Messiah comes: "Go and tell John what you have seen and heard: the blind receive their sight, the lame walk, lepers are cleansed, and the deaf hear, the dead are raised up, the poor have good news preached to them" (Luke 7:22).

The anticipation of a Messiah is by no means the predominant theme in what the Prophets are on record as saying to the people of Israel, but it is a persistent one. To quote the Orthodox catechism again:

> *Seeker*: Christ is not the name of Jesus?
>
> *Sage*: No. The name "Christ" [i.e. Messiah]—designated someone unknown, awaited and hoped for, who was described by the prophets before His actual appearance. They knew what His function would be, some of His characteristics, and the role which He would be called upon to play; but they did not know who would fill the role. When Jesus came, some people recognized in Him the Christ for whom they had waited.

Christians see prophetic images of the coming of Jesus as evident in particular in the writings of the prophet Isaiah, as in the following passage:

> Behold My servant, whom I uphold, My chosen, in whom My soul delights; I have put My Spirit upon him, he will bring forth justice to the

nations. He will not cry or lift up his voice, or make it heard in the street; A bruised reed he will not break, and a dimly burning wick he will not quench; he will faithfully bring justice. He will not fail or be discouraged till he has established justice in the earth; And the coastlands wait for his law. (Isaiah 42:1–4)

In another passage in Isaiah, God's servant—the Messiah, the anointed one— speaks in the first person:

The Spirit of the Lord God is upon me, Because the Lord has anointed me to bring good tidings to the afflicted; He has sent me to bind up the brokenhearted, To proclaim liberty to the captives, And the opening of the prison to those who are bound. . . . (Isaiah 61:1)

In Luke's Gospel (Luke 4:21), Jesus reads this text from a scroll in the synagogue in Nazareth, and applies it to himself, saying: "Today this scripture has been fulfilled in your hearing." This theme—the anticipation of a Messiah in the discourses of the prophets—is continued in chapter 8 of "The Story."

Before moving to that chapter, a few comments on particular linguistic challenges encountered in chapter 7. The first one was of course the concept of "prophet" itself—in the sense in which it is used in the Hebrew Bible. The main components with the help of which this concept has been articulated here are these four: (1) "someone not like many other people" (it should be noted that this is different from "someone not like other people," which implies uniqueness); (2) when someone like this spoke to people of Israel, God was with this someone (i.e., something like "divine inspiration"), and (3) often "prophets" spoke like this: "something will happen" (i.e., a "prophetic" quality, related to the future and to God's plans).

Another point worth commenting on is the concept of "virgin" in Isaiah's prophecy about the Messiah's mother. As has often been pointed out, the underlying Hebrew word, *alma*, could refer to a young woman in general, but the word used in the Greek translation of the Hebrew scriptures called the Septuagint (third century bc) is *parthenos* "virgin." In "The Story" the idea of a mother who is also a virgin has been rendered like this: "a woman will be this someone's mother, this someone will be her son, no man will be this someone's father."

Commentary on chapter 8: "It all happened as the prophets said"

As Benedict XVI (2012a: 64) writes in his *Jesus of Nazareth: The Infancy Narratives*, "It was not with a timelessness of myth that Jesus came to be born among us. He belongs to a time that can be precisely dated and a geographical area that is precisely defined." One historical fact that anchors Jesus's birth in time is the death of King Herod the Great, who is known to have died in the year 4 bc. Jesus was born not long before that. (It was a sixth-century monk, Dionysius Exiguus, who miscalculated the date, placing the beginning of the new era a few years after Jesus's birth.)

Matthew's Gospel grounds Jesus's birth in time and place with reference to King Herod, to the town of Bethlehem—where King David was born and where, according to prophet Micah, the Messiah would be born—and with reference to Jerusalem, which as *The Oxford Companion to the Bible* (1993: 352) puts it, "was integral to Judaism since the time of king David." (The *Oxford Companion* notes, on the same page, that "the name Jerusalem occurs 660 times in the Hebrew Bible.")

As described vividly by Men' in his *Son of Man*, Herod, who was a usurper and suspected treason everywhere, murdered his own sons, his wife, his wife's mother and brother, and many other relatives and courtiers. So when he heard that a new "King of the Jews" was born in Judea, he was alarmed and determined to act quickly. Matthew's Gospel recounts Herod's response like this (see chapter 10 of "The Story"):

> Then Herod summoned the wise men secretly and ascertained from them what time the star appeared; and he sent them to Bethlehem, saying, "Go and search diligently for the child, and when you have found him bring me word, that I too may come and worship him." When they had heard the king they went their way; and lo, the star which they had seen in the East went before them, till it came to rest over the place where the child was. When they saw the star, they rejoiced exceedingly with great joy; and going into the house they saw the child with Mary his mother, and they fell down and worshiped him. Then, opening their treasures, they offered him gifts, gold and frankincense and myrrh. And being warned in a dream not to return to Herod, they departed to their own country by another way. (Matthew 2:7–12)

Thus Matthew, who was addressing his Gospel mainly to Jews, places the birth of Jesus in the context of the history of the people of Israel. Luke, who was writing mainly for Gentiles, places Jesus's birth in the context of world history. His main historical point of reference is not King Herod but the Roman emperor Caesar Augustus (see chapter 10 of "The Story"):

> In those days a decree went out from Caesar Augustus that all the world should be enrolled. This was the first enrollment, when Quirinius was governor of Syria. And all went to be enrolled, each to his own city. And Joseph also went up from Galilee, from the city of Nazareth, to Judea, to the city of David, which is called Bethlehem, because he was of the house and lineage of David, to be enrolled with Mary, his betrothed, who was with child. And while they were there, the time came for her to be delivered.

And she gave birth to her first-born son and wrapped him in swaddling cloths, and laid him in a manger, because there was no place for them in the inn. (Luke 2:1–7)

Commenting on this passage from Luke's Gospel, Benedict XVI (2012a) highlights the convergence of the universal and the concrete:

Augustus' instruction regarding the registration, for tax purposes, of all the citizens of the *ecumēnē* leads Joseph, together with Mary, his betrothed, to Bethlehem, the city of David, and thus it helps to bring to fulfilment the promise of the prophet Micah that the shepherd of Israel would be born in that city (cf. 5:1-3). The Emperor unwittingly contributes to the realization of the prophecy: the history of the Roman Empire is interwoven with the history of the salvation that God established with Israel. The history of God's election, hitherto confined to Israel, enters the wider world, it enters world history. God, who is the God of Israel and of all peoples, shows himself to be the true guiding force behind all history. (p. 64)

Chapter 10 presents the circumstances of Jesus's birth. In chapter 8, the focus is on history and geography, and so the semantic challenges include, in addition to the meaning of the name "Jesus," concepts like "empire," "Caesar," and "temple," and ideas such as Israel's subordination to Rome, Herod's status as a protégé of the Romans, the role of the temple in Jewish religious life, and the special status of Jerusalem, as the city of David (it was David's capital, independent of the twelve tribes, the place where the all-important Ark of the Covenant was kept) and the "city of God."

To start with the name of Jesus, traditionally explained as "God saves," I have paraphrased it with a much longer but cross-translatable sentence: "when something very bad happens to people, God does very good things for them." The complex notion of "empire" (in fact, "Roman empire") has been paraphrased with two sentences, anchored in the concept of "country": "(Palestine) was one small part of something very very big, this something was called the Roman empire. It was something not like anything else at that time, many countries in many parts of the earth were part of it." (The concept of "country" was introduced earlier in "The Story" in chapters 4, 5, and 6.) The concept of "Caesar" has been introduced via the simpler concept of "king" (introduced earlier in chapter 7); and the concept of "temple," via the concept of "house." Herod's status as a protégé of Rome, imposed on the country as a king by the Romans, against the wishes of the Jews, is captured in the sentence "Herod was at that time King of Judea, as the Romans wanted, (not as the people of Israel wanted)."

Jerusalem is described, in Minimal English, as "a city not like any other city"—a perception shared by Jews and Christians. As *The Oxford Companion* (1993) notes, "The idea of the centrality of Jerusalem has been a mainstay in Christianity, in various ways, since its inception" (p. 660). In chapter 8, this centrality of Jerusalem to the story of God and people is linked, first, with King David and the Temple, and then, with the person of Jesus: "[Jesus] often spoke to people in Jerusalem . . . ; he felt something very good toward Jerusalem (he knew that very bad things would happen to Jerusalem, that the Romans would do very bad things to it; when he thought about it, he wept); many things happened to Jesus in Jerusalem; he died in Jerusalem."

In modern times, the particularity of these times and these places—Bethlehem and Jerusalem, "in the days of Herod the king," "in the days of Caesar Augustus" (the birth of Jesus, Matthew 2:1; Luke 2:11), "in the fifteenth year of the reign of the Emperor Tiberius" (the beginning of Jesus's public ministry, Luke 3:1)—has often been viewed with suspicion. Can "a particular moment in history" be of unique significance for "God's saving action for all people?," asks philosopher and theologian Vernon White (1991: 115–116). He replies with a clear yes: "In order to touch the whole world effectively, God did indeed enter deeply and uniquely into one part of it."

This is how Christians have always seen the interplay of the universal and the particular in the story of God and people; and before them, the prophets, especially Isaiah, who, eight centuries before Jesus, spoke to the people of Israel on Yahweh's behalf: "You are my servant, Israel, in whom I will be glorified. (. . .) I will give you as a light to the nations, that my salvation may reach to the end of the earth" (Isaiah 49: 4, 6).

According to Matthew's Gospel, the birth of Jesus in Bethlehem in the days of King Herod "took place to fulfil what the Lord had spoken by the prophet [Isaiah]: 'Behold, a virgin shall conceive and bear a son, and his name shall be called Emmanuel, God with us'" (Matthew 1:22; Isaiah 7:14). Jesus was born to the Israelite girl Mariam in Bethlehem in Judea, in the days of King Herod, but (to use Minimal English) God wanted him to be the Emmanuel, "God with us," for all people, everywhere on earth.

Commentary on chapter 9: "A woman called Mary says 'yes' to God"

Commenting on a Russian icon known as "The Virgin of the Sign," the Orthodox catechism *The Living God* (1989) writes:

> The icon represents Mary bearing in her womb the Son of God. It is called "the Virgin of the Sign" because it illustrates the prophecy of Isaiah: "Hear then, O house of David! . . . the Lord Himself will give you a sign. Behold, a virgin shall conceive and bear a son, and shall call his name Immanuel [that is, God is with us]. (Is 7:13-14)"

This prophecy is accomplished on the day of the Annunciation. The Virgin receives the angel's announcement by declaring her acceptance. This is "Mary's *fiat*." In Latin, *fiat* means "let it come to be." Mary's answer to the angel, her freely given "yes," enables her to become the Mother of God. Without this free acceptance, God could not have become incarnate, for God never forces a person's conscience and always waits for us to respond of our own free will.

The angel Gabriel said to the Mother of God: "Hail, O favoured one [or "much graced one"], the Lord is with you" (Lk 1:28). A little later, when Mary meets her cousin Elizabeth, the mother of John the Baptist, the latter sees her as the Virgin with child. She recognizes the "sign" of Isaiah by the joyful leaping in her womb of the child who is to be the prophet of the Most High and the forerunner of the Lord. Then Elizabeth completes the angel's salutation by adding: "Blessed are you among women, and blessed is the fruit of your womb" (Lk 1:41-42). The message of the angel now coincides with the prophecy of Isaiah. This prophecy was made more precise by the Septuagint translation, done two centuries before Jesus Christ, which rendered the Hebrew word *alma*, "young woman," by the Greek *parthenos*, "virgin." (p. 24)

As discussed by the scientist and Anglican theologian John Polkinghorne, "modern thought" has tended to find it difficult to accept the idea of a virginal conception. Quoting another theologian's, J. A. T. Robinson (1984), opinion that "the only choice open to us is between a virgin birth and an illegitimate birth" (p. 4) Polkinghorne (1994) comments: "A certain type of modern mind can find it quite appropriate to suppose that Jesus was born as a fruit of an illicit union but I cannot share the view that this is so" (p. 145). (As Polkinghorne notes, "In Mark 6.3. he [Jesus] is described as 'son of Mary', which is totally contrary to Jewish usage which habitually associated a son with his father.") After carefully considering the subject, Polkinghorne accepts the formulae of the creeds: "born of the Virgin Mary" (the Apostles' Creed) and "he became incarnate of the Virgin Mary and became man" (the Nicene Creed), and concludes:

> Such considerations, together with the symbolic appropriateness of the fusion of divine initiative and human co-operation which the virginal conception would signify as the origin of Emmanuel ('God with us'), along with the recognition, already referred to, that the incarnation is the union of the mythical and the historical, persuade me that the words 'born of the Virgin Mary' can be a proper part of the creed of a bottom-up thinker. (p. 145)

Benedict XVI (2012a) in his book *Jesus of Nazareth: The Infancy Narratives* stresses in particular the fact that Jesus's genealogy in Matthew's Gospel ends with a woman: Mary.

> Throughout the generations, we find the formula "Abraham was the father
> of Isaac . . . ". But in the end, there is something quite different. In Jesus'
> case there is no reference to fatherhood, instead we read: "Jacob [was] the
> father of Joseph the husband of Mary, of whom Jesus was born, who is
> called Christ." (Mt 1:16) (p. 7)

There seems to be hardly any doubt that Matthew saw Jesus's conception in
the same way as Luke: "That which is conceived in Mary is of the Holy Spirit"
(Matthew 1:20).

In the same book, Benedict XVI (2012a: 56–57) quotes the pre-eminent
Swiss Reformed theologian Karl Barth, who "pointed out that there are two
moments in the story of Jesus when God intervenes directly in the material
world: the virgin birth and the resurrection from the tomb, in which Jesus
did not remain, nor see corruption. These two moments are a scandal to the
modern spirit. God is 'allowed' to act in ideas and thoughts, in the spiritual
domain—but not in the material. That is shocking. He does not belong there."

Opposing such a "modern" way of thinking, Benedict XVI goes so far as
to put the virgin birth on the same level as the real resurrection from the tomb,
and to call it "a fundamental element of our faith":

> If God does not also have this [creative] power, then he simply is not
> God. But he does have this power, and through the conception and resur-
> rection of Jesus Christ he has ushered a new creation. So as the Creator
> he is also our Redeemer. Hence the conception and birth of Jesus from
> the Virgin Mary is a fundamental element of our faith and a radiant sign
> of hope. (p. 57)

In chapter 9 of "The Story of God and People" Mary says to the angel: "I
want it to happen to me as you say. I want it to happen to me because God
wants it." In chapter 10, "The Story" continues: "When Mary said to the
angel: 'I want it to happen to me as you say' something happened in her body.
Because of this, some time after this, she gave birth to a child (a son); she called
him Jesus, as the angel said."

Commentary on chapter 10: "Jesus is born"

From a semantic point of view, the main challenges in chapter 10 are related to
those we encountered in the three preceding chapters: the question of Jesus's
conception, and his mother's virginity. The sentences "something happened in
her [Mary's] body" and "because of this, some time after this, she gave birth to
a child" could of course apply to any child's conception and birth: What is unusual is the statement that "no man was Jesus's father," which matches Isaiah's
prophecy about the "Emmanuel."

It should perhaps be noted here that according to Jewish law, Mary was already married (betrothed to Joseph) at the time when she saw the angel, although they had not yet lived together as husband and wife. This means that there was never any doubt about Joseph's legal status as Jesus's father. This was particularly important in view of Jewish understanding of descent: Joseph was a descendant of King David, and since he was seen as Jesus's (legal) father, Jesus, too, legally belonged to the "house of David" and was seen as a descendant of David ("a son of David," fulfilling the prophesy about "the son of David" who would be "king forever").

At the same time, Joseph—like Mary—was a conscious and willing participant in the execution of God's plan: Jesus needed to have a legal guardian, Mary needed to have a husband, and Joseph's consent was crucial. As the third line of chapter 10 puts it, "Before Joseph was Mary's husband, he knew that no man was this child's father, he knew it because God wanted him to know it." Joseph agreed to play the role that God wanted him to play. What Polkinghorne (1994: 145) says about "the fusion of divine initiative and human cooperation" applies not only to Mary but also to Joseph.

According to the New Testament, Joseph's "Davidic descent" explains also why Jesus was born in Bethlehem and not in Nazareth, where Mary and Joseph lived before he was born. Since Bethlehem was "David's city" and since the Messiah was expected to be born in Bethlehem, this explanation is an important part of the story. The factual truth of this account (though doubted by sceptics) is supported by many details of history and archeology. *The Oxford Companion to the Bible* (1993) writes:

> Christian tradition, perhaps as early as the second century CE, identified a cave as the site of Jesus' birth. About 338 CE, [Caesar] Constantine had a church built over the grotto (and Justinian reconstructed it in the early sixth century). Jerome settled in Bethlehem in 386; here he made the Latin Vulgate translation of the Bible. (p. 78)

The cave mentioned in this quote deserves a comment. Tourists who come to Bethlehem in the third millennium can still see numerous rocky caves around the town, and it has been established that "in the area around Bethlehem rocky caves had been used as stables since ancient times" (cf. Stuhlmacher, *Die Geburt des Immanuel*, 2006: 51, quoted in Benedict XVI 2012a: 67). The belief that Jesus was born in such a cave is supported not only by the early Christian tradition but also by a historical fact concerning the Romans. To quote Benedict XVI (2012a):

> As early as Justin Martyr († 165) and Origen († 254), we find the tradition that Jesus was born in a cave, which Christians in Palestine could point to. The fact that after the expulsion of the Jews from the holy Land in the second century, Rome turned the cave into a shrine of Tammuz-Adonis,

thereby evidently intending to suppress the Christian memorial cult, confirms the age of this shrine and also shows how important it was thought to be by the Romans. Local traditions are frequently a more reliable source than written records. So a considerable measure of credibility may be assigned to the tradition that Bethlehem was Jesus' birthplace, a tradition to which the Church of the Nativity also bears witness. (p. 67)

A few linguistic aspects of this chapter particularly worth noting include the occurrence of several universal or near-universal semantic molecules, such as "born," "child," "mother," "father," "husband," "star," and "sing," as well as several culture-specific molecules such as "shepherd," "king," "money," "oxen," and "cave." From a syntactic point of view, the line "you will feel something very very bad because of this" deserves a comment. It is cross-translatable but does it capture adequately the meaning of Simeon's words directed to Mary the child's mother: "and a sword will pierce through your own soul"? Perhaps not. I have added, therefore, another line: "You will feel something like someone can feel when something very bad is happening to their body."

Simeon's other prophetic words referred to in this chapter (10) are these: "mine eyes have seen thy salvation which thou hast prepared in the presence of all people, a light for revelation to the Gentiles, and the glory of the people Israel" (Luke 2:30–32), recalling words of the prophet Isaiah such as these: "I will also give thee as a light to the Gentiles, that thou mayst be my salvation onto the end of the earth" (Isaiah 49:6). In "The Story" these words have been rendered in the lines "Because this child was born, all people can know you well; first, the people of Israel can know you well, after this, people in all parts of the earth can know you well because of this; this child will be like the light." (The sentence: "he [Simeon] said this with the words of the prophet Isaiah" is an abbreviation, and may not be fully cross-translatable; it will be cross-translatable, however, if it is "unpacked" with the help of a reference to what Isaiah said, to the specific words he used and to what Simeon said, and the words *he* used.)

This "Story" will return to Simeon's (and Isaiah's) prophecy in chapter 19, and the commentary on it. Here, I will end with another quotation from *Jesus of Nazareth: The Infancy Narratives*, in which Simeon's prophetic words are referred to as "a canticle":

This canticle contains two Christological statements: Jesus is "the light to enlighten the Gentiles," and he gives "glory to your people Israel" (Lk 2:32). Both expressions are taken from the prophet Isaiah. The reference to the "light to enlighten the Gentiles" comes from the first and second Suffering Servant songs (cf. Is. 42:6; 49:6). Jesus is identified as Isaiah's Suffering Servant—a mysterious figure, pointing toward the future. Central to the Servant's mission is universality, revelation to the Gentiles, to whom he brings God's light. The text referring to the glory of Israel is found in the prophet's words of consolation to suffering Israel, for whom help is promised through God's saving power (cf. Is 46:13). (Benedict XVI 2012a: 84)

Commentary on chapter 11: "Jesus lives in Nazareth"

The years when Jesus lived in Nazareth are often referred to as "the hidden years." The framework of his external life is quite clear, but what was happening in his thoughts? The *Catechism of the Catholic Church* (1994) writes:

> *The mysteries of Jesus' hidden life*
> During the greater part of his life Jesus shared the condition of the vast majority of human beings: a daily life spent without evident greatness, a life of manual labor. His religious life was that of a Jew obedient to the law of God, a life in the community. From this whole period it is revealed to us that Jesus was "obedient" to his parents and that he "increased in wisdom and in stature, and in favour with God and man." (p. 134)

In "The Story," the statement that Jesus was "obedient" to his parents has been translated into cross-translatable language like this: "when they wanted him to do something, he did it, when they wanted him not to do something, he didn't do it."

In fact, however, (as Luke's Gospel tells us) on one occasion Jesus did something which from Mary's and Joseph's point of view did not look like obedience at all, and which caused them a great deal of anguish. When Jesus was twelve years old, he accompanied his parents on their pilgrimage to Jerusalem for the feast of the Passover. (The Torah required that every Israelite visited the Temple in Jerusalem three times a year, at Passover, Pentecost, and Feast of Tabernacles.) In his *Infancy Narratives,* Benedict XVI (2012a) writes about what happened as follows:

> On the journey home, something unexpected happens. Jesus does not travel with the others, but stays behind in Jerusalem. His parents become aware of this only at the end of the first day's journey. For them it was evidently quite normal to assume that Jesus was somewhere among the group of pilgrims. Luke uses the word *synodia*—"pilgrim community", the technical term for the traveling caravan. (. . .) The twelve-year-old was free to spend time with friends and children his own age, and to remain in their company during the journey. Naturally, his parents expected to see him when evening came. (p. 122)

But when the evening came, Mary and Joseph found that Jesus was not with other children, and realized that they needed to go back to Jerusalem to look for him. As Benedict XVI puts it: "These are days spent suffering the absence of Jesus, days of darkness, whose heaviness can be sensed in the mother's words: 'Child, why have you treated us so? Behold, your father and I have been looking for you anxiously' (*Lk* 2:48)" (Benedict XVI 2012a: 123).

Jesus's answer (which one presumes Luke heard from Mary) was completely unexpected and incomprehensible to his parents: "How is it that you sought me? Did you not know that I must be in my Father's house?" (Luke 2:49) To quote Benedict XVI again:

> There are two principal elements to note in this reply. Mary had said: "Your father and I have been looking for you anxiously." Jesus corrects her: I *am* with my father. My father is not Joseph, but another—God himself. It is to him that I belong, and here I am with him. Could Jesus' divine sonship be presented any more clearly?
>
> The second element is directly linked with this. Jesus uses the word "must," and he acts in accordance with what *must* be. The Son, the child, *must* be with his father. (. . .) what might seem like disobedience or inappropriate freedom vis-à-vis his parents is in reality the actual expression of his filial obedience. He is in the Temple not as a rebel against his parents, but precisely as the obedient one, acting out the same obedience that leads to the Cross and the resurrection. (p. 124)

From a theological point of view, two most interesting questions arising from this part of the Gospel story have to do with Jesus's self-knowledge, and the notion of the kingdom of God. To begin with the first of them, one may ask: Did Jesus always know who he was and what his mission was? As we have seen, the *Catechism of the Catholic Church* emphasizes Jesus's "total consecration to a mission that flows from his divine sonship." One can ask, however: Did he know at that stage that he was "God's Son"?

In this connection, it is worth noting that Benedict XVI draws attention to Luke's statement (following the account of the episode of staying behind in Jerusalem) that "he grew in wisdom." The full sentence is: "he grew in wisdom and in stature, and in favour with God and people" (Luke 3:51–52). Quoting this sentence in his *Infancy Narratives* Benedict XVI comments first that evidently the twelve-year-old Jesus "knew the Father—God—intimately" and was with him "on familiar terms," and then he adds:

> And yet it is also true that his wisdom *grows*. As a human being, he does not live in some abstract omniscience, but he is rooted in a concrete history, a place and a time, in the different phases of human life, and this is what gives concrete shape to his knowledge. So it emerges clearly here that he thought and learned in human fashion. (p. 127)

"The Story," too, emphasizes that during his "hidden years" Jesus lived like other people lived in that place at that time, and that he worked as a carpenter, like Joseph. It adds another motif, however: Jesus's interest in reading the Bible, and (presumably) trying to understand who he was and what his mission was. In Luke's account, when Mary and Joseph finally found Jesus in the temple, he was "sitting among the teachers, listening to them and asking them questions; and all who heard him were amazed at his understanding and his answers" (Luke 2:46–47). This deep familiarity with the Hebrew Bible that Jesus already had as a twelve-year-old boy suggests that throughout his childhood he was eagerly studying it and thinking about it.

Turning now to the second question, the proclamation of the kingdom of God, we may start with a quote from Mark's Gospel: "Jesus came into Galilee, preaching the Gospel of God, and saying: 'The time is fulfilled, and the kingdom of God is at hand: repent, and believe in the gospel'" (Mark 1:14–15).

In the Gospel accounts, and in many other retellings of Jesus's life, the first thing that is mentioned after the description of Jesus's hidden years in Nazareth is Jesus's encounter with John the Baptist, near the Jordan river. The proclamation of the kingdom of God comes after that. In this "Story," however, the idea of that proclamation is mentioned first (in chapter 11), because one imagines that this was what prompted Jesus to leave Nazareth in the first place. This means that the challenge of explaining this idea in simple and cross-translatable words needs to be faced in chapter 11, before the chapters devoted to John the Baptist (12 and 13).

As the catechism of the Ukrainian Catholic Church *Christ Our Pascha* (2016: 141, English version) puts it, "Christ began his public ministry with the proclamation: 'The time is fulfilled, and the Kingdom of God has come near; repent and believe in the good news' (Mk 1:15)." As discussed in the "Introduction" to the present book, the idea behind that proclamation is not self-evident, and commentaries which try to explain it in complex theological language do not make it any clearer. In chapter 11 of "The Story" this idea is introduced with reference to what the prophets were saying for a long time: "At some time some things will happen in this country not like at any other time, at that time God will do something very good for all people"; this is followed by the good news: "these things are happening now," and an explanation, both revelatory and cryptic: "It is like this: people can now live with God like never before, people can know now that God is near."

Whether or not this phrasing renders what Jesus meant as well as it can be done is debatable, and there is certainly room for adjustments here. It would be an illusion, however, to think that the phrasing proposed here can be made clearer and more accurate by means of learned, technical, and non-cross-translatable words.

Commentary on chapter 12: "The prophet called John the Baptist"

In the Gospel of Matthew (3:1–3) we can read:

In those days came John the Baptist, preaching in the wilderness of Judea, "Repent, for the kingdom of heaven is at hand." For this is he

who was spoken of by the prophet Isaiah when he said, "The voice of
one crying in the wilderness: Prepare the way of the Lord, make his
paths straight."

We know exactly when this happened: as Luke's Gospel (3:1–2) tells us, it
happened "in the fifteenth year of the reign of Tiberius Caesar, Pontius Pilate
being governor of Judaea, and Herod [Antipas] being tetrarch of Galilee,
and his brother Philip Tetrarch of Ituraea and the reign of Trachanitis, and
Lysanias the tetrarch of Abilene, Annas and Caiaphas being the high priests."
The Orthodox catechism *The Living God* (1989) writes about John's activities
"in the wilderness of Judea" like this:

> John, inspired by the Spirit of God, retires to the banks of the Jordan.
> There the last of the prophets of the Former Covenant announces the im-
> minent coming of the Kingdom of God, that is, the Kingdom of which
> God's Christ will be king. He preaches repentance, for only those who are
> converted and who turn away from evil towards God can become part of
> this kingdom. "Repent, for the Kingdom of heaven is at hand", he repeats
> constantly (Mt 3:2; see also Mk 1:4; Lk 3:3). All those who were converted
> to the Lord, John prepared for entrance into the Kingdom of God by
> washing them of their sins, that is, by "baptizing" them in the Jordan by
> immersion in the waters. (vol. 1, pp. 54–55)

As the Gospel of Matthew presents it, the crowds of people who came to
John to listen to him and to be baptized were from Judea. But one day, Jesus
came from Galilee and also asked John to baptize him. The encounter between
the two is mysterious. First, John says to Jesus: "I need to be baptised by you,
and [do] you come to me?," and then Jesus responds: "Let it be so now; for
thus it is fitting for us to fulfil all righteousness" (Matthew 3:15). As this exchange between John and Jesus is portrayed in Minimal English in chapter 13,
John says to Jesus: "I can't baptize *you*, you can baptize *me*," to which Jesus
responds: "I *want* you to do it. It will be good if it happens like this now. It will
be as God wants." The biblical concept of "righteousness" is explained here by
means of the cross-translatable phrase "as God wants."

The exchange is puzzling for two reasons. First, it is not clear (at this point)
who John thinks Jesus is, and why he initially protests at Jesus's request to baptize him. As we will see in chapter 13, Jesus's identity becomes clear to John
during the baptism, but evidently even before that he regards Jesus as being
"someone above me." Second, it is also mysterious why Jesus, who knows that
he is *not* a sinner, wants to be baptized by John. Benedict XVI (2007a: 16)
writes about it like this: "So far, nothing has been said about pilgrims from
Galilee; the action seemed limited to the region of Judea. But the real novelty
here is (. . .) the fact that he—Jesus—(. . .) blends into the grey mass of sinners
waiting on the banks of the Jordan."

Benedict XVI develops here a complex and multifaceted commentary from which I will single out only two ideas, linked with two key words: "solidarity" and "identification." Thus, speaking of Jesus's "Yes" to God's will expressed in his request for baptism, Benedict XVI writes:

> In a world marked by sin (. . .), this Yes to the entire will of God also expresses solidarity with us, who have incurred guilt but yearn for right-eousness (. . .) Jesus loaded the burden of all mankind's guilt upon his shoulders; (. . .) He inaugurated his public activity by stepping into the place of sinners. (p. 18)

Referring to the Christian baptism as practiced later by Jesus's disciples and their successors, Benedict XVI writes: "To accept the invitation to be baptised now means to go to the place of Jesus' Baptism. It is to go where he identified himself with us and to receive there our identification with him" (p. 18). The idea of "solidarity" with sinners, that is, with the whole of humankind, is also strongly developed by Balthasar (1990).

But how to understand and explain these ideas of "solidarity" and "iden-tification" through languages which have no such words? Chapter 12 of "The Story" attempts to do so by means of two lines, framed as a message that Jesus wanted to convey by undergoing the baptism (which he did not need): "I want this to happen to me as it happens to other people. I want to be with other people, I feel something very good toward all people."

It could be argued that in this context, the expression "I want to be with other people" is used figuratively. What matters, however, is that this expression is cross-translatable, and also, that framed as it is here (between "I want this to happen to me as it happens to other people" and "I feel something very good to-ward all people") it is intuitively clear. Jesus "identifies himself" with sinners and expresses "solidarity" with them not by saying "I am like you" but by expressing his love for them and his desire "to be with them" in what happens to them.

Commentary on chapter 13: "John the Baptist baptizes Jesus"

In the Orthodox catechism *The Living God* (1989, vol. 1) we read:

> While in the desert John, the greatest of the prophets, receives the mes-sage: "he on whom you see the Spirit descend and remain, this is He who baptizes with the Holy Spirit" (Jn 1:33). Thus God lets John know (. . .) the sign by which he would recognize the Son of God. (. . .) This sign, which shows clearly that He is the anointed one (. . .) will be the descent and indwelling of the Holy Spirit. John will see the invisible Spirit Himself anointing God's Elect, the One whom He has chosen to reign forever on the throne of David. (p. 54)

When Jesus of Nazareth comes to John, John doesn't consider himself worthy to baptize him, although he doesn't recognize him immediately as the Messiah. But Jesus insists, and John does baptize him, as he baptizes everyone else. *The Living God* (1989) writes about it like this:

> As soon as John baptizes Him, he sees "the Spirit of God descending like a dove, and alighting on Him" (Mt 3:13-17). This is the long-awaited sign. Jesus is the One anointed by the Spirit of God; thus it is Jesus who is revealed to be the Christ. From heaven a voice is heard exclaiming: "This is My beloved Son, with whom I am well pleased" (Mt 3:17). John understands. He recognizes Jesus to be the Messiah, the Christ, and proclaims that the promise of His coming has been fulfilled.
>
> The baptism of Jesus is not only His epiphany or manifestation to the world as Christ. It also manifests Him as the Son of God. As such He *is* the "theophany," the manifestation of God, for He reveals to us the great mystery of God as Holy Trinity.
>
> John saw the Holy Spirit descend upon Jesus in the form of a dove and remain upon Him. The word "remain" expresses the idea that, from all eternity, the Holy Spirit dwells in Him of whom the heavenly voice said, "This is My beloved Son."
>
> Accordingly, St Cyril of Jerusalem [4th century] tells us that in manifesting Jesus as Christ, the baptism of Jesus reveals to us at the same time the mystery of the divine Trinity. (vol. 1, pp. 56–57)

So this is what Christians mean when they talk about the "Holy Trinity." The phrase does not occur in the New Testament, and it does not occur in the Apostles' Creed or in the Nicene Creed. Nor does it occur in "The Story." Nonetheless, the idea of God manifesting himself as the Father, the Son, and the Holy Spirit is present in all four Gospels in relation to Jesus's baptism. It is also present in the Christian creeds. To quote from the Nicene Creed:

> I believe in one God, the Father almighty (. . .)

> I believe in one Lord Jesus Christ, the Only Begotten Son of God, born of the Father before all ages (. . .)

> I believe in the Holy Spirit, the Lord, the giver of life, who proceeds from the Father and the Son (. . .)

Speaking of the "epiphany" of God at the moment of Jesus's baptism, *The Living God* draws attention to the famous icon painted by fifteenth-century Russian monk Andrew Rublev and known as "The Holy Trinity." In this icon, Rublev illustrates an enigmatic episode from the Hebrew Bible (Genesis 18), where three angels visit Abraham. Mysteriously, Abraham addresses these angels sometimes in the plural, and sometimes in the singular, as "Lord."

> And the Lord appeared to him by the oaks of Mamre, as he sat at the door of his tent in the heat of the day. He lifted up his eyes and looked, and

behold, three men stood in front of him. When he saw them, he ran from the tent door to meet them, and bowed himself to the earth, and said, "My Lord, if I have found favor in your sight, do not pass by your servant. . . ." (Genesis 18:1–3)

Christians speak in such cases of the Hebrew Bible "prefiguring" (anticipating) the New Testament. So *The Living God* (1989) links this mysterious scene at Mamre, as represented in Rublev's icon, with the scene of Jesus's baptism:

Let us return to the baptism of Jesus, to the moment when He comes up out of the water. We have already described how John the Baptist sees the Christ upon whom the Spirit remains, and hears the voice of the Father call Jesus His beloved Son. John recognizes one God in three Persons. At the Jordan the Trinity is manifested for the first time. The Church describes this manifestation to us through the icon and the troparion [hymn] of the feast of the Epiphany (or Theophany) [6 January]. (vol. 1, p. 57)

When John understands that Jesus is the long awaited Messiah—the Son of God—he describes him to all those present as "the lamb of God." Thus *The Living God* continues:

He remembers as well that Isaiah had prophesied, saying: "He was wounded for our transgressions, he was bruised for our iniquities, . . . like a lamb that is led to the slaughter, . . . [he was] striken for the transgression of my people . . ." (Is 53:5, 7, 8). That is why, in identifying Jesus with this Suffering Servant, John add: "Behold the Lamb of God who takes away the sin of the world!" (Jn 1:29). (p. 55)

After the baptism and the "epiphany," Jesus goes into the desert. What happens there is described in the Gospels in a different genre than the earlier events based on John's testimony and the recollections of other eyewitnesses. In "The Story," too, what happens in the desert is framed differently from the events at the river Jordan. One word which is conspicuously absent from this account is "temptation" (a word which is not cross-translatable); but the idea is clearly there. It is conveyed mainly by means of different configurations of simple and universal concepts "say," "want," "happen," "good," and "bad." The outcome of the exchange builds mainly on the concepts "know," "want," and "do": Jesus "knew what God wanted him to do. He wanted to do it."

Commentary on chapter 14: "What Jesus did when he didn't live in Nazareth anymore"

One of the most widely accepted facts about Jesus is that, as it is often put, he was an itinerary Galilean preacher. The themes at the heart of Jesus's preaching were God (what God is like), people (what is good for people), and something that he called "the kingdom of God." He often called his teaching "the good news." Trying to capture that "good news" in simple and cross-translatable words, I have posited these two main components: "something very good is happening now," and "people can live with God now like never before, God is near." In addition to teaching, Jesus healed people of their various illnesses, and "disabilities," physical and mental. Polkinghorne (2011) writes:

> Perhaps the most certain fact about the deeds of Jesus is that he was an outstanding healer. There are many healing stories in the Gospels and they could not be excised without destroying the whole fabric of the narrative. A repeated theme is controversy about the propriety of healing on the Sabbath. This was clearly a point of sharp contention between Jesus and the Jewish authorities and this could not have been the case unless there actually were such healings. Quite often these healings are depicted in terms of exorcism, the casting out of evil spirits (Mark 1.21-28, 32-34 and so on). Of course this is not how we would understand them today. It is important to remember that Jesus was a first-century Jew and so he and his contemporaries naturally interpreted his deeds in terms of the idiom of their day. (p. 66)

These healings were always asked for: Jesus responded to people's faith in him. ("I know that you can do something very good for me, I know that if you do it, I will not be like this anymore"). In his hometown, Nazareth, he couldn't heal people because of their lack of faith: he "could do no mighty work there, except that he laid his hands upon a few sick people and healed them. And he marvelled because of their unbelief" (Mark 6:5–6). As Polkinghorne (1989: 53) puts it, Jesus's healings "were not just naked acts of power imposed without the collaborative assent of those to be healed." This is why in chapter 14 of "The Story" I have formulated the nature of the "disability" in the first person: "I can't see," "I can't hear," "I can't move." (The other most typical case was that of parents begging Jesus to do something good for their child. In Minimal English: "something very bad is happening to his/her body, because of this, I want you to do something good for him/her, I know that you can do it").

But what exactly are miracles—and what exactly do Christians mean when they speak of Jesus's miracles in general and miraculous healings in particular? Polkinghorne (1989) writes:

> Miracles must be perceptions of a deeper rationality than that which we encounter in the everyday occasions which make visible a more profound level of divine activity. They are transparent moments in which the kingdom is found to be manifestly present. (p. 51)

Trying to say something about the subject in simple and cross-translatable words, chapter 14 of "The Story" focuses on two simple questions: "what did Jesus do?" and "why did he do it?" The basic answer to the first of these questions is that "wherever he went, Jesus did very good things for people," and that "nobody else could do things like this." As for the second question, the basic answer offered here is that Jesus did these things because he wanted to do something very good for people (when he saw that they felt something very bad because something very bad was happening to them). This simple answer is elaborated in a negative way: we know well that he did *not* do these things because he wanted people to know that he *could* do them; and he never did them because he wanted something good to happen to him, or something bad not to happen to him. We also know that when he did very good things for people (of the kind that no one else couldn't do) he often didn't want other people to know about it.

It is true that from the perspective of John the Evangelist, Jesus's healing miracles were, above all, "signs." From this perspective, when people knew what Jesus did they could think: "no one else can do things like this" and they could know that what Jesus was saying about God, and about himself, was true. This doesn't mean, however, that Jesus healed people in order to show that he could do it. There is a tension here, perhaps, which this commentary will not try to solve. Using Minimal English, however, we can make the different perspectives on Jesus's "healing miracles" clear.

In the section entitled "The Meaning of the Evangelical Acts of Healing" of his posthumous book *The Fourth Gospel*, Anglican theologian Edwyn Hoskyns (1940) writes this about the last part of chapter 4 of John's Gospel:

> The earlier synoptic tradition contains the record of many acts of healing. These actions had led to a tumultuous acceptance of Jesus by the crowds (Matt. iv. 23-5); but, since they were often done on the Sabbath and accompanied by a peculiar claim to authority, they led also to serious and deadly opposition on the part of the Jewish authorities (Mark ii.6-10, iii. 1-6, 22). Hitherto, the fourth Evangelist had recorded no acts of healing. But now, aware that they are still being misunderstood, he includes two in his narrative, and sets out both their false and their true meaning. Miracles of healing are not the goal of faith nor are they the means by which Jesus sought to exalt Himself. The claim *I am*, first asserted in iv. 26, must be protected against the accusation of arrogance (v. 18). (p. 273)

The verse 5:18 to which Hoskyns is referring at the end of this section says "But Jesus answered them: 'My Father is working still, and I am working,'" which is followed by the Jewish religious authorities' attempt to kill him "because he not only broke the Sabbath but also called God his own Father, making himself equal with God."

When Hoskyns suggests that by appealing to his "works" Jesus is defending himself against the accusation of arrogance, he appears to attribute to Jesus the following meaning: "I do very good things for people, like God does very good things for people. People can't do things like this. Because of this, when I say: 'God is my Father,' people can know that it is true."

Commentary on chapter 15: "Jesus teaches people what is good for them"

Arguably, the most remarkable feature of Jesus's moral teaching is its tone: it is not formulated in terms of prohibitions ("you shall not"), but, rather, in terms of something like guidance: "it is good for you if." The comparison with sheep without a shepherd is helpful here, as are also the metaphors of "light" and "the way" (sheep don't know where to find good grass to eat, people don't know where to go, they are like someone who wants to find their way in the dark). In Minimal English, this overall tone of Jesus's moral instruction has been rendered in "The Story" through the phrase "it is good for you if . . .," supplemented by the equally personalized and concerned warning: "it is bad for you if . . . "

In keeping with the overall tone of love, concern, and compassion, Jesus's teaching addressed to crowds which look to him like sheep without a shepherd takes as its starting point people's existential condition: they cannot lead fully autonomous lives and they suffer. Jesus's loving "advice" is to think often about God, to think: "I want to live with God," to talk to God every day, to recognize that "I can live because every day God does good things for me" (and remind oneself of this daily), to always trust that "God knows what is happening to me" and that "God knows what I feel now," and to always try to understand "what God wants me to do now."

Next to such essential and continuing thoughts about God, it is good for me if I try to relate to other people in a way which imitates God's attitude to people: it is good for me if I want to do good things for other people (as God wants to do good things for all people).

This is a continuation of the key biblical injunction: "love your neighbour as yourself" (Mark 12:31; Leviticus 19:18). In Jesus's teaching, however, the scope of this injunction is broadened to embrace everyone, including one's enemies or persecutors; and those who "hate God." Thus, not only is it good for you if you want to do good things for other people, and if you want good things to happen to them, but also, it is bad for you if you want bad things to happen to anyone. In this respect, Jesus's teaching is a radical departure from the ethos of the Hebrew Bible, including the Psalms. To illustrate, one of the most beautiful and profound psalms, which continues to nourish Christian, as well as Jewish, prayers (cf., e.g., Mayne 2006), nonetheless includes the following lines:

O that you would kill the wicked, O God (. . .)
Do I not hate those who hate you O Lord?
And do I not abhor those who rise up against you?
I hate them with perfect hatred,
I count them my enemies. (Psalm 139:19–22)

One could say that Jesus's teachings on what is good for people are in constant dialogue with the psalms. Jesus makes many themes and even phrases of the psalms his own, while at the same time rejecting others, such as hatred of one's enemies and of "the wicked," as well as the conviction of one's own innocence and purity.

Jesus warns people against pharisaic smugness: "When you are doing something good for someone, it is good for you if you don't think like this: 'I want people to know that I am doing something good for someone.'" This is the meaning behind the metaphor "But when you give alms, do not let your left hand know what your right hand is doing" (Matthew 5:3).

The next segment of chapter 15 refers to Jesus's teaching about body and "soul" (in Hebrew, "nepesh," see Wierzbicka 2016). Naturally, Jesus was not philosophizing on this subject in the abstract but teaching people how to live, and toward that end, teaching them how to think. The key sayings on this point can be found in Matthew's Gospel: "And do not fear those who kill the body but cannot kill the soul" (Matthew 10:28); and "For what is a man profited, if he shall gain the whole world, and lose his own soul?" (Matthew 16:26, KJV). In Minimal English, the meaning of these sayings is reflected in the last three lines of the first half of the chapter (introduced in the frame "He [Jesus] wanted them [people] to know what is good for them"), that is the lines which encourage people to think as follows: "It is not like this: if something bad happens to my body, this is bad for my soul. It is like this: if I think something bad, if I want to do something bad, if I feel something very bad towards someone, this is bad for my soul."

This chapter on Jesus's teaching about how to live cannot possibly be exhaustive, and neither can my commentary. I will therefore mention only briefly two things that Jesus particularly strongly warned against: revenge and love of money, and say a little (but only very little) about the theme of "men, women and marriage."

"Revenge" is a complex and culture-specific word (as is also its positive counterpart, "forgiveness"), but the essence of Jesus's warning against revenge (and of his injunction to always forgive) can be easily rendered in cross-translatable words. It entails a rejection of the thought: "this person did something bad to me, because of this I want to do something bad to this person," and of any bad feelings toward that person. In fact, Jesus appears to be in dialogue with Genesis when he tells Peter that one must forgive people "not seven times, but seventy times seven," echoing in this way Genesis, chapter 4:

Matthew's Gospel (18:21-22, 35)
Then Peter came up to him, and said, Lord, how often shall my brother sin against me, and I forgive him? As many as seven times? Jesus said to him, I do not say to you seven times, but seventy times seven. (18:21-22)

So also my heavenly Father will do to every one of you, if you do not for-give your brother from your heart. (18:35)

Genesis (4: 15, 23-24)
And the Lord said unto him, Therefore whosoever slays Cain, vengeance shall be taken on him sevenfold. (. . .)

And Lamech said unto his wives, Adah and Zillah, Hear my voice ye wives of Lamech (. . .) for I have slain a man (. . .) If Cain shall be avenged sevenfold, truly Lamech seventy and sevenfold.

The phrase "from your heart" in Matthew's Gospel makes it clear that Jesus's teaching repudiates not only "wanting to do something bad to someone who has done something bad to us," but also "wanting something bad to happen to this someone" and "feeling something bad towards this someone." (I will return to this point in the commentary on chapter 16.)

As for the love of money, I will note that while the word "money" is not en-tirely cross-translatable, it is very common in the language of the New Testament and of course throughout most of the twenty-first-century globalized world; so there are good reasons to allow it into the Minimal English of "The Story of God and People." Arguably, Jesus's warning "You cannot serve God and Mammon" (Matthew 6:24) can be reasonably rendered as: "It is bad for you if you often think like this: 'I want to have a lot of money.'"

Turning now to Jesus's teaching which relates directly to the theme "men, women and marriage," one aspect of it which is particularly striking is his con-cern for women. This has to do, above all, with marriage and divorce. In the patriarchal society in which he lived, a man could divorce his wife by simply writing a "certificate of divorce" and then "putting her away" (Mark 10:4). Jesus strongly condemned such a practice, saying that Moses allowed it only "for your hardness of heart" (Mark 10:5).

In complex English, we could say that Jesus's teaching about marriage included two ideas totally at variance with the norms and practices of his times: that the sexual union between two people should be exclusive, and that it should be lifelong. (Given the nature of the society in which he lived, he addressed this message above all to men.)

Speaking about Jesus's "new attitude to women" Men' (1969: ch. 5) sin-gles out marriage as one of the points where "the Gospel opposed the Old Testament."

The law gave the husband the right to leave his wife for any reason, some-times quite trivial. It was a reflection of the patriarchal law prevailing in the East. (. . .) The position of women didn't differ much from that in other countries. The husband was called "baal", "lord"; the wife was al-most his property, like the servants and domestic possessions (. . .) Jesus categorically rejected the thought that Moses' law *approves* of divorce. As he put it, in this case Moses made a concession to people's [in this case, men's, A.W.] "hardheartedness". And Jesus was opposing this concession, as unjust to women, and contrary to God's will.

Restating Jesus's message in Minimal English, we can say that its main point was this: "If a man says to his wife: 'I don't want to live with you anymore,' he is doing something very bad to her." At the same time, in the context of Jesus's teaching (as remembered in Matthew's "Sermon on the Mount") there appears to be a concern for men too: it is not the case that by abandoning his wife a man is doing something bad to his wife while at the same time benefiting himself. Rather, he is doing harm to himself, too. Hence the phrasing of the relevant lines in chapter 15: "it is bad for a man if he says to his wife: 'I don't want to live with you anymore.'" This double focus of Jesus's teaching directed at men is particularly clear in what he says about "lust" and adultery (Matthew 5:27–29):

> You have heard that it was said, "You shall not commit adultery." But I say to you that every one who looks at a woman lustfully has already committed adultery with her in his heart. If your right eye causes you to sin, pluck it out and throw it away; it is better that you lose one of your members than that your whole body go into hell.

The Revised Standard Version renders the Greek word *symferei* as "it is better," but the King James Version is closer to the Greek original when it says "it is profitable for thee," that is, "it is good for you."

Words like "lust," "adultery," and "divorce" are of course very complex in meaning and highly culture-specific. In chapter 15, the essence of Jesus's teaching on these matters is rendered through relatively simple and cross-translatable words, such as "man," "woman," and "wife," and through the universal semantic primes "body" and "live (with)."

Commentary on chapter 16: "How Jesus lived, what he was like"

In *Jesus of Nazareth*, in the chapter on the "Beatitudes" (the first part of Jesus's "Sermon on the Mount" in Matthew's Gospel), Benedict XVI (2007a: 250) writes: "Beatitudes (Mt, Lk)—in a way, this is Christ's autobiographical synthesis." In a sense, this is no doubt true: What Jesus taught others, he also showed them in his own life. Chapter 16, "How Jesus lived, what he was like," however, is not organized according to the schema of the Beatitudes, whether in Matthew (5:3–11) or in Luke (6:20–23). Rather, it is organized according to Jesus's attitude toward people—first of all, toward people in general, and then, to despised ethnic groups such as Samaritans; to outcasts, women, and children; toward special friends, his mother, and his people Israel; with the final section focusing on his attitude to God.

Jesus's attitude to people in general corresponds to his teaching as sketched in chapter 15: Jesus told people that (to use Minimal English) it was good for them if they wanted to do good things for other people and felt something good toward other people, and that it was bad for them if they wanted to do something bad to someone or felt something bad towards someone (even if that someone had done something very bad to them). Both these attitudes were clearly demonstrated by Jesus himself, for example, in the healing of the sick (see chapter 14) and in the absence of bad feelings toward the Roman soldiers who were nailing him to the Cross (see chapter 26).

Speaking in conventional English, one might say that a key moral value that Jesus emphasized in his teaching and demonstrated in his own life was "forgiveness." (As Benedict XVI (2007a: 157) notes, "forgiveness is a theme which pervades the whole Gospel.") Chapter 16 seeks to explain this value, as taught and demonstrated by Jesus, in cross-translatable words. It seems likely that the concept of "forgiveness," which modern European languages share and for which they have a special word, is in fact a Christian concept and that this concept developed in the context of Jesus's teaching. (See Appendix A.)

Apparently, there was no word with such a meaning in classical Greek: There was a word meaning "reconciliation," which will be discussed in the commentary on chapter 28 of "The Story," but not one meaning "forgiveness." The word *aphiemi*, used, for example, in what came to be known as the Lord's Prayer ("And forgive us our trespasses, as we forgive those who trespass against us") is usually listed in Greek–English dictionaries (e.g., Liddell & Scott 1940) with meanings such as "to let go, set free, and acquit," but not "forgive." Further, it would appear that there was no such word in biblical Hebrew. The Hebrew Bible does use some words and phrases which the King James Bible translates sometimes as "forgive," but evidence suggests that these words, usually used about God and not in relation to equals, are closer in some ways to "pardon" and "have mercy" than to "forgive," in the sense in which the Greek word *aphiemi* is used to render Jesus's teaching in the Greek original of Matthew's and Luke's Gospels.

Benedict XVI (2007a) asks: "What is forgiveness, really? What happens when forgiveness takes place?" and replies: "Guilt is a reality, an objective force; it has caused destruction that must be repaired. For this reason, forgiveness must be more than ignoring, or merely trying to forget. Guilt must be worked through, healed, and thus overcome" (p. 158). He also says, poetically, that "the person who forgives (. . .) must overcome within himself the evil done to him; he must, as it were, burn it interiorly, and in so doing renew himself" (p. 159). Using Minimal English, we can try to explain the sense of the two sentences with "forgive" (*aphiemi*) in the Lord's Prayer in a transparent and cross-translatable way. First, the sentence addressed to "Our Father":

1. Forgive us our sins (Luke 11:4); Forgive us our debts (Mt. 6:12)

We know that we did very bad things.
We know that You want us not to do such things.
We know that something very bad can happen to us because we did these
   things.
We know that it will not happen if You say: "I don't want it to happen."
We know that You are good, because of this we say:
   We want You to say it, we want it very much.

The component "we know that something very bad can happen to us because
we did these things" does not have to be understood in terms of "punishment": Rather, the bad consequences of "doing very bad things" may lie in a
person's inability to "live with God."

Turning now to the injunction to "forgive one's 'debtors,'" I will note that
it is not entirely symmetrical with the prayer request to God: "forgive us our
sins (debts)," if only because people can't "do something bad to God," as they
can "do something bad to other people." Further, in "forgive us our debts" the
focus is on "forgive *what*," whereas in "we forgive everyone who is indebted to
us" the focus is on "forgive *whom*." The components posited in the "we say now"
frame below are consistent with Benedict's comments about the need of the forgiving person (me) to "burn" the other person's guilt toward me within myself,
and also, to "renew" myself (by starting to think about that other person in a
new way). The two versions of Jesus's injunction to "forgive our debtors" (i.e.,
those who have wronged us), Matthew's and Luke's, are slightly different, but
the core is clearly the same and can be set out along the following lines:

2. . . .for we also forgive everyone who is indebted to us. (Luke 11:4, KJV)
. . . as we have forgiven our debtors (Mt. 6:12, NRSV)

We think like this about some people:
   "These people did some very bad things to us."
We feel something bad towards these people because of this.
We say now:
   We don't want to think like this about these people anymore.
   We don't want to feel anything bad towards them anymore.
   We want to think about them in another way.

This may not be a paraphrase which would quite fit every sentence in
the New Testament where the word *aphiemi* is used, and we can assume that
the concept of "forgiveness" was still *in statu nascendi* in the New Testament
Greek. But with time, the concept, anchored in Jesus's teaching and example
and stabilized in the Christian conceptual vocabulary is now (in a slightly modified form) part and parcel of the conceptual heritage of European languages.
Crucially, this concept implies an intentional change in one's attitude toward
another person, a change which is unconditional (does not require that the other

person do or say anything), and which involves a new way of thinking about that person: one wants not to think about that person anymore in terms of the bad things that they have done to us, but to think about them in another way.

Trying to understand Jesus's words in their historical and cultural context, we should note that the psalms, which he grew up with, often quoted from, and clearly identified with, regularly express very bad feelings toward one's enemies and call on God to punish them. (For example, in psalm 69, verses 24 and 28 read, in part: "let thy wrathful anger take hold of them," "let them be blotted out of the book of the living.") Evidently, Jesus was urging his listeners not to think of anyone in this way; and in so doing, he was, in "the Lord's Prayer," introducing a distinct new concept, for which there was not yet a ready-made word.

To test this interpretation against another example, I will adduce Jesus's exchange with Peter in Matthew's chapter 18 (which is followed by the highly relevant parable of the Unforgiving Servant), and I will try to explicate Jesus's words which follow that parable:

Jesus' exchange with Peter (Mt. 18:21)
Then came Peter to him, and said, Lord, how oft shall my brother sin against me, and I forgive him? till seven times? Jesus said unto him, I say not unto thee, until seven times, but: until seventy times seven. (Mt 18:21, RSV)

(. . .)

. . . So likewise shall my heavenly Father do also unto you, if ye from your hearts forgive not every one his brother their trespasses. (Mt 18:35, KJV)

The apparent threat of God's punishment, which follows the parable, belongs to the genre of biblical "Drohrede" (prophetic "warning speech," see Wierzbicka 2001), but Jesus's intended meaning is clear from context, and can be summed up as "forgive your brother from your heart."

Jesus' implicit injunction
. . . forgive your brother from your heart. (Mt. 18:35; cf. Luke 17:3-4)
Maybe it is like this:
You think like this about someone:
"This person did something very bad to me."
You feel something bad towards this person because of this,
you want something bad to happen to them because of this.
I say to you:
If it is like this, it is very bad for you.
It will be good for you if it is like this:
You say (not because you want other people to hear it):
"I don't want to think like this about this person anymore";
after this, you think about this person in another way;
you don't feel anything bad towards this person anymore.

Here (in Matthew 18:35 and Luke 17:3–4), no "debts" or "trespasses" are mentioned at all, and the only object of the verb "forgive" (*aphiemi*) is one referring to a person: it is a matter of how I relate to my "brother."

Speaking of the whole "Sermon on the Mount," which includes both the "Lord's Prayer" and the Beatitudes, and describing it as "the most important and most controversial biblical text," Canadian theologian Clarence Bauman (1985) complains about "a thousand commentaries whose function it is to explain by the art of theological science why the plain words of Jesus mean the opposite of what they say" (420). One can sympathize with Bauman's exasperation. At the same time, it must be said that to speak of "the plain words of Jesus" is to ignore the speech culture to which he belonged. Often, his words are not "plain," and even if they do seem plain on the surface, their apparent "plain" surface meaning is rarely all there is to them. (Cf. Chesterton 1925.)

This is why we need reliable methods to interpret Jesus's words, and also, reliable means of interpreting Jesus's own way of living: If, through simple and cross-translatable words, we can grasp how Jesus lived his own life, this will allow us to verify our understanding of what he taught. So this is what chapter 16 of "The Story" attempts to do: to test our understanding of Jesus's teachings against our understanding of how he lived his own life.

Chapter 16 is an attempted portrait of Jesus. We don't know what Jesus looked like, but we do know enough about his characteristic ways of thinking, feeling, and relating to people to be able to attempt a portrait of what he was like as a person. As far as feelings are concerned, perhaps the most arresting and unusual feature is that, although Jesus did sometimes say things which make him appear angry, even very angry, there is no evidence in the Gospels suggesting that Jesus ever felt something bad *toward* someone. Evidently, he did feel something very bad when he saw people desecrating the Temple (Mark 11:15–19), or when he was deploring the hypocrisy and spiritual blindness of the "scribes and Pharisees" who through their excessive demands were "shutting the kingdom of heaven against men [people]" (Matthew 23:13); but the use of Minimal English allows us to distinguish between "feeling something very bad" (or even "very very bad") and "feeling something very bad *toward* someone." (See Wierzbicka 2018b.)

Further, Jesus evidently didn't feel anything bad toward any particular "kinds of people," including those despised and shunned by most of his compatriots: Samaritans, "sinners," tax collectors, "untouchables" (such as lepers), or women who today would be called prostitutes.

Jesus's unusual attitude toward women has been much discussed, but the use of Minimal English allows us to make this attitude clearer, and to articulate it in cross-translatable words: "He didn't think about women as many men thought about women in that country at that time," "he felt something good toward women," "he wanted men not to do bad things to women," "he often wanted to be with women," "he often wanted to speak to women about God."

Jesus's unusual way of relating to children is described in chapter 16 in terms of how he felt toward them: "He felt something very good toward children," and more particularly, in terms of how he thought about them: "Someone like this can be very close to God."

Jesus's close friendships with particular men and women and his special love for them are represented in chapter 16 by a formulation which may seem not just simple but simplistic: "He felt something very very good toward them"; but again, the strength of this formulation lies in its cross-translatability, as well as intuitive intelligibility. The fact that, as evidence suggests, in most if not all languages people can distinguish between "good," "very good," and "very very good" feelings allows us a good deal of flexibility in describing human emotions and attitudes. At the same time, as chapter 16 illustrates, additional distinctions can also be made, in clear and cross-translatable ways, by referring to someone's ways of thinking and acting (for example, in the case of Jesus's attitude to his mother Mary: "When she said to him: 'I want you to do something good for these people,' she knew that he would want to do it").

Finally, in the case of Jesus's attitude to God, the component "he felt something very very good toward God" may sound naïve, and obviously doesn't tell the whole story, but arguably, it does point—in a clear and cross-translatable way—to what is of the essence here. The additional message conveyed by the word "Abba"—Jesus's unique way of addressing God—is also crucial: "I feel something very good toward you, I know that you feel something very good towards me." Equally important is his desire to know, and do, God's will: "He always wanted to know what God wanted him to do. He always wanted to do it."

Needless to say, the portrait of Jesus drawn here can only be a sketch. In particular, it leaves out some distinct aspects of his style of speaking such as that reflected in his idiosyncratic use of "Amen, I say to you . . ." and especially (in John's Gospel) "Amen, amen, I say to you . . ." at the beginning of a sentence—a characteristic which features prominently in the portrait of Jesus drawn by Polkinghorne (1994) in his *Faith of a Physicist*. Polkinghorne speaks in this context of Jesus's tone of "unshakeable certainty" and comments that this use "testifies to one who was conscious of possessing a particular and true insight, so that 'he taught them as one who had authority, and not as the scribes' (Matthew 7:29)." Using Minimal English, we can hypothesize that in saying "Amen, amen" Jesus was conveying the following message:

Amen, amen
I want you to know that I will say something to you now
    not like other people can say something to people.
When I say it, you can know that it is true.

I agree with Polkinghorne that this is an important aspect of "what Jesus was like." I have not included this in chapter 16 of "The Story," however, because this chapter seeks to focus, above all, on features of Jesus that people could, in principle, try to emulate. Theologian T.W. Manson (1960: 68) speaks for many Christians when he says in his book *Ethics and the Gospel*, "The living Christ is there to lead the way for all who are prepared to follow him (. . .) so the Christian ideal lies before us, not as a remote and austere mountain peak, an ethical Everest which we must scale by our own skill and endurance, but a road which we walk with Christ as guide and friend." Chapter 16 of "The Story" focuses, for the most part, on those aspects of Jesus's life which can be understood in this spirit.

To conclude, do we know what Jesus was like? Do we have a sense of his personality? On this point, I'd like to quote a comment by the famous twentieth-century German theologian Rudolf Bultmann (1952), adduced by C. S. Lewis in his essay "Fern-seed and Elephants," and then C. S. Lewis's mordant response to it.

> Finally, from the same Bultmann: "The personality of Jesus has no importance for the kerygma [proclamation of the Gospel] either of Paul or of John. . . . Indeed the tradition of the earliest Church did not even unconsciously preserve a picture of his personality. Every attempt to reconstruct one remains a play of subjective imagination." (Bultmann 1952: 30)

Now, C. S. Lewis's response:

> So there is no personality of our Lord presented in the New Testament. Through what strange process has this learned German gone in order to make himself blind to what all men except him see? What evidence have we that he would recognize a personality if it were there? For it is Bultmann *contra mundum* [Bultmann against the whole world]. If anything whatever is common to all believers, and even to many unbelievers, it is the sense that in the Gospels they have met a personality. (Lewis 1978: 109–110)

To re-state C. S. Lewis's main point in Minimal English: if we read the Gospels, we *can* know what Jesus was like.

Commentary on chapter 17: "The people who were with Jesus"

The people who often were with Jesus when he lived in Nazareth were, above all, Mary and Joseph. According to tradition (not to the New Testament), Joseph died when Jesus was nineteen years old, and since (as Men' 1969, chapter 2, points out), legends usually mention symbolic numbers, the non-symbolic number nineteen is likely to be accurate in this case. Men' also notes Jesus's words recorded only in the apocryphal "Acts of Peter" but regarded as likely to be authentic (and presumably referring to the extended family): "Those who are close to me don't understand me"; and he adds that only his mother was close to Jesus and that she was the only witness of what was happening in him, and to him. (See chapter 10 of "The Story.")

When Jesus didn't live in Nazareth anymore those who were with him most of the time included, above all, "the Twelve," that is, the twelve men whom Jesus named "the Apostles." In addition to the Twelve, there was also a continued presence of some women, who wanted to care for Jesus and the Apostles, and who were among his most faithful and most loving disciples. As chapter 17 puts it, they "felt something very good toward Jesus; they wanted to be with him; when he spoke about God, they wanted to hear it; they wanted to do many good things for him . . . ; they were with him when he was dying." I will briefly return to the presence of women among Jesus's disciples later. For the moment, I want to focus on the Apostles, starting with one extract from Dietrich Bonhoeffer (1959), *The Cost of Discipleship*, and one from Benedict XVI (2007a), *Jesus of Nazareth*. Bonhoeffer writes:

> Let us picture the scene: Jesus on the mountain, the multitudes, and the disciples. The *people* see Jesus with his disciples, who have gathered around him. Until quite recently these men had been completely identified with the multitude, they were just like the rest. Then came the call of Jesus, and at once they left all and followed him. Since then they have belonged to him, body and soul. Now they go with him, live with him, and follow him wherever he leads them. Something unique had occurred to them. They have publicly left the crowd to join him. He has called them, every one, and they have renounced everything at his call. (p. 95)

This key event of the "call" is rendered in chapter 17 of "The Story" with the words that Jesus addresses to the disciples: "I want you to be with me wherever I go" (not an exact quote).

Benedict's emphasis is different from, and complementary to, Bonhoeffer's. While Bonhoeffer's focus is on the individual disciples who had been called by Jesus, Benedict's (2007a: 169) emphasis is on "the 'we' of the 'new family' that Jesus gathers by his proclamation and action": and which "is in principle intended to be universal. This 'we' of the new family is not amorphous. Jesus calls an inner core of people specially chosen by him, who are to carry on his mission and give this family order and shape. That was why Jesus formed the group of the Twelve." The "we" emphasized by Benedict is also present in chapter 17 of "The Story," in the line which portrays the Apostles' way of thinking about Jesus ("You are someone above us"). It will become much more central in chapter 37, "The church: people who want to live with Jesus, with other people."

Another aspect of Benedict's (2007a) commentary which resonates with chapter 17 of "The Story" has to do with the *witnessing* of the Apostles—not only with their witnessing to events in Jesus's life, but also, with their being sufficiently close to Jesus to get insight into his relationship with God.

Jesus appoints the Twelve with a double assignment: "to be with him, and to be sent out to preach." They must be with him in order to get to know him; in order to attain that intimate acquaintance with him that could not be given to the "people' (. . .). The Twelve must be with him so as to be able to recognize his oneness with the Father and thus become witnesses to his mystery. (p. 172)

In chapter 17 of "The Story," this is reflected in the line "he wanted them to know who he was, to know that he said to God: 'Father,' 'Abba.'"

Further, Benedict explains the symbolic significance of the number twelve, in the context of Jesus's choice of his closest companions:

Twelve was the symbolic number of Israel – the number of the sons of Jacob. From them the twelve tribes of Israel were descended, though of these practically only the tribe of Judah remained after the Exile. In this sense, the number twelve is a return to the origins of Israel, and yet at the same time it is a symbol of hope: The whole of Israel is restored and the twelve tribes are newly assembled.

Twelve – the number of the tribes – is at the same time a cosmic number that expresses the comprehensiveness of the newly reborn People of God. (p. 171)

I quote this passage here in order to explain why the word "twelve" – which is not universally cross-translatable – has been nonetheless allowed to appear in the Minimal English of "The Story."

As mentioned earlier, in addition to the Twelve, Jesus was also accompanied by a number of women. Luke (8:1–3) writes:

Soon afterwards he went on through cities and villages, preaching and bringing the good news of the Kingdom of God. And the twelve were with him, and also some women who had been healed of evil spirits and infirmities: Mary, called Magdalene, from whom seven demons had gone out, and Joanna, the wife of Chuza, Herod's steward, and Susanna, and many others, who provided for them out of their means. (RSV)

Commenting on this passage in Luke's Gospel, Benedict XVI (2007a) writes:

The difference between the discipleship of the Twelve and the discipleship of the women is obvious; the tasks assigned to each group are quite different. Yet Luke makes clear – and the other Gospels also show this in all sorts of ways – that "many" women belonged to the more intimate community of believers and that their faith-filled following of Jesus was an essential element of that community, as would be vividly illustrated at the foot of the Cross and at the Resurrection. (p. 180)

"The Story" returns to the loving presence of the women at the foot of the Cross and at the Resurrection in chapters 27 and 30, and their friendships with Jesus were already mentioned in chapter 16. Chapter 17 emphasizes, in Minimal English, that many women "felt something very good toward Jesus [and] wanted to be with him [and] when he spoke about God, they wanted to hear it; [and] they wanted to do many good things for him." Jesus's attitude to women, "without precedent in contemporary Judaism" (Förster 1964: 124), is also reflected in chapters 15 and 16.

If, as Russian Orthodox theologian Alexander Men' (1969) puts it, "Christianity elevated women" (with lasting consequences for Christian, and post-Christian, societies in many parts of the world), this elevation no doubt had its roots not only in Jesus's teaching but also in his own countercultural life, as remembered by his followers and recorded in the Gospels. Perhaps the most unusual aspect of Jesus's attitude to the women was that, as the Evangelists make clear, he often wanted to speak to them about God.

Commenting specifically on Jesus's conversation with the Samaritan woman (already mentioned in chapter 16), Men' (1969: ch. 5) notes how surprised the Apostles were "that it was not to them but to that simple woman, at that a heretic and a 'loose woman', that Jesus first told plainly that he was the Messiah, and revealed to her the mystery of the eternal religion of the spirit." Then Men' goes on to make a more general observation:

> For Socrates, the woman was only a stupid annoying creature, and Buddha didn't allow his followers even to look at women. In the pre-Christian world women had to be for the most part like silent slaves whose life was limited to exhausting work and domestic cares. Christ gives the woman back the human dignity of which she had been deprived, and the right to have spiritual needs.

Chapter 17 tries to capture some of these points in cross-translatable words and phrases.

Commentary on chapter 18: "What happened on Mount Tabor"

As we saw in chapter 17, Jesus wanted the Apostles to know who he was—and he wanted them to know it well, so that they would understand how he fulfilled Israel's expectations, and how he transcended them. This is why, as Benedict XVI (2007a: 305) emphasizes, the timing of the Transfiguration (as related in the Gospels) is very significant: "All three Synoptic Gospels create a link between Peter's confession ['You are the Messiah, the Son of the Living God'] and the account of Jesus' Transfiguration by means of a reference to time." This is how chapter 18 starts, too. It places the Transfiguration event a short time after Peter's confession. At the same time, as Benedict XVI also emphasizes, the question of who Jesus was is linked in both cases with the Passion motif. Jesus's "glory" "belongs with the Cross—only when we put the two together do we recognize Jesus correctly. John expressed this intrinsic interconnectedness of Cross and glory when he said that the Cross is Jesus' 'exaltation'" (p. 305). The interconnection between "who Jesus was" (as the three Apostles could glimpse on Mount Tabor) and how he would die is also highlighted in chapter 18, both at the beginning and at the end.

The event of the Transfiguration is mysterious. Before commenting on the Minimal English formulations of chapter 18, I will first adduce here a few helpful explanations offered in non-minimal language by the "Sage" in the Orthodox catechism *The Living God* (1989). The first concerns what theologians call the "two natures of Christ":

> *Sage:* Never forget that there are two natures in the person of Christ: He is at the same time both God and man. And it is this union of two natures in Christ that God permitted the apostles to see for a moment. They saw Jesus illumined by a divine Light that shone through His human body. Moreover, the uncreated divine energy is also transmitted to matter, for the Gospel adds that Jesus' clothing took on a brilliance which no earthly product could have given: "And His garments became glistening, intensely white, as no fuller on earth could bleach them." (Mk 9:3). (vol. 1, p. 79)

The word "nature" is not cross-translatable, and neither is "persons" (let alone "union"). But the second sentence in the extract above is, essentially, cross-translatable: As Christians believe, Jesus was a man, and at the same time, he was God. This is not, however, how the Apostles thought at the time of the Transfiguration, and this is why chapter 18 doesn't try to fully explain the meaning of the event that Peter, John, and James witnessed (as Christians understand it). Instead, it tries to say (following the Gospels) what they saw at the time, what they heard, and what they felt.

For Christians reading the accounts of the Transfiguration, the light represents what *The Living God* calls "divine glory"—something that was later expressed in the Nicene Creed with the words "God from God, Light from Light, true God from true God." Chapter 18 has to rely on a more austere— and more cross-translatable—language, but the references to "light" are essential. Fortunately, as evidence suggests, "light" is a universal human concept, and thus the word is fully cross-translatable. To quote *The Living God* again:

> The divinity of Christ was not visible in any way. He manifested Himself as God only twice in His life: at His Baptism and at His Transfiguration. The Baptism in the Jordan revealed that Jesus is the Son of God (. . .). John the Baptist saw this and bore witness to it. At the Transfiguration on Mount Tabor the three apostles, Peter, James and John, saw Jesus resplendent in His divine glory, in the presence of two great witnesses who

had seen this same glory in the time of the Old Covenant. On the day of the Transfiguration Moses and Elijah confirmed that this was indeed the same Light and the same God. (vol. 1, p. 76)

The full significance of the presence of Moses and Elijah is likely to be lost on modern readers of the Gospels, but the symbolism of "the Law" (Moses) and "the Prophets" (Elijah) is clear enough. *The Living God* comments on this significance by linking the Gospel story with the composition of an old Russian icon called "The Transfiguration."

The icon is divided into two sections: three persons are seen in the upper part and three in the lower. The two groups of men demonstrate very different attitudes. At the summit of the mountain, Moses and Elijah stand upright next to Christ; they have entered into the radiant circle and participate in the glory of God, in full harmony with Him. On the other hand, the apostles, who are seen at the bottom of the icon at the foot of a cliff, are staggered, and their whole attitude expresses disorder and disarray. This contrast reminds us that we cannot see God with carnal eyes.

Moses and Elijah appear on the mountain and are able to bear the light of God because, together with Isaiah, God had granted to them the privilege of seeing Him during their earthly life (Ex 33:18-23; 1 Kings 19:9-13; Is 6:1-5). (vol. 1, p. 79)

The attitude of the Apostles shown in the icon and commented on in this extract is captured in chapter 18 with the line "The Apostles didn't know how it could be like this, they didn't know what to think." What *The Living God* says about Moses and Elijah for the benefit of readers, would have been known to the Apostles, but clearly, it was only adding to their confusion.

They both bow low before Jesus. Moses personifies the Law, while Elijah comes in the name of the prophets who bear witness with him to the divinity of Christ, He who fulfils the Law and the prophets. (. . .) By contrast, the three apostles prostrate on the earth are part of living humanity. Despite their astonishment at the sight of Christ in glory they are filled with joy and would like to prolong this moment. Peter asks to stay forever on the mountain; that is why he suggests that they build tents, in order to retain the vision of God for all eternity. Nevertheless, they had to experience death, like Christ Himself, in order to see Him again in glory after His Resurrection. (. . .) (vol. 1, p. 80)

In chapter 18, the significance of the appearance of Moses and Elijah on the scene, and the effect this appearance has on the three Apostles, are hinted at in two lines: "These two don't live on earth anymore; at the same time, they know Jesus, they are speaking to him, speaking *about* him. How can this be?" The Apostles' confusion is also reflected in the line about Peter: "He didn't know what he was saying, he didn't know what he wanted to say."

What did the Apostles feel at that extraordinary time? The accounts of Mark, Matthew, and Luke do not all say exactly the same. It seems clear, however, that these feelings included something like confusion, fear, awe and ecstasy. Benedict XVI (2007a: 313) comments: "The three disciples are shaken by the enormousness of what they have seen. (. . .) 'They were terrified' (Mark 9:6)." Commenting specifically on Peter's words "Rabbi, it is good that we are here," Benedict XVI says that "Peter speaks in a sort of ecstasy, in the midst of fear yet also in the joy of God's closeness" (p. 313). Chapter 18 tries to capture something of that emotional mix with cross-translatable phrases "feel something very good" and "feel something very bad", combined with some specific (also cross-translatable) thoughts.

Orthodox theologian Alexander Men' (1969) gives a slightly different interpretation of the order and the "logic" of the Apostles' emotions, but he too sees them as a mix of "very good" and "very bad" feelings:

When they had somehow grasped that the ancient prophets came to Jesus from another realm, fear gave way to a sense of peace, happiness, God's closeness. When they saw that the two were leaving, the disciples thought, with trepidation, that they might lose the inexpressible bliss of that minute. (ch. 10)

The Living God (1989) illustrates these different interrelated threads of the story of the Transfiguration by quoting from the "Kontakion" (special liturgical text) prescribed in the Orthodox church for the feast of the Transfiguration:

On the mountain wast Thou transfigured, O Christ God,
And Thy disciples beheld Thy Glory as far as they could see it;
So that when they would behold Thee crucified,
They would understand that Thy suffering was voluntary,
And would proclaim to the world
That thou are truly the radiance of the Father.

The Sage comments:

Sage: Jesus prepares His disciples for His death. For He must suffer a terrible, outrageous death; a death on the cross, devoid of glory. That is why He chose Peter, James and John, so that they might see Him in His glory and not despair at the moment of trial. (p. 81)

As the last few lines of chapter 18 state, the three Apostles thought about that light which they saw on Mount Tabor to the end of their lives. In the "Prologue" of the Gospel of John we read: "And the Word became flesh and lived among us, and we have seen his glory, the glory as of a father's only son full of grace and truth" (John 1:14). When commentators write about the Transfiguration, they feel compelled to use words like "glory," "splendour," "resplendent," "radiance," "dazzled," and "beauty" (see, e.g., *Readings in St John's*

Gospel, Temple 1961: 13). These words are not cross-translatable, but they capture an important aspect of the story. Chapter 18 seeks to express the intention behind all these words with the lines: "This light was not like any other light (. . .). They knew one thing: when they saw this light, they felt something very very good, they couldn't not feel it." As for John's (the Evangelist's) personal testimony (" . . . we have seen his glory"), I have sought to reflect it in chapter 18 in the line "we saw that light when we were with him [on Mount Tabor]."

Turning now from John's to Peter's recollection of the Transfiguration, in "the Second Letter of Peter" we read:

> we were eyewitnesses of his majesty. For when he received honor and glory from God the Father and the voice was borne to him by the Majestic Glory, "This is my beloved Son, with whom I am well pleased," we heard this voice borne from heaven, for we were with him on the holy mountain. And we have the prophetic word made more sure. You will do well to pay attention to this as to a lamp shining in a dark place, until the day dawns and the morning star rises in your hearts. (2 Peter 1:16–19, NRSV)

The Living God (1989: 85) comments: "One day the sun will cease to shine (as we are told by both the Scripture and astronomy), but the true Light, the divine Light, will never fail. In Christ we contemplate the Light which will shine eternally upon us after the Second Coming." In this context, *The Living God* cites one of the "Fathers of the Church," Saint Basil the Great [fourth century], who "in a sermon on the Transfiguration (. . .) teaches us that this feast is an anticipation of the second and glorious coming" (1989: 85).

The expression "The Second Coming" refers to the "end of times," when (as Christians believe) all people will see Jesus as the Judge (see the last chapter of "The Story"). Chapter 18 hints at the idea that the Transfiguration is "an anticipation of the second and glorious coming" in the final line, which rephrases, in simple words, Peter's confident expectation: "One day, when you don't live on earth anymore, you will all see Jesus, then you will all see this light."

Commentary on chapter 19: "What people said about Jesus, what people thought about Jesus"

The topic of what people in Palestine were saying about Jesus during the three years of his public ministry is quite complex, and it is difficult to reduce it to one page if all the complex concepts involved are to be fully explained. Obviously, in this one page there is hardly any room for an account of the changes in many people's attitudes which occurred during that period, and the overall picture has to be simplified and somewhat schematic.

In a broad outline, though, the contrast between the people who said "good things" about Jesus and those who said "bad things" about him is clear enough, as is also the presence of three distinct groups of opponents, without a similar differentiation among the supporters.

To begin with the latter (of whom there were a great many, especially in Galilee), what these crowds of supporters were mainly struck by was that Jesus spoke "like no one had spoken before," and that he did things "like no one had done before." Only with time, the idea spread among people that Jesus was indeed the Messiah promised by the prophets, the "son of David," in the Roman governor Pilate's words, the "king of the Jews," an idea which dominated the crowd of pilgrims coming to Jerusalem shortly before Jesus' arrest and execution.

As for the three main groups of opponents, I have identified by name the "scribes," the "Pharisees," and the "priests," each introduced by a label and defined, minimally, by its self-image. Thus, the scribes are presented in terms of their expertise ("they thought like this: we are not like other people; we know well what the Law says, what the Bible says"), the Pharisees, in terms of their superior fidelity to the Law, in all its minutiae ("they thought like this: we are not like other people, we do everything as the Law says, not like other people"), and the priests, in terms of their privileged role in the Temple rituals ("they thought like this: we are not like other people, we can do some things in the Temple as God wants, other people can't do these things").

In the account of the controversies between Jesus and his opponents, chapter 19 emphasizes the exchanges in the Temple, with as many direct quotations or near quotations as possible (given the constraints of Minimal English). These exchanges present many interpretative challenges. One of them is the saying "I am the light of the world" (John 8:12), on which I will focus in the remainder of this commentary. What does this saying mean, in simple and cross-translatable words?

In *Jesus of Nazareth* Pope Benedict XVI (2007a) writes:

> The sayings of Jesus that the Gospels transmit to us include (. . .) a group of "I am" sayings. They fall into two different categories. In the first type, Jesus simply says "I am" or "I am he" without any further additions. In the second type, figurative expressions specify the content of the "I am" in more detail: I am the light of the world, the true vine, the Good Shepherd, and so on. If at first sight the second group appears to be immediately intelligible, this only makes the first group even more puzzling. (p. 345)

It is interesting to note that Benedict XVI describes the words "the light of the world" as a figurative expression. In chapter 19, this "figurative" character is captured by means of the word "like." Benedict notes that Jesus's "I am" sayings, including the "light of the world," can cause confusion, as well as division, among his listeners: "some started asking themselves whether he might really be the awaited Prophet after all, whereas others pointed out that no prophet is supposed to come from Galilee (cf. Jn 7:40, 52." (pp. 345–346).

Benedict asks, on his own and other readers', behalf: "What does this mean? We want to ask: What are you, then? Who are you? And that, in fact, is just how the Jews respond: 'Who are you?' (Jn 8:25)" (p. 346).

It seems clear that to understand Jesus's key saying about the "light of the world" in John (1:12) we need to consider it together with the sentence which follows: "I am the light of the world. Whoever follows me will never walk in darkness but will have the light of life" (John 1:12). Rephrased in non-figurative and cross-translatable language, the second sentence of John 8:12 appears to mean: "people don't know how to live" (cf. also the line in the Prologue: "The light shines in the darkness," John 1:5).

Accordingly, the first sentence ("I am the light of the world") means – at least in part – that "if someone wants to live as I say, this someone can know how to live" – an interpretation which is supported by Jesus's words given later in the same chapter: "Very truly, I tell you, whoever keeps my word will never see death" (John 8:51). Following this path, we can arrive at a coherent sequence which can be formulated in Minimal English like this: "People don't know how to live, like people don't know where to go in a place where there is no light. I am the light. If people live as I say, they can live with God. If they live with God, they can live forever."

One might say, then, that in one sense at least, it is Jesus's teaching that "gives the light to the world," in other words, answers people's deepest existential longing to know how to live. It is important to bear in mind, however, that (as noted by many Christian theologians) Jesus's words about the light in John's chapter 8 belong together with the words about the light in the Prologue: "the true light, which enlightens everyone, was coming into the world" (John 1:9, NRSV) and "in him was life, and the life was the light of all people. The light shines in the darkness (. . .)" (John 1:4–5, NRSV).

These lines suggest that while Jesus's teaching uniquely articulates knowledge about how it is good for people to live, in part at least this knowledge can also be revealed to people in other ways. It is important to emphasize, therefore, that the critical line of chapter 19 says "if people **want** to live as I say, they can know how to live," and not, "if people **know** what I say, they can know how to live." One doesn't have to **know** what Jesus said in order to have insight into "how to live." This means that some people (e.g., saintly people of the Old Testament) could know how to live without knowing what Jesus said. But history shows that this is rare, and that at many times, in many societies, people "lived in darkness," believing in revenge, in the value of human sacrifice, the inferiority of women, the inequality of human races, and so on. Christians believe that Jesus's teachings on forgiveness, love of enemies, the (positive) golden rule ("do good things for others as you want others to do good things for you"), are, potentially, an incomparable source of light for everyone and every human group. (For my earlier attempts to render those teachings in Minimal English, see Wierzbicka 2001.)

Chapter 19 touches on a number of other things said by Jesus which are difficult to render in cross-translatable words. I will only comment here on one of them: the question of "freedom," and its relation to "truth." Many languages of the world don't have words like "freedom" and "truth" and many don't even have a word like "free" (although evidence suggests that they all have an equivalent of "true"). In chapter 19, "freedom" is dealt with by means of the concrete word "slaves," which had to be introduced in an earlier chapter of "the Story" anyway. (Roughly, to be "free" means in this context to be able to live not like a slave.) As for truth (which, Jesus says, "will make you free"), it is only referred to in chapter 19 by means of the adjective "true": "When I say some things to people, these things are true. My Father has said these things to me before." So "freedom" is, so to speak, anchored in God's words, which are always true. As Jesus says to God in John's Gospel, "Thy word is truth" (John 17:17). As chapter 19 suggests, then, the key logical connections in what Jesus tells his listeners can be outlined as follows:

People don't know how to live: if people want to live as I say, they *can* know how to live.

I say some things to people; these things are true: God has said these things to me before. (If God says something about something, it is always true.)

If people want to live as I say, they can live with God; they can then live not like slaves.

If people live with God, they can live forever.

Commentary on chapter 20: "The Romans"

Speaking of the birth of Jesus in Bethlehem ("the city of David"), Luke (2:1) writes: "In those days, a decree went out from Caesar Augustus that all the world [in Greek, "oikomene"] should be enrolled." In his book *Infancy Narratives*, Benedict XVI (2012a) comments:

With these words, Luke introduces his account of the birth of Jesus and explains how it came to take place in Bethlehem. A population census, for purposes of determining and collecting taxes, was what prompted Joseph to set off from Nazareth for Bethlehem, together with Mary, his betrothed, who was expecting a child. The birth of Jesus in the city of David is placed within the overarching framework of world history. . . . (p. 98)

Thus, Luke's reference to the census is important not only because it explains why Jesus was born in Bethlehem rather than in Nazareth but also because it places the birth of Jesus in a wider context of the Roman empire and world history.

Emphasizing Caesar Augustus's aspirations to universality and universal peace (not only "Pax Romana," "Roman peace," but more specifically "Pax Augusti" "Augustus' peace"), Benedict (2012a) points to the opportunities that these aspirations offered for Jesus's "message of universal salvation":

> For the first time, "all the world," the *ecumēnē* in its entirety, is to be enrolled. For the first time there is a government and an empire that spans the globe. For the first time, there is a great expanse of peace in which everyone's property can be registered (. . .). Only now, when there is a commonality of law and property on a large scale, and when a universal language has made it possible for a cultural community to trade in ideas and goods, only now can a message of universal salvation, a universal Saviour, enter the world: it is indeed the "fullness of time." (p. 59)

Chapter 20 of "The Story" does not address all these points directly, but it does hint at them, by noting the status of Greek as the universal language of the empire. At the same time, these references to Greek help explain many aspects of the Gospel story (including the possibility of a direct conversation between Pilate and Caiaphas, and Pilate and Jesus, as well as the fact that the New Testament was written in Greek, and the rapid spread of Christianity in the first century).

From a linguistic (and cross-linguistic) point of view, perhaps the greatest challenge in this chapter presents the word "Sanhedrin": a "collective body" which can make decisions as one person. Neither phrases like "a collective body" nor words like "group" have their counterparts in most languages of the world, and a word like "Sanhedrin" is not easy to explain in cross-translatable English. The solution adopted in chapter 20 uses the phrase "some people" (which is readily cross-translatable), "gluing" these people together by means of a label (they are called "the Sanhedrin") and a reference to their ability to, roughly speaking, make joint decisions ("when these people wanted something to happen, they could say: 'we want it to happen,' as one person can say about something: 'I want it to happen'").

I would also like to draw attention to the deliberate vagueness of the phrase "people like Caiaphas." For the purposes of "The Story," it would be unnecessary (as well as futile) to try to specify everywhere who exactly is being referred to (e.g. the Temple authorities, or the members of the religious elites more broadly). So the phrase "people like Caiaphas" is, I think, very useful, and in most contexts entirely adequate. For example, in chapter 19, this phrase is used in the line "when people like Caiaphas knew what Jesus was saying in the Temple, they thought like this: 'This man has to die.'" It is also used two lines down, with reference to what Jesus said in the Temple "to some people like Caiaphas" (presumably, in this case the Temple officials). In some contexts, however, "The Story" needs to be more specific, and the label "Sanhedrin" needs to be used. For example, this applies to the line about the meeting of "the whole Sanhedrin" in Caiaphas's house in the last segment of chapter 20.

One last point. A reader who is familiar with the story of Lazarus may well ask: Why has the memorable reproach of his sisters not been faithfully reproduced in "The Story"? Thus, in John (11:21) Martha says to Jesus, "Lord, if you had been here, my brother would not have died," and Mary echoes these words in John (11:32). But in chapter 20, we find a different phrasing: "Lord, you were not here when he was dying, he died because you were not here." Why not stay faithful to the biblical text?

The answer is that the so-called counter-factual construction, used in John's Gospel, is not universally cross-translatable (contrary to what I have hypothesized in an earlier publication, see Wierzbicka (1997)). Hopefully, the phrasing used here (in chapter 20) allows us to stay very close to the intended sense of Martha's loving reproach to Jesus, without using a construction which, as we now know (cf. Hasada 1997) is not universally available.

Commentary on chapter 21: "Passover"

In this chapter, the greatest challenge is to capture, as clearly and precisely as possible, the parallel between the two "Passovers": the one in Egypt and the one in Jerusalem; and to make this parallel transparent for the reader of "The Story." The essence of this parallel seems clear:

1. A long time ago in Egypt, at the time of Passover,
   God did something very good for the people of Israel.
   After this, the people of Israel could live not like before,
   they were not slaves anymore.
2. This year in Jerusalem, at the time of Passover,
   God will do something very good for all people.
   After this, all people can live not like before,
   they can live not like slaves anymore.

But the difference between the past tense in the first case, and the future tense, in the second, presupposes the point of view of someone for whom the second Passover was still in the future, although it was clearly a very near future ("this year").

Clearly, at the time before Jesus's crucifixion and resurrection (the "second Passover") this point of view could have only been Jesus's: other people didn't yet think about the events unfolding in Jerusalem around the time of Jesus's last Passover on earth as "the second Passover."

Given everything that Jesus says in the relevant chapters of John's Gospel, it seems very likely that Jesus was indeed thinking along those lines, and that the parallel between the two Passovers – the one in Egypt and the one in Jerusalem – was indeed present in his mind. It seems, however, presumptuous and inappropriate to attribute to Jesus any particular thoughts, unless he himself expressed those thoughts in words. Hence the somewhat complicated phrasing of the indented passage about what Jesus may have thought at the time:

> People can now think like this: we don't know how Jesus thought about it at that time; maybe he thought like this: . . .

Providing a short summary of Isaiah's four "Servant songs" is also a challenge: What to choose? And how best to phrase it? In chapter 21, I have focused on the image of the lamb, which takes up the motif of the lamb introduced in chapter 7 (on the prophets) and chapter 13 (on Jesus's baptism), and which will be taken up again in chapter 22.

In recalling John the Baptist's words "This is the Lamb of God," spoken the day after Jesus's baptism, the chapter is trying to explain for the reader some of the meaning, and of the resonances, of this image in the New Testament. The parallel between the two Passovers, the one in Egypt and the one in Jerusalem, raises the question of the counterpart of the lambs killed in Egypt during the new Passover; and it is easy to see how Jesus can be seen to fit that role.

The lambs in Egypt were innocent (didn't do anything bad, didn't want to do anything bad to anyone), and yet according to Exodus they died, because God wanted to do something very good for the people of Israel. As the Christian liturgical texts put it, Jesus, too, was "a spotless victim" (a Passover lamb had to be without blemish); he didn't do anything bad, he didn't want to do anything bad to anyone, and yet he was to die because God wanted to do something very good for all people.

The Orthodox catechism *The Living God* (1989) links John the Baptist's words "This is the Lamb of God" with the prophet Isaiah's four "Servant Songs" and the image of the sacrificial lamb in one of them as follows:

> Like all Jews, the prophet Isaiah received the heritage of the paschal lamb from his forefathers. When he describes the afflictions of the Suffering Servant, humiliated and outraged, a man of sorrows who does not resist evil, who gives his back to scourging and accepts buffeting and spitting without turning his face (Is 50:4-9), Isaiah makes this voluntary and expiatory sacrifice of the future Messiah or Christ (Is 53:4-5) coincide with the sacrificial lamb of Mosaic tradition. In fact, the fourth song of the Servant of God ends with the death of the innocent Lamb: "Like a lamb that is led to the slaughter, and like a sheep that before its shearers is dumb, so he opened not his mouth." (vol. 2, p. 154)

This identification of the "Suffering Servant of God" with the Paschal Lamb is further developed in the Catechism in the following passage:

> The image of the redemptive lamb, passed on from father to son, inspired the prophet of the Most High, John the Baptist. He cried

out on the banks of the Jordan at the sight of a man of modest appearance: "Behold, the Lamb of God, who takes away the sin of the world!" (Jn 1:29). He thus identifies Jesus as the Suffering Servant described by Isaiah, who will be given over to death for the sins of many. (vol. 2, p. 155)

But as the Catechism's reference to the "voluntary and expiatory sacrifice of the future Messiah" indicates, the "Suffering Servant of God" was not just a victim, like a lamb led to the slaughter. As chapter 21 puts it, Jesus—the Suffering Servant of God—died because he wanted to do something very good for all people; he died because he wanted all people to live with God. The double role of Jesus—as someone to whom people do very bad things and as someone who wants to do very good things for people—is in focus in the next chapter: "What Jesus said to the Apostles on the night before he died."

Commentary on chapter 22: "What Jesus said to the Apostles on the night before he died"

On Holy Thursday, 2017, my six-year-old granddaughter Therese copied on a sheet of paper Jesus's words from the account of the Last Supper in Matthew's Gospel: "Then he took a cup, and after giving thanks he gave it to them, saying, 'Drink from it, all of you; for this is my blood of the covenant, which is poured out for many for the forgiveness of sins" (Matthew 26:27). Then she said to me, half thinking aloud, half asking: "It is so-oo sad, I guess God wanted it." My heart skipped a beat, and I didn't say anything in response then and there: Although I had thought about it hundreds of times before, I felt I needed to think again before answering my small granddaughter.

Having re-read the next day all the New Testament accounts of the Last Supper, and of the night in the Garden of Olives, I found the account in Mark's Gospel the most helpful at that point: "Abba, Father, for you all things are possible; take away this cup from me; yet not what I want, but what you want" (Mark 14:36, KJV). First, the intimate, childlike address form, "Abba," implies (like "Daddy" in English) a bond: "I feel something very good toward you, I know that you feel something very good towards me" (cf. Wierzbicka 2017b). Second, the sentence "for you all things are possible" (in Mark's Greek, *panta dunata soi*) conveys, I believe, the kind of "almightiness" which was phrased in chapter 1 of "The Story" like this: "If God wants something to happen, it can happen because of this." This leaves us with the two questions: (1) what does "what I want" mean here? and (2) what does "what you want" mean?

In chapter 23 of "The Story" I interpret "what I want" as "if this can not-happen to me, I want it not to happen." As for the words "what you want," in my interpretation they refer neither to anything that God wants to do nor to what Jesus's persecutors want to do (i.e., kill him). Rather, they refer to what God wants Jesus to do, that is, not to defend himself against those who come to arrest him, to speak the truth to those in power (Caiaphas, see chapter 24, and Pilate, see chapter 25), not to oppose those who are nailing him to the cross. Jesus, despite his terror of what is going to happen to him, nonetheless wants to do everything that God wants him to do, and does so. Consequently, just before he dies on the cross, he is able to say to God: "It is accomplished," which I interpret in Minimal English as "I did everything as you wanted" (see chapter 27). The use of Minimal English allows us to distinguish, with clarity and precision, between two possible readings of Jesus's words: (1) "everything happened as you wanted" (wrong) and (2) "I did everything as you wanted" (right).

It would be deeply wrong, I believe, to say that on that first Good Friday (in the Jewish calendar 14 nissan, presumably in the year 30 a.d.) everything happened as God wanted: God did not want Judas to betray Jesus, Caiaphas and Pilate to sentence Jesus to death, or the Roman soldiers to crucify him. It is true, however, to say that "Jesus did everything as God wanted"—a formula echoing the Minimal English version of God's words at Jesus's baptism (chapter 13), at the Transfiguration (chapter 18), and elsewhere.

Inevitably, the question comes to mind at this point: Why didn't God prevent those things from happening? Couldn't God stop Caiaphas and Pilate from passing the death sentence on Jesus, or Judas from telling the Jewish authorities where Jesus was? Here (in light of the discussion in the Commentary on chapter 1), the answer appears to be: no, not having given them free will (that is, the freedom to choose doing something bad over doing something good), and, as Simone Weil (1963: 33) puts it, "tying his hands in the presence of evil." What God *could* do—and did do—was to raise Jesus from the dead after the Crucifixion. This will be discussed in chapter 28 and the commentary on it. Here, the main point is that when Jesus says at the Last Supper, "This is my body that is [given] for you. (. . .) This cup is the new covenant in my blood" (1 Corinthians 11:24–25), he wants to explain to the Apostles, and through them, to other people, the meaning of what he was doing and what was going to happen to him. I will return to this meaning very shortly.

Crucially, in addition to what Jesus did with bread and wine at that Last Supper, and what he said about that bread and wine at the time, he also said that he wanted his disciples to do the same when he wasn't with them on earth anymore. In his First Letter to the Corinthians, Paul writes:

> For I received from the Lord what I also handed on to you, that the Lord Jesus, on the night he was betrayed, took a loaf of bread, and when he had given thanks, he broke it and said, "This is my body that is [given] for you. Do this in remembrance of me." In the same way he took the cup also, after supper, saying, "This cup is the new covenant in my blood. Do this, as

often as you drink it, in remembrance of me." For as often as you eat this bread and drink this cup, you proclaim the Lord's death until he comes. (1 Corinthians 11:23–26)

It is generally agreed that this is the oldest account of what happened on that last Thursday, the day before Jesus died on the cross. It was written around the year 56, and it recorded what Paul had learned from other disciples upon his conversion more than two decades before. As Benedict XVI (2011a: 119) puts it in his *Jesus of Nazareth*, "The Eucharistic texts belong to the earliest strand of tradition. From the point of view of historical evidence, nothing could be more authentic than the Last Supper tradition." As Benedict XVI (2011a) also says, "the so-called institution narrative, namely, the words and actions by which Jesus gave himself to the disciples in the form of bread and wine, lies at the heart of the Last Supper tradition" (p. 115) and "concerns the very heart of Christianity" (p. 103).

These so-called Eucharistic words and actions have been repeated in Christian liturgy (during what Christians call "the Eucharist," or "the Mass") for two thousand years, bringing with them, as Christians experience it, a real presence of Christ. In *Science and Providence*, John Polkinghorne (1989: 92) speaks in this connection of "the Christian experience that the Eucharist is the real presence of Christ in a way most perplexing but undeniable." He also notes that "Testimony to the real presence is by no means confined to the Catholic and Orthodox tradition alone; it is to be found, for example, in Luther and Calvin, and it has been a continuing tradition within Anglicanism also."

What exactly happens in Christian liturgies when Jesus's "Eucharistic" words and actions are repeated is seen by Christians as one of the deepest mysteries of their faith, and the reflection on this mystery is ongoing. Polkinghorne (1989: 93) speaks for many Christians when he writes that "modern Eucharistic thought places emphasis not solely on the elements [bread and wine], but rather upon the whole Eucharistic action, taking place in the gathered community of believers." Elsewhere, referring to the last sentence in Paul's testimony quoted above (1 Corinthians 11:26) and speaking of the Eucharist as "both the commemoration of Calvary (Golgotha) and the anticipation of the heavenly banquet of the Kingdom of God," Polkinghorne (1994: 1584) writes: "I would want to add my own testimony of the mysterious but undeniable experience of the sense of the meeting of past event and future hope in the present reality of the Eucharist." (And I would want to add my own testimony, too, A. W.) To portray how most Christians understand the words "This is my body . . .," "This is my blood . . ." (uttered by the celebrant in the context of a Eucharistic celebration shared with a community of believers), we can propose the following:

> I am with you here now, as I was with the Apostles on the day before I died. In the same way, I can be with you when you are with God, with other people, after you die.

In his book *Jesus of Nazareth: Holy Week*, Benedict XVI (2011a: 117) comments:

> Given the uniquely powerful event described in the Last Supper accounts, in terms of its theological significance and its place in the history of religions, it could hardly fail to be called into question in modern theology: something so utterly extraordinary was scarcely compatible with the picture of the friendly rabbi that many exegetes draw of Jesus. It is "not to be believed of him". Neither, of course, does it match the picture of Jesus as a political revolutionary. Much present-day exegesis, then, disputes the claim that the words of the institution [of the Eucharist] go back to Jesus himself.

As Benedict notes, such skepticism is not based on historical evidence. Chapter 22 of "The Story" agrees with Benedict that what happened at the Last Supper was "something utterly extraordinary," and it emphasizes that what was so extraordinary was above all Jesus's words.

As noted, for example, by the Orthodox catechism *The Living God* (1989), what Jesus did with the bread and the wine was nothing out of the ordinary—but the accompanying *words* were indeed extraordinary: In breaking and distributing the bread, and then passing around the cup, "Jesus followed the gestures traditionally performed by the head of a Jewish family. However, He gives them a completely new meaning, identifying the bread with his body, which will be sanctified for the life of the world upon the Cross" (p. 281). So this is why in chapter 22 the words "he broke the bread into pieces, as he often did, he wanted all the Apostles to eat pieces of one bread" are followed by: "then he said something to the Apostles like no one had ever said before."

The last two sections of chapter 22 try to explain what Jesus said, and what he appears to have meant, without using complex and not cross-translatable words and phrases like "sacrifice," "covenant," and "forgiveness of sins," and without words like "expiation" (not to mention "propitiation,") which are potentially misleading and may distort the New Testament image of God as love ("God is love," 1 John 4:8). I will return to this point in the commentary on chapter 28, "Why Jesus died on the cross", and in Appendix C. At the same time, those last two sections of chapter 22 preserve the symbolism inherent in Jesus's words and actions at the Last Supper while emphasizing that in the light of what Jesus said about himself, he was not being "offered" by someone else, but was giving his life for people, out of love: "I lay down my life that I may take it up again. No one takes it from me, but I lay it down of my own accord. I have power to lay it down and I have power to take it again" (John 10:18); "Greater love has no man than this, that a man lay down his life for his friends" (John 15:13).

This is the "eternal covenant" (as the Letter to the Hebrews 13:20 calls it): not a covenant between God and God's chosen people (the people of Israel), "sealed in the blood of animals," but a covenant between God and *all* people, "sealed" by Jesus, willingly, in his own blood. It is a covenant offered by God to all people to be accepted, willingly, through faith (cf. Paul's Letter to the Romans 3:25). In the "old covenant" Moses said to God, on behalf of the people of Israel, "we want to do everything as God wants." In the "new covenant" Jesus says to God, on behalf of all people, "I want to do everything as you want." (The key idea that Jesus wanted all people to *want* to live with God, and that he was willing to die for this, will be developed more fully in chapter 28.)

To return to little Therese's question, on further reflection I have written the following answer for her: "God didn't want people to kill Jesus. God wanted Jesus to tell people two things, like this: that God loves all people, and that Jesus is the Son of God. God knew that if Jesus told people these two things, people would kill him, he knew that Jesus would die on the cross. Jesus knew the same. Jesus could have said: 'I don't want people to kill me, I don't want to die on the cross.' He didn't say it, because he wanted to do something very good for all people. He wanted people to know that he loved all people, he wanted people to know that God loves all people. We can know now that because Jesus died on the cross, all people can live with God, with other people, forever. At the same time, we can know that while we live on earth, we can eat the bread, drink the wine with other people in the way the Apostles did on the night before he died and that this helps us to live with Jesus with other people, as eating bread every day helps us to stay alive."

For Christians, these are mysteries, yet as Polkinghorne's testimony illustrates, these mysteries resonate with their experience.

Commentary on chapter 23: "Gethsemane"

In his novel *Doctor Zhivago*, Russian writer Boris Pasternak (1973) includes a cycle of poems written (we are told) by the hero, Jurij Zhivago. One of them, entitled Gethsemane, sets the scene, beginning with Jesus's and the Apostles' nocturnal passage from the house where the Last Supper took place to the Mount of Olives:

> The turn of the road was lit
> By the unconcerned shimmer of distant stars.
> The road circled the Mount of Olives;
> Beneath it flowed the Kedron.
>
> The field tailed off
> Into the Milky Way,
> Grey-haired olive trees tried to walk the air
> Into the distance.

> Across the way was a vegetable garden.
> Leaving his disciples outside the enclosure,
> He said to them: "My soul is sorrowful unto death."
> Stay here and watch with me. (p. 603)

The sentence "My soul is sorrowful unto death" included in this translation of Pasternak's poem is a variation of the rendition of Jesus's words in Mark's Gospel (14:34) as given in the King James Bible (KJV), the Revised Standard Version (RSV), and the New Revised Standard Version (NRSV):

> Mark's Greek: perylyptos estin he psykhe mou eos thanatou.
> KJV: My soul is exceeding sorrowful, even unto death.
> RSV: My soul is very sorrowful, even to death.
> NRSV: I am deeply grieved, even to death.

Chapter 23 of "The Story" seeks to be faithful to the Greek original and to stay close to Jesus's own way of thinking, as reflected in his words and phrases remembered (we presume) by Peter and passed on by Peter to Mark. At the same time, it chooses words and phrases which are both clear in meaning and cross-translatable. This results in the sentence: "It is like this in my soul now: I feel something very very bad; someone can feel like this when they are dying." This rendering is of course far from idiomatic, and may seem strange to the English reader. Yet to dispense with the word "soul" and to replace it with a phrase like "deeply grieved," as the New Revised Standard Version does, distorts Jesus's way of thinking (as well as losing the echoes of Psalm 42 which no doubt were in Jesus's mind), whereas the phrase "even unto death" is not fully understandable to the modern reader. The Minimal English rendering, while not idiomatic, is semantically transparent, and does not introduce any meanings absent from the original Greek of Mark's Gospel or (we must presume) from Jesus's Aramaic.

We could easily make the Minimal English rendering of Jesus's words more idiomatic by simply omitting the first clause, with its reference to "soul," and say: "I feel something very very bad; someone can feel like this when they are dying." This would, however, significantly alter the meaning preserved in Mark's Gospel. One can feel something very bad (perhaps even very very bad) while at the same experiencing some other feelings too (as illustrated by the combination of something like terror and something like ecstasy in the scene of the Transfiguration, see chapter 18 of "The Story"). The frame: "it is like this in my soul now" excludes any possibility of mixed feelings.

It might be asked, however: is the word "soul" itself cross-translatable? The answer is: Yes, up to a point; as cross-linguistic evidence suggests, all languages have a word identical in meaning to "body," and another, comparable (though not identical) to "soul." The Hebrew and Aramaic word that Jesus would have used for the invisible counterpart of "body" was "nepesh." The Greek word was "psykhe" (as in Mark 14:34), the Russian word is "duša," the Yolngu (Australia) word—"birrimbir," and so on (see Wierzbicka 2016). The full meaning of each of these words may be different from its counterparts in other languages, but evidence suggests that the core meaning is the same. On present indications, the quasi-locative phrase "in my soul" is also cross-translatable.

In the synoptic Gospels (Mark, Matthew, and Luke), Jesus's appeal to his closest friends to stay with him and to be awake when, to phrase his words in Minimal English, "it was like this in his soul," is followed by his turning in prayer to God. To quote Mark (in the King James Version):

> And he went further a little, and fell on the ground and prayed that, if it were possible, the hour might pass from him. And he said, "Abba, Father, all things are possible unto thee; take away this cup from me; nevertheless not what I will, but what thou wilt." (Mark 14:35–36)

In "The Story," these words of Jesus, which are at the heart of Christian faith, are represented as follows:

> Abba, my Father, if this can not-happen to me, I want it not to happen.
> At the same time I want everything to happen as *you* want, not as I want.

The phrase "if this can not-happen to me . . ." may sound awkward in modern English, but it is both intelligible and cross-translatable, as is everything else in this rendering.

The words in Mark's Gospel: "all things are possible unto thee" ("for you everything is possible," RSV) could be interpreted in a few different ways. The context in which they occur in Mark, where they are followed by the words "take this cup away from me," suggests the following interpretation: "I know that if you say: 'I want it not to happen,' it *will* not-happen." But this sounds too analytical to be included in the text of "The Story." The phrasing chosen instead—"if this can not-happen to me"—is shorter and simpler, and it comes close to Jesus's actual words in Matthew's Gospel.

As noted by Benedict XVI (2011a: 157) in *Jesus of Nazareth*, Christians have always struggled to understand the meaning, and the mystery, of Jesus's prayer in Gethsemane and "the early Church's efforts to arrive at an understanding of the figure of Jesus Christ took their final shape as a result of faith-filled reflection on his prayer on the Mount of Olives." In this connection, Benedict recalls the comments of the famous seventh-century Byzantine theologian Maximus the Confessor, who spoke of the "irreducible duality of human and divine willing in Jesus" and of Jesus's two wills, his "natural will" and his "personal will."

But discussions framed in terms of "two wills," however helpful they may be for speakers of languages which do have a word for "will," are certainly not cross-translatable. The same applies to words like "obedient" and "obedience," which, in addition to being not cross-translatable, can also be misleading. For example, German theologian Christoph Schönborn (1994: 126–127), in his book *God's Human Face*, states: "the transition between the two wills from opposition to union is accomplished through the sacrifice of obedience. In the agony in Gethsemane, this transition occurs."

As chapter 23 illustrates, the use of Minimal English allows us to stay much closer to Jesus's actual words, as well as speaking in ways which are both clear and cross-translatable. It also prevents the impression that Jesus thought: "I have to do this" (i.e., "I can't not do this"), which would be quite inconsistent with the rendering of Jesus's prayer given by Matthew, Mark, and Luke. Relying on the simple and universally cross-translatable words "want," "don't want," "do," and "happen," we can portray Jesus's inner struggle without abstract and potentially misleading words like "will" and "obedience." It is true that the word "will" (in Greek, *thelema*) does occur in Matthew's rendering of Jesus's prayer in Gethsemane, and indeed in the Lord's Prayer ("thy will be done"), but in translating the Gospel into languages which don't have an abstract noun like "will" the meaning of "thy will be done" needs to be clarified via a verb meaning "want." In addition to the universal concept "want," the universal syntactic construction "as you want" is also very important here. Jesus was not saying to God: "I have to do it, because you want me to do it." Rather, he was saying: "I want to do [everything] as you want."

The prayer in Gethsemane does not contradict what Jesus says in John's Gospel (John 10:17–19): "I lay down my life, that I may take it again. No man takes it from me, but I lay it down of my own accord." I stress this point because in many accounts of what happened in Gethsemane that night the phrases "had to" or "have to" are used about Jesus. But this is a misinterpretation. When Jesus says (in Matthew 26:54): "But how then should the scriptures be fulfilled, that it must be so," he doesn't mean "I know that I have to do it [drink this cup]." This is evident from the preceding sentence: "Do you think that I cannot appeal to my Father, and he will at once send me more than twelve legions of angels?" It is clear, then, that after his plea "let this cup pass from me" Jesus freely accepts the "cup," in the following sense: "I say: I want everything to happen as you want, not as I want"; and "I want to do everything as you want."

After the prayer to God about "the cup" and before the words addressed to Peter, a change evidently occurs in Jesus's thoughts. As Alexander Men' writes, "Finally, Jesus rose. Love to his Father had triumphed and strengthened in Him an accord of human and divine will." A very short time later, when the soldiers and guards appear in the garden and when Peter tries to defend Jesus with a sword, Jesus says to Peter: "Put your sword into its sheath; shall I not drink the cup which the Father has given me?" (John 18:11). In chapter 23 of "The Story" the corresponding line reads: "Jesus said to Peter: 'Don't do anything with a sword. My Father wants me to drink this cup, I want to do everything as he wants."

Using Minimal English we can make it clear that at no point does Jesus say, in effect: "I don't want to drink this cup," although (speaking in Minimal English) he evidently does for some time *feel* like someone can feel when they think like this: "something very bad will happen to me now, I don't want it to happen." What Jesus does say is, first (to paraphrase Mark 14:36): "If this can not-happen to me, I want it not to happen," and later (to paraphrase John 18:11): "I want to do everything as God wants." As we can understand it, what God wants Jesus to do at this stage is (as Jesus sees it) not to oppose those who have come to arrest him, not to run away, and not to deny who he is:

> Then Jesus, knowing all that was to befall him, came forward and said to them: "Whom do you seek?" They answered him, "Jesus of Nazareth". Jesus said to them, "I am he" [ego eimi, I AM] (. . .) When he said, "I am he," they drew back and fell to the ground. (John 18:4)

As Men' (1969: ch. 16) notes, it must have been the Jewish guards who drew back, shocked, when they heard Jesus replying "with the sacred formula of God's name [I AM]." It is the same sacred formula with which Jesus was to reply to the High Priest's question later that night—a reply that was to be followed by a sentence of death.

Commentary on chapter 24: "Jesus before Caiaphas"

Chapter 24 has two main themes: the trial of Jesus before the Jewish leaders and Peter's denial. In this commentary, I will only comment on the first of the two, where the most challenging concept is that of "blasphemy." The readers of the Gospels are well aware that by the time Jesus is brought to trial in the High Priest Caiaphas's house, the Sanhedrin has already decided what the outcome of the trial must be: a death sentence. To maintain the appearance that the matter has not been decided in advance, witnesses are brought in, but their testimonies are not consistent. Then Caiaphas reaches for the weapon which he has reasons to expect will not fail: a charge of "blasphemy."

He knows that people call Jesus "the Son of God," and that Jesus calls God "Father." He asks him, then, in front of the whole Council: "Are you the Messiah, the Son of the Blessed One [i.e. God]?" (Mark 14:62) Jesus answers in a way which from Caiaphas's point of view could not be more self-incriminating. Not only does he say, "I am," but he goes on to identify himself with the "Son of Man seated at the right hand of Power [i.e. God] and coming on the clouds of heaven," using the words from Psalm 110 and the vision of prophet Daniel (7:13).

As Benedict XVI (2011a: 180–181) writes, "Jesus accepted the title Messiah, with all the meanings accruing it from the tradition, but at the same time he qualified it in a way that could only lead to a guilty verdict, which he could have avoided (. . .) He left no room for political or military interpretation of the Messiah's activity. No, the Messiah—he himself—will come as the Son of Man on the clouds of heaven." At this point Caiaphas ritually tears his robe and says: "He has blasphemed! Why do we need witnesses? You have now heard his blasphemy" (Matthew 26:65–66)

But what is "blasphemy" (in the sense in which Caiaphas uses it to condemn Jesus) and how can it be explained in cross-translatable words?

According to the *Dictionary of the Bible* (Browning 2009) "blasphemy" is "a deliberate assault on the majesty of God." This may seem intuitively convincing, but it is hardly transparent in meaning and in any case it is anything but cross-translatable.

Mark's Gospel (14:63) uses the Greek word "blasphemia," thus no doubt rendering Caiaphas's Hebrew word "ne'âtsâh." It is not absolutely clear what exactly this word would have meant in first-century Palestine. *The Greek-English Dictionary of the New Testament* (1983) glosses "blasphemia" as "speaking against God, blasphemy."

But what exactly is "speaking against God"? In the part of the Bible called Leviticus, "blasphemy" is explained in terms of "cursing the name of God" (Leviticus 24:11) and "cursing God" (Leviticus 24:15). Evidently, however, this word was used in the Bible far more broadly (as shown, for example, by the entry "Blasphemy" in the *Oxford Companion to the Bible* 1993). Presumably, speakers had a certain prototype in mind and extended the use of the word in various ways which seemed to them compatible with the prototype. One thing is clear: according to Leviticus (24:10–16), "blasphemy" was punishable by death, and evidently, this passage in Leviticus is the key reference point for Caiaphas and the whole Sanhedrin.

Using Minimal English, I have formulated the essence of Caiaphas's charge against Jesus with the help of the clause "if someone says something very bad about God." Presumably, the point is not that, according to Caiaphas, Jesus did indeed say something very bad about God, but rather, that he said something of the same kind as that. *The Oxford Companion to the Bible* (1993: 91) links "blasphemy" in particular with a situation "when a person speaks against God in a way that fails to recognize the sacredness and honour of God's person and name." It is not clear, however, how exactly such a failure to recognize "the sacredness and honour of God" would manifest itself, other than by someone deliberately saying something bad, or very bad, about God.

As for Caiaphas's gesture of tearing his robe, it is not clear how its full meaning should be articulated (especially for the cultural outsider). The phrasing used in chapter 24—"when I hear this, I feel something very very bad"—is no doubt incomplete, but it is consistent with the situation, and presumably, valid, as far as it goes.

One final comment: the justification of the last two lines of chapter 24, which go beyond what the Gospels say. How do we know that Caiphas spoke to Pilate on Thursday night, or that Pilate spoke about Caiaphas's late-night visit to his wife? The answer is that we do not know, but that these are very plausible conjectures based on what the Gospels do say. These conjectures draw on the very fine "forensics" undertaken by the lawyer-historian Frank Morison (1958) in his book *Who Moved the Stone?* Without these hypotheses it is not clear why Pilate would have received the Jewish leaders on Friday early morning in the way he did, as if he was expecting them (John 18:28), or why Pilate's wife would have sent him, during the time when he (Pilate) was interrogating Jesus in the Praetorium, urgent notes referring to her dreams about Jesus. As we will see very shortly, all these elements of the story are recounted, on the basis of the Gospels, in chapter 25. Morison's conjectures clarify the logic of the situation, simply putting two and two together, and as the last two lines of chapter 24 show, they can be easily formulated in cross-translatable words and phrases of Minimal English.

Comment on chapter 25: "Jesus before Pilate"

The cock's crow, when Peter denied Jesus, announced the arrival of the day-break, when the Roman governor would start holding court in the Praetorium. In John's Gospel (18: 28–33, RSV) we read:

> Then they led Jesus from the house of Caiaphas to the praetorium. It was early. They themselves did not enter the praetorium, so that they might not be defiled but might eat the passover. So Pilate went out to them and said, "What accusation do you bring against this man?" They answered him, "If this man were not an evildoer, we would not have handed him over." Pilate said to them, "Take him yourselves and judge him by your own law." The Jews said to him, "It is not lawful for us to put any man to death." This was to fulfil the word which Jesus had spoken to show by what death he was to die. Pilate entered the praetorium again and called Jesus, and said to him, "Are you the King of the Jews?"

In the trial before the Sanhedrin, Jesus was found guilty of blasphemy, but in presenting the case to Pilate, Caiaphas and those with him have obviously emphasized the political aspect: Jesus's apparent claim to kingship, which from the point of view of the Roman governor would have been a political offense, to be punished by Roman justice. Hence Pilate's first question to Jesus: "Are you the king of the Jews?" The conversation continues as follows:

> Jesus answered, "Do you say this of your own accord, or did others say it to you about me?" Pilate answered, "Am I a Jew? Your own nation and the chief priests have handed you over to me; what have you done?" Jesus

answered, "My kingship is not of this world; if my kingship were of this world, my servants would fight, that I might not be handed over to the Jews; but my kingship is not from the world." Pilate said to him, "So you are a king?" Jesus answered, "You say that I am a king. For this I was born, and for this I have come into the world, to bear witness to the truth. Every one who is of the truth hears my voice." Pilate said to him, "What is truth?"

In chapter 25, I have rendered Jesus's words "My kingship is not of this world" by means of the three sentences: "I am a king not like other kings" and "I am not the king of a country on earth" and "No soldiers have to do as I say." As noted in *Jesus of Nazareth. Holy Week* (Benedict XVI 2011a), this last point must have been decisive for Pilate: Jesus was accused of claiming kingship and a kingdom (in Greek, *basileus* and *basilea*). And yet, "No one is fighting for this kingship. If power, indeed military power, is characteristic of kingship and kingdoms, there is no sign of it in Jesus' case. And neither is there any threat to Roman order. This kingdom is powerless" (p. 199).

There are many other striking aspects in the conversations between Jesus and Pilate, but here I will focus only on one: Jesus's words about the purpose of his life on earth. In response to Pilate's question: "Are you the king of the Jews?" Jesus says: "To this end was I born, and for this cause came I into the world, that I should bear witness unto the truth" (John 18:38). Many readers of the Gospels find this answer puzzling: wasn't Jesus born in order to save people, rather than to bear witness to the truth? If Jesus's saving mission is understood in terms of "ransom" (something done by the "saviour" for the people who are "kidnapped," without any participation or response from these people themselves), then indeed Jesus's emphasis on giving witness to the truth may seem strange. If, however, Jesus's purpose was to bring people to living with God by appealing to people's own will and as it were "winning them over" for God, then the appeal to truth becomes understandable.

In another famous reference to the truth Jesus says: "ye shall know the truth and the truth shall make you free" (John 8:32). This sounds as if it wasn't "ransom" that would make people free but the truth (that is, presumably, their own recognition of the truth). This is indeed the interpretation suggested by the passage in Paul's First Letter to Timothy, where the word "ransom" is used and explained by Paul himself as a metaphor:

> God our Saviour, who desires all men to be saved and to come to the knowledge of the truth. For there is one God, and there is one mediator between God and men, the man Christ Jesus, who gave himself as a ransom for all. . . . (1 Timothy 2:4–5)

I will return to the use of the word "ransom" in the New Testament in the commentary on chapter 28 ("Why Jesus died on the cross"). Here, I will note the importance of the reference to the word "voice." If people hear Jesus's voice then they can know what is true; but in order to hear his voice, they have to really want to know what is true. (Obviously, "voice" refers here not only to what people can hear with their ears, but also, to what they can hear in their heads and in their hearts when they read the Gospels and seek the truth.)

Another arresting aspect of Jesus's words about the "truth" (rendered in Minimal English with the cross-translatable adjective "true") is the reference to "giving witness" (in Greek, *martyreo*, a verb cognate with the noun *martyros*—first "witness" and then "martyr"). The implication here appears to be that Jesus was not only *speaking* the truth but also confirming it with his life and his person. I have not spelled this implication out in chapter 25, except for the reference to Jesus's "voice." If someone really wants to know what is true, they will *hear* Jesus's voice and recognize that he is trustworthy and that what he says must be true.

Pilate, as presented in John's Gospel, does "hear" Jesus to some extent, and recognizes that this man is not lying; at the same time, he doesn't sufficiently *want* to know what is true to accept that everything that Jesus says is true, and to draw the consequences. One thought is clear in his mind: "If I don't say: 'this man has to die,' something very bad can happen to me"; and this thought prevents him from doing what he knows justice demands. Benedict XVI (2011a) comments:

> Finally, Pilate takes his place on the judgment seat. Once again he says: "Here is your King!" (Jn 19:14). Then he pronounces the death sentence. Indeed the great "Truth" of which Jesus had spoken was inaccessible to Pilate. Yet the concrete truth of this particular case he knew very well. He knew that this Jesus was not a political criminal and that the kingship he claimed did not represent any political danger—that he ought therefore to be acquitted. (p. 200)

Translating the outcome of the trial into simple and cross-translatable words, chapter 25 puts it like this: "Pilate said: 'this man has to die'; then he said to the soldiers: 'kill him.'"

Pilate's final gesture, washing his hands, is symbolic, as was Caiaphas's gesture of tearing his robe. Chapter 25 explains this meaning in simple and cross-translatable words as follows: "I know that something very bad is happening here. It is happening because someone wanted it, I didn't want it." (Was Pilate thinking at the same time, "I did something very bad"? We have no grounds for thinking that he did, although we do have good reasons to think that his wife did.)

To return to Pilate's exchange with Jesus, an obvious question is: in what language did Pilate speak to Jesus, and Jesus to Pilate? Since Greek was the lingua franca of the Roman Empire and since we have no reasons to think that Pilate could speak Aramaic, it seems likely that the exchange was in Greek. Admittedly, we don't know that Jesus could speak Greek either, but as argued persuasively by historians such as John Dickson (2010), anyone who was involved in trade or business in Palestine needed to speak some Greek. This included carpenters and builders like Joseph and Jesus, and fishermen and fishsellers like Zebedee and his sons. We can presume, then, that the exchange between Jesus and Pilate was in Greek.

And who witnessed that exchange? German Lutheran scholar Gottfried Voigt (1991: 261), in his beautiful book-length commentary on John's Gospel, writes: "There were no eyewitnesses. But John writes like someone who has learnt in Jesus' school. The 'Son of Thunder' has understood his Lord very well and could therefore describe the exchange between the accused and the judge very well."

Thus, like many other commentators Voigt assumes that there were no eyewitnesses and that John must have *imagined* what was said between Pilate and Jesus. But is this assumption justified? Is it not possible that John himself was actually present? After all, unlike the members of the Sanhedrin, *he* didn't have to fear "defilement" which would have prevented him from eating the Passover meal that evening because he had already eaten that meal (with Jesus and the other Apostles). We know that John was in Caiaphas's house when the Sanhedrin was conducting its trial of Jesus, and undoubtedly, he would have followed Jesus when the guards were taking him to the Praetorium. When Jesus was led inside (presumably by the guards) could John perhaps have got inside with them?

There was also Claudia Procula, Pilate's wife, who was intensely interested in the proceedings against Jesus. As we know from Matthew's Gospel (27:19), Claudia was at that time inside the Praetorium, and was trying to prevent Pilate from passing a death sentence on Jesus. We also know that in the third century, Origen suggested in his "Homilies on Matthew" that Pilate's wife had become a Christian, and that this view was shared by several theologians of Antiquity and the Middle Ages (*Catholic Encyclopedia* 1913). Further, we know that Claudia is venerated as a saint in the Greek Orthodox Church and the Ethiopian Orthodox Church.

Finally, there is a literary quality to the exchange between Jesus and Pilate which makes this exchange ring true. One can readily say about this exchange what C. S. Lewis said about several other dialogues between Jesus and other people in John's Gospel (and in particular, about the "woman caught in adultery" passage in John 8:1–11):

> I have been reading poems, romances, vision-literature, legends, myths all my life. I know what they are like. I know that not one of them is like this. Of this text there are only two possible views. Either this is reportage—though it may no doubt contain errors—pretty close up to the facts (. . .). Or else, some unknown writer in the second century, without known predecessors or successors, suddenly anticipated the whole technique of

modern, novelistic, realistic narrative. If it is untrue, it must be a narrative of that kind. The reader who doesn't see this has simply not learned to read. (Lewis 1978: 108)

In John's Gospel, Jesus tells Pilate: "Everyone that is of the truth heareth my voice" (John 18:36, KJV) (to which Pilate famously replies: "What is truth?"). Many readers of John's Gospel believe that they can "hear Jesus' voice" in Jesus's exchange with Pilate, and that, for example, the sentences "My kingdom is not of this world" and "For this I was born, and for this I have come into the world, to bear witness to the truth" (John 18:36–37, KJV) cannot be someone's else's literary inventions.

Christians can wonder: Do we hear in the Greek versions of these sentences (Ego eis touto gegennemai kai eis touto elelytha eis ton kosmon, hina martyreso te aletheia . . .) something that Jesus actually said? (Not in translation, but his very words?)

Benedict XVI (2011a: 184) comments, cautiously: "Certainly no one would claim that John set out to provide anything resembling a transcript of the trial. Yet we may assume that he was able to explain with great precision the core question at issue and that he presents us with a true account of the trial." Christians can wonder, though: perhaps this is not just a matter of precision in explaining the core question at issue but also of some words and sentences being actually remembered by an eyewitness—whether John himself, or Claudia Procula, or possibly one of the guards in the Praetorium who later became a Christian? Be that as it may, for Christians, the intended meaning of Jesus's own explanation of "why I was born, and why I have come into the world" (John 18:37) is of utmost importance. Chapter 25 of "The Story" tries to capture that meaning in simple and cross-translatable words.

Commentary on chapter 26: "Jesus is nailed to the cross"

In *Encountering Scripture: A scientist explores the Bible*, John Polkinghorne (2010) writes:

Crucifixion was devised by the Romans to be a lingering and torturing death, imposed on rebels, slaves and felons. To the criminal hanging on the cross, every breath was excruciating as he had to press on the nails to raise his chest in order to breathe. The perpetual pain, together with the loss of blood, the heat, the flies and the public exposure, made crucifixion a particularly horrible form of death. (. . .) In addition to this suffering, a first-century Jew would have seen crucifixion as a sign of divine rejection, for it says in Deuteronomy 21.23, "anyone hung on a tree is under God's curse." (p. 71)

Among the "indisputable facts" about Jesus, historian E. P. Sanders (1985: 11) includes the fact that "Jesus was crucified outside Jerusalem by the Roman authorities." It is not easy to describe in cross-translatable words what a Roman cross was, and what this "particularly horrible form of death" looked like. To give someone who knows nothing about it an idea of the cross and the cruci-fixion we need a number of concrete words, some of them universal or near universal (such as "long," "head," "arms," "face," "ground") and some not ("to tie," "to nail," "to hang"). More challenging than the words, however, is the task of explaining, through words alone (i.e., without any pictures), the struc-ture of the cross, its relation to the place where it stood and the body which hung on it, and the logistics of it all. I hope I have achieved this in the third segment of the text, but I do not expect the full content of this segment to be easy to grasp without a picture of the cross (†).

In this commentary, I will not discuss the logistics of the crucifixion any further, commenting instead on the meaning of the cross, on Jesus's prayer for his executioners, and on the love and suffering of God (the Father).

In addition to the physical aspects of the cross, there are also the symbolic ones, which are important to Christian faith, but again, not easy to articulate in cross-translatable words and sentences. I will mention here two attempts to ar-ticulate the symbolic significance of the cross, one by the contemporary Jewish theologian Pinchas Lapide, and the other by a fifth-century Christian theolo-gian known as "Pseudo-Hippolytus."

In his book *Er predigte in ihren Synagogen: Jüdische Evangelienauslegung* ("He taught in their synagogues: a Jewish interpretation of the Gospels"), Pinchas Lapide (1980) writes this about the cross as a "sign of reconciliation" ("Versöhnungszeichen"):

> I have often reflected on the cross—that cross that once was the sadistic instrument of martyrdom of the cruel Romans; on which thousands upon thousands of pious Jews before Jesus, together with Jesus, and after Jesus had to bleed to death. That cross (. . .) that later became the heart of Christian teaching about salvation. (. . .) Shouldn't we finally reinterpret that cross? (pp. 95–96)

What Lapide suggests at this point is that the cross could become "an em-bodiment of the faith of both our Bible-based religions." More specifically, Lapide suggests that the vertical beam of the cross "is like a stake rooted in the earth but pointing to heaven—just as the biblical commandment to love God; whereas the horizontal part, which points, impartially, to the left and to the right, is like the commandment to love one's neighbours, who find the best guarantee for the meaning and hope of their life in the same God and Father." I find this a powerful idea, which underscores the symbolic significance of the shape of the cross seemingly pointing to heaven and embracing the whole earth (and the whole of humankind).

A somewhat different but analogous way to think about the cross could be to link the "arms" of the cross with love (for people) and the vertical stake with faith (in God). Drawing on the resources of Minimal English we could say that when looking at the horizontal part of the cross people can think about all people, and when looking at the vertical part, they can think about God, and that when looking at the cross as a whole people can think about God and about all people at the same time.

It is interesting to note that, as discussed by British theologian Alister McGrath (1995: 179) in his *Christian Theology Reader*, "the means in which the death of Christ on the cross enabled humanity to be redeemed was the subject of considerable speculation in the early patristic period." One example is the anonymous Easter homily known as "Pseudo-Hippolytus on the Cosmic Dimensions of the Cross," which, as McGrath puts it, "views the cross against a cosmic background, arguing that the redemption achieved by Christ affected every aspect of the universe":

> This tree of heavenly proportions rises up from the earth to heaven. It is fixed, as an eternal growth, at the midpoint of heaven and earth. (. . .) Established by the invisible pegs of the Spirit, it holds together the various aspects of human nature in such a way that, divinely guided, its nature may never again become separated from God. By its peak which touches the height of the heavens, by its base which supports the earth, and by its immense arms (. . .) it exists in its totality in every thing and in every place. (Pseudo-Hippolytus, in McGrath 1995: 179)

We can see the same cosmic perspective in *One World: The interaction of science and theology* by the scientist John Polkinghorne (1986: 80). Speaking of the "agonizing question" of human suffering he writes: "At the deepest level I believe that the only possible answer is to be found in the darkness and dereliction of the cross, where Christianity asserts that in that lonely figure hanging there we see God himself opening his arms to embrace the bitterness of the strange world he had made."

Trying to capture something of that symbolic significance of the cross in clear and cross-translatable words while staying as close as possible to the biblical text, I have included in chapter 26 of "The Story" the following lines: "When people saw Jesus on the cross, above the earth, his arms on both sides of the cross, they could think like this: 'A short time before, Jesus said: "When I am above the earth, I will draw all people to myself."'" This is based on Jesus's words in John (12:32), which in John's Gospel are followed immediately by the narrator's explanation: "He said this to show by what death he was to die" (John 12:33). In chapter 26, the line with Jesus's words is followed by a line based on both verses 32 and 33 of John's Gospel: "He wanted people to know how he would die, he wanted people to know why he would die like this."

Turning now to Jesus's words: "Father forgive them . . .," we must first note their close correspondence to Jesus's teaching on forgiveness: "Love your enemies and pray for those who persecute you" (Matthew 5:44); "but I say to you that listen, Love your enemies, do good to those who hate you, bless those who curse you, pray for those who abuse you" (Luke 6:27–28). This is precisely what Jesus is doing when he is being nailed to the cross: praying for the Roman soldiers who are doing it. "Forgiveness" is not a word cross-translatable into all languages. In Minimal English, we can explain the meaning of Jesus' prayer for his executioners with the following, fully cross-translatable words: "Father, I don't want anything bad to happen to them because of this, I don't feel anything bad towards them." At the same time, Jesus, the "advocate of sinners" (cf. John 14:15), pleads with the Father: "They don't know what they are doing." (For further discussion of "forgiveness," see commentary on chapter 16, and Appendix A.)

In his book *The Mystery of God's Suffering,* Belgian theologian Jean Galot (1975: 45) writes: "One should recognize here the vertex of God's revelation. In the human life of Jesus, everything is a revelation of God. But suffering is the most intense human experience. It is therefore the most effective in demonstrating what God is." This leads Galot to the conclusion that we must accept, in accordance with the revelation of the New Testament, "an image of God that transcends and overturns our concepts":

> One cannot begin with the idea of omnipotence, the principle of which excludes every possibility of suffering. The true point of departure lies in the fact that the Omnipotent did suffer. Above all, it draws attention to the primacy of God's love. Omnipotence is not the first absolute attribute [of God]. (. . .) Love is primary, and the divine power is that of love. For this reason, such power is capable of abasing itself to the ultimate depth of suffering. (Quoted in Rossé 1987: 130)

This resonates with the First Letter of John: "God is love, and he who abides in love abides in God, and God abides in him" (1 John 4:16). "This love was revealed to us in this way: God sent his only Son into the world so that we might live through him. In this is love, not that we loved God but that he loved us" (4:10). "So we have known and believe the love that God has for us" (4:16). But love is inseparable from suffering—suffering oneself and suffering with others.

Thinking along similar lines as Galot, Polish Catholic theologian Wacław Hryniewicz (2001) emphasizes Jesus's words on the cross: "Who sees me, sees the Father" (John 14:9; 12:45). He comments: "who sees Christ crushed by suffering, sees also the Father marked by suffering. These words undermine the vision of an immutable God who cannot be touched by suffering. From early on, these words generated this intuition [of a co-suffering God], contrary to the widespread, even official, ideas about an 'impassible' God" (p. 305). Crucially (according to Hryniewicz), the God who co-suffers at the crucifixion of his Son can also be seen as the God who shares in all human suffering. "The suffering is not imposed on God from outside. (. . .) God, out of his own will and love, can share the suffering of others, showing in this way his sovereignty over suffering. It is the omnipotence of co-suffering Love!" (Hryniewicz 2001: 312–313) This is also the perspective of the German Protestant theologian Jürgen Moltmann, "widely regarded as one of the most important modern exponents of a 'theology of the cross.'" (McGrath 1995: 117).

> The early Fathers insisted on God's inability to suffer in opposition to the Syrian Monophysite heresy. An essential inability to suffer was the only contrast to passive suffering recognized in the early Church. There is, however, a third form of suffering – active suffering, the suffering of love, a voluntary openness to the possibility of being affected by outside influences. If God were really incapable of suffering, he would also be as incapable of loving, as the God of Aristotle, who was loved by all, but could not love. Whoever is capable of love is also capable of suffering, because he is open to the suffering that love brings with it (. . .) God (. . .) loves from the fullness of his being and suffers because of his full and free love. (Moltmann 1972, quoted in McGrath 1995: 118)

Following the line of thought of theologians like Galot, Hryniewicz, and Moltmann, we might conclude—provisionally—with two points. First, when Jesus was dying on the cross, God was not a bystander and an onlooker: God was suffering *in* Jesus, and *with* Jesus (as Jesus said, "My Father and I are one" (John 10:30) and "I am in the Father and the Father in me" (John 14:10)). As the great third-century theologian Origen put it, "God has taken our ways upon himself, just as the Son of God bore our sufferings. The Father himself is not impassible (*Ipse Pater non est impassibilis*)" (quoted in McGrath 1995: 97).

Second, Jesus died on the cross because for many people who have either suffered terribly themselves or have witnessed the terrible suffering of others, only a suffering God is credible. People have always suffered, and will always suffer, if only because of human freedom: since God gave people free will, some people have always inflicted suffering on others, and always will. But at some point, everyone may come to the realization that, through Jesus, "God-made-man," God suffered on the cross. Isaiah describes the Suffering Servant of God as "a man of sorrows and acquainted with grief" (Isaiah 53:3); but through Jesus, and in Jesus, God himself (God the Father) was acquainted with grief, with suffering. The realization that it is so may be sufficient to overcome many people's reluctance to accept the invitation to live with God, with other people, for ever.

Christians do not claim that they fully understand the cross; rather, they tend to regard it as a mystery. They are convinced, however, that love and forgiveness are at the heart of this mystery, and that there is a deep connection between Jesus's death on the cross and his love for all people (epitomized in his prayer for his executioners). I will probe this connection through Minimal English in chapter 28, and the commentary on it.

Commentary on chapter 27: "Jesus dies on the cross"

The idea of a crucified Messiah was inconceivable to first-century Jews. Early Christians, a large proportion of whom were Jews, did accept the idea, but for a long time they found the image too shocking to contemplate. As Polkinghorne (2010: 71) notes: "There is no depiction of a crucified Christ in Christian art until the centuries in which crucifixion was no longer a contemporary reality. The earliest Christians preferred to represent Jesus as the Good Shepherd." He goes on to comment: "Crucifixion is the death that Jesus died, after crying out, 'My God, my God, why have you forsaken me?', as if to say that Jesus' mental and spiritual suffering was as great as physical." Since I cannot touch on all the different aspects of Jesus's agony on the cross here, I will focus my comments on this cry.

Like Polkinghorne, Benedict XVI (2009), in his book *Credo for Today*, also sees that "cry of abandonment" as the most extreme point in Jesus's ordeal: "The most terrible moment in the story of Jesus' Passion is doubtless the one in which he cries aloud in his extreme torment on the Cross: 'My God, my God, why have you forsaken me?'" (p. 73). In his more recent book *Jesus of Nazareth*, Benedict XVI (2011a: 213) continues his reflections on this moment in the story of Jesus' Passion, and on its significance: "This prayer of Jesus has prompted constant questioning and reflection among Christians: How could the Son of God be abandoned by God? What does this exclamation mean?" His main point is that in their accounts of Jesus's Passion, all four Gospels contain a multitude of Old Testament allusions and quotations: "Word of God and event are deeply interwoven" (p. 202).

As Benedict (2011a) notes, two Old Testament texts are widely recognized as being of fundamental importance to the Passion narratives: Psalm 22 and prophet Isaiah's chapter on the Suffering Servant (Isaiah 53). In view of certain differences between Matthew's and Mark's accounts of Jesus' cry of distress (to be discussed shortly), it is particularly interesting to note Benedict's comment on Psalm 22: "Psalm 22 is Israel's great cry of anguish, in the midst of its sufferings, addressed to the apparently silent God. The word 'cry,' which is of central importance, especially in Mark's account, for the story of Jesus' crucifixion, sets, as it were, the tonality of this psalm" (p. 204). As for Isaiah's "Suffering Servant" chapter, Benedict (2011a: 206) quotes German theologian Marius Reiser: "In Marius Reiser's meticulous analysis of this mysterious passage, we can relive the early Christians' astonishment on seeing how one step after another of the path of Jesus Christ is foretold here. The Prophet—viewed through the lens of all the methods of modern critical textual analysis—speaks as an evangelist." Coming back to Jesus's "cry of abandonment," I will start with the disputed question: In what language did Jesus address God in this case, in Aramaic or in Hebrew? Polkinghorne (2010) writes:

> Both Matthew 27.46 and Mark 15.34 are honest enough to report the cry of dereliction from the cross, "My God, my God, why have you forsaken me?" Mark feels that this is of such solemn significance that he must record the actual Aramaic words that Jesus would have spoken, "Eloi, Eloi, lema sabachthani?", but Matthew reduces the shock a little by turning the words into Hebrew, suggesting a quotation of Psalm 22.1. (p. 58)

Thus the question, who was more accurate here, Mark or Matthew? is linked with a larger one: Did Jesus, or didn't he, have psalm 22 in mind as he uttered that cry? This in turn is linked with an even larger question: Was Jesus in despair when he uttered these words, or did he still trust in God? Evidently, Polkinghorne believes that Jesus uttered the Aramaic words: *Eloi, Eloi, lema sabachthani?* and that he thought at that moment that God had deliberately abandoned him ("the cry of dereliction"). Benedict XVI's (2011a) perspective is different:

> It is no ordinary cry of abandonment. Jesus is praying the great psalm of suffering Israel, and so he is taking upon himself all the tribulation, not just of Israel, but of all those in this world who suffer from God's concealment. He brings the world's anguished cry at God's absence before the heart of God himself. He identifies himself with suffering Israel, with all who suffer under "God's darkness"; he takes their cry, their anguish, all their helplessness, upon himself—and in so doing he transforms it. (p. 214)

In support of this interpretation, Benedict XVI (2011a) shows, through careful textual analysis, that "Psalm 22 pervades the whole Passion story":

> The public humiliation, the mockery and shaking of heads by the scoffers, the pain, the terrible thirst, the piercing of Jesus' hands and feet, the casting of lots for his garment—the whole Passion is, as it were, anticipated in the psalm. Yet when Jesus utters the opening words of the psalm, the whole of this great prayer is essentially already present—including the certainty of an answer to prayer, to be revealed in the Resurrection, in the gathering of the "great assembly", and in the poor having their fill (cf. vv. 24-26). The cry of extreme anguish is at the same time the certainty of an answer from God, the certainty of salvation—not only for Jesus himself, but for "many." (p. 214)

Eminent Russian theologian and Bible translator Sergei Averintsev (2007: 222) also thinks that "the quotation ['My God, my God . . .'] refers to the psalm as a whole, and so should not be unequivocally understood as a cry of despair." In this connection, Averinstsev notes that the Hebrew word "Eli" is much closer to the name of the prophet "Elijah" (Elia) than the Aramaic word "Eloi," so if some people near the cross thought that Jesus was calling Elijah, it is far more likely that Jesus was actually saying "Eli" (as in Matthew) rather than "Eloi" (as in Mark).

Similarly, E. A. Knapp (n.d.), who has devoted a whole article to the question of whether Jesus uttered his "cry of abandonment" in Aramaic or in Hebrew, strongly supports the latter: "Thus, the original version of what Yeshua said is Matthew's "Eli," which must have been spoken in Hebrew in order for the bystanders to mistakenly think he was calling out to Elijah." Knapp concludes: "You may find it thought-provoking to revisit the scene of the Messiah's crucifixion knowing that the words He spoke at one of the most pivotal moments in history were clearly spoken *in Hebrew*."

I assume then, with Benedict XVI, Averintsev, and Knapp (and contra Polkinghorne), that in his cry to God Jesus uttered the Hebrew word "Eli" (as in Matthew's Gospel) and not the Aramaic word "Eloi" (as in Mark's). I also assume, with Benedict XVI and Averintsev, that Jesus's "cry of abandonment" was a quote from psalm 22, and that it invoked the psalm as a whole. I would add that Jesus's inner speech of prayer must have included many phrases from psalms (as in fact it does for many Christians today, but incomparably more so). Further, I assume that Jesus's cry expressed a terrible feeling, rather than a terrible thought: He could have felt like someone may feel when they think that they are totally cut off from God, without actually thinking so himself.

The use of Minimal English helps us to clarify the debates around Jesus's "cry of abandonment" and to pinpoint the difference between the two interpretations: "Jesus thought like this at that moment: 'God is not with me anymore'" (wrong) and "Jesus felt at that moment like someone can feel when they think like this: 'God is not with me anymore'" (right).

The actual words uttered by Jesus are rendered in the Minimal English of "The Story" as "My God, my God, why are you not with me anymore?" I have chosen this phrasing, in preference to "why are you not with me now?" to account for Jesus's feeling of complete abandonment: It is not just a feeling of God's absence (perhaps temporary) but a feeling of being abandoned by God forever ("not anymore"). As commentators such as Balthasar and Moltmann have suggested, Jesus shared at that moment the experience of people who feel that they are in hell.

Speaking of this subjective experience of hell, Balthasar (1983: 281) quotes St John of the Cross's description of just such an experience. Citing from a psalm (psalm 116): "the torments of hell have . . . seized me," St John of the Cross says: "The soul feels keenly the shadows of death, mortal anguish and the torments of hell. It feels itself as being without God . . . and more: it seems that this state will last forever." This chimes in with the way another German theologian, Ernst Käsemann (quoted in Benedict XVI 2007a: 86) describes Jesus's cry of abandonment: "a prayer sent up from hell." A prayer sent up from hell, yes; a cry of despair—no (cf. Rossé 1987).

To further support this conclusion, I will now turn to the additional utterances of Jesus on the cross, one included in John's Gospel, and two, in Luke's. Thus, in John's account, Jesus's final words on the cross were "It is accomplished," in Greek "tetelestai." Very unfortunately, these words are rendered in the King James Bible and its successors (including the Revised Standard Version) as "It is finished"—a misleading translation, which loses the element of "completion" or "a task accomplished," present in the meaning of the Greek word (and in St Jerome's Latin translation, "Consummatum est"). I have tried to convey what I take to be the intended meaning like this: "I have done everything as you wanted."

Luke's account of the crucifixion includes not one but two additional utterances of Jesus on the cross (Luke may have heard about them from Mary, Jesus's mother, to whom he is believed to have been close). First, there is the episode of two criminals dying on the cross on Golgotha at the same time as Jesus (to be discussed more fully in chapter 28). When one of them says to Jesus: "Jesus, remember me when you come into your kingdom," Jesus replies "Truly, I say to you, today you will be with me in Paradise" (23:43). Thus, even though Jesus didn't feel his Father to be with him throughout his agony on the cross, he evidently did not doubt that he would be with his Father ("in Paradise") after he died.

The other vignette included in Luke's Gospel is Jesus's final cry on the cross, just before he died: "Father, into your hands I commit my spirit." Significantly, these words, too, come from a psalm (psalm 31), except that in this case Jesus added the word "Father" before these words (in the psalm these words are not preceded by any form of address, but they are followed by "O Lord").

It is important to note that in many psalms, David cries out to God in utter distress but at the same time expresses trust in God. For example:

"In my distress I cried unto the Lord, and he heard me." (Psalm 120)
"In the day when I cried thou answered me." (Psalm 138)
"Lord, I cry unto thee: make haste unto me (. . .) mine eyes are unto
    thee, O God the Lord; in thee is my trust." (Psalm 141)
"I called upon the Lord in distress: the Lord answered me."
    (Psalm 118)
"Unto thee will I cry, O Lord my rock." (Psalm 28)

However, while many psalms combine a cry of utter distress with an expression of trust, God is addressed in them as either "Eli" ("my God") or "Adonai" ("Lord"), never as "Father." The fact that in his last words Jesus replaces the "Lord" with "Father" (perhaps "Abba") seems to me highly significant.

Commentary on chapter 28: "Why Jesus died on the cross"

The first line in chapter 28 which may give some readers a jolt is: "God didn't want people to kill Jesus." How so? they may think. Christians often say, in relation to Jesus's death on the cross, that it happened according to God's "plan"— a statement that may seem to suggest cruelty and lack of love on God's part. Such use of the word "plan" (and its equivalents in other languages) is thought to go back to Apostle Peter's first speech to the Jews in Jerusalem on Pentecost (Acts 2:23). In the Greek original of the Acts of the Apostles, Peter uses here the phrase "boule kai prognosis," which can be glossed as "purpose and foreknowledge." Using Minimal English we can replace the complex and misleading word "plan" with two simpler words, "want" and "know," which actually correspond more closely to Peter's two-word phrase than the single English word "plan." This allows us to ask two very precise questions—(1) What did God want? and (2) What did God know?—which can help clarify the confusion.

The word "plan" referring to the whole situation blurs the distinction between "want" and "know" and leads many people to think that God both **knew** and **wanted** everything that was going to happen. Relying on these two simpler concepts we can say that (as suggested by the parable of the vineyard and the tenants told by Jesus in Matthew's Gospel (21:33–46)), God **didn't** want people to kill Jesus, while at the same time God **knew** that if Jesus did what God wanted him to do, people would kill him. (The fact that God **knew** what was going to happen and what people would do to Jesus, does not mean that God **wanted** people to do it, and Peter's word "foreknowledge" is very significant here.)

It can be asked at this point: Why then did God want Jesus to do things which, as he knew in advance, would result in people killing him? And why did Jesus agree to do these things (if he too knew what the result would be)? Christians believe that God wanted Jesus to do these things, and that Jesus agreed to do them, because of God's, and Jesus's, love for people. As Anglican theologian Alister McGrath (1992: 14) puts it in his book *A Journey Through Suffering*: "For the Christian, the extent of the love of God is not in doubt: the Son of God dies in order that we might know its full depth."

A central theme in the New Testament is that Jesus wanted to do something very good for all people, in accordance with God's will. For example, in the First Letter to Timothy, Paul (if it was indeed Paul who wrote it), says: "God our Saviour . . . desires all men [people] to be saved and to come to the knowledge of the truth. For there is one God and there is one mediator between God and man, the man Christ Jesus, who gave himself as a ransom for all" (1 Timothy 2:4–5). Accordingly, Paul urges "that supplications, prayers, intercessions and thanksgivings be made for all men [people]" (1 Timothy 2:1).

Was Paul referring to **all** people or only those who lived after Jesus was born, and thus could respond to his teaching about the "kingdom of God"? Numerous passages in the New Testament indicate quite clearly that what is meant by the authors of the New Testament is **all** people (all humankind), and not only those who were born after Jesus. For example, when Paul says in another letter (again, if Paul wrote it): "For the grace of God appeared for the salvation of all men [people]" (Titus 2:11), he clearly refers to **all** people, and not only to some. The biblical use of the word "world," as in the famous passage in the third chapter of John's Gospel, points in the same direction: "For God so loved the world that he gave his only Son, that whoever believes in him should not perish but have eternal life. For God sent the Son into the world, not to condemn the world, but that the world might be saved through him" (John 3:16–17).

The word "ransom" in the first quote from Paul's letter to Timothy above is potentially misleading: Indeed it has sometimes been taken to mean that Jesus was as it were "paying ransom" to God for people who otherwise could not "be saved" (i.e., in Minimal English, could not live with God, with other people, forever). Such a literal interpretation of Paul's use of the word "ransom" would imply both that God was the one enslaving people and that the people in question were passive objects of something done by Jesus and did not have to respond personally to his (and God's) "offer of salvation." That would be incompatible, however, with the New Testament's (and Paul's in particular) insistence that this "offer of salvation" requires that one "believes in" Jesus (as in the quote from John's Gospel above). This is how it was with the "good thief" on the cross next to Jesus: At some moment, he came to "believe in" Jesus and to want to be with him and with God. So obviously Jesus didn't just "ransom" that criminal without any participation of the criminal himself. Rather, as this man was looking at Jesus on the cross, he realized who Jesus was and then freely turned to Jesus and to God. Jesus then accepted the man's inner conversion and promised: "it will be as you want" (not Jesus's exact words, but a paraphrase in Minimal English).

But of course that criminal on the cross next to Jesus lived at the same time as Jesus, not before him. How could such an inner conversion occur in someone who lived long before Jesus? According to many Christian thinkers and mystics, the only coherent overall interpretation is to accept that God wants **all people** "to be saved" (to live with God, with other people, forever), whether they lived after Jesus or before, that the Good News (that all people can live with God if they want to) was offered not only to the living but also to the dead, and that the dead, too, can undergo an inner conversion and come to believe in Jesus and to want to "live with Jesus and with God."

This in fact is what the First Letter of Peter says, in relation to Jesus's "descent to hell" on the day after he died ("Holy Saturday"): "Christ also died for sins once and for all, the righteous and the unrighteous, that he might bring us to God, being put to death in the flesh but made alive in the spirit; in which he went and preached to the spirits in prison, who formerly did not obey, when God's patience waited in the days of Noah, during the building of the ark . . ."

(1 Peter 3:18–20). The "spirits in prison" who lived "in the days of Noah" were people who lived long before Jesus and who, according to some translations, were "rebellious," i.e. (in Minimal English), did not want to live with God. When Jesus "descended to hell" (as the Apostles' Creed puts it, using the word "hell" to render the Hebrew word "Sheol," the "underworld," the "land of the dead"), his purpose was, according to Peter's First Letter, to bring the Good News to the dead: "For this is why the gospel was preached even to the dead, that though judged in the flesh like men, they might live in the spirit like God" (1 Peter 4:5).

What was the "good news" (the gospel) proclaimed by Jesus to the dead, on that Saturday between the Crucifixion and the Resurrection? As many Christian theologians and mystics believe, Jesus was saying to those dead people, that if they wanted, they too could live with God. Thus, Swiss theologian Hans Urs von Balthasar (1982) writes (*The von Balthasar Reader*):

> on Holy Saturday there is the descent of the dead Jesus to hell, that is (put very simply) his solidarity (. . .) with those who have lost their way from God. (p. 153)

> there really have been, especially in earlier periods of theology, in the fathers of the church, numerous approaches that sought to do justice to the biblical statements (. . .) of the *descensus Christi ad inferos* (Christ's descent to the deepest hell), which regarded the descent as the decisive act of the redeemer (cf. the Byzantine and Russian pictures of the journey to hell). (. . .) These manifold attempts at beginning could not be brought into a convincing unity (. . .) And yet Holy Saturday stands as the mysterious middle between cross and resurrection, and consequently properly in the center of all revelation and theology. (pp. 403–404)

This is, in part, what chapter 28 of "The Story" is about. Using traditional Christian language, we can say that this chapter links the key New Testament themes of God's love for all people (of all times), Jesus's desire to do God's will and at the same time to do something very good for all people (the living and the dead), the power of God's love to overcome human resistance, the limitlessness of God's love, mercy and patience, and God's respect for human freedom.

There are now and there have always been considerable differences among Christians in how they think about these themes. In his book *Mere Christianity*, C. S. Lewis (2001 [1952]) wrote about it like this:

> The central Christian belief is that Christ's death has somehow put us right with God and given us a fresh start (. . .) A good many different theories have been held as to how it works; what all Christians are agreed on is that it does work (. . .) We believe that the death of Christ is just that point in history at which something absolutely unimaginable from outside shows through into our own world. (pp. 54–55)

Arguably, "Christ's [or Jesus'] willingness to die on the cross" would be a more fitting phrase here than "Christ's death," but apart from that, this is a helpful comment, as it highlights something that has united Christians for two thousand years—something that has always been at the centre of their meditation, prayer, and worship.

Chapter 28 of "The Story" doesn't aim at a comprehensive picture of what has been said on this point at different times. Rather, it follows that strand of Christian tradition which embodies a hope for all people, the whole of humanity, as reflected in the following quote from the writings of German Jewish philosopher and Carmelite nun Edith Stein, who was murdered at Auschwitz. (I will not try to explain the sense of the Christian words "redemption" and "grace" as used in this quote because I think they are sufficiently clear from the context):

> We attempted to understand what part freedom plays in the work of redemption. For this it is not adequate if one focuses on freedom alone. One must investigate as well what grace can do and whether even for it there is an absolute limit. This we have already seen: grace must come to man. By its own power, it can, at best, come up to his door but never force its way inside. And further: it can come to him without his seeking it, without his desiring it. The question is whether it can complete its work without his cooperation. It seemed to us that this question had to be answered negatively. (. . .) Grace is the Spirit of God who descends to the soul of man. It can find no abode there if it is not freely taken in. That is a hard truth. It implies (. . .) the possibility, in principle, of excluding oneself from redemption and the kingdom of grace. It does *not* imply a limit to divine mercy. For even if we cannot close our minds to the fact that temporal death comes for countless men without their ever having looked eternity in the eye and without salvation's ever having become a problem for them. (. . .) we still do not know whether the decisive hour might not come for all of these somewhere in the next world, and faith can tell us that this is the case.
>
> All-merciful love can thus descend to everyone. We believe that it does so. (Quoted in Balthasar 1988: 218–219; and in Wild 2015: 45–46)

And one more quote, this time from the Catechism of the Russian Orthodox Church published in France in 1989 under the title *Dieu est vivant*, and then in an English translation as *The Living God* (1989, vol. 2):

> *Seeker*: You're talking about those who live in Christ, but what about all the others, those who died before the coming of Christ or those today who don't believe in Him? What happens to them after death?
>
> *Sage*: The apostle Peter answers your question: ". . . He [Christ] went and preached to the spirits in prison, who formerly did not obey, when God's patience waited in the days of Noah, during the building of the ark . . ." (1 Pet 3:19–20).

Those who were, are, or will be rebels, become "spirits in prison" after death. They are in Sheol, the "place of perdition," the "land of forgetfulness," of which the psalms and Isaiah spoke. [...]

But "what is impossible with men is possible with God" (Lk 18:27). And Christ, God made man, descends from heaven, not only down to earth but also into the abyss. He looks for us in the lowest depths, even in Sheol or hell, so that He might break the eternal bonds, liberate Adam and Eve from their prison, and allow those who hear His voice to participate in "the resurrection of Life" which had been promised to the just who accept His love. (vol. 2, pp. 369–370)

When Christians reflect on the question: Why did Jesus die on the cross? (as they have done for two millennia), they often ask themselves: What did Jesus himself think (and say) about it? And many reach the conclusion that the clearest answers to this question can be found in chapter 12 of the Gospel of John. According to this chapter, on the last occasion when Jesus spoke to people in Jerusalem (on the eve of his arrest), he said the following five things, which are clearly interconnected:

1. "The hour has come for the Son of Man to be glorified." (John 12:23)
2. "Truly, truly, I say to you, unless a grain of wheat falls into the
   earth and dies, it remains alone; but if it dies, it bears much fruit."
   (John 12:24)
3. "And I, when I am lifted up from the earth, will draw all men [people]
   to myself." He said this to show by what death he was to die. (John
   12:32–33)
4. "And he who sees me sees him who sent me." (John 12:45)
5. "I came not to judge the world but to save the world." (John 12:47)

A partial translation of these utterances into Minimal English could look like this:

1. In a very short time, I will die.
2. Something very good will happen because of this, as something very
   good can happen if a grain of wheat falls into the ground.
3. When I am above the earth [on the cross], many people will see me.
4. When someone sees me, this someone sees God.
5. I want all people to live with God forever, I was born because of this.

In a somewhat more expanded form, these sayings of Jesus can be interpreted like this:

I will die very soon, I will die on the cross.
Something very good will happen because of this,
    as something very good can happen
    if a grain of wheat falls into the earth.

When I am on the cross, I will feel something very very bad.
Many people will see me on the cross, these people will know what I feel.
Some of them will know that when they see me they see God.
They will know then who I am.
At some time *all* people will see me.
They will *all* know then that when they see me, they see God.
They will all know then who I am.
At the same time, they will know how I died, they will know
    why I died like this.
They will know that I wanted to do something very good for all people.
They will know that I wanted all people to live with God.
They can feel something very good toward me then.
They can think then: "I want to live with Jesus, I want to live with God."
If someone thinks like this, they can live with God, with other people,
    forever.

This interpretation seems to me to be in accordance with what Christians profess in the Nicene Creed: "He will come again in glory to judge the living and the dead and his kingdom will have no end," and in the Apostles' Creed: "I believe in the forgiveness of sins and (. . .) life everlasting." It also accords with the words of Revelation: "To him who loves us and has freed us from our sins by his blood and made us a kingdom (. . .), to him be glory and dominion for ever and ever" (Revelation 1:5–6), and with the vision that follows: "Behold, he is coming with the clouds, and every eye will see him, every one who pierced him" (Revelation 1:7). It is consistent with Jesus's words included in John chapter 12 and quoted earlier in the present commentary. It is also consistent with, and supported by, many other sayings of Jesus in earlier chapters of John's Gospel, such as those listed below. Above all, it is consistent with Jesus's words uttered at the Last Supper: "Greater love has no man than this, that a man lay down his life for his friends" (John 15:13).

1. And as Moses lifted up the serpent in the wilderness, so must the Son of Man be lifted up, that whoever believes in him may have eternal life. (John 3:15)
2. Truly, truly, I say to you, the hour is coming (. . .) when the dead will hear the voice of the Son of God, (. . .) the hour is coming when all who are in the tombs will hear his voice . . . (John 5:25–28)
3. For this is the will of my Father, that everyone who sees the Son and believes in him should have eternal life . . . (John 6:40)
4. When you have lifted up the Son of man, then you will know that I am he (. . .) and that he who sent me is with me. (John 8:28–29)
5. I and my Father are one. (John 10:30)

The first of these five sayings, referring to Moses, requires an explanation. To provide it, I will quote a passage from the posthumous book of the Anglican theologian Edwyn Clement Hoskyns (1940):

> The mission of the son of man is the mission of the Son of God dedicated to be *lifted up*. (. . .) Here an anticipatory Old Testament incident, another prophetic analogy or parable or sign or whatever other term be used to denote that a thing does not exist by itself and in its own right, becomes important and relevant. The children of Israel sinned—in fact, they rejected Moses—and were punished by death in the desert. But Moses, in order to save them, fashioned a serpent—serpents had been the instruments of God for their destruction—and set it up, lifted it up, on a pole or stake like a condemned criminal for all to see. The people looked and—*lived* (Num. xxi.4-9) (vol. 1, pp. 219–220)

As Hoskyns further notes, with reference to another book of the Hebrew Bible (2 Kings 18:4), the bronze serpent fashioned by Moses became later an object of superstition and was destroyed. Then he continues:

> But the biblical story remained imperishable; it lay waiting till apt times and circumstance should give it an opportunity to discharge its office, and now it comes into its own. The son of man must so be lifted up. The Evangelist and his Christian readers know, of course, what this means. It means that the son of man, the visible historical Jesus, must be lifted up on a cross and die in public for all to see as a dangerous disturber of the public peace. But for all those who have eyes to see, for those who believe, the place of death is the place of revelation. (vol. 1, p. 220)

Chapter 28 of "The Story" quotes Jesus's utterance: "When I am lifted up from the earth, I will draw all people to myself," while at the same time trying to elucidate its meaning through simple and cross-translatable phrases such as "above the earth," "people can see," and "live with God."

Commentary on chapter 29: "What happened with Jesus's body after he died"

In the Gospel of John, we first hear John's solemn eyewitness testimony about the crucifixion ("He who saw it has borne witness—his testimony is true, and he knows that he tells the truth," John 19:35), and then his account of the burial of Jesus:

> After this Joseph of Arimathea, who was a disciple of Jesus, but secretly, for fear of the Jews, asked Pilate that he might take away the body of Jesus, and Pilate gave him leave. So he came and took away his body. Nicodemus

also, who had at first come to him by night, came bringing a mixture of myrrh and aloes, about a hundred pounds' weight. They took the body of Jesus, and bound it in linen cloths with the spices, as is the burial custom of the Jews. Now in the place where he was crucified there was a garden, and in the garden a new tomb where no one had ever been laid. So because of the Jewish day of Preparation, as the tomb was close at hand, they laid Jesus there. (John 19:38–42)

For Christians, what happened to Jesus's body after he died is extremely important, because it bears on how they understand Jesus's subsequent resurrection, which is the cornerstone of Christian faith. In his first letter to the Corinthians, written some twenty years after the crucifixion, Paul writes: "I delivered to you as of first importance what I also received, that Christ died for our sins in accordance with the scripture, that he was buried that he was raised on the third day" (1 Corinthians 15:3). As Polkinghorne (1994) notes, the fact that Paul refers to the burial in his extraordinarily concise summary of what happened indicates how important it was to early Christians that Jesus was buried, and buried in a separate tomb, and not in an anonymous common grave in accordance with the normal Roman practice. If Jesus was buried in a separate tomb, and, moreover, one about which a good deal was known, then there could be no mistake as to which tomb was found empty on the morning of the resurrection.

There is archaeological evidence from Palestine later in the first century which shows that a crucified man was, in that case, buried separately and not assigned to a common grave. Thus the story of Jesus' separate burial is not impossible. If it were a made-up story, it is hard to see why Joseph of Arimathea and Nicodemus are the names associated with it, since these figures do not play any prominent part in the subsequent story of the Christian movement. The most natural explanation of their assignment to an honoured role is that they fulfilled it. (p. 116)

Despite the doubts expressed by some modern skeptics, the conviction held by the early Christians that there was indeed a separate tomb—a tomb which was found empty on Sunday morning—is corroborated by the well-attested first-century accusations aimed at Jesus's disciples by their opponents:

Whatever difficulties twentieth-century scholars may feel about the empty tomb stories, they do not seem to have been shared by critics of Christianity in the ancient world. As a bitter polemical argument sprang up between Judaism and the Church, it was always accepted that there was a tomb and that it was empty. The critical counter-suggestion was that the disciples had stolen the body in an act of deception. (. . .) There is clear evidence, then, that in the first century those hostile to Christianity nevertheless accepted that the tomb had been found empty. (Polkinghorne 1994: 117)

The importance of the empty tomb may explain, up to a point, why the names of Joseph of Arimathea and Nicodemus are mentioned. First, Joseph was rich, which is why he owned his own new tomb (as well as the enormous quantities of the sweet-smelling spices which he bought). This rules out any confusion over which tomb Jesus's body was lain in, and which tomb was found empty on Sunday morning. Nicodemus, "a leader of the Jews" (John 3:1), was a witness far more credible, in that patriarchal society, than the women disciples. The involvement of these two prominent Israelites also has broader, symbolic significance, highlighted in *Jesus of Nazareth. Holy Week: From the Entrance into Jerusalem to the Resurrection*:

> After the drama of the trial, in which everything seemed to conspire against Jesus and there seemed to be no one left to speak up for him, we now encounter the other Israel: people who are waiting, people who trust God's promises and await their fulfilment. (. . .) Up to this point in the Gospel, we have encountered such people mainly among simple folk. (. . .) Now—after Jesus' death—we meet two highly regarded representatives of the educated class of Israel who had not yet dared to profess their discipleship, but who nevertheless were blessed with the kind of simple heart that makes man capable of the truth. (cf. Mt 10:25-26) (Benedict XVI 2011a: 227)

From this perspective, the "absurd amount" (Voigt 1991: 274) of costly spices that Joseph of Arimathea brought is also symbolic: "The quantity of balm is extraordinary and exceeds all normal proportions: this is a royal burial." As Benedict XVI (2011a: 228) further comments, Jesus is now "revealed to us as king by the manner of his burial: just when it seems that everything is finished, his glory mysteriously shines through."

Thus, on Friday, before the sunset, Jesus's body was in the tomb, wrapped in linen, and the entrance to the tomb was secured with a very big stone. On Saturday—Christians' "Holy Saturday"—Jesus's body was still in the tomb, and (according to Matthew's Gospel) the tomb was guarded by Roman soldiers, posted there by Pilate, at the request of the Jewish authorities. On that day, as the great third-century theologian Origen put it, "Christ was with the dead" (quoted in Balthasar 1993: 179), and as the Apostles' Creed puts it, "descended into hell." What exactly this mysterious formulation means will be discussed in the commentary to chapter 33.

Turning now to questions of cross-translatability, it will be noticed that this chapter abounds in concrete nouns, such as "tomb," "cave," "garden," "stone," "linen," and "cloth," which are not readily cross-translatable. A few of them have been introduced here as labels ("something called a tomb," "something called myrrh," "something called aloes," "a day called the Sabbath"), but the others have not. There are also two concrete verbs, which may not have exact equivalents in all languages: "push" and "wrap." Because of the presence of such words when this chapter is translated into other languages, it may require the use of either some approximations or some glosses in a cultural glossary, but any resulting divergences between different language-specific versions of this chapter would, I believe, be minor and insignificant.

Commentary on chapter 30: "Jesus lives"

In his First Letter to the Corinthians (1 Corinthians 15:14–15), St Paul writes: "If Christ has not been raised, then our preaching is in vain and your faith is in vain. We are even found to be misrepresenting God, because we testified of God that he raised Christ." Commenting on these words, Benedict XVI (2011a: 241) is equally emphatic: "with these words, Saint Paul explains quite drastically what faith in the Resurrection of Jesus Christ means for the Christian message overall: it is its very foundation. The Christian faith stands or falls with the truth of the testimony that Christ is risen from the dead."

The Anglican bishop N. T. Wright (2008), author of the monumental work *The Resurrection of the Son of God*, agrees. Emphasizing that the idea of one person's (Jesus's) resurrection was a radical innovation in the ancient world (both pagan and Jewish), Wright comments that in the classic Jewish belief, the resurrection was "something that was going to happen to all God's people at the end," and that "no first-century Jew (. . .) believed that there would be one person raised ahead of everybody else" (p. 199). He also explains that the idea of resurrection (at the end of times) was rather marginal to Judaism, and not even generally accepted. By contrast, "we find that in early Christianity 'resurrection' has moved from being one doctrine among many others—important, but not that important—which is where it is in Judaism, to become the center of everything. Take it away from Paul, say, or 1 Peter, Revelation, or the great second-century fathers, and you will destroy their whole framework" (Wright 2007: 199).

From this and other historical considerations Wright concludes that "something must have happened to bring 'resurrection' in from the periphery to the center, to the focal point" (p.199). In a nutshell, what happened was, first, the discovery of the empty tomb, and second, the astonishing "appearances" of the living Jesus to his disciples and his interactions with them. "The Story" focuses on the discovery of the empty tomb in chapter 30, and then reviews the "appearances" in chapters 31, 32, 33, and 34. To begin with the tomb, in the Gospel of John we read:

> Now on the first day of the week Mary Magdalene came to the tomb early, while it was still dark, and saw that the stone had been taken away from the tomb. So she ran, and went to Simon Peter and the other disciple, the one whom Jesus loved, and said to them, "They have taken the Lord out of the

> tomb, and we do not know where they have laid him." Peter then came out with the other disciple, and they went toward the tomb. They both ran, but the other disciple outran Peter and reached the tomb first; and stooping to look in, he saw the linen cloths lying there, but he did not go in. Then Simon Peter came, following him, and went into the tomb; he saw the linen cloths lying, and the napkin, which had been on his head, not lying with the linen cloths but rolled up in a place by itself. Then the other disciple, who reached the tomb first, also went in, and he saw and believed; for as yet they did not know the scripture, that he must rise from the dead. Then the disciples went back to their homes. (John 20:1–10)

John's account says nothing about the resurrection itself, and neither do the other Gospels (although Matthew imagines an earthquake happening in the place where the tomb was). What the first witnesses did see was not the event of the resurrection but its visible effects: no stone at the entrance to the tomb, no body inside the tomb.

John's account concentrates on the experiences of two key witnesses: Mary Magdalene and himself. The other Gospels mention "women" in the plural, and indeed even in John's report, Mary Magdalene speaks in the plural: "We do not know where they have laid him." Neither she nor her companions conclude from their discovery of the empty tomb that Jesus lives. As Polkinghorne (2010: 75) says, "It is striking that the initial reaction of the women is not joy but fear." Mary Magdalene thought that somebody had taken Jesus's body. N. T. Wright (2007: 210) comments: "Tombs were regularly robbed [in the ancient world], especially if the people were rich or famous; there might be jewels in there, there might be something worth stealing." According to Wright, then, without some further evidence, people would have said what Mary Magdalene said later on that morning (see chapter 31): "They have taken away my Lord [i.e., Jesus' body]." "They would never ever have talked about resurrection, if all that had happened was an empty tomb" (Wright 2007: 210). When Simon Peter, alerted by the women, runs to the tomb (together with the "beloved disciple," that is, according to the tradition, John son of Zebedee), he doesn't make that connection either. It is only the "beloved disciple" who has the sudden overwhelming insight: "he saw and he believed." As John the Evangelist tells the story, however, even in John's case, it was not the empty tomb as such that gave rise to that sudden intuition but the question of the linen used in Jesus's burial.

What exactly did John believe at that moment? Presumably, above all, this: "Jesus lives." John's understanding of what happened, and what to expect, could not have been very clear at that point, or even very secure, as we will see in chapter 31. According to the account in John's Gospel, however, this was the first moment of insight, and apparently it was then that the thought "Jesus lives" crossed his mind for the first time. We don't know whether he dared to express it openly to himself and to others before they saw Jesus with their own eyes. I will return to this point in chapter 33.

The fact that it was the women who first discovered that the tomb was empty is widely regarded to be of fundamental importance: Since in first-century Palestine women's testimony was not regarded as reliable, if Christians wanted to invent a story of the empty tomb, they would not have attributed the discovery to women. Since nonetheless all four Gospels (Matthew 28:1–8; Mark 16:1–8; Luke 24:1–10; John 20:1–10) agree that the women saw and reported the empty tomb first, the most likely explanation is that this was simply a fact. I will return to this theme in the commentary on chapter 31.

Commentary on chapter 31: "Mary Magdalene sees Jesus"

In John's Gospel, the story of the resurrection continues with the spotlight on Mary Magdalene, who didn't go away from the empty tomb after Peter and John "had gone back to their homes."

> But Mary stood weeping outside the tomb, and as she wept she stooped to look into the tomb; and she saw two angels in white, sitting where the body of Jesus had lain, one at the head and one at the feet. They said to her, "Woman, why are you weeping?" She said to them, "Because they have taken away my Lord, and I do not know where they have laid him." Saying this, she turned round and saw Jesus standing, but she did not know that it was Jesus. Jesus said to her, "Woman, why are you weeping? Whom do you seek?" Supposing him to be the gardener, she said to him, "Sir, if you have carried him away, tell me where you have laid him, and I will take him away." Jesus said to her, "Mary." She turned and said to him in Hebrew, "Rabboni!" (which means Teacher). Jesus said to her, "Do not hold me, for I have not yet ascended to the Father; but go to my brethren and say to them, I am ascending to my Father and your Father, to my God and your God." Mary Magdalene went and said to the disciples, "I have seen the Lord"; and she told them that he had said these things to her. (John 20:11–18)

John doesn't tell us how, as he remembers, the disciples responded to Mary Magdalene's revelation, but in the Gospel of Luke (which mentions her companions too) we read: "Now it was Mary Magdalene and Joanna and Mary the mother of James and the other women with them who told this to the apostles; but these words seemed to them an idle tale, and they did not believe them" (Luke 24:10–11).

In chapter 31 of "The Story" I have kept John's focus on Mary Magdalene, while drawing in some small measure on the other Gospel accounts as well.

Four aspects of this chapter deserve special comment, the physical (to do with bodies), the psychological (to do with thoughts and feelings), the verbal (to do with words), and the social (to do with "many people").

First, there is the physical aspect of the encounter. Mary Magdalene certainly sees Jesus—the risen Christ. Does she touch him? John's account doesn't say so explicitly, but in Matthew's Gospel (28:9, RSV), we read: "they [the women] (. . .) took hold of his feet and worshipped him." In the Greek text of John (20:17), Jesus says to Mary Magdalene: "me mou haptou," which was rendered in the Vulgate as "noli me tangere" (where *tangere* means "touch") and translated into numerous European languages with a verb meaning "touch": "Do not touch me." (In the King James Version, "Touch me not.") The interpretation "Do not touch me" was reflected in numerous European paintings, for example, in Giotto's "Resurrection," where Jesus as it were recoils from Mary Magdalene's touch. The Greek word *hapto*, however, could mean not only "touch" but also "take hold of," and it was this latter interpretation which was followed (broadly) by the "New Vulgate" (1926), where "tangere" was replaced with "tenere": "noli me tenere." As a result, many recent European translations of the Gospels abandoned the equivalents of "touch" (*tangere*) in favor of something else, usually either "hold" (or expressions derived from "hold") or something like "detain." For example, the New Revised Standard Version says "do not hold on to me," whereas the French translation "Le Nouveau Testament" says *ne me retiens pas*, i.e., "do not detain me."

The element of "holding" suggested by the Greek verb *hapto* is supported by Matthew's version of the story, where the women (more than one) "ekrastesan autou tous podes" (from *krateo* "hold, hold fast"), in the King James Version, "held him by the feet," in the New Revised Standard Version, "took hold of his feet," and in the Polish Millennium Bible *objęły go za nogi*, literally, "embraced him by the legs."

It would appear, then, that Jesus was not objecting to Mary Magdalene touching or holding his feet but, rather, to her holding them for too long—either, because by doing so she was somehow detaining Jesus, or because she was delaying her task of letting the Apostles know that Jesus is alive. Matthew's version (Matthew 28:7), where an angel appears to the women and says: "Go quickly and tell the disciples that he has risen from the dead," would suggest that it is not a matter of "detaining" Jesus but rather, of the need to tell the Apostles the news quickly. This double nuance of "holding" and "detaining" is rendered very felicitously by the English phrase "to hold on to someone," but that phrase is not cross-translatable. Chapter 31 tries to achieve a similar effect through cross-translatable words.

Trying to harmonize the accounts of the two Gospels, John's and Matthew's, while retaining John's spotlight on Mary Magdalene, I have used the phrases "she wanted to touch him, she wanted to hold his feet, she wanted to hold his feet for some time," which are compatible with Jesus's words to her as interpreted in chapter 31 of "The Story" ("Don't do this"), and also, with the account in Matthew's Gospel rendered in English in the Revised Standard Version as "they took hold of his feet."

Moving now from the physical to the psychological aspect of the encounter (and noting that the two are of course closely related), I will quote from the dialogue between "Seeker" and "Sage" in the Orthodox catechism *The Living God* (1989):

> *Seeker:* Why didn't Mary Magdalene recognize Jesus at once? Why did she at first take Him for a gardener?
>
> *Sage:* Mary Magdalene did not recognize Jesus by His features but only by His voice, by hearing Him call her name. The meeting in which she recognized Him is a deeply personal one—"Mary", "Rabboni!"—on a much deeper level than mere physical recognition. Jesus returned from another world. He no longer belongs to the world in which one grows old and dies. He is already part of an eternal world. He returns into this world in such an unheard-of and disconcerting way that only those who had loved and believed in Him could recognize Him in a personal relationship full of love and faith. That is why, several hours after Mary Magdalene sees Him, two other disciples would not be able to recognize Him at first sight. Only Saint Luke gives a detailed account of the second appearance of the Lord Jesus, although Mark (16:12) briefly alludes to it. (p. 211)

Chapter 31 of "The Story" tries to capture some of the key elements emphasized in this passage by means of the components "Jesus said her name to her then," "At that moment [she] knew that it was Jesus," "she knew that it was Jesus's voice," and "she thought: 'this is true,'" "she felt something very very good toward Jesus."

To some extent, Mary's feelings at that moment are reflected in the word "Rabboni," which clearly comes straight from her heart. Biblical scholar Edwyn Clement Hoskyns (1940) comments on this word as follows:

> *Rabboni.* In the older Jewish literature the word *Rabboni*, as distinct from *Rabbi*, is hardly ever used in reference to men, and never in addressing them. The word is reserved for address to God. (. . .) Mary's use of it here is therefore probably to be understood as a declaration of faith, parallel to that of Thomas. (vol. 2, p. 648)

Thomas's encounter with the risen Jesus is the subject of chapter 34, and of the commentary on that chapter. Here, I will note that the encounter between Jesus and Mary Magdalene illuminates not only her attitude to Jesus but also Jesus's attitude toward her. To quote Hoskyns (1940, vol. 2) again, "The Lord appeared first neither to the beloved Disciple, who already believed [as we saw in chapter 30 of "The Story"], nor to Peter (. . .), but to the woman who stood by the Cross and discovered the empty tomb, and who announced her discovery to the disciples" (p. 646). Clearly, Mary Magdalene's role in the story of the Cross and the Resurrection was unique, but so also was Jesus's way of relating to the women who loved him and were his true disciples. Like John, Mary Magdalene was a beloved disciple, too.

Turning now to the main content of what Jesus says to Mary Magdalene, it can be rendered in Minimal English in the following simple sentences: "I want you to say something to my brothers [i.e. the Apostles]," "I want them to know that I say this to them: . . . ," "You will see me in a short time" and "I will now go to my Father, my Father is your Father." The only word in these sentences which is not universally cross-translatable is "brothers" (as discussed in chapter 4 of the Introduction). I have left out from my account Jesus's references to his "ascending to his Father," which are much debated in the literature and whose meaning in this context is not quite clear to me.

The third aspect of this chapter on which I want to comment, the social one, has to do with the place of women in the accounts of the resurrection. As noted by most commentators, in the ancient world, both pagan and Jewish, women were not regarded as reliable witnesses, and in Palestine only men could be admitted as witnesses in court. N. T. Wright (2008: 207) mentions in this context the second-century pagan writer Celsius, who "pours scorn on the resurrection by saying, 'This faith is just based on the testimony of some hysterical women.'" Wright himself draws a diametrically opposed conclusion from the role of women as the first witnesses to Jesus's resurrection:

> it's fascinating that in Matthew, Mark, Luke, and John we have Mary Magdalene, the other Marys, and the other women. (. . .) To put Mary there is, from the point of view of Christian apologists wanting to explain to a sceptical audience that Jesus really did rise from the dead, like shooting themselves in the foot. But to us as historians this kind of thing is gold dust. *The early Christians would never, never have made this up.* The stories—of the women finding an empty tomb and then meeting the risen Jesus—must be regarded as solidly historical. (p. 207)

Speaking as a scientist, John Polkinghorne (2010: 77) concurs: "the most powerful argument for the authenticity of the empty tomb is that it is the women who are the witnesses. In the ancient world women were not regarded as being reliable witnesses in a court of law and anyone simply making up a tale would make sure it was men who played the key role in it. The women are there, I believe, because they were indeed the ones who made the startling discovery."

It is interesting to note in this context that Paul, who wants to present convincing evidence concerning the appearances of the risen Jesus, leaves out the women from his list of witnesses. Benedict XVI (2011a) distinguishes here two traditions, which he calls the "confessional tradition" and the "narrative tradition":

in the confessional tradition only men are named as witnesses, whereas in the narrative tradition women play a key role, indeed they take precedence over the men. This may be linked to the fact that in the Jewish tradition only men could be admitted as witnesses in court – the testimony of women was considered unreliable. So the "official" tradition, which is, so to speak, addressing the court of Israel and the court of the world, has to observe this norm if it is to prevail in what we might describe as Jesus' ongoing trial. (p. 262)

The confessional tradition "authoritatively condenses the shared faith of Christianity in fixed formulae and insists on their binding character" (p. 260). The narrative tradition is, according to Benedict XVI, quite different:

The narratives, on the other hand, do not feel bound by this juridical structure, but they communicate the whole breadth of the Resurrection experience. Just as there were only women standing by the Cross – apart from the beloved disciple—so too the first encounter with the risen Lord was destined to be for them. (p. 263)

What can we learn about the risen Jesus from his encounter with Mary Magdalene as recounted in chapter 31 of "The Story"? First of all, obviously, this encounter confirms John's insight: "Jesus lives," mentioned in the commentary on chapter 30. Beyond that, it tells us that those who loved him could see him, that they could touch him, and that they could speak to him.

We can also learn that those who loved him could recognize him—though not immediately. His body was transformed in some mysterious ways. Evidently, it was "not like it was before," and yet, visibly, "it was the same body." All these are themes which emerge also—and more clearly—in Jesus's subsequent encounters, as I will discuss in the commentaries on chapters 32, 33, and 34.

Commentary on chapter 32: "Two other people see Jesus"

On the same day when Mary Magdalene saw the risen Jesus, before all the Apostles saw him, two other people saw him on the road to Emmaus. For the reader, it is natural to ask: who were those two people?

Mark's Gospel, where this encounter is mentioned only in passing, does not mention any names, and Luke's Gospel mentions only one: Cleopas. Who was Cleopas's companion, and why is his (or her) name not mentioned? In the popular literature on the New Testament, the speculation is rife.

The author of the two-volume commentary on Luke's Gospel, Joseph Fitzmyer (1981–1985, vol. 2: 1555) notes quite convincingly that if Luke had invented the name, he would undoubtedly have done the same for the other disciple as well." Since, however, Luke doesn't add: we don't know the name of the other disciple, some commentators have sought to find in this omission a clue to the other disciple's identity. Dorothy Sayers (1969 [1949]), in her play based on the Gospels, "The man born to be king," assumes that it was Cleopas's wife. But appealing as this suggestion is, it seems hard to reconcile with Cleopas's reference to "our women," which reflects a man's perspective, rather than that of a couple, and also, with the Gospel's reference to "Mary the wife of Cleopas" as one of the women who came with Jesus to Judea from Galilee, and who stood at the cross with Jesus's mother Mary and Mary Magdalene (John 19:25).

There is some confusion about the various women named Mary in the Gospels. What matters most, however, is that *many* women followed Jesus from Galilee to Jerusalem and stood by him to the end; and Mary wife of Cleopas was one of them. The disillusionment and dejection of "the two" on the way to Emmaus seems more consistent with the attitude of Jesus's male disciples at that time than with the loving sorrow of the women. As Robert Wild (April 3, 2018) puts it in his Easter homily, "The Gospel witnesses to the doubt of the apostles and the faith of the women." However, since the evidence is inconclusive, I have used in chapter 32 the expression "the two," despite some stylistic awkwardness, avoiding the more natural-sounding expressions "the two men" and "the two people."

Leaving aside the question of the identity of the two disciples, perhaps the most striking feature of the encounter on the road to Emmaus is the fact that the two disciples are walking with Jesus, and talking with him, for some time, and yet do not recognize him—until, seated at the table with them, "he took the bread, and they recognized him, and he vanished from their sight" (Luke 24:30–31). Evidently, Jesus is now both the same and different. N. T. Wright (2008: 199) speaks in this connection of "a different physicality," but what exactly does that mean? "The early Christians (. . .) talked about a new sort of physicality (. . .)—a new type of embodiedness that is definitely bodily in the sense of being solid and substantial, but seems to have been transformed so that it is now not susceptible to pain or suffering or death."

Strictly speaking, of course, early Christians—such as those who wrote the Gospels—did not speak about the risen Jesus in terms like "embodiment," "physicality," "solid," or "substantial"; rather, they spoke in words much closer to Minimal English, often as simple as "see," "eyes," "touch," "hands," and "fingers." In relation to people like Lazarus, who were brought back to life shortly after they died and who would die again later, they used simple words like "body," "living," and "dead." They also spoke of Jesus as "being risen" or "having risen," meaning that after he died, he lived and that he wouldn't die again.

Trying to think through the Emmaus story with slightly modified Minimal English, we could say this: "The two saw someone in the place where they were, they saw this someone for some time, this someone was going with them along the same road; they knew that this someone was alive (they didn't for a moment think otherwise), they spoke to this someone, this someone spoke to them; for some time (not a short time) they didn't know who this someone was; after some time, they knew it, they knew it not because anyone said anything about it; at some moment, they thought like this: 'this is Jesus'; they thought like this when he did something as he had often done before: he was holding some bread in his hands, he broke it into pieces, he wanted them to eat these pieces. After this, this someone—Jesus—was not with them anymore; they didn't know how it happened."

One particularly arresting feature of the encounter of these two disciples with Jesus is their evident astonishment when they realized that it was Jesus ("why didn't we know that it was him? didn't we feel something very good inside when he was speaking to us about the prophets?"). Evidently, something happened that was completely unexpected, and what was happening as a result was utterly unusual.

Paul grappled with this new "physicality" (new kind of body) of the risen Jesus in his First Letter to the Corinthians, where he sought to explain the inextricable link between Jesus's resurrection and the resurrection of all people, which—as he expected—would occur at the end of times. Evidently, some of the Corinthians did not fully believe that God raised Jesus from the dead, and some did not fully believe that God would raise people from the dead too:

> Now if Christ is preached as raised from the dead, how can some of you say that there is no resurrection of the dead? But if there be no resurrection of the dead, then Christ has not been raised. If Christ has not been raised, then our preaching is in vain, and your faith is in vain. (. . .) For if the dead are not raised, then Christ has not been raised. If Christ is not raised, your faith is futile. (. . .) But in fact Christ has been risen from the dead, the first fruits of those who have fallen asleep [i.e. were dead]. (1 Corinthians 15:12–20)

As Jesus (the risen Christ) proclaims himself in the opening vision of the book of Revelation (1:18), "I was dead, and see, I am alive for ever and ever, and I have the keys of Death and Hades." The metaphor of "the keys of Death and Hades" means, in the first place: "I will not die anymore"; but it also means something about other people: they, too, can live after they die, and their bodies, too, will not be as they were before.

What kind of body will people have when God raises them, too, from the dead? Paul tries to answer this question throughout chapter 15 of his letter to the Corinthians, using figurative language which is not very easy to understand. His conclusion however is clear:

> But someone will ask, "How are the dead raised? With what kind of body do they come?" (. . .) "When the perishable puts on the imperishable, and the mortal puts on immortality, then shall come to pass the saying

that is written: "Death is swallowed up in victory." "O death, where is thy victory? O death, where is thy sting?" (. . .) But thanks be to God, who gives us the victory through our Lord Jesus Christ. (1 Corinthians 15:35, 54–55, 57)

Trying to express some of Paul's ideas in Minimal English, I would venture:

We can know that is *not* like this:
    after we die, we will not live anymore, we will be dead forever.
It is like this: after we die, something will happen to us;
    it will happen because God wants it to happen.
We can't know when it will happen, we can't know how it will happen;
    we can know that it *will* happen;
We can know that after it happens, we will live,
    that after this we will never die again.
We can know that when Jesus died, it was like this:
    For some time (a short time) he was dead;
    then something happened to him,
    After this, he wasn't dead anymore, he was alive.
    Many people saw him; many spoke to him; some touched him.
    After these people were with Jesus for some time,
    they could know that his body was not as it was before.
    They could know that his body was not like other people's bodies.
    At the same time they could know that it was his body;
    when he spoke to them they could know that it was him.
We can think like this: "The same will happen to us all;
    it can happen to us all because it happened to Jesus first."

Did the two disciples who encountered Jesus on the way of Emmaus think about all this as they were hurrying, joyfully, back to Jerusalem? Obviously not: They were just beginning to try to make sense of what had happened to them and what the implications of it might be. Yet when Paul was writing about the resurrection to Corinthians some twenty years later, he was clearly building on the experiences of those who saw Jesus on earth between his resurrection (return to earth from the dead) and ascension (return to his Father). The accounts of those who saw Jesus at that time became no doubt part and parcel of what was transmitted to Paul after his own encounter with the risen Jesus on the way to Damascus. (See chapter 39 of "The Story.")

Commentary on chapter 33: "The Apostles see Jesus"

In the Gospel of John (20:19–20), we read:

When it was evening on that day, the first day of the week, the doors of the house where the disciples had met were locked for fear of the Jews, Jesus came and stood among them and said, "Peace be with you!" After he said this, he showed them his hands and his side. Then the disciples were glad when they saw the Lord.

In Luke's Gospel, the account of that first evening after Jesus's resurrection is somewhat different. It begins with the arrival of the two disciples who met Jesus on the way to Emmaus: "they found the eleven [the Twelve minus Judas] and their companions gathered together. They were saying, "The Lord has risen indeed, and he has appeared to Simon!" Then the two told the eleven what had happened to them on the road and in Emmaus." Then Luke continues:

> As they were saying this, Jesus himself stood among them. But they were startled and frightened, and supposed that they saw a spirit. And he said to them, "Why are you troubled, and why do questionings rise in your hearts? See my hands and my feet, that it is I myself; handle me, and see; for a spirit has not flesh and bones as you see that I have." (Luke 24:36–40)

Neither John's account nor Luke's has been copied here in full because the rest of each passage would take us too far from the points on which I want to focus.

The main linguistic challenges that we meet in recounting Jesus's appearance to the disciples in the evening of that "first day" include these: How to avoid using the (not cross-translatable) word "appear," which usually features as a matter of course in commentaries relating to these passages in John's and Matthew's Gospels, and which is in fact also used in Luke 24:34? How to avoid using the word "ghost," used in Matthew's account of the Apostles' experience? How to express, in cross-translatable words, what the Apostles felt at that moment, and also, what Jesus meant when he said, "Peace be with you"? Finally, how to avoid abstract speculations about Jesus's "physicality" while capturing the Apostles' understanding of what happened?

John's Gospel says, "Jesus came and stood among them," but Luke's Gospel simply says, "Jesus himself stood among them." The fact that no movement is mentioned (at least not in Luke) implies that the Apostles didn't see Jesus move before he "stood among them," and so a sense of something like amazement, as well as fear, is conveyed in both accounts, even though only Luke's says "they were startled and terrified." (The King James' Bible says: "terrified and affrighted"; the Latin Vulgate says "conturbati vero et conterriti," the original Greek says "ptochethentes de kai emphoboi," and the Revised Standard Version: "startled and frightened.")

Chapter 33 of "The Story" says simply: "They felt something very bad because of it." Jesus's greeting, rendered in English (KJV, RSV) as "Peace be with you," used in all probability the Hebrew word "Shalom," or its Aramaic counterpart. Using Minimal English, I have rendered the meaning of this greeting as "I say: I want it to be like this: you feel something good in your soul, you don't feel something bad in your soul." However, given the key place of the concept of "peace," and of Jesus's gift of "peace" in the Gospels, it is likely that he conveyed far more with this greeting. Thus, in chapter 14 of John's Gospel (14:27), just before his arrest, Jesus says: "Peace I leave with you, my peace I give to you, not as the world gives do I give to you." And in his letter to the Philippians (4:7), Paul refers to this peace as "the peace of God, which passes all understanding." Accordingly, chapter 33 of "The Story" includes also the line: "It *can* be like this because I say I want it to be like this."

In both accounts (John's and Luke's) Jesus refers to his hands, in Luke's also to his feet, and in John's, to his side. He wants the Apostles to see him (and in Luke, touch him)—not only because he wants them to know that he lives but also that he does still have a body, in some sense the same body that was nailed to the Cross and pierced—even though evidently this body is not like it was before.

Speaking of this and other "appearances" of the risen Christ in the Gospels, Polkinghorne (2007: 81) writes: "At once we enter a strange dream-like realm in which Jesus appears in rooms with locked doors, disappears at will and is found hard to recognize, although those whose eyes are opened can perceive that it is the Lord." Yet to those who were there, the meetings with the risen Jesus were extremely real, and not at all like dreams. Commenting on the nature of these experiences, Polkinghorne writes:

> It is important to recognize that the New Testament seems quite able to distinguish between these appearances of the risen Christ which only happened for a limited period, and the sort of visions of Jesus which have been a continuing phenomenon for ecstatically sensitive people in the Church down the ages. (. . .) The latter also occurs in the New Testament (for example, Acts 18:19, where the Lord speaks words of comfort to Paul in a dream). However, there is no attempt to attach any special significance to them." (p. 83)

Similarly, Wright (2008: 210–211) stresses that the disciples "all knew about hallucinations and ghosts and visions. Ancient literature—Jewish and pagan alike—is full of such things. (. . .) the crunch is that the early Christians knew about phenomena like this as well." Speaking of both the empty tomb and the appearances of Jesus to the disciples, Wright (2008: 212) comments: "The easiest explanation by far is that these things happened because Jesus really was raised from the dead, and the disciples really did meet him, even though his body was renewed and transformed (. . .)." He concludes: "The resurrection of Jesus does in fact provide a *sufficient* explanation for the empty tomb and the meetings with Jesus. Having examined all the other possible hypotheses I've read about anywhere in the literature, I think it is also a *necessary* explanation" (p. 213).

Wright uses the phrase "the resurrection of Jesus," and this is how the early Christians spoke about what had happened. In the Gospels, the key words appear to be, above all, "live" and "living" (Luke 24:51, 24:46), and the key thoughts, "Jesus lives," and "he has risen from the dead" (Matthew 28:6–7). What exactly this "rising from the dead" means is not clear, except that evidently Jesus "is living" in a new way, not like before. Benedict XVI (2011a) writes about it like this:

> The dialectic of recognition and non-recognition corresponds to the manner of the apparitions. Jesus comes through closed doors; he suddenly stands in their midst. And in the same way he suddenly withdraws again, as at the end of the Emmaus encounter. His presence is entirely physical, yet he is not bound by physical laws, by the laws of space and time. In this remarkable dialectic of identity and otherness, of real physicality and freedom from the constraints of the body, we see the special mysterious nature of the risen Lord's new existence. Both elements apply here: he is the same embodied man, and he is the new man, having entered upon a different manner of existence. (p. 266)

I am not sure to what extent such ideas about the life of the risen Jesus can be translated from the somewhat poetic language of commentators like Benedict XVI and N. T. Wright into cross-translatable English (that is, Minimal English), beyond what has already been said here. One further clear idea, though, emerges from Peter the Apostle's speech at Pentecost (Acts 2:31–32), where Peter draws on Psalm 16, understood as prophetic: "God (. . .) foresaw and spoke of the resurrection of the Christ, that he was not abandoned to Hades, nor did his flesh see corruption. This Jesus God raised up and of that we are all witnesses." This means that after Jesus died, nothing bad happened to his body; and that after some time (during which his body was in the tomb and he was with the dead in "Hades") he was alive; the Apostles saw him; that they knew that he was never going to die.

Commentary on chapter 34: "The Apostle called Thomas sees Jesus"

The story of Thomas, "one of the twelve," and his encounter with the risen Jesus, is so remarkable, and so dramatic, that I will not try to retell it in my own words but will simply quote John's Gospel:

> Now Thomas, one of the twelve, called the Twin, was not with them when Jesus came. So the other disciples told him, "We have seen the Lord." But he said to them, "Unless I see in his hands the print of the nails, and place my finger in the mark of the nails, and place my hand in his side, I will not believe."
>
> Eight days later, his disciples were again in the house, and Thomas was with them. The doors were shut, but Jesus came and stood among them, and said, "Peace be with you." Then he said to Thomas, "Put your finger

here, and see my hands; and put out your hand, and place it in my side; do not be faithless, but believing." Thomas answered him, "My Lord and my God!" Jesus said to him, "Have you believed because you have seen me? Blessed are those who have not seen and yet believe." (John 20:24–29)

There is much to comment on in this passage and in chapter 34 of "The Story" which is based on it. I will restrict myself, however, to discussing (admittedly, at some length) the meaning of Thomas's words: "My Lord and my God," which are the subject of extensive literature.

I will start with a quote from "Does the New Testament Call Jesus God?" by Catholic biblical scholar Raymond Brown (1965; see also Brown 1968).

> This is the clearest example in the New Testament of the use of "God" for Jesus (. . .). Here Jesus is addressed as God (*ho theos mou*) (. . .). The scene is designed to serve as a climax to the Gospel: as the resurrected Jesus stands before the disciples, one of their number at last gives expression to an adequate faith in Jesus. He does this by applying to Jesus the Greek equivalent of two terms applied to the God of the Old Testament. The best example of the Old Testament usage is in Psalm 35:23, where the psalmist cries out: "My God and my Lord." (p. 565)

But what could Thomas have meant by the words "My Lord and my God" (which reverse the order of "My God" and "my Lord" in the psalm)? Trying to address this question, I will first of all note that the word "God" in Greek (as used in the Bible or Septuagint) can be used in two different ways: either as what linguists call a "referring expression" or as a "predicate." For example, when Genesis (1:1) says: "In the beginning God created the heaven and the earth," "God" is used as a referring expression. When, on the other hand, Christians say "I believe that Jesus is God," they are using the word "God" (or rather, the expression "is God") as a predicate. One can say "Jesus is God," but one cannot say "God is Jesus," because "Jesus"—a proper name—is always a referring expression, whereas the word "God" has two meanings, one as a referring expression and another, a predicative one. (Roughly speaking, a "referring expression" is a pointer, whereas a "predicate" is a description: one can describe someone as "God," but not as "Jesus.")

In the New Testament, the Greek word *Theos* ("God") is used nearly always as a referring expression, and this is how Jesus uses it. For example, when Jesus says to Mary Magdalene (as recounted in chapter 31 of this "Story"): "I am ascending to my Father and your Father, to my God and your God" (John 20:17), he is using the phrase "my God" as a referring expression, to refer to his Father. However, when in the mid-second century early Christian homily known as "2 Clement" the author says, "Brethren, we must think of Jesus Christ as God" (2 Clement 1:1, quoted in Brown 1965: 568), he is using the word "God" in a predicative sense: "when we think about Jesus Christ, we must think like this: he is God."

It appears that this second, predicative use of the word "God" (*Theos*) was virtually absent during Jesus's lifetime, and that it developed gradually later, among Christians, becoming well established only in the second century.

The reason why such a predicative use of the word "God" was virtually absent during Jesus's lifetime seems obvious: Generally speaking, first-century Jews did not ask "Who is God?" because they felt they knew this: "God" was that someone who spoke to their father Abraham in Harran: "Go from your country and your kindred and your father's house to the land that I will show you" (Genesis 12:1). "God" was for them "the God of Abraham, Isaac, and Jacob." But Jesus was a puzzle to his contemporaries, and the question: "Who is he?" was very much in people's thoughts. For many, at least up to the moment of Jesus's death on the cross, the answer was: "the Messiah." After the resurrection, however, the question: "Who is he?" presented itself with a new urgency, especially in the form: "How must we think about him?" (as reflected in "2 Clement's" words: "Brethren, we must think about Jesus Christ as God").

As McGrath (2013: 69) notes in his book *Faith and Creeds*, the first form of Christian confessions of faith was simply "Jesus is Lord!" (Romans 10:9; Corinthians 12:3). Before long, however, this was expanded, following the risen Christ's "great commission" to his disciples: "Go therefore and make disciples of all nations, baptising them in the name of the Father, of the Son, and of the Holy Spirit" (Matthew 28:19). Accordingly, for a long time, at baptism, believers were asked to respond to three questions (McGrath 2013: 67):

1. Do you believe in God the Father Almighty?
2. Do you believe in Jesus Christ, the Son of God?
3. Do you believe in the Holy Spirit?

As McGrath further notes, throughout the first three centuries, the search for understanding of who Jesus was continued: The Apostles Creed was the final outcome of this long process of reflection and refinement across the Christian world." (McGrath 2013: 69)

In the fourth century, however, controversies arose that, it was felt, required further elaboration. To quote Polish Orthodox theologian Henryk Paprocki (2009):

> The Church in the first centuries faced an extremely difficult task of defining the relation between Christ and God the Father, which caused long-term theological disputes. The most important result of these debates was the emergence of Arianism. Arius (. . .) taught that only the Father is God. (. . .) Arius' teaching was extremely popular. The church of the early III century was, in effect, Arian. (. . .) Who is Christ? This question dominated the whole period of ecumenical councils. (p. 103)

The formulations of the Nicene Creed need to be understood in the context of the fierce debates which were going on at the beginning of the fourth century and which led to the Nicene Council in 325. When the 318 bishops from the East and West agreed in Nicea on the formulations "God from God," "true God from true God," they agreed on them in the context of a Christian confession of faith: that is how we, Christians, must, and want to, think about Jesus. It is only in this new context that the word "God" fully acquired its new, predicative meaning; and even then this meaning was used mainly—as it still is now—in phrases like "acknowledging Jesus Christ as God" or "recognizing the divinity of Christ" rather than in the form of the plain sentence "Jesus is God." In fact, not even the Nicene Creed says plainly: "Jesus is God," using instead the more abstract phrases: "God from God," "true God from true God."

This intention of stating a shared way of thinking about Jesus is echoed in modern statements such as that of the inaugural Conference of the World Council of Churches held in Amsterdam in 1948: "the World Council is composed of churches which acknowledge Jesus Christ as God and Saviour" (quoted in Brown 1965: 545). The implication is: "We say: we think about Jesus Christ like this: 'Jesus is Saviour, Jesus is God'; we want to think like this; we think about it like this: 'this is true.'"

A little earlier, the outstanding Christian writer and theologian Dorothy Sayers (1969 [1949]: 35) wrote: "We must unite with Athanasius (. . .) that the God who lived and died in the world was the same God who made the world." In a poetic form, this insight was already present in the Prologue to John's Gospel, but it took Christians a long time to reach the clarity of the Creed, as successfully defended against Arianism by the great fourth-century theologian Athanasius.

Returning to the words "My Lord and my God" attributed to Thomas in John's Gospel, biblical scholars agree that it was an extraordinary thing for a first-century monotheistic Jew to say. As, for example, Meeks (1983: 74) states, commenting on these words: "It was precisely their devotion to One God, their abhorrence of sharing his worship with that of any other, that gave Jews their sense of being a unique people." Yet somebody must have said these words for the first time. Could Thomas have blurted them out to Jesus, under a sudden inspiration from the Holy Spirit? Or did John dream them up, thinking back to that evening when they saw Jesus in the Upper Room just one week after the resurrection? Quoting Meeks's comments on Thomas's words, another biblical scholar, Timothy Radcliffe (1984: 56) notes that we don't find any such words in Paul's letters, and comments: "It would have been unthinkable for Paul to confess the divinity of Christ." He also says: "Thomas' claim that this man [Jesus] is God is undoubtedly odd."

But was Thomas really making a claim? Or was he rather saying aloud (*to Jesus*) a word which somehow forced itself on his mind or on his lips at that moment? It seems to me that whoever first said the words "my God" about Jesus was not making a claim (because the word "God" didn't yet have the predicative meaning needed to make such a claim) but was saying something spontaneously, without perhaps knowing clearly what they wanted to say. Of course John, writing his Gospel late in the first century, could only say these words *about* Jesus, not *to* Jesus. Thomas, however, was able to say them *to* Jesus. Is it not possible that it was Jesus's presence which brought to Thomas's lips these extraordinary words, and that John, who was there too, remembered it to the end of his life?

According to Radcliffe (1984: 54), John's Gospel "works a transformation of the meaning of the word 'God.'" Perhaps another way to describe what happened to the word "God" would be to say that in addition to its meaning as a referring expression (applicable only to Yahweh, whom Jesus himself referred to as either "God" or "Father," and addressed as "Father") it acquired a second meaning, as a predicative expression. At the same time, Jesus often used about himself the iconic formula "I AM," which (as God revealed to Moses (Exodus 3:14)) was "the name of God." It seems likely that what Jesus meant with the words "I AM" was not "I am God," but rather, "when I am with you, God is with you"—in accordance with his own prophetic name, "Emmanuel," that is, "God with us" (Isaiah 7:14). This would mean that Jesus used this form of words ("I AM") so that the disciples could recognize God in him, rather than in order to identify himself, explicitly, as God (an identification for which they were not yet ready). According to the hypothesis presented here (in chapter 34 of "The Story"), the flash of recognition in Thomas's mind is likely to have taken an analogous form: not "Jesus is God" but "when I see Jesus, I see God."

There are good reasons to think that it took the disciples a long time to start thinking about Jesus as God. This is why chapter 34 of "The Story" does not render the meaning of the phrase "My Lord and my God" with the words: "You are God," or "Jesus is God"—a rendering which I think would be anachronistic. On the other hand, the paraphrase given in chapter 34, i.e., "I know now: when I see you, I see God" seems to me plausible enough— especially given that (according to John's Gospel) a few days before, Jesus him- self said: "Whoever sees me sees him who sent me" (John 12:45), and "Whoever has seen me has seen the Father" (John 14:9).

As discussed very persuasively by Polkinghorne (1994) in his book *The Faith of a Physicist*, at first the disciples must have grappled with words and meanings, trying to find ways of speaking that would fit their experience—the experience of meeting the risen Jesus. Thus, he writes: "When we turn from the gospels to the other writings of the New Testament, which overtly present a post-Easter account of the impact of Jesus, we enter a realm of discourse where the dominant impression is of people groping for concepts capable of doing justice to their experience" (p. 124). Polkinghorne's emphasis on the dis- ciples' experience as what seems to have forced them to search for new ways of speaking is particularly persuasive:

I do not think these developments in first-century Christian thought rep- resent the results of unbridled metaphysical speculation. Rather, we see the struggle to do justice to the encounter with this man, in his life and death and resurrection, which nevertheless simply cannot adequately be expressed in human terms alone. (p. 125)

These new ways of speaking included, first of all, the new use of the word "Lord" (in Greek, *Kyrios*), which Christians started to use in relation to Jesus— a word which in Paul's letters alone occurs 230 times (Polkinghorne 1994: 125). In the Greek translation of the Hebrew Bible called the Septuagint this word ("Adonai" in Hebrew) was used exclusively about God, as a substitute for "Yahweh," which pious Jews could not speak aloud. So it seems that this use of the word "Lord" (*Kyrios*) about Jesus in the second half of the first century paved the way to the emergence of the predicative use of "God" (*Theos*) and its application to Jesus later. Polkinghorne (1994) comments:

> Yet New Testament writers, however much their language about Jesus carries overtones of divinity, are extremely discreet and reserved about actually calling him "God". (. . .) The clearest New Testament statement of Jesus' unqualified divinity is Thomas' confession, "My Lord and my God!" (John 20:28) (p. 126)

This brings us back to Thomas's words and what they meant. Again, Polkinghorne's conclusion, "The New Testament writers raise the question of Jesus' relation to the divine without resolving it," seems apt, as is also his further comment referring in particular to opening formulae in Paul's letters such as "God our Father and the Lord Jesus Christ," which bracket together God and Jesus:

> They clearly result from a struggle to do justice both to the "Christ-event" and to that fundamental Israelite assertion that "The Lord our God is one Lord" (Deut. 6.4). Their intellectual instability is manifest. Further thought must lie ahead, grappling with how the Lordship of Christ and the Lordship of God are to be reconciled and understood. (p. 126)

Thus, when in the fourth century the Council of Nicea adopted the formula "God from God, Light from Light, true God from true God," this was the end of a long process of reflection and of a long search for new ways of thinking and new ways of speaking, adequate to these new experiences. Speaking of his own experience as a Christian, Polkinghorne concludes:

> Thus I am driven by the necessity of finding a Christology adequate to the Christian experience of new life in Christ, to seek an understanding along the orthodox and traditional lines which speak in terms of the presence of both true humanity and true deity in Jesus. (. . .) The thrust of this argument-from-below has been to start with the human figure of Jesus and to recognize that adequate talk of him is driven to employ also the language of the divine. (pp. 141–142)

But words like "deity" and "the divine" are not intuitively clear, and it is not clear what exactly they intend to say about Jesus (or how they could be rendered in other languages). What does seem clear is that Polkinghorne wants to distinguish between the meaning of the word "God" as used in the Nicene Creed's phrase "I believe in one God, the Father almighty" and the meaning of "God" as the first word in the phrase "God from God." To speak of "one God" is to use the word "God" in the sense explicated in chapter 1 of "The Story." To speak of "the presence of true divinity in Jesus" means, I take it, believing that "Jesus is God" in the second, predicative sense of the word "God," i.e., as in "to be God." (It appears to be the same distinction which John draws in the famous first sentence of his Gospel, at the beginning of the Prologue: "In the beginning was the Word, and the Word was with God [in Greek, *ho Theos*, with a definite article], and the Word was God [in Greek, *Theos*, without an article]."

The subtitle of Polkinghorne's book *The Faith of a Physicist* is "Reflections of a bottom-up thinker." While the language "of the divine" is neither clear nor cross-translatable, Polkinghorne's "bottom-up" approach seems to me very helpful: It is helpful to try to articulate one's faith in Jesus as "true God from true God" in terms of one's own experience. Trying to think along these lines, I would propose the following partial explication, focussing not so much on "who Jesus is" as on "how I think about Jesus and why I want to think like this" (that is, not on "ontology" as such but on belief motivated by experience).

I believe in one Lord, Jesus Christ, . . . God from God . . ., true God from true God
When I think about Jesus, I think like this: When I hear Jesus' voice (in the Gospels), I know that I hear God's voice; when I see Jesus on the cross, I know that I see God; when I am with Jesus, I know that I am with God; when I speak to Jesus, I know that I am speaking to God. I think like this at the same time: "this is all true"; I want to think like this.

A final point. On the last day before the crucifixion, Jesus (in John's Gospel) seeks to comfort the Apostles and tells them that he is departing to prepare a place for them, adding: "And you know the way to the place where I am going" (John 14:4). Thomas, "whom we know as 'doubting Thomas' [and who] is the spokesperson for those who struggle with faith" (Johnson 2017), pleads: "Lord, we do not know where you are going. How can we know the way?" To this, Jesus replies: "I am the way, and the truth, and the life. If you know me, you will know my Father also" (John 14:5–7). These words too must have been puzzling to Thomas at that moment. But it is not inconceivable (or so it seems to me) that when he found himself in the presence of the risen Jesus ten days later, and saw his wounds, something happened in him, and he could only say, without yet clearly knowing what he meant, "My Lord and my God."

During Jesus's Transfiguration, when the three disciples (Peter, John, and James) "saw his glory," Peter said to Jesus: "'Master, it is well that we are here; let us make three booths, one for you and one for Moses and one for Elijah'— not knowing what he said" (Luke 9: 34). In chapter 18 of "The Story" this is rendered like this: "He didn't know what he was saying, he didn't know what he wanted to say." So in the presence of Jesus in his glory, Peter said something not knowing what he was saying. Couldn't Thomas also have said something not knowing what he was saying?

In her article on John's Gospel in the prestigious *New Jerome Biblical Commentary*, theologian Pheme Perkins (1990: 984) writes: "John creates a separate story of Jesus' appearance to Thomas. (. . .) Thomas' confession is the culmination of the Gospel's christology, since it acknowledges the crucified/exalted Jesus as 'Lord and God.'" This could be interpreted as implying that the whole encounter between Jesus and Thomas was more or less invented by John. But the intuition of many ordinary Christians resists any such notion: To them, the story of this encounter rings true. If the words "My Lord and my God" were as "odd," and as extraordinary, as the biblical scholars agree they were, then it seems plausible that they were first spoken in an unprecedented situation deeply affecting the speaker. Such was the situation of Thomas in that unique encounter recounted in John's Gospel. If so, then "Thomas the Doubter" may in fact have been "Thomas the first believer," or at least, the first disciple who, in the presence of the risen Jesus, under the guidance of the Holy Spirit, dared to say the word "God."

Commentary on chapter 35: "People can't see Jesus on earth anymore"

According to the Acts of the Apostles, "until the day when he [Jesus] was taken up, (. . .) he presented himself alive [to the Apostles] after his passion (. . .), appearing to them during forty days, and speaking of the kingdom of God" (Acts 1:2–3). Then he told them to stay in Jerusalem and await the coming of the Holy Spirit: "you will receive power when the Holy Spirit has come upon you; and you will be my witnesses in Jerusalem, in all Judea and Samaria, and to the ends of the earth. When he had said this, as they were watching, he was lifted up, and a cloud took him out of their sight." And in the words of the Apostles' Creed: "he ascended into heaven and is seated at the right hand of the Father almighty."

In this commentary I want to focus on three points: first, what happened on the Mount of Olives on that day (the "Ascension"), second, what Jesus told the Apostles to do (the "commission"), and third, Jesus's new way of thinking about God as the Father, the Son, and the Holy Spirit.

As for the first point, the main challenge is how to distinguish, in cross-translatable words, the factual from the symbolic. In *The Faith of a Physicist* John Polkinghorne (1994) writes:

> The language of the creed, and the New Testament passages on which it is based (. . .) is heavily symbolic at this point. We are not committed to the quaint picture, sometimes found in medieval stained glass, of the Lord's feet projecting from the underside of a cloud, as he sets out on his space-journey to the heavenly realm. In scripture a cloud is the symbol of the presence of God (. . .) and its role in the story of the ascension is to emphasize the divine authority of the exalted Christ. A similar purpose is served by the mythological language of the heavenly session [i.e. "is seated at the right hand of the Father"]. (p. 123)

The phrase "seated at the right hand of the Father" derives from psalm 110, where David says mysteriously: "The Lord says to my Lord: 'Sit at my right hand.'" According to Christian tradition, beginning with Peter's speech to Israelites on the day of Pentecost, these are prophetic words in which God speaks of Christ, David's descendant. The language is indeed "mythological," because obviously David didn't think of God as, literally, having hands, or as sitting in heaven on a throne. Likewise, Peter didn't think of Jesus as sitting at the right hand of God, and when Christians recite the creed, they do not see Jesus as, literally, "seated at the right hand of the Father." (As Jesus said to the Samaritan woman: "God is spirit," John 4:24.) What did Peter mean, then, when he spoke of Jesus "exalted at the right hand of God" (Acts 2:33)?

Chapter 35 of "The Story" says that when the Apostles who were gathered on the Mount of Olives on that day of the "Ascension" realized that Jesus "was not in that place anymore," "they thought: Jesus is with God now." This seems right, as far as it goes. But clearly, this is not the whole meaning, for the word "exalted" and the image of the special place "on the right hand of God" suggests some other semantic component, which is difficult to formulate. Polkinghorne interprets this image as representing "the divine authority of the exalted Christ," and given the symbolism of the "right hand" in the biblical world, this seems right. In Minimal English, I have rendered this idea in the same way in which I presented God's "almightiness" in chapter 1: "they [the Apostles] knew that they could think about him like they thought about God, they knew that they could think like this: 'If he wants something to happen on earth, it can happen because of this. If he wants something to happen in other places, it can happen because of this.'" (In Matthew's Gospel, Jesus says on the day of his Ascension: "All authority in heaven and on earth has been given to me," Matthew 28:18).

Turning now to the image of the cloud, I think we need to recognize that while this image too, is symbolic, it is not mythological, in the sense in which the image of God's right hand is: Neither Luke (the author of "The Acts of the Apostles") nor the other New Testament writers thought that God had hands, but presumably they did think that on the day of the Ascension the Apostles saw a cloud (we have no reason to think otherwise). That cloud was not *just* a cloud (as Polkinghorne says, in scripture a cloud is the symbol of the presence of God), but it was *also* a cloud. Thus, according to chapter 35 of "The Story," "They couldn't see him because there was a cloud in the place where he was a moment before. After a very short time, the cloud wasn't there anymore. They couldn't see Jesus anymore then. They knew that he was not there anymore."

What about the image of "ascension," that is, the upward movement of some kind? Chapter 1 of Acts says: "as they were watching, he was lifted up, and a cloud took him out of their sight." It also says that "they were gazing up towards heaven," and the ending of Luke's Gospel says: "while he was blessing them, he withdrew from them and was carried up into heaven" (Luke 24:51). I agree with Polkinghorne that the image of Jesus being "lifted up" is best interpreted as symbolic, and accordingly, there is no mention of a "lifting up" in chapter 35. At the same time, it seems to me that the image of the Apostles gazing toward the sky after the cloud "took him out of their sight" can be understood quite literally: It is entirely plausible that as a cloud covered Jesus and then lifted, they kept looking toward the sky.

Turning now to the "commission," there can be little doubt that this is how the Apostles remembered what Jesus said he wanted them to do: "Go therefore and make disciples of all nations" (Matthew 28:19); "Go into the world and proclaim the good news to the whole creation" (Mark 16:15); "you will be my witnesses in Jerusalem, in all Judea and Samaria, and to the ends of the earth" (Acts 1:8). In chapter 35 of "The Story," I have phrased this "commission" like this: "Because you were always with me, you know what I did, what I said, what happened to me. I want people in all parts of the earth to know it. Go to many places, say it to people in these places. At the same time, baptise people in these places."

It is a distinctive feature of Christianity that it is a "missionary religion": Christians have always believed that Jesus wanted them to be his witnesses and to tell people in all parts of the earth "the good news about the kingdom of God." In the postcolonial world this conviction is often viewed negatively and what Christians see as their mission of "evangelization" is often attributed to an "imperialist" impulse and seen as something incompatible with values such as cultural and religious pluralism, human diversity, interfaith dialogue, and so on. It is true that the way this mission was carried out in the course of the last two millennia was often totally incompatible with Jesus's teaching and with Christian values which arose from it. Yet there can be no doubt that the command to proclaim the Gospel "to the ends of the earth" was an inherent and inescapable part of that teaching. In a sense, the present attempt to tell "the story of God and people" in a version cross-translatable into all languages can be seen as a small part of the ongoing Christian project of trying to make Jesus' "good news" available to all people on earth.

Since I am writing in Australia, in the remainder of this chapter I will discuss this theme with special reference to the work of the Australian Bible translator John Harris (who received a prestigious Lambeth honorary doctorate for his scholarship and advocacy on behalf of Aboriginal Australians). In his massive book *One Blood*, which is a history of Christian missions in Aboriginal Australia, Harris (1990) quotes Pope Paul VI's encyclical *Evangelii Nuntiandi*, "Evangelization in the Modern World" (1982 [1975]) and writes: "The person who has been evangelised goes on to evangelise others. Here lies the test of truth, the touchstone of evangelisation: it is unthinkable that a person should accept the word and give himself to the kingdom without becoming a person who bears witness to it and proclaims it in his turn." (p. 861)

Telling the story of how Aboriginal people in Australia "have become confident bearers of the gospel" (p. 867), Harris also quotes Charles Harris (no relation), the first national President of the Christian Aboriginal and Islander Congress in Australia, who explained the aim of the Congress in these terms: "The primary aim of the Congress is evangelism. Aboriginal and Islander Christians want to respond to the command of Jesus to 'Go and make disciples.'" (p. 866)

Pointing out that long before the arrival of the Europeans, Aboriginal people "were a God-seeking people" who believed that "they inhabited a spiritual world," John Harris (1990) writes:

> Christians believe that Christ was born, died and rose again for all humankind, including Aboriginal people. The missionaries believed that, and believed it against the tide of popular and scientific opinion.
>
> Yet Aborigines did not live in some remote corner of the earth where the Spirit of God did not dwell. Those of us recent arrivals who see the handiwork of God in the gold of the wattle, the red of the desert, the blues of the sky, in parrot and kangaroo and kookaburra, are acknowledging that God was here before us. So few European Christians, until recently, recognised that God was here and that he was discernible to the Aboriginal people—that they, in their way, were reaching out for him.
>
> Aboriginal people needed to hear of Christ who died to fulfil the longings of their culture as much as he did to fulfil the longings of mine. (p. 867)

It is easy for secular modern Westerners to criticize Christian efforts of "evangelization" over the centuries, and it is true that the record of this evangelization is tragically mixed. Yet as Harris's history of missions in Australia shows (deeply critical as he is of many aspects of that history), the perspective of many Aboriginal people is different from that of many critics of European descent, especially since Aboriginal Christians took charge of their Christianity themselves. To quote Harris (1990: 852): "The missionaries, however imperfect, brought the gospel. People responded, but real growth in the Christian community had to wait until Aboriginal people themselves assumed responsibility for evangelisation."

As Harris's book documents, missionaries in Australia, whatever their limitations and biases, held the view that Aboriginal people were "descendants of Adam" just like Europeans, were fully human, had immortal souls, and were (in the words of Anglican clergyman Robert Cartwright (1824) "deserving of compassion and fraternal respect"—and also, that the missionaries "held this view against powerful and unrelenting opposition." Indeed, "they were assailed by a secular press claiming Aborigines to be a race of 'the monkey tribe,' or 'the orang-utan species'" (Harris, p. 3).

As pointed out by Harris, "The association of blackness with inferiority was already strongly implanted in the European mind in 1788. Together with nakedness, it came to symbolise Aboriginal degradation." It is particularly interesting to read that the French scholar and philosopher Ernest Renan ("eulogized after his death as the embodiment of the progressive spirit in Western culture," Wikipedia) held that Aborigines had no soul. Against this background, one can better appreciate the appeal of Christianity in Aboriginal Australia. Tellingly, Harris quotes in this context a pastoral letter written by Catholic Archbishop John Bede Polding and his fellow bishops in 1869:

> [Some of our fellow colonists] have, in justification of a great crime, striven to believe that these black men are not of our race, are not our fellow creatures. We Catholics know assuredly how false this is: we know that one soul of theirs is, like one of our own, of more worth than the whole material world, that any human soul is of more worth, as it is of greater cost, than the whole mere matter of this earth, its sun and its system or, indeed, of all the glories of the firmament. (p. 33)

The title of Harris's book, *One Blood*, comes from a line in the Acts of the Apostles (from Paul's speech to the Greeks, in Athens), as rendered by the King James Bible (Acts 17:26): "[God] hath made of one blood all nations of men to dwell on all the face of the earth." In the New Revised Standard Version it reads, "From one ancestor he made all nations to inhabit the whole earth." So this is an inherent part of the message which Jesus commanded his disciples to proclaim "to the ends of the earth" (Acts 1:8). It is a message which, Christians believe, people everywhere on earth need to hear.

Relatedly, in a recent lecture given at the Australian National University (Canberra, April 21, 2017) John Harris quoted a speech by the Nobel Prize winner Archbishop Desmond Tutu given at an event organized by "Jesus House for all the Nations" in London in 2008. Drawing on his experiences in apartheid-dominated South Africa, Desmond Tutu told a conference of UK

Christians and church leaders: "The Bible has revolutionary power to free the poor, (. . .) If you want to keep people subjugated, the last thing you place in their hands is a Bible. (. . .) There is nothing more radical, nothing more revolutionary, nothing more subversive against injustice and oppression than the Bible." (Incidentally, as I write this commentary, *The Economist,* April 26, 2018, online, reports that "The Chinese government has recently stepped up efforts to block the sale of bibles online.") These points about the Bible, and more particularly about the New Testament, are inseparable from the content of Jesus's message, which can be stated clearly and cross-translatably in Minimal English:

> It is like this:
>> God feels something very good towards all people,
>> God wants to do good things for all people.
>> God wants people everywhere on earth to know this.
>> Jesus was born because of this, Jesus died because of this.
> At the same time, it is like this:
>> Jesus lives. People everywhere on earth can live with Jesus,
>> with other people.
>> If they live with Jesus, with other people, they live with God.

Thus, Jesus's command that his disciples should be his messengers everywhere on earth was inherently related to the content of his message.

The record of those who tried to implement this command over the centuries is tragically mixed. As Polkinghorne (1983: 102) writes in his book *The Way the World Is,* "Any Christian must feel deep penitence and shame at the thought of the Crusades, the Inquisition, the blasphemy of the wars of religion. The record of Christian colonial powers in contact with 'primitive' people is not always one of which we can feel proud." At the same time, as Polkinghorne also notes, "the account is not all written on the debit side of the ledger. In the pioneering of hospitals and education, in the improvement in the status of women (whatever blind spots still remain), the Church has a record in which the Christian can take some comfort. To an extent that we seldom appreciate, we people in the West are living on inherited moral capital which is being consumed as the Christian fabric of society diminishes." (As discussed in Appendices A and B, this inherited moral capital includes, inter alia, the concepts "to love" and "to forgive," as well as the injunction "love your neighbor as yourself," in the universal and global sense of the word "neighbor.")

Arguably, it is this inherited moral capital which motivates some Western critics of the historical record of Christianity to judge that record as they do—sometimes unaware that their very standards have their origins in Jesus's teaching. As I see it, there is an interesting paradox here: the most passionate critics of the Christian missionary record appear to be, for the most part, post-Christians (at least in a cultural sense). Their critique may be entirely justified, but if at one time St Paul had not embarked on his missionary journeys, they would probably not be familiar with the Gospels, and would be very unlikely to have arrived at the exacting standards against which they judge the past. It seems to me that this point is often overlooked, or not given the weight that it deserves. To note the obvious, it is not an accident that the name of the organisation responsible for the event in London in 2008 where the South African Archbishop Desmond Tutu spoke about "the revolutionary power of the Bible to free the poor" is "Jesus House for All the Nations." This name resonates with Jesus' words at the Ascension: "Thus it is written that the Christ should suffer and on the third day rise from the dead, and that repentance and forgiveness of sins should be preached in his name to all nations" (Luke 24:47).

In the twenty-first century, Christians on the whole still believe that the task of evangelization entrusted by Jesus to his disciples remains, while at the same trying to conceive it in new ways. To quote Vernon White's (1991) book *Atonement and Incarnation*:

> we do not have to believe that other people's final fulfilment depends wholly on our faithfulness in preaching the Gospel effectively. Few can seriously believe that without being either crushed by a sense of impotence, or driven by guilt. The point is, it is a belief that need never have been attempted. (p. 114)

Speaking in the abstract language of academic theology, White (1991) further describes the aim of his own book as follows: "I have simply and solely sought ways to conceive how the Christ event might be constitutive of God's saving action for all people in, and beyond, the whole world of space and time; ways of believing an ancient claim in a modern world" (p. 115). This is also the aim of the present book—except that the story told here tries to use cross-translatable words which can make that "ancient claim" really accessible "to all nations."

This brings us to the third point to be discussed in this commentary, which is Jesus's new way of thinking about God: God seen as one and at the same time as a "community" embracing the Father, the Son, and the Holy Spirit.

In his book *The Mystery of the Triune God*, Catholic theologian John O'Donnell (1988: 100) writes: "The traditional formula which the non-professional believer has learned to express his faith in the Trinity is 'one God in three persons.'" Looking at this formula in a historical perspective, O'Donnell asks "whether it is still a useful formula for Christians today." He concludes (p. 105): "However much Christianity retains the monotheism of the Old Testament, the last word is not (. . .) on unity. (. . .) For Christians the ultimate is the community. The One also includes the We. The Christian doctrine of God constrains us to think multiplicity within unity."

The startlingly simple formulation "the One also includes the We" is not only more cross-translatable than "multiplicity within unity" but also reflects a different perspective: A theologian can think about God as "multiplicity within unity" (implying "many, as well as one"), but who can think about God as "we"? Obviously, only Jesus. In the light of John's Gospel, at times Jesus did think about God as "we," because at times he did speak in this way about the Father and the Son. For example, in John 10:30, Jesus says: "I and the Father [we] are (first person plural) one," in John 14:23, "If a man loves me, he will keep my word, and my Father will love him, and we will come to him and make our home with him," and in John 17:11, "we are one." (If someone were to suggest that it was the author of the Gospel rather than Jesus himself who invented this new way of referring to God as "we," I would say that it was totally implausible.)

Chapter 35 places the words "we are one" in a line which says: "They [the Apostles] knew that when Jesus said 'the Father' he sometimes said 'we'"—a line which comes almost on the heels of Jesus's command: "Go therefore and make disciples of all nations, baptising them in the name of the Father, he Son, the Holy Spirit." The two intervening lines in chapter 35 say: "They [the Apostles] didn't know well then what Jesus wanted to say with the words 'the Father, the Son, the Holy Spirit'" and "They didn't know then that Jesus was speaking in this way about God."

The baptismal formula introduces a new way of thinking about God, which, we must presume, reflects Jesus's own way of thinking about God, combining, so to speak, "community" and "unity" (not **multiplicity** but **community**), and Jesus's "insider perspective": not "*they* are one" but "*we* are one." There is no explicit reference in the Gospels to "the Father, the Son, the Holy Spirit" as "we," but the notion formulated by modern theologians such as Mühlen (1966), O'Donnell (1988), and Benedict XVI (2011a) (and derived from the treatise "On the Trinity" by the twelfth-century theologian Richard of St Victor) that "the One includes the We," is clearly anchored in that "we" used by Jesus himself and remembered by the Apostles.

Incidentally, the line "They didn't know then that Jesus was speaking in this way about God" is compatible with the interpretation of Jesus' "we" as "we two" rather than "we three," as argued by Mühlen. According to Mühlen, the inclusion of the Holy Spirit in the phrase "the Father, the Son, and the Holy Spirit" can be interpreted along the lines of the liturgical formula "in the unity of the Holy Spirit": Jesus can say "I and the Father, we are one" because Jesus' spirit is God's Spirit: It is one Spirit.

In a chapter entitled "The hidden God" of his book of interviews *On the Edge of the Precipices of Faith*, Catholic theologian Hryniewicz (2001) writes:

We are helpless before the mystery of God, who is hidden from us and transcending our reality. Perhaps we do repeat the old, worn trinitarian formulas too unfeelingly. Perhaps we behave as though we already owned the Trinity, rather than realizing that we've only caught a gleam of its light. Christian faith is genuinely demanding. It presents an enormous challenge to the human mind. (p. 262)

Like many other contemporary theologians, Hryniewicz stresses "the need [for Christians] to re-think our faith in God, our traditional categories, by means of which we are trying to describe the amazing mystery of Jesus Christ," also with a view "to search for paths towards a better understanding between Christianity and other religions" (p. 261). From this perspective, too, the word "we," which Jesus himself used about God, is likely to be less misleading than the word "three," which he did not use; and Jesus's formula "we are one" may be more helpful than the theologian's formulae "God is three," or "one God in three persons." (The faith in God expressed in the Apostles' Creed and the Nicene Creed was also formulated as a faith in the Father, in the Son, and in the Holy Spirit, without the word "three.")

Chapter 35 of "The Story" tries to capture Jesus's startling new way of thinking about God—not as "two," "three," or "many," but as "we" (as well as "one")—in simple and cross-translatable words.

Commentary on chapter 36: "The Holy Spirit"

The chapter on "The Holy Spirit" in *I Believe in One God: The Creed Explained* (Benedict XVI 2012b: 57), begins with the question: "Who or what is the Holy Spirit?" This commentary will focus not so much on the various answers to this question that Christian theologians have offered, as on the question itself: Which interrogative word should it be, "who?" or "what?"

The first answer to this question must be that the New Testament speaks about the Holy Spirit in two ways: sometimes as "something" ("what") and sometimes as "someone" ("who"). The first way of speaking represents continuity with the Old Testament, the second reflects a change. For example, in Luke's Gospel, chapter 4 ("the temptation of Jesus") starts with the words: "Jesus, full of the Holy Spirit, returned from the Jordan and was led by the Spirit in the wilderness" (Luke 4:1, NRSV). The phrase "full of the Holy Spirit" appears to construe this Spirit as "something," but the phrase "led by the Spirit" appears to construe the same Spirit as "someone." In the same chapter, Jesus begins his public life by speaking on a Sabbath in the Synagogue in Nazareth. As Luke (4:16–21) describes it:

> He stood up to read, and the scroll of the prophet Isaiah was given to him. He unrolled the scroll and found the place where it was written: "The Spirit of the Lord is upon me, because he has anointed me to bring good news to the poor (. . .)
>
> And he rolled up the scroll, gave it back to the attendant and sat down. The eyes of all in the synagogue were fixed on him. Then he began to say to them: 'Today this scripture has been fulfilled in your hearing.'"

In this memorable passage, in which Jesus evidently applies Isaiah's visionary prediction to himself, Jesus seems to be speaking about the Spirit of God as "someone": "He has anointed me to bring the good news to the poor." In presenting Jesus's words in this way, Luke was evidently relying on the Greek translation of the Hebrew Bible known as the Septuagint (produced two centuries earlier in Egypt, for the benefit of Jews who could no longer understand Hebrew).

In the Septuagint version, we read: "Pneuma Kyriou ep' eme, hou heineken ekhrise me," that is, "The Spirit of the Lord is upon me, therefore he has anointed me." But Jesus was reading from a Hebrew scroll, in which Isaiah's words were rendered differently, in a form retained by the King James Bible (where "the Old Testament" was translated from the original Hebrew): "The spirit of the Lord God is upon me; because the Lord hath anointed me to preach good tidings unto the meek."

This means that in the passage from Isaiah that Jesus was reading in the synagogue in Nazareth the Spirit of God was construed as "something" rather than "someone." But when the same passage was repeated in Luke's Gospel (and presented by Luke as Isaiah's words quoted by Jesus), the Spirit of God was referred to as "someone" rather than "something."

Presumably, when the Jewish translators of the Hebrew Bible rendered the relevant passage from Isaiah into Greek in the way they did (implying that the Spirit of the Lord did the anointing), this was for them a manner of speaking: They didn't really think of God's Spirit as "someone" rather than "something," because from their point of view, there was only one "someone": God (Yahwe). But for Luke, who was writing his Gospel in the eighties, speaking of God's Spirit—the Holy Spirit—as "someone" rather than "something" was presumably not just a way of speaking but also a way of thinking. For Christians, too, there was only one God, so they didn't think about the Holy Spirit as "someone *else*" (i.e., someone other than God). Hence the apparent paradox, which chapter 36 tries to preserve: not "someone *else*" and yet "*someone.*" Evidently, this is how the first generations of Christians came to think about the Holy Spirit, and how they remembered Jesus's way of speaking, as presented, in particular, in the Gospel of John:

> These things I have spoken to you, while I am still with you. But the Counsellor, the Holy Spirit, whom the Father will send in my name, he will teach you all things and bring to your remembrance all that I have said to you. (John 14:25–26)

Evidently, this way of thinking about God's Spirit (as "someone") gradually established itself in Christian thinking in the first, second, and third centuries, and was codified by the great councils of the undivided church in Nicaea in 325 and Constantinople in 381, becoming part of the Christian Creed in the East and in the West. To quote Polish Catholic theologian Hryniewicz (2009):

The Nicene-Constantinopoletan Creed expressed the belief that God's Spirit acting in the history of humankind is not some impersonal power of God or God's personal closeness to people, but truly a Divine Person, as is God's Son incarnate in Jesus Christ. Early Christian generations believed that the same Spirit that appeared at the very beginning of the world (see Genesis 1:2), and spoke through the prophets, was also bringing about the new beginning of the history of humankind in the incarnation of God's Son (Luke 1:35). (p. 201)

So there was clearly a continuity between the Old Testament and the New Testament thinking about the Spirit (God's Spirit), but at the same time, as scientist and theologian John Polkinghorne emphasizes, there was a significant difference. Having discussed the difficulty that the early Christian generations had in grasping who Jesus was in relation to God, Polkinghorne (2007) writes:

More slowly still, the Church became aware of the presence of God in yet another way. It felt in its midst the power of God which is referred to as his Spirit. In Old Testament times men had often spoken of the spirit of the Lord. (. . .) It came upon the prophets as the source of their inspiration. It had been brooding on the chaos of the deep in creation (Gen. 1:2). The Church felt the activity of the Spirit with such intensity that it no longer seemed appropriate to speak of it as if it were just an emanation of power from God but rather it seemed necessary to recognize it as the presence of God himself. The spirit had become the Spirit, so to speak. (p. 77)

Polkinghorne (2007) comments further:

The Spirit was (and is) the most elusive element in the experience of God. (. . .) The much more characteristic New Testament phrase is the binitarian "God our Father and the Lord Jesus Christ" rather than the Trinitarian "the grace of our Lord Jesus Christ, the love of God and the fellowship of the Holy Spirit" (2 Cor. 13:14). It took several centuries for a recognition of the Spirit's divinity and distinctiveness to gain universal acceptance in the Church. Nevertheless, in the end there did not appear to be a stable position, adequate to experience, which did not take account of this fact. (p. 97)

I think Polkinghorne's emphasis on *experience* is very helpful here. As chapter 36 of "The Story" puts it, on the day of Pentecost the Apostles *knew* that the Holy Spirit was with them, they *knew* that the Holy Spirit was in them (italics added). They knew it not on the basis of intellectual speculation, or because someone else told them this was the case—they knew it from inner experience: "they couldn't not know it." Speaking as a Christian, Polkinghorne (2007) puts it like this: "We know God at work within us, in the depth of our own being" (p. 98). He also comments: "I think it is important to recognize that the doctrine of the Trinity arose in this way, as a response to phenomena rather than an ungrounded metaphysical speculation. It is a summary of experience rather than a puzzling piece of divine arithmetic" (p. 98). The "summary of experience" fitted in with Jesus's words, as the Apostles remembered them: "the Counselor, the Holy Spirit, whom the Father will send in my name, he will teach you all things."

Chapter 36 tries to capture something of that experience, and of that emerging new understanding, in simple and cross-translatable words. It avoids, therefore, complex phrases like "divine persons," "indwelling," or "sanctifying agent," which are often used in commentaries on the Holy Spirit. It also shuns arcane explanations such as "the Holy Spirit has both a poetic and ontological function," offered in O'Donnell's (1988: 78) otherwise highly illuminating book *The Mystery of the Triune God*. It does not try to explain more than what can be explained in simple words and phrases. Like Polkinghorne (1994: 147), I believe that "this elusive character of our thought and expression about the Spirit is the reflection of a deep theological truth. He is the *deus absconditus*, the hidden God, because his working is from within."

Chapter 36 tries to capture something of the "elusiveness" of the Holy Spirit in Christian thought and this Spirit's perceived reality in Christian experience in the lines about the Apostles: "When they were doing these things they *knew* that the Holy Spirit was with them, they *knew* that the Holy Spirit was in them." The Holy Spirit was invisible but the Apostles knew that when they were trying to do what Jesus told them to do, the Holy Spirit was with them, the Holy Spirit was *in* them. They couldn't not know it.

Commentary on chapter 37: "The Church: people who want to live with Jesus, with other people"

In his book *The Faith of a Physicist* John Polkinghorne (1994: 160) says about the Church that "it is a company of sinners on the way to salvation." This succinct formula reflects two aspects of the concept "church" which Polkinghorne is particularly keen to emphasize: (1) "human solidarity" and (2) "eschatological orientation." What he means by these expressions is close to what chapter 37 tries to capture with (1) the word "we" (repeated more than ten times) and (2) with the word "forever."

As Polkinghorne (1994: 16) further writes, "A real condition of the Christian life is the recognition of our heteronomy [opposite of "autonomy"]. We are not able to go it alone." In Minimal English, the key phrase is "with other people" in the baptizing formula: "You can live with Jesus, with other people."

But the unity implied by the concept "church" goes further than what the phrase "with other people" may imply. When Jesus spoke about "my church" he called it "something" (something that he wanted to build on rock). He also spoke of all Christians, to the end of days, when he prayed that they should be "one" (John 17:20–23).

Of course all the divisions among Christians show clearly that this "oneness" of what Jesus called "my church" (*ekklesia mou*, see chapter 38 and the commentary on it) which he *wished* for has not yet, in the first two millennia of Christianity, become a reality. Yet the vision of that oneness was enough to allow Jesus to think of those who would come to believe in him the (because of the Apostles' words) as being "one something" and not just "many many people."

Are Christians "parts" of that one "something"? Chapter 37 carefully avoids using the word "parts" in relation to people: Christians do not see themselves as "parts of something" in the sense of cogs in a machine. Chapter 37 does not say that Christians thought (and think): "we are parts of one something." Instead, it uses the more personal language of "one" and "many," while at the same time drawing an analogy between the "many" who are "one" and the many parts of a living body which are one body. As the chapter further says, from very early on, Christians understood their "oneness" with the help of Paul's image of "the body of Christ," and of Jesus' words: "This is my body which will be given up for you."

In his Letter to the Romans (12:4–5) Paul wrote: "as in one body we have many members, (. . .), so we, though many, are one body in Christ"; and similarly, in his First Letter to the Corinthians:

> For just as the body is one and has many members, and all the members of the body, though many, are one body, so it is with Christ. For by one Spirit we were all baptised into one body—Jews or Greeks, slaves or free —and we all were made to drink of one Spirit. (1 Corinthians 12:12–13)

This "we" in Paul's letter is revealing: the church is a community of people united, in the first place, through their faith in Jesus's resurrection and their acceptance of "Christ the Lord." The line in chapter 37 which refers to the image of the church as the body of Christ reads, in part: "Christians thought like this: (. . .) we are something like Christ's body."

For people who are not Christians the idea that the church is "something like Christ's body" may seem strange and incomprehensible. For Christians, on the other hand, the word "like" may seem unnecessary, perhaps even improper: usually, Christians say simply: "the church *is* the Body of Christ," not "the church *is like* the body of Christ."

For example, the Orthodox catechism *The Living God* (1989) includes a section entitled "The Church is the Body of Christ," which starts like this:

> St Paul tells us that this Body is the Church (Eph. 1:22-23; Col. 1:18, 1 Cor 12:12-27). We must not think that St Paul uses this expression only as a

literary image. He means that the Church is the mystical embodiment of believers in the cosmic Body of the risen Christ through the power of the Holy Spirit. (p. 277)

Most Christians would probably agree that Paul uses the expression "the body of Christ" as more than a literary image. But the sentence in the Catechism which seeks to explain what Paul meant by means of the expression "mystical embodiment" is far from clear (even for Christians). Furthermore, the phrase "like the body of Christ" used in chapter 37 is cross-translatable, whereas "mystical embodiment" is not.

This is not to say that Paul's expression is to be seen as a mere figure of speech. For Christians, this expression captures something of their experience as participants in the liturgy. The Catechism *The Living God* (1989: 279) puts it quite simply elsewhere: "One can understand how the Church is the Body of Christ only by eating this Bread which is in itself the Body of Christ." We might add: One can understand it intuitively, experientially. This is consistent with the experience of many Christians who during church services sing hymns like "One bread, one body" and who often do so with evident deep feeling and conviction:

One bread, one body
One bread, one body,
one Lord of all,
one cup of blessing which we bless.
And we, though many,
throughout the earth,
we are one body in this one Lord.
Servant or free,
woman or man, no more.
One bread, one body,
one Lord of all (. . .)
(John Foley, 1 Corinthians 10:16, 17; 12:4; Galatians 3:28)

When one bears in mind that the equation between "one bread" (the Eucharistic bread) and "one body" (the church) is based on experience rather than logic it is easier to understand the intention of further explanations such as those offered by the same Orthodox catechism (1989):

The Church is the Eucharistic Bread, the Body of Christ
This perplexing mystery is realized and experienced in the mystery of the Eucharist. The New Testament reveals a double equation: the eucharistic Bread = the Body of Christ = the Church. The Body of Christ is the Church, but it is also the living Bread descended from heaven (Jn 6: 51) which "gives life to the world" (Jn 6: 33). (. . .) This is the Bread which Jesus gave to His disciples on the eve of His death saying, "Take, eat, this

is My Body which is broken for you for the remission of sins" (Mt 26: 26; 1 Cor 11: 24). (p. 279)

The Orthodox catechism links Paul's image of the church as the body of Christ with Jesus's own words spoken in the temple at the beginning of his ministry (John 2:19):

The Lord Jesus Himself told us that His Body would become the meeting place of the faithful, in a phrase which was distorted by the false witnesses at His trial before Caiaphas. (. . .) Actually, Jesus had said, "Destroy this temple, and in three days I will raise it up" (Jn 2:19). And the evangelist adds: "But He spoke of the temple of His body. When therefore He was raised from the dead, His disciples remembered that He had said this; and they believed the scripture and the word which Jesus had spoken" (Jn 2:21-22). In fact an attempt was made to destroy Jesus' body by nailing it to the Cross, and forty years later the Temple of Jerusalem was destroyed by Roman armies. Henceforth, the only temple, the only place where the true worshipers of the Father (Jn 4:23) assemble, is the Body of the Risen One. (vol. 2, pp. 277–278)

The catechism acknowledges that the church, which the Nicene Creed calls "one" and "holy," is in fact sinful and divided. Mainly for this reason, no doubt, the "Seeker" in the catechism says: "I believe in God, I believe in Jesus Christ, but I don't believe in the Church" (vol. 2, p. 264) But the "Sage" replies:

If you cannot recognize the Holy One hidden among the sinners of His Church and in the shame of His Passion, you will not be able to recognize Him at His glorious Second Coming. (. . .) (vol. 2, p. 264)

If you had been in Jerusalem on that Friday when Pilate presented Christ to the crowd, covered with blood and spit, you would have thought that He looked repulsive. (. . .) His face was marked by all the ugliness of this world. The spitting of men disfigured Him and yet He remained the same Christ, the only Holy One. It is the same with the Church. It is disfigured by our spitting, our pettiness, our crimes, by the sins of those who belong to it, including yours and mine. (vol. 2, p. 264)

For Christians, the true nature of the Church, as the Catechism puts it, "is defined by what God calls it to be." The formulations of the Orthodox catechism linking Christians' understanding of the church with their experience of the Eucharist are consonant with what Polkinghorne (1994) says in his *Faith of Physicist:* "A bottom-up thinker will want to ask what is the anchorage in experience which leads the Church to speak of itself not only in historical terms, but also in terms which look beyond history. The answer must be its participation in the Eucharist" (p. 158).

In other words, people who participate in the Eucharist with others and who share both in "historical remembrance" and "eschatological hope," experience "present participation in past reality" and "a common sharing in Christ's everlasting life" (Polkinghorne 1994: 158). Polkinghorne (1994) quotes here from Paul's letter to the Corinthians, "For as often as you eat this bread and drink the cup, you proclaim the Lord's death until he comes" (Corinthians 11:26), and comments: "It is both the commemoration of Calvary and the anticipation of the heavenly banquet of the kingdom of God." He also adds his personal testimony: "I would want to add my own testimony to the mysterious but undeniable experience of the sense of the meeting of past event and future hope in the present reality of the Eucharist" (p. 158).

Chapter 37 of "The Story" uses words and phrases quite different from those of either Polkinghorne or the Orthodox catechism, but in content, it is consistent with them both.

One final point, concerning the formula "in the name of the Father, of the Son, of the Holy Spirit." This formula is so familiar that many Christians take it for granted and do not ask themselves what it really means. It is not self-explanatory, however, and it is not cross-translatable. Nor is it easy to disentangle the meaning of that formula from the meaning of "I baptize you." But when we look, for example, at the words of Peter addressed to a lame man: "In the name of Jesus Christ of Nazareth, rise up and walk" (Acts 3:6), the meaning of the phrase "in the name of . . ." becomes clearer. Essentially, Peter is saying: "I say: I want you to rise up and walk." In saying this, however, he is not relying on his own power but on the power of Jesus. It is not his, Peter's, will which brings about a miracle, but Jesus. So, more fully: "I say: I want you to rise up and walk, you can do it now because Jesus Christ wants it."

This reference to what Jesus wants brings to mind Jesus's own miracles, such as cleansing the leper (in Matthew 8:2). When the leper says to Jesus: "Lord, if you will [want], you can make me clean," Jesus replies: "I will [want], be clean." Thus, when Jesus says about something: "I say: I want it to happen," it happens. When Peter says about something: "In the name of Jesus Christ, I say: I want it to happen," it *can* happen: because Jesus wants it.

Commentary on chapter 38: "The Apostle Peter"

The chapter on Apostle Peter presents a number of linguistic as well as theological challenges. In this commentary, I will only comment on two. I will above all continue to probe the concept of "church" and, relatedly, to reflect on the metaphor of "rock." What exactly did Jesus mean with these words, and how can their presumed meaning be expressed in cross-translatable words and phrases?

To start with "church" (*ekklesia*), it has often been pointed out that in Greek, *ekklesia* meant simply "gathering" and didn't have any of the senses that the word "church" has in the Christian creeds. As Cyril of Jerusalem wrote in the fourth century, "the word 'church' [ekklesia] has different senses. It can refer to the crowd which filled the theatre at Ephesus (Acts 19: 41) . . . or to gatherings of heretics . . . And because of this variation of the word 'church,' the article of faith: 'and [I believe] in one holy Catholic church' has been given to you" (quoted in McGrath 1995: 263).

The meaning of this "article of faith" (included in both the Apostles' and Nicene creeds) can also be misleading. I will return to this point shortly. For the moment, however, what matters is the "oneness" and the all-embracing character ("catholicity") of the new, Christian meaning of the word *ekklesia*.

In the older meaning (as used to refer to a crowd in the theater at Ephesus), *ekklesia* referred to a group of people who gathered in one place at one time. These people could be thought of as "something" because they were in one place at one time and wanted to do the same things. This one "something," however, was limited to that particular place and time. By contrast, in the new Christian sense, *ekklesia* referred to people living in many different places, and at many different times. What gave these people their unity, then? This question was often addressed by early Christians, including many Fathers of the Church. In the fourth century, Saint Augustine answered this question as follows: "What the soul is to the human body, the Holy Spirit is to the Body of Christ, which is the Church" (Sermon 267, quoted in the *Catechism of the Catholic Church,* 1994: 213).

There can be little doubt that the phrases "the body of Christ," "the Holy Spirit," and "the spirit of Christ" played a key role in the early Christian understanding of the new concept *ekklesia*, "the church," as something embracing people from many parts of the earth, and living at different times, who are nonetheless "one."

No matter how this "oneness" anchored in Christ and the Holy Spirit is formulated, it is clear that the new concept of *ekklesia* had its origin in Jesus's words addressed (in Aramaic) to Peter, in response to Peter's declaration of faith in him: "You are the Christ, the Son of the living God" (Matthew 16:16). When Jesus responds to Peter with the words "You are Peter [rock] and on this rock I will build my church" (Matthew 16:18), he is using the word rendered in Greek as *ekklesia* in a new, universal sense, transcending time and space.

How exactly should this new sense be understood? In the entry on "Church" in *The Oxford Companion to the Bible* American theologian David Schowalter (1993: 122) states that "this verse conveys a sense of the church as a universal institution." But the word "institution" is also misleading, not only because it may suggest social hierarchy and earthly power but also because it leaves out the community of believers. The interpretation offered by Russian theologian Alexander Men' (1969) seems more to the point, and more consonant with the early Christians' image of the church as the Body of Christ, animated by the Holy Spirit (the Spirit of God, and at the same time, Christ's spirit):

With these words the Saviour announced to his disciples the founding of his universal community—the Church. He ties this founding to Peter— the first among the Apostles, who, receiving "the keys to the kingdom of Heaven", becomes as it were the leader of the Church in its historical exist- ence, and in its struggles with "the gates of hell." It is not Peter's personal qualities ("flesh and blood") which led him to this insight [that Jesus is "the Messiah, the Son of the living God"], but a revelation from the Father in Heaven. Peter is the first to recognise Christ in Jesus—a feat of worldwide- historical significance.

By using the word "community" (*obščina*) rather than "institution" Men's ac- count balances the "it" (of something built on a rock) and the "many people" (of the older *ekklesia*); and suggests that the "many people" in question see themselves as "we." Further, in Men's account what is shared by people in- cluded in that "we" is their faith that Jesus is indeed "the Christ, the Son of the living God"—as Peter was the first to recognize and profess.

Evidently, a full understanding of this new concept of *ekklesia* developed later, no doubt largely through Paul's letters. Some key components of that concept, however, can be discerned in what Jesus said to Peter, in response to Peter's "confession of faith." In Minimal English, the gist of what Jesus said can be rendered as follows:

> You Simon (Peter, Rock) say to me: "You are the Christ, the Son of the living God."
> After some time many people in many parts of the earth will say the same.
> They will say: "we want to live with Jesus, with other people."
> This will happen as long as there are people on earth.
> I want all these people to be one [something], as many stones are one something if someone builds a house with these stones.
> At the same time, I want this something to be like something built on rock.

Later, Jesus introduced two other, inter-related, metaphors which linked the concept of church with his own person: the metaphor of the temple and the metaphor of his own body. Thus, in the episode of the "cleansing of the temple" in Jerusalem (when Jesus overturns the tables of the money- changers and drives out the sellers of oxen, sheep and pigeons from the temple) we read:

> The Jews then said to him: "What sign have you to show us for doing this?" Then Jesus answers: "Destroy this temple, and in three days I will raise it up." The Jews then said: "It has taken forty six years to build this temple, and you will raise it up in three days?" But he spoke of the temple of his body. When therefore he was raised from the dead, his disciples remembered that he had said this. (John 2:18–22)

Evidently, Paul's repeated references to the church as the body of Christ (Colossians 1:17, 1:24; Ephesians 1:22–23; Romans 12:4–5) built both on Jesus's words to Peter ("on this rock I will build my church") and on his words about his own body as a (new) "temple." As the Orthodox catechism *The Living God* quoted earlier puts it, "The Lord himself told us that His Body would become the meeting place of the faithful."

As noted earlier, when Jesus said: "I will be with you always, to the end of times" he couldn't have been talking only to the Twelve (or, strictly speaking, Eleven), because they would all die within decades. Evidently, when Jesus said this, he was addressing all the future generations of Christians. They will all be "one something," and the Apostles are the first, "foundational" part of this something. As Benedict XVI (2012b: 77) puts it, "the Church was built on the foundation of the Apostles." In Minimal English this means that the Twelve are not only "part of this something" but that they are part of it "before other people can be part of it."

This relates to Jesus's promise to the Apostles included in chapter 36: "When the Holy Spirit is with you, you will know well what I wanted to say to you before." In Jesus's intention, the church would preserve his teaching for all the future generations, and the "Apostolic tradition" would provide guidelines for the interpretation of that teaching.

And Peter? What did Jesus mean when he called him the rock on which he would build his church? It is interesting to note that Benedict XVI in writing about the church is always careful to say that it was built "auf dem Fundament der Apostels" (on the foundation of the Apostles), rather than "on Peter." So what exactly was Peter's place in that edifice, in Jesus' intention?

As the last lines of chapter 38 indicate, Christians have often argued about this in the past; and they still argue about it now. After the miraculous catch of fish, Peter himself asked Jesus to leave his boat: "Depart from me for I am a sinful man, O Lord" (Luke 5:8). Peter was, by his own admission, "a sinful man." Yet it was to this "sinful man" that Jesus said: "on this rock I will build my church, and the gates of hell shall not prevail against it." This means, Christians believe, that the Holy Spirit can act in the church regardless of the sinfulness and unworthiness of Christians (church leaders not excepted).

Catholic theologian Wacław Hryniewicz (2009: 224) interprets the article of the creeds concerning the church as follows: "We believe in God, and trust Him, at the same time we profess our faith in the existence of one, holy, universal and apostolic church. This faith is trust that within this human and sinful community the Holy Spirit acts, transforming it." He also writes: "It is not power and authority which determine the nature of the church, but the Holy Spirit, thanks to whom Christ does not become a distant historical memory, but continues to be [for everyone in the community of believers] a living presence."

Authority in the church should be exercised at all levels to *serve* people, and not to rule. Hryniewicz invokes Jesus's words on this point: "The kings of the

Gentiles exercise lordship over them. But I am among you as one who serves" (Luke 22:24–27) and stresses that the church needs to "be a community of brothers [and sisters] under Christ and the Holy Spirit." (In the image of Peter as the rock on which the church was to be built, Peter is *below* the church, not above it.)

Commentary on chapter 39: "An Apostle called Paul"

In his essay "Christianity for the Twenty-First Century" Russian Orthodox theologian Alexander Men' (1996), sometimes called "the Apostle to Russia," notes that the New Testament has been described as consisting of two biographies, that of Jesus Christ and that of his follower, Paul of Tarsus, the Apostle Paul. This may be an overstatement, but no one can doubt the importance of Paul as "the Apostle to the nations" and "the Apostle to the Gentiles." As Men' further notes, "Paul never saw Jesus face to face during his earthly life (. . .). But Christ appeared to Paul with a vividness that surpasses any outward encounter. (. . .) This event changed not only his destiny, but also the destiny of the early church." The word "destiny" is an approximate translation of the untranslatable Russian word "sud'ba"—roughly, the "design" of what happens to someone in the course of their life. In relation to Paul, the main implication is that (to put it in Minimal English) many things happened to him as God wanted (not as he, Paul, wanted) because God wanted him to do some things; and also, that because Paul did those things, many things happened to the church as God wanted.

We can also say that for a long time before his encounter with Jesus Paul (then called Saul) "felt something very bad" toward Jesus and his followers.

> For you heard of my former life in Judaism, how I persecuted the church of God violently and tried to destroy it; and I advanced in Judaism beyond many of my own age among key people, as extremely zealous was I for the traditions of my fathers. (Galatians 1:13–14, RSV)

In the Acts of the Apostles, Saul's anti-Christian zeal is described in even stronger terms:

> But Saul was ravaging the church, and entering house after house, he dragged off men and women and committed them to prison. (Acts 8:3)

> But Saul, still breathing threats and murder against the disciples of the Lord, went to the high priest and asked him for letters to the synagogues at Damascus, so that if he found any belonging to the Way, men or women, he may bring them bound to Jerusalem. (Acts 9:1–2, RSV)

It is particularly interesting to note how the word "church" (*ekklesia*) is used in these passages. In Paul's own account, in his letter to the Galatians, he doesn't say "I persecuted Christians," he says: "I persecuted the church of God." As he saw it, then, he was not persecuting "people of one kind" (Christians), nor was he persecuting a particular "gathering of people" (*ekklesia* in the older sense of the word). Rather, he was persecuting the "something" that Jesus created, "the church" in the new sense of the word, "the church of Jesus." Luke speaks about Saul's actions in the same way: in the Acts' account, Saul was not persecuting "Christians" but ravaging "the church," *ekklesia*, in the new sense of the word.

Saul was a Pharisee. In the chapter "The Gospel, the law and the Pharisees" in his great work *The Son of Man*, Alexander Men' (1969: 4) points out that "The Pharisees" were closer to Christ's teaching than the other Jewish groups: the Sadducees, the Zealots, the Essenes," and he closes his survey of historical sources with the conclusion that it is unclear why they (the Pharisees) took a hostile position in relation to Jesus' teaching. Then he reviews various explanations which have been proposed by various scholars.

Judging by Paul's own explanation in the letter to Galatians, what motivated his early hatred of Christianity was his extreme zeal for "the traditions of [his] fathers," that is, for the law of Moses (and the traditions deriving from it). Presumably, what mattered for Saul most, was not just the letter of the Law, but its spirit; and as Jesus' parable of the Pharisee and the Tax Collector (Luke 18:9–14) shows, the spirit of Jesus's teaching was quite different from that encouraged by the teaching of the Pharisees. It seems likely that it was this new spirit that made Saul see Christianity as a threat to "the Law."

Accordingly, chapter 39 attributes to Saul the following way of thinking: "this man Jesus wants Israelites to live not as Moses said, he wants them to think not as they thought before; this is very very bad." As discussed in detail by Men', not all Pharisees had such an attitude to Jesus and his followers, and for example a Pharisee in the Sandedrin called Gamaliel, "a teacher of the law, held in honour by all the people" (Acts 5:34), recommended a patient and tolerant attitude to the new teaching. Saul, however, was obviously a man of great passion and couldn't take the attitude recommended by Gamaliel (who was in fact his teacher). But then, on the road to Damascus, he saw Jesus.

Did he really see him? The New Testament accounts vary. In Luke's account, Saul saw a light ("suddenly a light from heaven flashed about him, and he fell to the ground," Acts 9:3–4), whereas in his own letter to the Corinthians Paul says, "Have I not seen Jesus our Lord?" (1 Corinthians 9:1); and further in the same letter Paul includes himself among those to whom the risen Jesus *appeared* ("he appeared also to me," 1 Corinthians 15:8). Garry Wills (2006: ch. 1), in his book *What Paul Meant*, attaches a great deal of significance to this difference between the two accounts, Luke's and Paul's. I think, however, that they can be harmonized, as I have tried to do in chapter 39, and as artists have often tried to do in their paintings. If Saul, blinded by the light, couldn't see the ground before him, this doesn't mean that he didn't see Jesus, as he was evidently convinced he did.

Undoubtedly, during his encounter with Jesus on the way to Damascus "something happened to Saul like never before"; and when, blinded by the light, he heard Jesus's voice addressing him personally, in the words rendered in this "Story" as "Saul, Saul, why do you want to do very bad things to me?" ("Saul, Saul, why are you persecuting me?"), "something happened *in* Saul." After this, Saul didn't want to persecute Christians anymore. He became, as it were, a different person, as symbolized by his change of name from Saul to Paul.

Perhaps the most striking aspect of what Saul heard the voice say is the word "me." As Saul saw it, he was persecuting "the church," this new thing created by that man Jesus, but as Jesus saw it, Saul was persecuting "me," Jesus himself. No doubt Paul meditated all his life on the words that he heard on the road to Damascus, and on that identification between "the church" that he was persecuting and the "me" of the risen Christ. Presumably, this was how he conceived the idea of the church as "the body of Christ," an idea which struck a chord in the hearts of other Christians.

The main challenges of chapter 39 lie in condensing Saul/Paul's extraordinary life and thought into one page of text, and in doing so without any of the usual props on which entries on Paul of Tarsus in biblical reference works normally rely, that is, complex words like "conversion," "transformation," "persecution," "missionary," "journeys," "shipwreck," "epistles," and the like. Such props can compress a great deal of knowledge and interpretation into the space of one word, but they are not cross-translatable (or self-explanatory). Unpacking them would take a great deal of space, and would involve many unnecessary conceptual detours. What chapter 39 attempts to do instead, is to re-think Paul's life and thought in simple and cross-translatable words without any such detours, and to zero in, at every turn, on the main point. For example: "at that moment, something happened in Saul"; "he didn't want to do bad things to Christians anymore"; "often very bad things happened to him because of this," and so on.

As for Paul's writings and ideas, arguably, the best way to give some account of them in simple and cross-translatable words, and in the space of one page, is to identify their main themes through phrases like "to know what," "to know why," or "to know who," rather than trying to fully spell out their content. For example, "He [Paul] wanted people to know well who Jesus was, why he lived on earth, why he died on the cross."

Nonetheless, some of Paul's most important and most distinct ideas *have* been spelled out in this chapter. This applies, in particular, to the following lines:

> Paul wanted people to know that *all* people can live with Jesus:
> Greeks, Jews; men, women; slaves, not slaves; all people.
> He wanted people everywhere to know
> that if they live with Jesus they live with God.

In the final segment, the chapter tries to say something about Paul's place among the Apostles. In this context, it was necessary to identify the main goal which they all shared. There are various possible ways of doing so; chapter 39 settled on "[wanting many people] to know well who Jesus was, why he lived on earth, why he died on the cross." In Paul's and Peter's case, there is an added emphasis on the scope and effectiveness of their work, as seen from the perspective of the twenty-first century: "these two [Apostles] did more, there are many many Christians on earth now because of this."

Commentary on chapter 40: "What will happen to people, what God wants"

What will happen to me after I die? What will happen to other people? The New Testament's answer to such questions is that at some point, all people will see Jesus and that when they see him, they will know, like never before, how they lived when they lived on earth. This corresponds to the following lines of the Apostles' Creed: "he [Jesus Christ] ascended into heaven, and is seated at the right hand of God the Father almighty; from there he will come to judge the living and the dead." In the Nicene Creed the line about Jesus' "second coming" is slightly expanded: "He will come again in glory to judge the living and the dead."

Translated into Minimal English, the phrase "in glory" implies that "when someone sees Jesus, they will know that they see God" (cf. John 12:45). In the visionary language of the part of the Bible called "The Revelation to John," Jesus—"who loves us and has freed us from our sins by his blood" (Revelation. 1:5)—will come "with the clouds, and every eye will see him, every one who pierced him" (Revelation 1:7). In this vision, the author of "Revelation" actually *sees* Jesus ("one like a son of man," Revelation 1:12), and this "son of man" touches him and says: "Fear not, I am the first and the last, and the living one; I died, and behold I am alive for evermore, and I have the keys of Death and Hades" (Revelation 1:17–18). The reference to "the clouds" has a source in a prophecy of Daniel in the Hebrew Bible (Daniel 7:13), and also echoes a phrase from Matthew's Gospel about Jesus's "second coming," when the nations "will see the Son of man coming on the clouds of heaven with power and great glory" (Matthew 24:30, RSV).

This is then the Judge who "has the keys of Death": Jesus, whom people will see as "pierced" (on the cross) and yet living, and appearing to them "in glory." As many Christian thinkers have pointed out, the richest and most illuminating image of the Last Judgment is provided in the Gospels by the parable of the Prodigal Son, in which the younger son, having squandered his money, finally comes to his senses and sees his life in truth, in the light in which his father must have seen it—and passes judgment on it himself.

According to a long tradition in biblical interpretation, starting with the great third-century theologian Origen and continuing to the present, this self-judgment will be connected with a radical illumination by the light of Christ. For example, Basil of Caesarea (fourth century) says that "the face of the Judge radiates a divine light, which penetrates the depths of the hearts, and we will have no other accuser but our own sins, which through this light will have become present to us" (quoted in Balthasar 1983: 265).

In the parable of the Last Judgment in Matthew's Gospel (Matthew 25:31–46), the main criterion on which the Last Judgment will be based is how much love and compassion one has shown to other people:

When the Son of man comes in his glory, and all the angels with him, then he will sit on his glorious throne. Before him will be gathered all the nations, and he will separate them one from another as a shepherd separates the sheep from the goats, and he will place the sheep at his right hand, but the goats at the left. Then the King will say to those at his right hand, "Come, O blessed of my Father, inherit the kingdom prepared for you from the foundation of the world; for I was hungry and you gave me food, thirsty and you gave me drink, I was a stranger and you welcomed me, I was naked and you clothed me, I was sick and you visited me, I was in prison and you came to me." Then the righteous answer him, "Lord, when did we see thee hungry and feed thee, thirsty and give thee drink? And when did we see thee a stranger and welcome thee, or naked and clothe thee? And when did we see thee sick or in prison and visit thee?" And the King will answer them, "Truly, I say to you, as you did it to one of the least of my brethren, you did it to me." Then he will say to those at his left hand, "Depart from me, you cursed, into the eternal fire prepared for the devil and his angels; for I was hungry and you gave me no food, I was thirsty and you gave me no drink, I was a stranger and you did not welcome me, naked and you did not clothe me, sick and in prison and you did not visit me." Then they also answer, "Lord, when did we see thee hungry or thirsty or a stranger or naked or sick or in prison, and did not minister to thee?" And he will answer them, "Truly, I say to you, as you did it not to the least of these, you did it not to me." And they will go away into eternal punishment, but the righteous into eternal life.

As many Christian thinkers have argued over the centuries, the division of people into "sheep" and "goats" is to be understood against the background of biblical prophetic speech, and the threats of "eternal fire" and "eternal punishment" are to be taken as appeals rather than factual predictions. It is clear that the Apostles, familiar with the rhetorical tradition of the Hebrew prophets (and enlightened, as Jesus promised, by the Holy Spirit) did not take the threats of the parable literally. The ancient document called the Apostles' Creed, which is thought to be a distillation of the faith of the Apostles, does not say anything about a forthcoming division of all people into two groups, the "sheep" and the "goats," or about God rejecting some people forever. On the contrary, it states, as an article of Christian faith, "the forgiveness of sins."

Furthermore, according to the New Testament *all* people are sinners; only Jesus was not a sinner (and, many Christians believe, his mother Mary). This being so, the division of people into "sheep" and "goats" has to be understood as a metaphor: all people are in some respects like "goats," and in others like "sheep." The fourth-century Father of the Church Ambrose formulated this insight as follows: "Idem homo et salvatur ex parte et condemnatur ex parte," "the same human being is both partially saved and partially condemned" (quoted in Balthasar 1983: 293).

Nonetheless Christians believe that to some people (perhaps not very many) the Judge—Jesus—will say something like this: "You can now live with God as you are now," whereas others will hear something like this: "You can't live with God now as you are now." This suggests the need for many people, perhaps most, to undergo an inner transformation before they can be fit to live with God. The Fathers of the Church such as St Gregory of Nyssa (1993) spoke in this connection of a temporary process of purification, as if by fire, which can heal and transform a person:

> For it is not out of hatred or vengeance for an evil life (in my opinion) that God brings painful conditions upon sinners, when He seeks after and draws to Himself whatever has come to birth for his sake; but for a better purpose. He draws the soul to Himself, who is the foundation of all bless-edness. The painful condition necessarily happens as an incidental conse-quence to the one who is drawn. When goldsmiths purify gold by fire from the matter which is mixed with it, they do not only melt the adulterant in the fire, but inevitably the pure metal is melted away with the base admix-ture. When the latter is consumed the former remains. In the same way when evil is consumed by purifying fire, the soul which is united to evil must necessarily also be in the fire until the base adulterant material is removed, consumed by the fire. (pp. 83–84).

Again, it must be emphasized that there is nothing about any "eternal punishment" (or "everlasting hell") in the Apostles' Creed. Instead, the creed speaks of "the forgiveness of sins." This is consistent with the numerous references to God's love and concern for all people ("the world") in the letters of the Apostles: John, Peter, James, and above all, Paul. To quote just a few brief examples from Paul's letters: "Christ died and lived again, that he might be Lord of both the dead and the living" (Romans 14:9); "For the grace of God has appeared for the salvation of all men [people]" (Titus 2:11); "God our Savior desires all men to be saved and to come to the knowledge of the truth" (1 Timothy 2:4–5); "For in him [Christ] all the fullness of God was pleased to dwell and through him to reconcile to himself all things, whether on earth or in heaven." (Colossians 1:20).

This is why "The Story" is, I believe, justified in saying: "The Apostles thought like this: Jesus will not say to anyone: 'You can never live with God." The Apostles (and the Fathers of the Church) believed in "the forgiveness of sins," that is, in the limitlessness of God's, and Jesus', forgiveness.

Speaking of what will happen to all people "in the end," we need to distinguish two things: what God will do and what people will do. The two key questions are: "Will God reject anyone?" and "Will anyone reject God?" To the first question, many Christian thinkers and mystics reply: "No," in line with the Apostles' Creed: "I believe in the forgiveness of sins." The word usually used in this context is "mercy," and the usual way to frame the question is this: "Is there a limit to God's mercy?" Two Christian thinkers (from very different periods), St Isaac (seventh century) and Edith Stein (twentieth century, canonized in 1998) offer responses which are particularly worth listening to:

Isaac of Nineveh (1995), who was both a mystic and a biblical scholar, rejected a literalist reading of references to "everlasting damnation" as a deplorable misunderstanding and an insult to God:

> It is not (the way of) the compassionate Maker to create rational beings in order to deliver them over mercilessly to unending affliction (in punishment) for things of which He knew even before they were fashioned, (aware) how they would turn out when He created them – and whom (nonetheless) He created. (p. 165)

In view of this, the suffering Gehenna (hell) could only be, according to St Isaac, temporary, and part of God's overall love and mercy.

> That we should further say or think that the matter is not full of love and mingled with compassion would be an opinion full of blasphemy and insult to our Lord God. (By saying) that He will even hand us over to burning for the sake of suffering torment and all sorts of ills, we are attributing to divine Nature an enmity towards the very rational beings which He created through grace. . . . Among all His actions there is none which is not entirely a matter of mercy, love and compassion: this constitutes the beginning and the end of His dealings with us. (p. 172)

Edith Stein, a German Jewish philosopher and Carmelite nun who died in Auschwitz, in an essay, asking "what grace can do and whether even for it there is an absolute limit," replies: "the possibility, in principle, of excluding oneself from redemption and the kingdom of grace (. . .) does *not* imply a limit to divine mercy (. . .) The descent of grace to the human soul is a free act of divine love. And there are *no limits* to how far it may descend" (quoted in Balthasar 1988: 218–220).

But if there are good reasons to believe that God will not reject anyone, what about the possibility that some people will definitively (forever) reject God? Stein responds as follows (quoted in Balthasar 1988):

> All-merciful love can thus descend to everyone. We believe that it does so. And now, can we assume that there are souls that remain perpetually closed to such love? As a possibility in principle, this cannot be rejected. *In reality*, it can become infinitely improbable—precisely through what preparatory grace is capable of effecting in the soul. It can do no more than knock at the door, and there are souls that already open themselves to it upon hearing this unobtrusive call. Others allow it to go unheeded. Then it can steal its way into souls and begin to spread itself out there more and more.
>
> The more that grace wins ground from the things that had filled the soul before it, the more it repels the effects of the acts directed against it. And to this process of displacement there are, in principle, no limits. If all the impulses opposed to the spirit of light have been expelled from the soul, then any free decision against this has become infinitely improbable. Then faith in the unboundedness of divine love and grace also justifies *hope for the universality of redemption*, although, through the possibility of resistance to grace that remain open in principle, the *possibility* of eternal damnation also persists. (p. 210)

"The Story of God and People" as told here does not assert that in the end, all people will live with God. Rather, it highlights the message of the New Testament that this is what God wants. It is consistent with Isaac of Nineveh's and Edith Stein's evident conviction that "at the end of time" Jesus as a Judge will not say to anyone: "you can never live with God."

As for the final outcome—the possibility of some people rejecting God (refusing to live with God) forever, "The Story" makes no pronouncements on this point, emphasizing both human freedom ("all people can live with God *if they want to*") and God's love for all people ("God feels something very good *toward all people*," "God wants to do very good things *for all people*"). Let me end with a quote from the French theologian and biblical scholar Louis Lochet (1979), in his book *Jésus descendu aux enfers* ("Jesus descended to hell"), which Hans Urs von Balthasar (1988) includes in his book *Dare we hope that all men will be saved?*:

> If someone asks us, "Will all men be saved?" we answer in line with the Gospel: I do not know. I have no certainty whatsoever. That means just as well that I have no certainty whatsoever that all men will not be saved. The whole of Scripture is full of the proclamation of a salvation that binds all men by a Redeemer who gathers together and reconciles the whole universe. That is quite sufficient to enable us to hope for the salvation of all men without thereby coming into contradiction with the Word of God. (p. 113)

PART IV

Appendices

A. On the word "forgiveness"

The explanation of the English word "forgiveness" and its equivalents in other European languages formulated in chapter 16 of "The Story" in Minimal English is actually quite close to that given, in a more complex language, by the American Psychological Association (2006) and included in the Wikipedia article on "Forgiveness": "Forgiveness is the intentional and voluntary process by which a victim undergoes a change in feelings and attitude regarding an offense, lets go of negative emotions such as vengefulness, with an increased ability to wish the offender well." Arguably, defining "forgiveness" in this way, the American Psychological Association is being guided by the meaning of the English word "forgiveness," and thus, by a concept shaped by a particular cultural tradition. It is a misapprehension to think that, as the same Wikipedia article states, "Most world religions include teachings on the nature of forgiveness." It would be more accurate to say that most world religions include concepts comparable, in some respects, to the Christian (and post-Christian) concept of "forgiveness," though by no means identical to it.

For example, using the word "forgiveness" to describe Buddhism is to look at Buddhism through Christian spectacles—an approach which was critiqued by the Buddhist scholar Gananath Obeyesekere (1985) and which can be illustrated with the following statement from the same Wikipedia article: "In Buddhism, forgiveness is seen as a practice to prevent harmful thoughts from causing havoc on one's mental well-being." Having used the word "forgiveness" in this way, without providing any Buddhist equivalent, the article then goes on to offer such equivalents (or quasi-equivalents) for a number of other concepts: "Buddhism places much emphasis on the concepts of *Metta* (loving kindness), *karuna* (compassion), *mudita* (sympathetic joy), and *upekkha* (equanimity), as a means of avoiding resentments in the first place."

This suggests that there is no word meaning "forgiveness" (in the sense explicated in the present commentary) in the Buddhist moral vocabulary, although there are related and overlapping concepts. I would suggest that the overlap lies, above all, in the following components: "I don't want to think about this person like this: 'this person did something very bad to me,'" "I don't want to feel something bad toward this person." The main difference seems to lie in the component "I want to think about this person in another way," which appears to be absent in the Buddhist concept, where the focus is on freeing oneself from harmful thoughts. The focus on the other person is of course present in concepts like "loving kindness" (*Metta*) and "compassion" (*karuna*), but these differ from "forgiveness" in other respects.

In the book *The Sunflower: On the Possibilities and Limits of Forgiveness*, edited by Simon Wiesenthal (1998), the Dalai Lama responds to the question implicit in the title of the book with a true story:

> A few years back, a Tibetan monk who had served about eighteen years in a Chinese prison in Tibet came to see me after his escape to India. (. . .) During the course of that meeting I had asked him what he felt was the biggest threat or danger while he was in prison. I was amazed by his answer. It was extraordinary and inspiring. I was expecting him to say something else; instead he said that what he feared most was losing his compassion for the Chinese.

From a Christian point of view, this can be seen as a magnificent story illustrating the beauty and value of forgiveness. From a Buddhist point of view, however, the story illustrates something else: the beauty and value of something like compassion (in Tibetan, *nying je* ("compassion") and *nying je chenmo* ("great compassion")—words and glosses cited by the Dalai Lama (1999) in *Ethics for the New Millennium*). For all that it is understandable that Christians might respond in this way to the story, then, what is at issue here is the Tibetan Buddhist value of *nying je chenmo* rather than the Christian one of forgiveness.

In *The Sunflower*, an Austrian-American Catholic theologian, Eva Fleischner, writes (1998: 139): "forgiveness is no Christian invention. Along with so much else in our tradition we inherited from Judaism: the image of a loving, merciful God who waits eagerly and, as it were, with open arms, to welcome back the sinner (cf. Isa. 55:6-7; Joel 2:12-13; Ps. 130:7-8)."

One can certainly agree with Fleischner that forgiveness is no Christian invention. For example, as speakers of English we could easily say that the biblical Esau forgave his brother Jacob who had cheated him out of his birth-right (Genesis 27, 33). This doesn't mean, however, that the *concept* of "for-giveness" is not of Christian origin. Evidence suggests that while the concepts of something like "mercy" (in Hebrew, *hesed*) are prominently present in the Hebrew Bible, the concept of "forgiveness" as such is not—the concept of God "wiping out" people's sins (in Hebrew, *kipper*, see Barrett 1991: 73), yes, but the concept of "forgiveness" among equals, in the sense of people deliberately changing their way of thinking about their "brothers" and "neighbours" who have wronged them (as in Jesus's injunction to "forgive your brother from the heart," Matthew's Gospel 18:35), no.

This shift from abstract targets like "sins," "debts," and "trespasses" to *people* (e.g., "your brother," "your debtors," "everyone") is also significant. In "wiping out sins" or "cancelling debts," the focus is on objective states of af-fairs, whereas in "forgiving one's brother" those objective states of affairs are not even mentioned, the focus is entirely on the relationship between people (we and our "debtors," I and my brother).

The Oxford Dictionary of Jewish Religion (1997: 278) says, using the English words "forgive" and "forgiveness," that in Judaism "God is proclaimed as 'forgiving iniquity, transgression and sin' (Exodus 34:6-7). (. . .) Since the individual should imitate the attributes of God, forgiveness for injuries or offenses should be freely given by the injured party, but human forgiveness involves the added need for rectifying any wrong and appeasing the person injured." While this statement is framed in terms of the Christian and post-Christian concept of "forgiveness," the quote itself makes it clear that dif-ferent concepts are involved: A concept which requires rectifying the wrong and appeasing the person injured is different from the concept of "forgive-ness." (See also the entry on "Forgiveness" in *The Interpreter's Dictionary of the Bible* (1962).)

One can fully agree with Fleischner (1998: 140) when she says that "Jesus' well-known parable of the Prodigal Son stands squarely in the Jewish tradi-tion"—without agreeing with the sentence which follows: "The only require-ment for being forgiven by God is genuine repentance—*teshuvah,* metanoia. Such a 'turning' is required by Christian as much as by Jewish tradition. Without repentance, no forgiveness." Surely, not so: When Jesus was for-giving the Roman soldiers who were nailing him to the cross, he did not wait for them to repent first. (In *The Sunflower* (Wiesenthal 1998: 182), Cardinal Franz Köenig, Archbishop of Vienna, states: "For Christians, the binding an-swer is in the Gospels. The question of whether there is a limit to forgiveness has been emphatically answered by Christ in the negative.") For Jesus, the im-perative to think about others *not* in terms of the wrong they have done us, is unconditional.

"Repentance" may indeed be implied by the Greek word *metanoia* and by the Hebrew word *teshuvah*, but is not implied, for example, by the English words "forgiveness" and "forgive." As I see it, genuine dialogue between religions consists neither in reducing them all to the smallest common denominator nor in viewing them all through the lens of one of those religions. Instead, it requires an effort to understand others—which includes trying to understand the concepts that they think with—and to make oneself understood. To paraphrase Eva Fleischner's saying about forgiveness, without mutual understanding, no genuine dialogue.

This is why I think that when a religious Jew like the prominent American radio broadcaster and author Dennis Prager (1998) says (in *The Sunflower*) that he rejects "the Christian notions of forgiving everyone" (p. 227) and "the Christian doctrine of forgiveness" (p. 229), this may do more for interfaith dialogue and global understanding than well-meaning assertions that all world religions teach forgiveness.

B. On the word "love"

1. SETTING THE SCENE

Seen from a broad cross-linguistic perspective, the English word "love" is quite unusual. (For reasons of space, I will not be talking about the noun "love," but only about the verb, as in the sentence "She loves him.") What is unusual about this verb is its very broad scope: It can apply to a mother's love, a husband's love, a sister's love, a grandmother's love, a child's love, and so on, without any restrictions whatsoever.

It is true that the same broad and unrestricted scope is also characteristic of the German verb *lieben*, the French verb *aimer*, and the Russian verb *ljubit'*; so from the perspective of modern European languages there is nothing unusual about this English verb ("to love") as such. But from a broader historical and geographical perspective the concept *is* unusual. To begin with the historical perspective, in ancient Greece there was no verb that could be used across the board like this (as discussed, for example, by C. S. Lewis (1960) in his book *The Four Loves*). Instead, there were four verbs: *stergo, erao, phileo*, and *agapao* (first person singular) (the corresponding nouns are *storge, eros, philia*, and *agape*), linked with different prototypes. Thus, *stergo* had its prototype in the mutual love of parents and children; *erao*, in erotic love, and *phileo*, in the love between friends. As for *agapao*, it was often used in relation to short-term good feelings toward someone, rather than a long-term attitude. (Liddell and Scott's *Greek-English Lexicon*, 1963, glosses *agapao*, in the first place, as "to welcome, to entertain, to take leave of.")

Thus, even in Europe, the broad concept of "love" (as in "she loves him"), implying stability and not confined to one prototypical relationship, does not go back to antiquity. Further, linguists and anthropologists have shown that in other parts of the world, too, many languages also lack a word matching the English verb "(to) love." For example, for languages of Oceania, there are excellent accounts by Catherine Lutz (1985, 1988) of Ifaluk, Eleanor Gerber (1985) of Samoan, and Robert Levy (1973) of Tahitian. (For a broader survey, see *Semantics, Culture and Cognition* (Wierzbicka 1992).) As Lutz shows, in Ifaluk, the word closest to the English *love* is *fago*, which she glosses as "love/compassion/sadness," and which is linked with the prototype of misfortune, that is, with the thought "very bad things can happen to people." Furthermore, *fago* does not necessarily imply a long-term attitude: it can refer to a short-term feeling, like the English noun "compassion" or the phrase "to be sorry for someone."

Returning to the English verb "(to) love," I would explicate it, anticipating further discussion, as follows:

Rebekah loved Jacob.
Rebekah often thought about Jacob,
she felt something very good toward him,
she wanted to do many things because of this, she wanted to do good
    things for him.

The first component shows that the verb "(to) love" refers to a long-term attitude; the second component is self-explanatory; and the third component, based on "wanting," is composite, including an impulse to do many things, and a desire to do good things for the loved person. The first "want" subcomponent may have a prototype in erotic love, and the second, in the love of parents for their children; but unlike in the case of *eros* and *storge*, these two prototypes are as it were fused in one conceptual whole.

2. THE ORIGINS OF THE BROAD CONCEPT "TO LOVE (SOMEONE)"

Where does the broad concept encoded in the English verb "to love" (and also, in the German *lieben*, the French *aimer*, and the Russian *ljubit'*) come from?

My hypothesis is that this concept has its origin in the Greek verb *agapao*, not as used in classical Greek, but as used in New Testament Greek, and in particular, in the Gospels. The first point to note is that the verb *agapao* in Jesus's speech (as portrayed in the Gospels) is evidently quite different in meaning from *agapao* as used in classical Greek (as characterized, for example by Liddell and Scott 1963). Since Jesus was not a native speaker of Greek, and normally spoke to people in Aramaic, it is reasonable to assume that the verb *agapao* used in the Gospels stands for an Aramaic verb spoken originally by Jesus—an Aramaic counterpart of the Hebrew verb *'āhēb*, much discussed in the commentaries on the Hebrew Bible.

But what was the relationship between the concept as used by Jesus (and reflected in the Gospels in the new use of the Greek verb *agapao*) and the concept of *'āhēb* in the Hebrew Bible? A key point to note here is that Jewish scholars who translated the Hebrew Bible into Greek in the third and second century BC chose the Greek verb *agapao* to render *'āhēb*. Evidently the New Testament use of *agapao* built on earlier use. (I am referring here to the monumental translation known at the "Septuagint" or "LXX.")

In the New Testament, *agapao*, which (together with its derivatives) occurs 300 times, assumes a central place in its conceptual vocabulary. (Relative to length, *agapao* and *agape* occur in the New Testament over five times as often as in the Greek version of the Old Testament, that is, the Septuagint.)

But is the verb *agapao* used in the New Testament in the same sense in which it was used in the Septuagint? And further, what did Jesus mean when he used the Aramaic word rendered in the Greek Gospels with the verb *agapao*, and in the King James Bible, with the English verb "(to) love"?

I think these questions are of great interest not only to people who want to understand Christianity, but also to anyone interested in the concept of "love," as we know it from modern European languages such as English.

3. "LOVING" ANOTHER PERSON IN THE OLD TESTAMENT

Let us consider another biblical sentence: "Jacob loved (*'āhēb*) Rachel" (Genesis 29:18). An English reader who reads this sentence in an English translation is likely to interpret it in the way in which "Rebekah loved Jacob" was explicated in section 1. But is this what the sentence "Jacob 'loved' (*'āhēb*) Rachel" means in the Hebrew Bible?

There are good reasons to think that the answer is: no. As many dictionaries and biblical commentaries put it, *'āhēb* meant something like "preferential love" rather than simply "love" (see, e.g., McKenzie 1965). Jacob loved Rachel not like he loved anyone else, or, more precisely, he thought about her not like he thought about any other people, and felt something very good toward her not like toward anyone else.

This suggestion that *'āhēb* implies not just "love" (as in English) but a "preferential love," is supported by biblical sentences like the following one:

Isaac loved Esau (. . .) but Rebekah loved Jacob. (Genesis 25:28)

Isaac and Rebekah were the parents of two twin sons, Esau and Jacob; and there is no reason to doubt that both parents loved both sons. However, the use of *'āhēb* implies that Isaac loved Esau with a *special* love, whereas Rebekah had a *special* love for Jacob. In Minimal English, this can be represented as follows:

Rebekah "loved" Jacob (Hebrew, *'āhēb*, Old Testament Greek, *agapao*)
Rebekah often thought about Jacob, she thought about him not like she
    thought about anyone else.
She felt something very good toward him, not like toward anyone else.
She wanted to do many things because of this, she wanted to do good
    things for him.

Such "preferential" love (*'āhēb*) often goes to favorite sons (as in the case of Isaac's special love for Esau, and Rebekah's, for Jacob), and favorite wives (as in the case of Jacob's special love for Rachel, in contrast to his other wife, Leah). But the word *'āhēb* could also be used for one's "favorite person," so to speak.

Biblical scholar Susan Ackerman (2002) emphasizes that in the Hebrew Bible, the verb *'āhēb* is used predominantly about men in relation to women, and not the other way around, and also, about parents in relation to their children, and not the other way. The interpretation of *'āhēb* as, so to speak, "preferential love" explains this: in a patriarchal, polygamous society like ancient Israel, men could have favorite wives, but wives couldn't have favorite husbands. While both fathers and mothers could have favorite sons, sons of course couldn't have a favorite father or a favorite mother.

4. LOVING ANOTHER PERSON IN THE NEW TESTAMENT

Moving now to the New Testament, do we find the verb *agapao* being used, in relation to individuals, in the same way in which *'āhēb* was used in the Hebrew Bible and *agapao* in the Septuagint? For example, when Jesus asks Simon Peter (in the Gospel of John, 21:16) "Simon, son of John, do you love me?," is he using the verb translated into English as "to love" in the same sense in which it was used in Genesis about Rebekah and Jacob, or about Jacob and Rachel? In other words, is Jesus asking Peter about "love" (as in English), or about "special, preferential love," as in Genesis?

Since the conceptual world of Aramaic-speaking first-century Palestinian Jews like Jesus and his disciples was very much shaped by the conceptual world of the Hebrew Bible, it is very likely that the starting point of their thinking about "love" among people, and also, between God and people, was the same as that of the Hebrew Bible. Yet at some time it must have become clear to Jesus's companions that his (Jesus's) way of thinking about these things was quite different from that reflected in the Hebrew word *'āhēb,* and that new conceptual wine was bursting the old linguistic wineskins. What speaks most strongly in favor of this hypothesis is Jesus's deliberate conceptual innovation in relation to "love," highlighted in chapter 13 of John's Gospel. Thus, after the Last Supper, in his farewell speech to his disciples, Jesus said: "A new commandment I give to you, that you love one another, (. . .) as I have loved you, that you also love one another. By this everyone will know that you are my disciples, if you have love for one another" (John 13:34–35). The Greek verb used in this passage is *agapao,* which is obviously intended to render an Aramaic verb used by Jesus; but in what sense was Jesus using that verb here? In the same sense in which Genesis uses *'āhēb* about Rebecca and Jacob?

This doesn't seem possible, because the combination of components "not like anyone else" with the phrase "one another" would be semantically incoherent. One can hardly "love" eleven people (or more) with a special "preferential" love for each of them; so clearly, the meaning of *agapao* as used here is quite different from that which the translators of the Septuagint had in mind when they used *agapao* to render the Hebrew *'āhēb.*

One is led to conclude, therefore, that in Jesus's use of the Aramaic verb rendered in John 13:34 with the verb *agapao,* the proviso "not like toward anyone else" was absent, and that the meaning of this word in his "new commandment" was broader:

Love one another
I want it to be like this:
  every one of you often thinks about all the others,
  every one of you feels something very good toward all the others,
  every one of you wants to do many things because of this,
  everyone of you wants to do good things for all the others

5. JESUS'S DELIBERATE BROADENING OF THE CONCEPT OF "LOVE"

As discussed by the eminent nineteenth-century German linguist Hugo Schuhardt ([1972] 1885), changes can occur in language not only through unconscious imperceptible "shifts" in sounds and meanings but also under the influence of certain individuals such as actors, kings, or writers whose linguistic innovations or peculiarities of speech "catch on." Something like this undoubtedly occurred in the case of Jesus, and the broadening of the meaning of the Aramaic word which was the closest counterpart of the Hebrew word *'ahēb* is clearly a case in point.

My point here is that there not only was a new teaching on "love" reflected in the Gospels (a fact which is well known), but also a *linguistic* innovation: the meaning of the Aramaic verb rendered in the Greek New Testament with *agapao* (and later in English with "(to) love") was being deliberately and emphatically stretched.

Thus, in the case of a person's "love" for another person, Jesus was (so to speak) launching a new concept, without the components "you will think about (someone X) not like about anyone else" and "feel toward (someone X) not like toward anyone else." Presumably, Jesus's closest companions, like John and Peter, first "got" this new concept through Jesus's idiosyncratic use of Aramaic, but many early Christians acquired it through their encounter with the Greek verb *agapao* as used in the New Testament.

According to the *New Catholic Encyclopedia* (1967: 1040), which takes a historical perspective on the subject, "Christianity brought about a basic shift in man's thinking about love. The abundant generosity of love comes to the fore." Stated in this way, the claim can be disputed; it can also be criticized for vagueness. By taking a semantic perspective on these historical developments, and exploring them through the rigorous framework of NSM and Minimal English, we can be more precise, and arrive at clear and verifiable hypotheses about a theme which is of great general interest, regardless of one's own religious and philosophical views and commitments. The use of Minimal English allows us also to pinpoint the similarities and the differences between the concept of "loving someone" (as it developed in the New Testament) and the injunctions "love your neighbour as yourself" and "love your enemies" (see Wierzbicka in press).

C. On the word *hilastērion*

1. A "MERCY SEAT" OF PURE GOLD

The Greek word *hilastērion* has played, and continues to play, an important role in the debates over the interpretation of the New Testament. It is used by St Paul in his letter to the Romans as a metaphor for Christ: According to Paul, Christ is our *hilastērion*. Thus, in a highly condensed, even elliptical, Greek sentence, Paul wrote of Jesus Christ "whom God set forth, publicly, as a *hilastērion* through faith in his blood" (in Greek: ". . . *hon proetheto ho theos hilastērion dia pisteos en to autou haimati . . .*").

What did Paul mean by that? A good deal depends on the answer to this question, as it has implications for our image of God, our understanding of why Jesus died on the cross, and our interpretation of God's purposes in relation to Jesus and to all people. The matter is hotly debated. A key fact is that the Greek word *hilastērion* was, so to speak, invented by the Jews: There was no such word in classical Greek. There were morphologically related words, such as the noun *hilasmos*, and the verb *hilaskomai*, but the noun *hilastērion* was apparently invented by the Jewish translators of the Bible, who needed to create a *Greek* word to render a *Hebrew* concept, for the benefit of the Jewish diaspora in Greek-speaking countries. The suffix-*terion* indicated a place where something was done, e.g. *ergasterion* was a place where word (*ergon*) was done, i.e. a workshop.

The Hebrew word which the Septuagint was trying to render in this way was *kapporeth*. It was a word used in Exodus for the lid of the ark of the covenant, a sacred box which, as the *Oxford Companion to the Bible* (1993: 55) puts it, "symbolised the presence of the living God at one particular spot on earth; for the God who dwelled 'in the high and holy place' was also present in the ark in the minds of his people."

The King James Bible, following William Tyndale, translates the key word *kapporeth* in Exodus as "mercy seat." Thus, in the passage in which God instructs Moses to cover the ark of the covenant with a lid of gold, we read:

> And thou shalt make a mercy seat [*kapporeth, hilastērion*] of pure gold. (. . .) And thou shalt put on the mercy seat above the ark; and in the ark thou shalt put the testimony that I shall give thee. And then I will meet with thee, and I will commune with thee from above the mercy seat (. . .) of all things which I will give thee in commandment unto the children of Israel. (Exodus 25:17–22, KJV)

So the *kapporeth*, the *hilastērion*, was the lid of the ark of the covenant, which was a place where God was to meet with Moses, and through Moses, with the people of Israel. At the same time, it was the place where people's sins would be, in some way, "covered up" or "wiped away" by God: the noun *kapporeth* is derived from the verb *kipper* meaning "to cover up" or to "wipe away"; and both these words are cognate with the word *kippur*, as in "Yom Kippur" (the Day of Atonement): the day of the year (every year) when God "covers up" or "wipes away" people's sins. As *The Oxford Companion to the Bible* (1993: 156) explains, "According to Leviticus 25.9-10 Yom Kippur was the day of the jubilee year (i.e., the fiftieth year) when slaves were freed, debts cancelled, and land returned to the original owners." As *The Companion* also notes, "It was only on this day (every year) that the high priest entered the holy of holies, the most sacred part of the Temple enclosure in which the ark of the covenant was situated. He would enter bearing incense whose fragrance symbolized God's forgiveness of the sins of Israel" (p. 156).

When we bear these facts in mind, it seems clear that by calling Christ our *hilastērion*, that is, our *kapporeth*, Paul wanted to suggest two things: that Jesus was the true meeting place between God and people, and that he was, so to speak, the true place of forgiveness. In fact, that much most commentators agree on. Where they differ, is in the interpretation of *how* Jesus was the true place of forgiveness, and consequently, the true meeting place between God and people. Paul himself didn't say how—thus leaving room for others, who not only came up with their own interpretations but even incorporated these interpretations into their very translations of Paul's sentence. As a result, words and phrases like "propitiation," "expiation," "sacrificial death," and "expiatory sacrifice" crept into many translations of Paul's epistle—first in Latin, and then in German, English, and many other languages.

2. PAUL'S PHRASE "IN HIS BLOOD" AND ITS OVER-INTERPRETATIONS

A good example of commentary where the author's interpretation is unwittingly inserted into Paul's text under the guise of translation is C. K. Barrett's (1991) book *The Epistle to the Romans*. In this study, Barrett does at a certain point provide an accurate translation of Paul's vital verse 3:25, but unfortunately, he dismisses it in favor of an expanded rendering which introduces Barrett's own interpretation into Paul's verse. The expanded rendering reads: "He [Paul] says: This Christ Jesus God publicly set forth in his bloody sacrificial death as his means of dealing with sin, received through faith" (p. 73).

As Barrett himself acknowledges, in fact Paul doesn't say anything about Jesus's "bloody sacrificial death": The phrase that Paul uses is actually "in his blood," but, Barrett adds, "the notion of sacrifice is contained in the [nonexistent, A.W.] words 'his bloody sacrificial death' (literally, *his blood*, but the shedding of blood implies sacrifice)" (p. 73).

Surely, not so: the mention of blood doesn't necessarily imply "bloody sacrificial death," because both the Old and the New Testament also speak of blood as a seal of the covenant. This is how Jesus himself speaks of his blood at the Last Supper: "Drink of it, all of you; for this is my blood of the covenant" (Matthew 26:28); "this is my blood of the covenant" (Mark 14:24); "this cup which is poured out for you is the new covenant in my blood" (Luke 22:20). This echoes Exodus: "And Moses took the blood, and sprinkled it on the people, and said, Behold the blood of the covenant which the Lord hath made for you" (Exodus 24:8, KJV).

And where is the *hilastērion*, the "seat of mercy," in Barrett's translation? Barrett explains: "The death of Christ, thus understood [that is, understood as 'his bloody sacrificial death'] became God's 'means of dealing with sin.' This cumbersome phrase translates a single Greek word 'hilastērion.'"

As Barrett notes, the noun *hilastērion* is derived from the verb *hilaskesthai*, "of which the normal meaning [in classical Greek] is 'to propitiate,' 'to appease.' This verb is employed in the LXX [Septuagint], where, however, it commonly translates a Hebrew verb (*kipper*), whose original meaning is 'to cover over' or 'to wipe off'" (p. 73). But clearly, whatever the common use of the verb *hilaskesthai* might be in classical Greek, what matters for the interpretation of Paul's thought is that in the Septuagint, this verb is used to render the Hebrew verb *kipper*, referring to God's "wiping off," or "passing over" people's sins; and that the noun *hilastērion*, coined by the Jewish translators to render the Hebrew *kapporeth*, refers to the "mercy seat" or the "meeting place between God and people."

In fact, Barrett notes that the verb *hilaskesthai* is sometimes used of God, commenting that "the common Greek meaning 'to propitiate' becomes practically impossible when, as sometimes happens, God is the subject of the verb. God cannot be said to propitiate man." Relatedly, it is worth noting that in the New Testament, the verb *hilaskesthai* is used in the parable of the Pharisee and the Tax Collector (Luke 18:1–3), where we read: "And the publican, standing far off, would not lift so much as his eyes unto heaven, but smote upon his breast, saying, God be merciful to me [*hilastheti moi*], a sinner" (KJV). Clearly, the tax collector is asking God to have mercy on him, rather than to "propitiate" either him or himself.

3. WHERE DOES THE IDEA OF THE *HILASTĒRION* AS "PROPITIATION" COME FROM?

I don't think it would be unfair to suggest that the misinterpretations of the *hilastērion* (the symbol of God's love and forgiveness) as "propitiation" can be blamed, to a considerable extent, on the Western Father of the Church St Jerome: When in the fourth century Jerome translated the Greek New Testament into Latin (the Vulgate), disastrously he used the Latin word *propitiatorium* to render the Greek *hilastērion*. In doing so, Jerome introduced into the Western tradition a distorted image of God, alien not only to the New Testament but also to the Hebrew Bible (where God wanted to be loved, not "propitiated"). Arguably, Jerome's interpretation betrayed a lack of sufficient familiarity with the Jewish speech culture to which Paul belonged, and which the Eastern Fathers of the Church such as Origen, St Gregory of Nyssa, and St Isaac of Nineveh (Isaac the Syrian) were far more deeply familiar with.

It is true that in his letter to the Romans Paul spoke of God's "wrath" (e.g., 3:5). Yet he added: "I speak in the human way." To quote what the seventh-century theologian and saint of the Eastern Church, Isaac of Nineveh, had to say about the use of words like "wrath" in the Bible in relation to God:

> Just because the terms "wrath", "anger", "hatred" and the rest are used of the Creator in the Bible, we should not imagine that He actually does anything in anger, hatred or zeal. Many figurative terms are used of God in the Scriptures, of God, which are far removed from his true nature. (Brock 1997: 18)

> That we should imagine that anger, wrath, jealousy or the like have anything to do with divine Nature is something utterly abhorrent for us: no one in their right mind, no one who has any understanding (at all) can possibly come to such madness as to think anything of the sort about God. Nor again can we possibly say that He acts thus out of retribution, even though the Scriptures may on the outer surface posit this. (Bettiolo 1990: 162–163)

For a long time, these insights were largely lost in the Western tradition. As a result, the image of the loving God, eager to "cover up" his people's sins and to meet up with them on the "mercy seat," was replaced with the image of a wrathful God who needs to be "propitiated" with bloody sacrifices. Like many European translations of the Bible, the King James Bible (which in Exodus rendered *kapporeth* as "mercy seat") followed suit, rendering Paul's sentence in English as "[Jesus Christ] whom God set forth to be a propitiation through faith in his blood" (Romans 3:25). Sadly, in popular theology, "propitiation" is still widely used in connection with Paul's Letter to the Romans, in print and in internet discussions. For example, in the New American Standard Bible (on-line) we read: "[Jesus Christ] whom God displayed publicly as a propitiation in his blood through faith."

4. FROM "PROPITIATION" TO "EXPIATION"

As we have seen, in the King James Bible the key word *hilastērion* was rendered (following the Vulgate) as "propitiation." In the Revised Standard Version (1981), however, we read: "[Jesus Christ] whom God put forward as an expiation by his blood, to be received by faith."

The replacement of "propitiation" with "expiation" in the Revised Standard Version may have been due to the impact of *The Epistle to the Romans*, the influential monograph by Anglican theologian Charles Dodd (1935). In this book, Dodd argued that in Paul's letter *hilastērion* referred to something like a means by which guilt is annulled, and that there was no reference there to placating an angry God:

> In accordance with biblical usage, therefore, the substantive *(hilastērion)* would mean, not propitiation, but "a means by which guilt is annulled": if a man is the agent, the meaning would be "a means of expiation"; if God, "a means by which sin is forgiven." Biblical usage is determinative for Paul. The rendering propitiation is therefore misleading, for it suggests the placating of an angry God, and although this would be in accord with pagan usage, it is foreign to biblical usage. In the present passage it is God who puts forward the means whereby the guilt of sin is removed, by sending Christ. The sending of Christ, therefore, is the divine method of forgiveness. This brings the teaching of the present passage into exact harmony with that of verses 8-9. (p. 55)

But while we should be grateful for the partial victory of "expiation" over "propitiation" in many modern English translations and commentaries, it is still important to recognize that there is no mention of anything like "expiation" in Paul's key passage Romans 3:24–25 either. We do hear about Jesus's blood and [people's] faith, but the notion of "expiation" comes from the commentators and translators.

We do of course hear the word *hilastērion*, which stands for the Hebrew *kapporeth*, but if the *kapporeth* refers to a "mercy seat" and a "place where God meets people," then there are no grounds for reading the notion of "expiation" into this passage itself: While certainly better than "propitiation," it too is extraneous to what Paul himself is saying.

5. N. T. WRIGHT'S RECENT ONSLAUGHT ON THE NOTION OF "PROPITIATION"

The idea that that in his Letter to the Romans (Romans 3:25) Paul was talking about something like "propitiation" of God is vigorously disputed by Anglican theologian N. T. Wright (2016: 297) in *The Day the Revolution Began*. As Wright puts it, "the dense little paragraph we know as Romans 3:21-26 has regularly been read as the vital move *in the wrong story*—the story (. . .) in which, to put it crudely, humans sin, God punishes Jesus, and humans are let off." The key to the right understanding, Wright argues, is the proper understanding of the word *hilastērion*. If this key word is interpreted as "the place or means of 'propitiation,'" then Paul's intention is badly misunderstood.

Taken in context, Wright says, the keyword *hilastērion* "is far more likely to refer to the 'mercy seat' [Tyndale's English rendering of "kapporeth"/ "hilastērion"], the place in the tabernacle or Temple where God promises (. . .)

to meet with his people." (p. 302) As Wright further argues, the concept of *hilastērion* (as used by Paul) has nothing to do with God's "wrath" or the idea of punishment. In fact, "at the heart of this passage (Rom. 3:21-26) Paul says that God has passed over former sins in his forbearance" (p. 303).

Thus, according to Wright, "when Paul writes in Romans 3:25 that God put Jesus forth as a *hilastērion*, he does not mean that God was punishing Jesus for the sins of Israel or the world" (p. 330). Accordingly, "the *hilastērion* does not denote a 'propitiatory sacrifice', in which Jesus is punished for the sins of others" (p. 331). And further: "In Paul's revised Exodus narrative (. . .) I suggest that we are meant to see Jesus, 'put forth' by God as the *hilastērion*, as the revelation of God's personal presence" (p. 340). Thus, according to Wright, Paul's reference to Christ as the *hilastērion* does not refer to bloody sacrifices but to God's faithfulness to the covenant: the covenant with the people of Israel, and through Israel, with the whole world (a point to which I will return later). One doesn't have to accept every aspect of Wright's careful as well as passionate analysis to appreciate the force of his arguments against "the paganized vision of an angry God looming over the world and bent upon blood" (p. 349)—and against attributing anything like that vision to Paul.

The long tradition of translation which replaced Paul's "wiping out [sins]" with "propitiation" evidently distorted the intended sense. In the immediately preceding sentence (Romans 3:24) Paul speaks of people being "justified" by God "for free" (in Greek *dorean*, a word glossed by the *Greek-English Dictionary of the New Testament* (1971) as "as a free gift"). The word *dorean* (rendered in the NRSV as "the free gift") occurs in Paul's letter to the Romans several times, showing clearly that he wasn't thinking of God as someone demanding "ransom" or "propitiation" but, rather, as someone offering people salvation as a "free gift, through Jesus Christ."

6. BENEDICT XVI ON THE *HILASTĒRION* AS GOD'S PRESENCE IN CHRIST

In his book *The Spirit of the Liturgy*, Benedict XVI (2000) writes:

> St Paul saw the crucified Christ as the true and living "place of expiation" [in the original German, *Sühne*] of whom the "mercy seat", the *kapporeth* lost during the Exile, was but a foreshadowing. In him God has now, so to speak, lifted the veil from his face. The Eastern Church's icon of the Resurrection of Christ takes up this link between the Ark of the Covenant and the Paschal Mystery of Christ when it shows Christ standing on cross-shaped slabs, which symbolize the grave but also suggest a reference to the *kapporeth* of the Old Covenant. Christ is flanked by the cherubim and approached by the women who came to the tomb to anoint him. The fundamental image of the Old Testament is retained, but it is reshaped in the

light of the Resurrection and given a new center: the God who no longer completely conceals himself but now shows himself in the form of the Son. This transformation of the narrative of the Ark of the Covenant into an image of the Resurrection reveals the very heart of the development from Old Testament to New. (p. 116)

If we overlook the word "expiation" (in German *Sühne*) in the first sentence of this illuminating quote, we can follow the train of Benedict's exposition to its logical conclusion.

The image of the risen Christ as the *hilastērion*—the highly visible ("golden") part of the "ark of the covenant" which is the meeting place between God and people—is consistent with the view that sooner or later all people will be able to see the risen Christ, to see God's light in Jesus's face, to see God's love in the wounds on Jesus's hands and feet, and thus to know God. Although this personal meeting with Jesus will be for everyone a time of judgment (see chapter 40 of "The Story," Part II of this book), it can also be a time of coming to "believe in" Jesus, that is, of recognizing God in him and of being drawn to him: "and I, when I am lifted up from the earth, will draw all people to myself" (John 12:32).

Two passages in an earlier book by Benedict XVI (2011b) throw additional light on Paul's idea of Jesus as the true *hilastērion*. In the first, Benedict points out that in the faith of the New Testament, "the Cross of Jesus Christ (. . .) means the end of the old Temple":

> The Evangelists suggest this idea when they report that at the moment of Jesus' death the curtain of the Temple was torn in two. As the Evangelists understood it, this can mean, on the one hand, that the curtain that until then had veiled the Holy of Holies was taken away, so that now God's grace, no longer concealed, was accessible to all mankind. He, the Crucified One himself, is now the Holy of Holies, which is now set up for the general public worldwide; his outstretched arms are the open gesture of divine favour, which desires to "draw all men to himself" (cf. John 12:32). (p. 235)

The image of Jesus as the new *hilastērion* is closely related to the image of Jesus as a new temple: The temple in Jerusalem was the place where the ark of the covenant (earlier carried by Israelites in a portable tabernacle) was kept, and after the loss of the ark, the place where the holy of holies was—the most sacred part of the temple where God continued to meet with his people Israel. Jesus's words in John's Gospel (2:19): "Destroy this temple, and in three days I will raise it up" refer to Jesus himself as the new temple, the new tabernacle, and thus, by implication, the new *hilasterion*: God's meeting place with all of humankind.

The second passage elaborates the motif of the "real presence" of God in the Eucharist, echoing that of the presence of the living God in the ark of the covenant, where (as *The Oxford Companion to the Bible* 1993, puts it, with reference to Martin Luther) "the Lord 'sat' enthroned over [the mercy seat] in mercy, invisibly present where the wingtips of two cherubims met above it, guarding the divine presence (p. 56)":

> The new worship of God is rooted in the love of the Son. It is vitally dependent on it. This means, in turn, that the faith community of Jesus is vitally dependent on gathering around him, the crucified and risen Lord. This gathering, which we call Eucharist, is the heartbeat of its life. In it, the faith community remembers that central event of the Cross and Resurrection and, in remembering, receives the Presence. (Benedict XVI, 2011: 237)

7. "ATONEMENT" IN ANGLOPHONE THEOLOGY

What applies to the words "propitiation" and "expiation," also applies to the word "atonement," which is also often used in English translations of, and commentaries on, Paul's letter to the Romans. Thus, while in the King James Bible, *hilastērion* in verse 3:25 is translated as "propitiation," and in the Revised Standard Version (1971) as "expiation," in the New Revised Standard Version (1990, 2009) it is translated as "atonement" (more exactly, "a sacrifice of atonement").

The word "atonement" is also often used in English translations of another part of the Paul's letter to the Romans (verses 5:10–11), where Paul speaks of people being "reconciled to God by the death of his Son," "saved by his life," and (according to the King James Bible) "[having] joy in God through our Lord Jesus Christ, by whom we have now received atonement." Most present-day readers of the King James Bible are not aware that at the time when this word was used in the King James Bible (and before, in Tyndale's translation of the Bible, 1526, cf. Warren 2013), "atonement"—originally, "at-one-ment"—meant "being at one (again)," that is, reconciliation. The Greek word translated by the King James Bible as "atonement" is *katallage* (rendered in the Latin Vulgate as *reconciliatio*). The noun *katallage* is derived from the verb *katallasso* "reconcile" (the *Greek-English Dictionary of the New Testament* adds: "of man and wife"; and Barrett (1991: 100) notes that, for example, in his first letter to Corinthians (1 Corinthians 7:11) Paul uses this word to refer to "reconciliation of estranged husband and wife"). In his Second Letter to Corinthians (2 Corinthians 5:19) Paul uses it in the sentence rendered in the Revised Standard Version as: "God was in Christ reconciling the world to himself."

In the course of the eighteenth and nineteenth centuries, however, the word "atonement" changed its meaning and instead of "reconciliation" came to suggest something like "reparation." Unfortunately, the word "atonement" has taken root in Anglophone theology, so much so that even theologians who reject the idea of "atonement" as an explanation of why Jesus died on the cross still use the word "atonement" (which has no equivalents in, for example, French or German, cf. Williams 1996) as if it were a neutral term, rather than a loaded one. For example, Vernon White (1991) in his beautiful and profound book *Atonement and Incarnation* speaks of "different models of atonement," thus using the English word "atonement" (which reflects the vagaries of the history of English, rather than Paul's original thought) to mean "different explanations of why Jesus died on the Cross."

Both through Bible translations, some of which still use the word "atonement" in their rendering of Paul's letter to the Romans (either in 3:25 or in 5:10–11), and through the entrenched use of this misleading word in Anglophone theology, "atonement"—along with "propitiation," "expiation," and also "ransom"—for many people perpetuate an image of God distorted by long-term cross-cultural, cross-linguistic and cross-temporal misunderstandings.

As for the word "ransom" (in Greek, *antilytron*), it differs from "propitiation," "expiation," and "atonement" insofar as it was actually used by Paul, rather than being added to Paul's letters by translators and commentators. But Paul used it as a comparison expressed—in accordance with the conventions of Paul's speech culture, without the word "like"—a point lost on many commentators, who were inclined to take this word in a literal sense. For example, in his First Letter to Timothy (1 Timothy 2:6) Paul says: "For there is one God, and there is one mediator between God and men, the man Jesus Christ, who gave himself as a ransom for all." The apparent implication that God demanded "a ransom" for sinners is plainly refuted by the immediately preceding sentence, which speaks of "God our Savior, who desires all people to be saved and to come to the knowledge of truth" (1 Timothy 2:5). As Paul's letter to Timothy makes clear, salvation for all is what God *desires*, not something that either people, or Jesus, have to "buy" from God.

The idea that God the Father wanted a "payment"—a recompense—for people's sins was introduced into religious discussions by the fourth-century theologian Cyril of Jerusalem, and it is still to be found, here and there, in modern popular theology. Another literalist interpretation of "ransom" which was popular at one time saw *Satan,* rather than God the Father, as the supposed recipient of the payment. Today, it is increasingly well understood that in the New Testament, "ransom" (in Matthew 20:28, *lytron*, in 1Timothy 2:5-6 *antilytron*), was a figure of speech. (The *Catechism of the Catholic Church* (1994:155) speaks of Jesus's death as "a mystery of universal redemption, that is, as the ransom that would free men from the slavery of sin." Evidently, the word "ransom" is used here in a figurative sense.)

8. IN HIS BLOOD

As Polish theologian Wacław Hryniewicz (2009: 145) remarks in *Credo* (a book co-written by three theologians: one Catholic, one Lutheran, and one

Orthodox), "for centuries, the Western tradition was dominated by the notion of a propitiatory sacrifice, and of vicarious satisfaction for the sins of humankind offered to God [by Christ]." But this is not how Jesus himself spoke about his own life and death; and this is not how he spoke about his blood on the night before he died. As discussed in the commentary on chapter 22 of "The Story," (Part II of this book) at the Last Supper, Jesus called his blood ("which is shed for you") "the blood of the new covenant." As Hryniewicz puts it, "through Jesus' death, God's "covenant with the chosen people, Israel, was extended to the whole humankind" (p. 147).

Jesus does speak in the Gospels in words which justify the use of the word "sacrifice" (in the modern English sense of self-sacrifice), when he says, for example: "This is my body which is given for you. (. . .) This cup which is poured out for you is the new covenant in my blood" (Luke 22:19–20). But nothing in the Gospels justifies the addition of notions such as "vicarious" or "propitiatory." His sacrifice is voluntary and motivated by love:

> I am the good shepherd. The good shepherd lays down his life for the sheep. (. . .) I am the good shepherd. (. . .) I lay down my life for the sheep. (. . .) For this reason the Father loves me, because I lay down my life, that I may take it again. No one takes it from me, but I lay it down of my own accord. I have power to lay it down, and I have power to take it again; this charge I have received from my Father. (John 10:11–18)

So the sacrifice is there, and it is a sacrifice both on the part of Jesus and on the part of God (the Father), because as Jesus says, "I and the Father are one" (John 10:30). It is, however, a sacrifice made by both the Father and the Son out of love. As Jesus also says, first about the Father: "For God so loved the world that he gave his only Son" (John 3:16), and then about himself: "Greater love has no man than this, that a man lay down his life for his friends" (John 15:13).

But what was the point of that sacrifice? one might ask. I have not tried to discuss this question here in Appendix C because it has been discussed at length elsewhere in "The Story," especially in chapter 28 and the commentary on it (Parts II and III of this book; but also in chapters 3, 4, and 22, Part II of this book). The key line is the first line of chapter 28: "Jesus died on the cross because he wanted to do something good for all people: he wanted them to live with God."

9. THE *HILASTĒRION* AND THE FAITH IN JESUS

There are three key words in Paul's much discussed verse 3:25: *hilastērion*, "blood" and "faith." Throughout this appendix, I have focused on *hilastērion*, and I have also discussed "blood." But what about "faith"?

As many commentators have noted, in the Letter to the Romans there appears to be a tension between the universal scope of Paul's vision and his insistence on faith in Jesus. There seems to be little doubt that for Paul, access to God through Jesus is equally open to Gentiles as to Jews. But what of people who have never heard of Jesus? What of those who had lived and died before Jesus was born?

Well, one person who had lived and died a long time before Jesus was born was Abraham. Like other New Testament writers, Paul has no doubt that Abraham was "our father in faith" and a model of faith for all believers. Surely this shows that when Paul says that God sent Jesus as a *hilastērion* "through faith in blood" he does not mean an explicit faith in Jesus as the Son of God during one's life on earth. While Paul urged *his listeners* to open their hearts to faith in Jesus, he seemed to have full confidence that God would be able to reach *all* people through Jesus—if not before they die then after. Thus speaking of Jesus's death on the cross and his subsequent "exaltation" by God, Paul wrote:

> Therefore God has highly exalted him, and bestowed on him the name which is above every name, that at the name of Jesus every knee should bow in heaven, and on earth, and under the earth; and every tongue confess that Jesus Christ is Lord, to the glory of God the Father. (Philippians 2:9–11, RSV)

In saying this, Paul was obviously echoing the lines of the prophet Isaiah (45:22–23): "Look unto me and be ye saved, all the ends of the earth: for I am God and there is none else. I have sworn by myself, the word is gone out of my mouth in righteousness, and shall not return, that unto me every knee shall bow, every tongue shall swear." This is consistent with Jesus's own words quoted earlier: "And I, when I'm lifted up above the earth, will draw all people to myself" (John 12:32, NRSV). It is also consistent with the vision of thinkers like Edith Stein (see the commentary on chapter 27 in Part III) that to many people, faith in Jesus may come *after* their death, when, as the Nicene Creed puts it, the risen Jesus will "come again in glory to judge the living and the dead."

In an article entitled "Jesus as hilastērion in Romans 3:25," biblical scholar David Greenwood (1973: 321–322) writes: "It is generally agreed that Rom 3:25 is essentially a reasoned plea for universalism, in the sense of the inclusion of the Gentiles in the kingdom of God. But the *dia pisteos* [through faith] of verse 25 does in fact limit St Paul's universalism to a greater degree than some writers care to admit." For his own part, Greenwood hopes for more: "I would submit that, in the case of genuine nonbelievers, the *hilastērion* may be effective without explicit faith in Jesus" (p. 322).

These apparent tensions between Paul's universalism (cf. "God has consigned all men [people] to disobedience, that he may have mercy upon all," Romans 11:32) and his emphasis on faith (faith in Jesus) can be resolved if we accept, with early Fathers of the Church like St Ambrose and Basil of Cesarea, and modern theologians like Balthasar and Edith Stein, that at the "Second Coming" everyone, no matter when and where they have lived on earth, will see Jesus, with his hands, feet and side pierced, and with his face "radiating divine light" (Basil of Caesarea)—and will have a chance to believe in him and to enter the kingdom of God.

This brings me back to N. T. Wright's (2016) *The Day the Revolution Began*, which is, in effect, a book about the meaning of *hilastērion* in the Letter to the Romans. Wright's main idea can be read off his own translation of Paul's crucial verse 3:25: "God put Jesus forth as the place of mercy, through faithfulness, by means of his blood." We are bound to ask: Not through *faith*, but through *faithfulness*? Whose faithfulness?

Before Wright, the phrase *dia pisteos* ("through faith") in Paul's Letter to the Romans was generally understood as referring to people's faith in Jesus. Wright, however, in his translation renders the word *pistis* ("faith") as "faithfulness," arguing that what is at issue is not people's faith in Jesus but God's faithfulness to the covenant. Accordingly, verse 26, which explicitly speaks of "everyone who has faith in Jesus" (*ton ek pisteos Iesou*) is rendered by Wright as "everyone who trusts in the faithfulness of Jesus."

I fully agree with Wright when he says that "verses 25-26 really do seem to be talking about God's faithfulness to the covenant." But they do also seem to be talking about faith in Jesus. So why has "faith in Jesus" disappeared from Wright's translation (as well as from his commentary)?

Again, I think we must agree with Wright that God's faithfulness to the covenant with Abraham (and with Moses) cannot depend on people's coming to believe in Jesus during their lifetime on earth—if this was the condition then everyone who lived before Jesus would be excluded from the covenant. But no one needs to be excluded from the covenant, and from God's love, if all people can meet Jesus when, as both the Apostles' Creed and the Nicene Creed confidently expect, "He will come again in glory to judge the living and the dead." This "Second Coming" does not have to come at the same time for all people (as in Michelangelo's fresco in the Sistine Chapel). Rather, it may come to each of us as we die, when we see our life in the light of Jesus's presence. As I see it, it is this faith in the "Second Coming" of Jesus which allows Christians reciting the Creeds to accept verse 3:16 of John's Gospel (along with its sequel, 3:17) as the summary and the distillation of the whole New Testament: "For God so loved the world that he gave his only Son, that whoever believes in him should not perish but have eternal life. For God sent his Son into the world, not to condemn the world, but that the world might be saved through him."

In the language of the New Testament, "the world" (as used in this sentence) means *all people*. In the Hebrew Bible Israel is seen as God's chosen people, and the New Testament accepts this view. Wright's insistence on God's faithfulness to the covenants with Abraham and with Moses is justified. At the same time, Jesus's "new covenant" extends to humankind as a whole; and this must include people who never had a chance to hear about him and to believe in him (including those who lived before he was born).

In his book *Salvation for All*, Catholic theologian Gerald O'Collins (2008: 208) also invokes the image of the ark of the covenant representing God's presence amidst his chosen people, and he cites Moses's words (Deuteronomy 4:7): "What other great nation has a god so near to it as the Lord our God is whenever we call to him?" Acknowledging "the divine blessings lavished on Israel," O'Collins points at the same time to the universality of Jesus's mission as understood by Paul and other New Testament writers, and also by prominent early Christian writers such as St Irenaeus and Origen:

> In the second century of the Christian era, St Irenaeus (d. around 200) acknowledged the universal scope of the divine action for human salvation: "the Word of the all-powerful God . . . on the invisible plane is co-extensive with the whole of creation," "rules the universe," and as the Son of God "has traced the sign of the cross on everything" (*Demonstratio* 34). In the third century Origen (d. around 254) also highlighted the universal saving presence: "Christ is so powerful that, although invisible because of his divinity, he is present to every person and extends over the whole universe." (*In Ioannem* 6.15; italics mine [G.O'C])

This is in keeping with the words of the Nicene Creed: "I believe in one Lord Jesus Christ . . . For us men [people] and for our salvation he came down from heaven . . . and became man . . . For our sake he was crucified under Pontius Pilate, he suffered death and was buried, and rose again on the third day. . . . He will come again in glory to judge the living and the dead and his kingdom will have no end." It is also in keeping with Paul's vision of Jesus as the true *hilastērion*, the true ark of the covenant between God and humanity as a whole.

REFERENCES

Ackerman, Susan. 2002. The Personal Is Political: Covenantal and Affectionate Love (*'āhēb, 'ahăbâ*) in the Hebrew Bible. *Vetus Testamentum* LII (4): 437–458.

American Psychological Association. 2006. Forgiveness: A Sampling of Research Results. Archived from the original (PDF) on June 26, 2011. https://web.archive.org/web/20110626153005/http://www.apa.org/international/resources/forgiveness.pdf (accessed December 7, 2017).

Austin, John L. 1962. *How to Do Things with Words*. Oxford: Oxford University Press.

Averintsev, Sergei. 2007. *Sobranie sochinenij: Perevody*. Kiev: Dukh I Litera.

Balthasar, Hans Urs von. 1982. *The von Balthasar Reader* (edited by Medard Kehl & Werner Löser; translated by Robert J. Daly & Fred Lawrence). Edinburgh: T. & T. Clark.

Balthasar, Hans Urs von. 1983. *Theodramatik*. Einsiedeln: Johannes Verlag.

Balthasar, Hans Urs von. 1988. *Dare We Hope That All Men Be Saved?* San Francisco: Ignatius Press.

Balthasar, Hans Urs von. 1990. *Theologie der drei Tage*. Freiburg: Johannes Verlag.

Balthasar, Hans Urs von. 1993. *Mysterium Paschale* (translated by Aidan Nichols). Grand Rapids, MI: Eerdmanns.

Barclay, William. 1990 [1967]. *The Plain Man Looks at the Apostles' Creed*. London: Collins, Fontana Books.

Barrett, C. K. 1991. *A Commentary on The Epistle to the Romans*. London: A. & C. Black (Black's New Testament Commentaries).

Bauman, Clarence. 1985. *The Sermon on the Mount: The Modern Quest for Its Meaning*. Macon, GA: Mercer University, Liddell & Scott Press.

Benedict XVI. 2000. *The Spirit of the Liturgy*. San Francisco: Ignatius Press.

Benedict XVI. 2007a. *Jesus of Nazareth*. New York: Doubleday.

Benedict XVI. 2007b. *Christus und seine Kirche: Das Fundament der Apostel*. Rome: Libreria Editrice Vaticana.

Benedict XVI. 2009. *Credo for Today: What Christians Believe*. San Francisco: Ignatius Press.

Benedict XVI. 2011a. *Jesus of Nazareth. Holy Week: From the Entrance into Jerusalem to the Resurrection*. San Francisco: Ignatius Press.

Benedict XVI. 2011b. *Dogma and Preaching: Applying the Christion Doctrine to Daily Life*. San Francisco: Igantius Press.

Benedict XVI. 2012a. *Jesus of Nazareth: The Infancy Narratives*. London: Bloomsbury.

Benedict XVI. 2012b. *I Believe in One God: The Creed Explained*. Strathfield, NSW: St. Pauls Publications.

Bettiolo, P. 1990. Avec la charité comme but; Dieu et la création dans la mediation de l'Isaac de Ninivie. *Irenikon* 63: 323–345.

Bonhoeffer, Dietrich. 1959. *The Cost of Discipleship* (rev. 6th edn., translated by R. Fuller). London: SCM Press.

Borg, Marcus. 1999. Was Jesus God? In Marcus Borg & N. T. Wright (eds.), *The Meaning of Jesus: Two Visions*, pp. 145–170. San Francisco: Harper San Francisco.

Brague, Rémi & Jean-Pierre Batut. 2011. *Qui est le Dieu des chrétiens?* Paris: i Salvator.

Brock, Sebastian (ed.). 1997. *The Wisdom of Saint Isaac the Syrian*. Oxford: SLG Press.

Brown, Raymond. 1965. Does the New Testament Call Jesus God? *Theological Studies* 26 (4): 545–573.

Brown, Raymond. 1968. *Jesus, God and Man: Modern Biblical Reflections*. London & Dublin: G. Chapman.

Brown, Raymond. 1975. *Biblical Reflections on Crises Facing the Church*. London: Darton, Longman & Todd.

Brown, Raymond. 1994. *An Introduction to New Testament Christology*. New York: Paulist Press.

Browning, W. R. F. 2009. *A Dictionary of the Bible* (2nd edn.). Oxford: Oxford University Press.

Bultmann, Rudolf. 1952. *Theology of the New Testament,* vol. 1 (translated by Kendrick Grobel). London: SCM Press.

Butwin, Francis. 1958. Translator's Introduction to Sholom Aleichem *The Old Country*, pp. 7–11. London: André Deutsch.

Caird, G. B. 1980. *The Language and Imagery of the Bible*. London: Duckworth.

Catechism of the Catholic Church. 1994. Homebush, NSW: St Paul's Publications.

Catholic Encyclopedia. 1913. "Pontius Pilate." New York: Robert Appleton Company.

Chalmers, David. 2012. *Constructing the World*. Oxford: Oxford University Press.

Chesterton, G. K. 1925 [2008]. *The Everlasting Man*. Radford, VA: Wilder Publications.

Christ, Our Pascha: Catechism of the Ukrainian Catholic Church. 2016. Kyiv: Synod of the Ukrainian Greek-Catholic Church.

Collins, Adela Yarbro. 2007. *Mark: A Commentary*. Minneapolis: Fortress Press.

Collins, Francis. 2006. *The Language of God: A Scientist Presents Evidence for Belief*. New York: Free Press.

Compendium of the Catechism of the Catholic Church. 2005. Strathfield, NSW: St Paul's Publications.

A Concise Greek-English Dictionary of the New Testament. 1971. Prepared by Barclay Newman, Jr. London: United Bible Societies.

Contemporary English Version of the Bible. 1995. Bangalore: The Bible Society of India.

Dalai Lama XIV. 1997. Response in The Symposium. In Simon Wiesenthal (ed.), *The Sunflower: On the Possibilities and Limits of Forgiveness* (rev. and expanded 2nd edn.), p. 129. New York: Schocken Books.

Dalai Lama XIV. 1999. *Ethics for the New Millennium*. New York: Riverhead Books.

Darwin, Charles. 2003 [1871]. *The Descent of Man, and Selection in Relation to Sex*. London: Gibson Square Books.

Descartes, René. 1931 [1701]. The Search After Truth by the Light of Nature. In *The Philosophical Works of Descartes*, 1: 305–327 (translated by Elizabeth S. Haldane & G. T. T. Ross). Cambridge: Cambridge University Press.

Dickson, John. 2010. *Investigating Jesus An Historian's Quest*. Oxford: Lion.

Dodd, Charles. 1935. *The Epistle of Paul to the Romans*. London: Hodder and Stoughton.

Evans, Nicholas. 2010. Semantic Typology. In Jae Jung Song (ed.), *The Oxford Handbook of Linguistic Typology*, pp. 504–533. Oxford & New York: Oxford University Press.

Fitzmyer, Joseph A. 1981–1985. *The Gospel According to Luke: Introduction, Translation, and Notes*, 2 vols. Garden City, NY: Doubleday.

Fleischner, Eva. 1998. Response in The Symposium. In Simon Wiesenthal (ed.), *The Sunflower: On the Possibilities and Limits of Forgiveness* (rev. and expanded 2nd edn.), pp. 138–142. New York: Schocken Books.

Foley, John. *One bread, one body*. John B. Foley, SJ and OCP Publications, 1978. https://hymnary.org/tune/one_bread_one_body_foley, accessed 25 September 2018.

Förster, Werner. 1964. *Palestinian Judaism in New Testament Times* (translated by Gordon E. Harris). Edinburgh: Oliver & Boyd.

Funk, Robert W., Roy Hoover & Jesus Seminar. 1993. *The Five Gospels: What Did Jesus Really Say?* New York: Macmillan.

Galot, Jean. 1975. *Il mistero della sofferenza di Dio*. Assisi: Cittadella Editrice.

Gellner, Ernest. 1981. General Introduction: Relativism and Universals. In Barbara Bloom Lloyd & John Gay (eds.), *Universals of Human Thought: The African Evidence*, pp. 1–20. Cambridge: Cambridge University Press.

Gerber, Eleanor. 1985. Rage and Obligation: Samoan Emotions in Conflict. In Geoffrey M. White & John Kirkpatrick (eds.), *Person, Self, and Experience: Exploring Pacific Ethnopsychologies*, pp. 121–167. Berkeley: University of California Press.

Goddard, Cliff. 1996. *Pitjantjatjara/Yankunytjatjara to English Dictionary* (rev. 2nd edn.). Alice Springs: IAD Press.

Goddard, Cliff. 1998. *Semantic Analysis: A Practical Introduction*. Oxford: Oxford University Press.

Goddard, Cliff (ed.). 2008. *Cross-linguistic Semantics*. Amsterdam: John Benjamins.

Goddard, Cliff. 2010. The Natural Semantic Metalanguage Approach. In Bernd Heine & Heiko Narrog (eds.), *The Oxford Handbook of Linguistic Analysis*, pp. 459–484. Oxford: Oxford University Press.

Goddard, Cliff. 2011. *Semantic Analysis: A Practical Introduction* (rev. 2nd edn.). Oxford: Oxford University Press.

Goddard, Cliff (ed.). 2018. *Minimal English for a Global World: Improved Communication Using Fewer Words*. Cham: Palgrave Macmillan.

Goddard, Cliff & Anna Wierzbicka (eds.). 2002. *Meaning and Universal Grammar: Theory and Empirical Findings*, 2 vols. Amsterdam: John Benjamins.

Goddard, Cliff & Anna Wierzbicka. 2014a. *Words and Meanings: Lexical Semantics Across Domains, Languages, and Cultures*. Oxford: Oxford University Press.

Goddard, Cliff & Anna Wierzbicka. 2014b. Semantic Fieldwork and Lexical Universals. *Studies in Language* 38 (1): 80–127.

A Greek-English Lexicon (4th edn., Liddell and Scott). 1940. Oxford: Clarendon Press.

Greenwood, David. 1973. Jesus as Hilasterion in Romans 3:25. *Biblical Theology Bulletin* 3 (3): 316–322.

Gregory of Nyssa. 1993. *The Soul and the Resurrection* (translated and introduced by Catherine P. Roth). Crestwood, NY: St Vladimir's Seminary Press.

Harris, John. 1990. *One Blood: 200 Years of Aboriginal Encounter with Christianity: A Story of Hope*. Sutherland, NSW: Albatross Books.

Hasada, Rie. 1997. Conditionals and Counterfactuals in Japanese. *Language Sciences* 19 (3): 277–288.

Helm, Paul. 1992. Are There Few That Be Saved? In Nigel Cameron (ed.), *Universalism and the Doctrine of Hell*, pp. 257–281. Carlisle, UK & Grand Rapids, MI: Paternoster Press & Baker Book House.

Heschel, Abraham. 1962. *The Prophets*. New York: Jewish Publication Society of America.

Hill, Deborah. 2016. Bride-Price, Baskets, and the Semantic Domain of "Carrying" in a Matrilineal Society. *Oceanic Linguistics* 55 (2): 500–521.

Hoskyns, Edwyn Clement. 1940. *The Fourth Gospel* (edited by Francis Noel Davey), 2 vols. London: Faber and Faber.

Hryniewicz, Wacław. 1990. *A Hope of Salvation for All: From an Eschatology of Fear to an Eschatology of Hope*. Warsaw: Verbinum. (In Polish)

Hryniewicz, Wacław. 2001. *Nad przepaściami wiary. Z ks. Wacławem Hryniewiczem rozmawiają Elżbieta Adamiak i Józef Majewski* [On the Edge of the Precipices of Faith: Rev. Wacław Hryniewicz's Talks with Elżbieta Adamiak and Józef Majewski]. Kraków: Znak.

Hryniewicz, Wacław. 2009. In Wacław Hryniewicz, Karol Karski & Henryk Paprocki (eds.), *Credo*. Cracow: Znak. (In Polish)

Hryniewicz, Wacław. 2012. *God's Spirit in the World: Ecumenical and Cultural Essays*. Washington, DC: The Council for Research in Values and Philosophy.

The Interpreter's Dictionary of the Bible. 1962. New York: Abingdon Press.

Isaac of Niniveh. 1995. *"The Second Part"/Chapters IV–XLI* (edited and translated by Sebastian Brock). Lovanii: Peeters.

John Paul II. 1993. *Veritatis Splendor*. Homebush, NSW: St Paul's Publications.

Johnson, Brian. 2017. Finding Our Way. Majellan Sunday Bulletin for 5th Sunday Easter, Year A, May 14, 2017, by the Redemptorist Congregation. Brighton, Vic.: Magellan Publications. (Reproduced in the bulletin of St Joseph's Parish, O'Connor, ACT, May 14, 2017.)

Kaufman, Gordon D. 2005 [1987]. Religious Diversity, Historical Consciousness, and Christian Theology. In John Hick & Paul F. Knitter (eds.), *The Myth of Christian Uniqueness: Towards a Pluralistic Theology of Religions*, pp. 3–15. Eugene, OR: Wipf and Stock.

Knapp, E. A. n.d. Did the Messiah Speak Aramaic or Hebrew? (part 2). http://www.torahclass.com/archived-articles/412-did-the-messiah-speak-aramaic-or-hebrew-part-2-by-eaknapp (accessed April 3, 2017).

Kopenawa, Davi and Bruce Albert. 2013. *The Falling Sky: Words of a Yanomami Shaman*. Cambridge, MA: Belknap Press.

Küng, Hans. 1993. *Credo: The Apostles' Creed Explained for Today*. London: S.C.M. Press.

Lapide, Pinchas. 1980. *Er predigte in ihren Synagogen: Jüdische Evangelienauslegung*. Gütersloh: Gütersloher Verlagshaus G. Mohn.

Lapide, Pinchas. 1985. A Jewish Perspective. In Pinchas Lapide & Ulrich Luz, *Jesus in Two Perspectives: A Jewish-Christian Dialogue* (translated by Lawrence Denef), pp. 9–110. Minneapolis: Augsburg.

Leibniz, Gottfried Wilhelm. 1903. *Opuscules et fragments inédits de Leibniz* (edited by Louis Couturat). Paris: Presses universitaires de France (Reprinted 1961, Hildesheim: Georg Olms)

Levy, Robert. 1973. *Tahitians: Mind and Experience in the Society Islands*. Chicago: University of Chicago Press.

Lewis, C. S. 1977 [1960]. *The Four Loves*. London: Fount.
Lewis, C. S. 1978. *Fern-seed and Elephants, and Other Essays on Christianity*. Glasgow: Collins.
Lewis, C. S. 2000. *Essay Collection and Other Short Pieces*. London: Fount.
Lewis, C. S. 2001 [1952]. *Mere Christianity*. San Francisco: HarperSanFrancisco.
A Lexicon Abridged from Liddell and Scott's Greek-English Lexicon. 1963. Oxford: Clarendon Press.
The Living God: A Catechism for the Christian Faith (translated from the French by Olga Dunlop). 1989. Crestwood, NY: St. Vladimir's Seminary Press.
Lochet, Louis. 1979. *Jésus descendu aux enfers*. Paris: Cerf.
Longman Dictionary of the English Language. 1987. Harlow, Essex: Longman.
Lutz, Catherine. 1985. Ethnopsychology Compared to What? Explaining Behavior and Consciousness among the Ifaluk. In Arthur Kleinman and Byron Good (eds.), *Culture and Depression*, pp. 63–100. Berkeley: University of California Press.
Lutz, Catherine. 1988. *Unnatural Emotions*. Chicago: University of Chicago Press.
Manson, T. W. 1960. *Ethics and the Gospel*. London: SCM Press.
Mayne, Michael. 2006. *The Enduring Melody*. London: Darton, Longman & Todd.
McGrath, Alister. 1992. *A Journey Through Suffering*. London: Hodder and Stoughton.
McGrath, Alister (ed.). 1995. *The Christian Theology Reader*. Oxford: Blackwell.
McGrath, Alister. 2013. *Faith and the Creeds: A Guide for Study and Devotion*. Louisville, KY: Westminster John Knox Press.
McKenzie, John L. 1965. *The Dictionary of the Bible*. London: G. Chapman.
Meeks, Wayne. 1983. *The First Urban Christians: The Social World of the Apostle Paul*. New Haven: Yale University Press.
Men', Alexander.1969. *The Son of Man*. Online. http://www.alexandrmen.ru/books/son_max/son_max.html (accessed August 10, 2017) (In Russian).
Men', Alexander. 1991. *Istorija Religii* [History of Religion], vol. 2. Moscow: Slovo.
Men', Alexander. 1996. *Christianity for the Twenty First Century* (edited by Elizabeth Roberts & Ann Shukman). London: SCM Press.
Millennium Bible. 1971. Pismo Święte. Poznań: Wydawnictwo Pallottinum. (In Polish)
Moltmann, Jürgen. 1972. The Crucified God: God and the Trinity Today. In J. B. Metz (ed.), *New Questions on God*, 26–37. New York: Herder & Herder.
Morison, Frank. 1958. *Who Moved the Stone?* London: Faber and Faber.
Moyise, Steve. 2001. *The Old Testament in the New*. London & New York: T. & T. Clark.
Mühlen, Herribert. 1966. *Der Heilige Geist als Person*. Münster: Aschendorff.
Nerriere, Jean Paul. 2004. *Parlez Globish?* Paris: Eyrolles.
Newbigin, Leslie. 1989. *The Gospel in a Pluralist Society*. Grand Rapids, MI & Geneva, Switzerland: William B. Eerdmans & WCC Publications.
Newman, Barclay M. 1983. *The Greek-English Dictionary of the New Testament*. Stuttgart: United Bible Societies.
Norris, Kathleen. 2001. Foreword to C. S. Lewis, *Mere Christianity*. In C. S. Lewis, *Mere Christianity*, pp. XVII–XX. San Francisco: HarperSanFrancisco.
O'Collins, Gerald. 2008. *Salvation for All: God's Other Peoples*. Oxford: Oxford University Press.
O'Donnell, John. 1988. *The Mystery of the Triune God*. London: Sheed & Ward.

Obeyesekere, Gananath. 1985. Depression, Buddhism, and the Work of Culture in Sri Lanka. In A. Kleinman & B. Good (eds.), *Culture and Depression*, pp. 134–152. Berkeley: University of California Press.

Ogden, Charles Kay. 1930. *Basic English: A General Introduction with Rules and Grammar*. London: Paul Treber.

Ostler, Nicholas. 2016. *Passwords to Paradise: How Languages Have Re-invented World Religions*. New York: Bloomsbury NY.

The Oxford Companion to the Bible. 1993. (Edited by Bruce M. Metzger & Michael D. Coogan). Oxford: Oxford University Press.

The Oxford Dictionary of the Jewish Religion. 1997. (Edited by R. J. Zwi Werblowsky & Geoffrey Wigoder). New York: Oxford University Press.

Packer, J. I. 2001. *Concise Theology: A Guide to Historic Christian Beliefs*. Carol Stream, IL: Tyndale House.

Pailin, D. A. 1989. *God and the Process of Reality: Foundations of a Credible Theism*. London: Routledge.

Paprocki, Henryk. 2009. What Is Resurrection? [in Polish]. In Wacław Hryniewicz, Karol Karski & Henryk Paprocki (eds.), *Credo*. Cracow: Znak.

Pasternak, Boris. 1973. *Doctor Zhivago* (translated by Max Hayward & Manya Harari). London: Fontana.

Paul VI. 1982 [1975]. *Evangelii Nuntiandi* ["Evangelization in the Modern World"]. Homebush, NSW: St Pauls Publications.

Peeters, Bert (ed.). 2006. *Semantic Primes and Universal Grammar: Empirical Evidence from the Romance Languages*. Amsterdam: John Benjamins.

Perkins, Pheme. 1990. The Gospel According to John. In Raymond Brown, Joseph Fitzmyer & Roland Murphy (eds.), *The New Jerome Biblical Commentary*, pp. 942–985. Englewood Cliffs, NJ: Prentice Hall.

Polkinghorne, John. 1986. *One World: The Interaction of Science and Theology.* London: SPCK.

Polkinghorne, John. 1989. *Science and Providence: God's Interaction with the World*. Boston: New Science Library.

Polkinghorne, John. 1994. *The Faith of a Physicist: Reflections of a Bottom-up Thinker: The Gifford Lectures for 1993–4*. Princeton, NJ: Princeton University Press.

Polkinghorne, John. 1998. *Belief in God in an Age of Science*. New Haven: Yale University Press.

Polkinghorne, John. 2002. *The God of Hope and the End of the World*. New Haven: Yale University Press.

Polkinghorne, John. 1983 [2007]. *The Way the World Is: The Christian Perspective of a Scientist*. London: Triangle.

Polkinghorne, John. 2010. *Encountering Scripture: A Scientist Explores the Bible*. London: SPCK.

Prager, Denis. 1998. Response in The Symposium. In Simon Wiesenthal (ed.), *The Sunflower: On the Possibilities and Limits of Forgiveness*, pp. 225–229. New York: Schocken Books.

Radcliffe, Timothy. 1984. "My Lord and My God": The Locus of Confession. *New Blackfriars* 65(764): 52–62.

Robinson, J. A. T. 1984. *Twelve More New Testament Studies*. London: SCM Press.

Robinson, Marilynne. 2015. *The Givenness of Things: Essays*. London: Virago Press.

Rossé, Gerard. 1987. *The Cry of Jesus on the Cross: A Biblical and Theological Study*. New York: Paulist Press.

Sanders, E. P. 1985. *Jesus and Judaism*. London: SCM.

Sayers, Dorothy. 1969 [1949]. *Creed or Chaos? And Other Essays in Popular Theology*. New York: Harcourt Brace.

Sayers, Dorothy. 1990 [1943]. *The Man Born to Be King: A Play-Cycle on the Life of Our Lord and Saviour Jesus Christ Written for Broadcasting*. San Francisco: Ignatius Press.

Schuchardt, Hugo. 1972 [1885]. On Sound Laws: Against the Neogrammarians. In Theo Vennemann and Terence H. Wilbur, *Schuchardt, the Neogrammarians, and the Transformational Theory of Phonological Change*, pp. 39–72. Frankfurt: Athenäum.

Schönborn, Christoph. 1994. *God's Human Face: The Christ-icon* (translated by Lothar Krauth). San Francisco: Ignatius Press.

Searle, J. R. 1969. *Speech Acts: An Essay in the Philosophy of Languages*. Cambridge: Cambridge University Press.

Solov'ev, Vladimir. 1901. History of Theocracy. In Vladimir Solov'ev, *Sochinenya* (Works). St Petersburg: Obschchestvennaya Pol'za. (In Russian)

Sproul, R. C. 1992. *Essential Truths of the Christian Faith: 100 Key Doctrines in Plain Language*. Wheaton, IL: Tyndale House.

Stuhlmacher, Peter. 2006. *Die Geburt des Immanuel. Die Weihnachtsgeschichten aus dem Lukas- und Matthäusevangelium*. Göttingen: Vandenhoeck & Ruprecht.

Suddendorf, Thomas. 2013. *The Gap: The Science of What Separates Us from Other Animals*. New York: Basic Books.

Sweetman, Robert. 2011. Sin Has Its Place, But All Shall Be Well: The Universalism of Hope in Julian of Norwich. In Gregory MacDonald (ed.), *All Shall Be Well: Explorations in Universalism and Christian Theology, from Origen to Moltmann*, pp. 66–92. Eugene, OR: Cascade.

Temple, William. 1961. *Readings in St John's Gospel (First and Second Series)*. London: Macmillan & Co.

Tjukurpa Palya. Irititja munu Kuwaritja. 1987. Canberra: Bible Society in Australia.

Tutu, Desmond. 2008. "Bible has power to free the poor—Tutu." 2008. *Christian Today*, September 8, 2008. https://www.christiantoday.com/article/bible.has.power.to.free. poor.tutu/21378.htm (accessed April 24, 2017).

Voigt, Gottfried. 1991. *Licht, Liebe, Leben—Das Evangelium nach Johannes*. Göttingen: Vandenhoeck & Ruprecht.

Ward, Keith. 2015. *What Do We Mean by "God"?* London: SPCK.

Warren, James 2013. *Compassion or Apocalypse?: A Comprehensible Guide to the Thought of Rene Girard*. Alresford, Hants, UK: Christian Alternative.

Weigel, George. 2009 [1999]. *Witness to Hope: The Biography of Pope John Paul II 1920–2005*. New York: Harper Perennial.

Weil, Simone. 1963. *Gravity and Grace*. London: Routledge & Kegan Paul.

White, Vernon. 1985. *The Fall of a Sparrow: A Concept of Special Divine Action*. Exeter: Paternoster.

White, Vernon. 1991. *Atonement and Incarnation*. Cambridge: Cambridge University Press.

Wierzbicka, Anna. 1972. *Semantic Primitives*. Frankfurt: Athenäum.

Wierzbicka, Anna. 1985. *Lexicography and Conceptual Analysis*. Ann Arbor, MI: Karoma.

Wierzbicka, Anna. 1992. *Semantics, Culture and Cognition: Universal Human Concepts in Culture-Specific Configurations.* New York: Oxford University Press.

Wierzbicka, Anna. 1996. *Semantics: Primes and Universals.* Oxford: Oxford University Press.

Wierzbicka, Anna. 1997. Conditionals and Counterfactuals: Conceptual Primitives and Linguistic Universals. In Angeliki Athanasiadou & René Dirven (eds.), *On Conditionals Again*, pp. 15–59. Amsterdam: John Benjamins.

Wierzbicka, Anna. 2001. *What Did Jesus Mean? Explaining the Sermon on the Mount and the Parables in Simple and Universal Human Concepts.* New York: Oxford University Press.

Wierzbicka, Anna. 2004. Jewish Cultural Scripts and the Interpretation of the Bible. *Journal of Pragmatics* 36 (1): 575–599.

Wierzbicka, Anna. 2010. *Experience, Evidence and Sense: The Hidden Cultural Legacy of English.* New York: Oxford University Press.

Wierzbicka, Anna. 2014. *Imprisoned in English: The Hazards of English as a Default Language.* New York: Oxford University Press.

Wierzbicka, Anna. 2016. Two Levels of Verbal Communication, Universal and Culture-Specific. In Louis de Saussure & Andrea Rocci (eds.), *Verbal Communication*, pp. 447–481. Berlin: de Gruyter.

Wierzbicka, Anna. 2017a. *W co wierzą chrześcijanie? Opowieść o Bogu i o ludziach* [*What Christians Believe: The Story of God and People*]. Cracow: Znak.

Wierzbicka, Anna. 2017b. The Meaning of Kinship Terms: A Developmental and Cross-Linguistic Perspective. In Zhengdao Ye (ed.), *The Semantics of Nouns*, pp. 19–62. Oxford: Oxford University Press.

Wierzbicka, Anna. 2018a. Speaking About God in Universal Words, Thinking About God Outside English. In Paul Chilton & Monika Kopytowska (eds.), *Religion, Language, and the Human Mind*, pp. 19–51. Oxford: Oxford University Press.

Wierzbicka, Anna. 2018b. Emotions of Jesus. *Russian Journal of Linguistics* 22 (1): 38–53.

Wierzbicka, Anna. in press. The Concept of "Love" in a Historical and Cross-Linguistic Perspective (English, classical Greek, New Testament Greek, Hebrew, Ifaluk, Pitjantjatjara). *International Journal of Language and Culture.*

Wiesenthal, Simon (ed.). 1998. *The Sunflower: On the Possibilities and Limits of Forgiveness* (rev. and expanded 2nd edn.). New York: Schocken Books.

Wild, Robert (ed.). 2015. *A Catholic Reading Guide to Universalism.* Eugene, Oregon: Resource Publications.

Wild, Robert. 2018. Easter Homily. Unpublished.

Williams, James. 1996. The Anthropology of René Girard and Traditional Doctrines of Atonement. In James G. Williams, *The Girard Reader*. New York: Crossroad.

Williams, Rowan. 2015. *What Is Christianity?: A Little Book of Guidance.* London: SPCK.

Wills, Garry. 2003. *Why I Am a Catholic.* Mariner: Boston & New York.

Wills, Garry. 2007. *What Paul Meant.* New York: Penguin.

Wittgenstein, Ludwig. 1974 [1922]. *Tractatus Logico-Philosophicus* (with an introduction by Bertrand Russell). London: Kegan Paul, Trench, Trubner.

World Council of Churches. 2010. *Confessing the One Faith: An Ecumenical Explication of the Apostolic Faith as it is Confessed in the Nicene-Constantinopolitan Creed (381)*. Geneva: World Council of Churches Publications.

Wright, N. T. 2007. A Dialogue on Jesus with N. T. Wright. In Anthony Flew, *There Is a God: How the World's Most Notorious Atheist Changed His Mind*, pp. 185–214. San Francisco: HarperOne.

Wright, N. T. 2015. *Simply Good News: Why the Gospel Is News and What Makes It Good*. London: Society for Promoting Christian Knowledge (SPCK).

Wright, N. T. 2016. *The Day the Revolution Began: Reconsidering the Meaning of Jesus's Crucifixion*. New York: HarperCollins.

YOUCAT. Youth Catechism of the Catholic Church. 2010. San Francisco: Ignatius Press.

INDEX